Taxation under
the early Tudors
1485–1547

PATRI MATRIQUE

Taxation under the early Tudors 1485–1547

Roger Schofield

Blackwell
Publishing

BLACKWELL PUBLISHING
350 Main Street, Malden, MA 02148-5020, USA
108 Cowley Road, Oxford OX4 1JF, UK
550 Swanston Street, Carlton, Victoria 3053, Australia

First published 2004 by Blackwell Publishing Ltd

Library of Congress Cataloging-in-Publication Data

Schofield, Roger.
   Taxation under the early Tudors 1485–1547 / Roger Schofield.
      p. cm.
   Includes bibliographical references and index.
   ISBN 0-631-15231-8 (alk. paper)
   1. Taxation–Great Britain–History. 2. Great Britain–Economic conditions–16th century. 3. Great Britain–History–1066–1687. I. Title.

HJ2603.S26   2004
336.2'00942'09031–dc22

                                                                    2003026899

A catalogue record for this title is available from the British Library.

Set in 10/12½pt Sabon
by MHL Production Services Ltd, Coventry

The publisher's policy is to use permanent paper from mills that operate a sustainable forestry policy, and which has been manufactured from pulp processed using acid-free and elementary chlorine-free practices. Furthermore, the publisher ensures that the text paper and cover board used have met acceptable environmental accreditation standards.

For further information on
Blackwell Publishing, visit our website:
http://www.blackwellpublishing.com

Contents

v

Tables and Figures

Tables

ix

Figures

Preface

This study has been based primarily upon the original documents produced during the levy and account of each of the taxes granted by parliament to the crown during the reigns of two monarchs, Henry VII and Henry VIII. Originally this was submitted as a doctoral thesis for the University of Cambridge, under the title 'Parliamentary Lay Taxation, 1485–1547'. I then found that I was more employable, as a research assistant in the history of population, than as a scholar with some knowledge about taxation, in what appeared to many as a somewhat distant period of history. In fact, I then joined, and have worked all my life, in the Cambridge Group for the History of Population and Social Structure. But direct taxation has remained my first love. So I kept in touch with Geoffrey Elton, until his death, who right at the outset first suggested to me that taxation might indeed prove to be a worthwhile subject of investigation. In fact Geoffrey supervised my doctoral dissertation on that topic and, more recently, he has tried to encourage me to publish my findings. But before doing that, I tried to set the early Tudor experiment in its historical context. This exercise was printed as one of a set of 'essays presented to Sir Geoffrey Elton on his retirement', and it has now become an appropriate final chapter to this book.[1]

It so happens that the original documents of the history of taxation have, for the most part, been preserved amongst the records of the Exchequer and are at present deposited in the National Archives at Kew Gardens, London. In order to make this study as thorough as possible, it has proved necessary to work systematically through all the classes of documents in which references to parliamentary taxation might be expected to occur for all the sixty-three years covered by the early Tudor period.[2] Unfortunately it has proved impossible to extend this approach to documents in other repositories, mainly on account of their bulk, but also because only a very small percentage of them were, in fact, relevant to the subject of the thesis. For these documents recourse has been taken to guides, lists and indexes.[3] In this way it was hoped that as much as possible of the contemporary manuscript material might be covered, however inadequately. In the event, very few documents of independent value have been discovered outside the National Archives.

Since, therefore, the majority of references in this thesis are to documents in the National Archives, such references have been made simply by means of the call numbers now in use at that office. A full key to the official description of each class of document represented by these call numbers has been provided in the first section of the Bibliography. In order to distinguish these documents from documents in other repositories, references to the latter bear a prefix indicating the name of the repository. The prefixes, for example 'BM' for British Museum in London, are also listed and explained in the first section of the bibliography.

In the years after the thesis was completed a number of studies have appeared by other scholars, which also have been included in the bibliography. This has been restricted so as to include only those works which have been cited in the footnotes or which, although not cited, have been found directly helpful or relevant. Individual bibliographies, guides to record collections, and similar works, although extensively used, have not been listed in the bibliography, unless they have been cited in the footnotes. The lists of published works have been arranged so that the abbreviated forms of titles given in the footnotes may be identified directly.

In the course of this study I have gained much from the helpful discussion and kindness of many people. In particular, I should like to acknowledge my debt to Helen Miller (now deceased) for her generous permission to use her transcripts from the Corporation of London records. I should also like, above all, to acknowledge the size of my debt my research supervisor, Professor Sir Geoffrey Elton. His earlier guidance and encouragement was responsible both for the initial conception of the possibility of this study, and for whatever merits it may now possess. In fact, I owe everything to him; my debt to him is very great indeed.

Abbreviations

Apart from the usual conventional abbreviations, the following have been used:

Ad	'Adhuc', prefixed to 'It' and 'Res', q.v.
b.	Reverse side of a folio sheet
Bre. Dir.	'Brevia directa', section of the king's remembrancer's memoranda roll (E159)
Bre. Ret.	'Brevia retornabilia et irretornabilia', section of both memoranda rolls (E159, E368)
Cssn.	'Commissiones', section of the king's remembrancer's memoranda rolls (E159)
d.	'Dorso', reverse side of a rotulus or membrane
H.	'Hilary', one of the law terms
It.	'Item', a supplementary rotulus immediately following the main county rotulus on the pipe rolls (E372)
M.	'Michaelmas', one of the law terms
m.	'Membrane', used to denote a piece of parchment joined to other similar pieces at both the head and the foot, i.e., as part of a continuous roll. Compare 'r.'
n.s.	New Series
P.	'Pasche', one of the law terms
r.	'Rotulus', in accordance with sixteenth-century exchequer usage this abbreviation is used to denote a piece of parchment joined to other pieces of parchment at the head alone
r-.	Denotes that no numeration of the rotuli occurs in the original
Res.	'Residuum', a supplementary rotulus, or part of rotulus, to the main county rotulus on the pipe rolls (E372), but often to be found some way away from the main rotulus
s. a.	'Sine auctore', no known author

xv

xvi   *Abbreviations*

Scr. Recogn.   'Scripta Recognita', section of the king's remembrancer's
               memoranda roll (E159)
s. l.   'Sine loco', no known place of publication
SVC   'Status et visus compotorum', section of the Lord Treasurer's
               remembrancer's memoranda roll (E368)
T.   'Trinity', one of the law terms
TNA   The National Archives, Kew, Richmond, Surrey

1

Introduction

Scope of the Study

This study is concerned with those taxes granted by parliament to the first two Tudor monarchs, Henry VII and Henry VIII, between 1485 and 1547 and levied directly upon the assessed wealth of each individual taxpayer. It goes slightly beyond this definition to include loans levied on people to be paid back from parliamentary taxation, or 'forced loans', and payments without any parliamentary backing known as 'benevolences'.

It does not attempt to discuss indirect taxes granted by parliament to the crown, for example tonnage and poundage, or the clergy, except in so far as they were liable to parliamentary taxation of the laity. The scope of this study is, therefore, restricted to one aspect of taxation in the early Tudor period for three reasons.

First, parliamentary taxation under the early Tudors has received inadequate attention from historians of taxation. The complexity of the subject and the diffuseness of the materials available for its study are such that any partial approach produces results that are inaccurate and misleading. Second, parliamentary taxation was both more extensive in its incidence and more systematically administered than most other forms of taxation. Thus it has left an unrivalled mass of personal assessments, the potential value of which to social, economic and local historians is so great as to demand a full study of the legislative and administrative framework in which these records were produced. Third, parliamentary taxation occupies a somewhat critical position in constitutional history, for it reflects both the theoretical relationships of the different parts of the constitution, and the political conditions and attitudes prevalent in the country at large. The constitutional position becomes clearer if the circumstances in which non-parliamentary 'forced loans' and 'benevolences' were levied are examined.

1

The General Nature and Incidence of the Taxes

The taxes granted by parliament to the crown between 1485 and 1547 were of two distinct types: the fifteenth and tenth, and the directly assessed subsidy. By 1485 the fifteenth and tenth had been levied in a standard form for 150 years.[1] The grant by parliament of a fifteenth and tenth was the grant of a specified sum of money, fixed in 1334 and little altered thereafter, from every 'vill' and urban ward in the country. The fifteenth and tenth was thus a very simple tax, of fixed yield, and levied in the first instance on communities rather than on individuals.[2]

In contrast the directly assessed subsidy was a tax, of varying rates, levied on each individual according to criteria specified in the act granting each tax. It was thus a more complex tax, of open yield, and being levied upon the assessed wealth of each taxpayer, and reflected far more accurately than the fifteenth and tenth the distribution of wealth in the country. Directly assessed subsidies had been levied in England many times before 1485, indeed for a brief period the fifteenth and tenth had been such a tax.[3] But, during the fifteenth century, directly assessed subsidies were both regarded with suspicion by parliament and were singularly unsuccessful as sources of revenue to the crown. As a result they were therefore rarely granted.[4] The history of parliamentary taxation from 1485 to 1547 is the history of a successful attempt to replace the fifteenth and tenth as the main form of taxation by a more viable directly assessed subsidy. This change in the relative frequency of grants of the two forms of taxation in the early Tudor period is clearly shown in Table 1.1. It is also clear from the table that fifteenths and tenths were by no means superseded by directly assessed subsidies. And after 1512 fifteenths and tenths were never granted without an accompanying grant of a directly assessed subsidy, while about half of the grants of directly assessed subsidies were made without any accompanying grant of a fifteenth and tenth.

It is also apparent that one act of parliament might grant more than one tax, that is both a fifteenth and tenth and a directly assessed subsidy, or more than one of either or both of these. In the case of multiple grants of either fifteenths and tenths, or of subsidies, difficulties arise as to how to refer to each tax. Reference by the year of the act granting the taxes, while having much to recommend it, has two serious drawbacks. First, multiple grants of taxes were usually arranged so that they were collected and paid to the crown, not all at once; but with intervals of up to a year between each payment.[5] To refer to a tax collected in 1527, as 'the fourth part of the 1523 subsidy' is both clumsy and uninformative. Second, although the acts themselves referred to multiple payments of subsidies as one 'subsidy', the usage is misleading, for it masks the fact that every payment of the 'subsidy' involved a completely fresh assessment, admittedly according to the same rates and criteria, but no less

Table 1.1 Relative frequency of grants of fifteenths and tenths and directly assessed subsidies

Year of grant	No. of taxes granted	
	XV & X	Subsidy
1487	2	1[a]
1488	–	1
1490	1	–
1491	3[b]	–
1497	2	2[c]
1504	–	1
1512 (3 H. VIII)	2	–
1512 (4 H. VIII)	1	1
1514	–	1
1515 (6 H. VIII)	–	1
1515 (7 H. VIII)	1	1
1523	–	4
1534	1	2
1540	4	2
1543	–	3
1545	2	2
Total	18	20

Notes:
[a] A poll tax on aliens.
[b] 3rd XV & X never levied.
[c] 2nd subsidy never levied.
Sources:
See appendix I.

independent for that. In order to remove this confusion each levy and payment of a tax will be referred to by the year in which payment was made to the crown.[6] But in discussing the acts that granted the taxes, reference will be made to the year of the enactment. Thus the act of 1523 specified a series of rates and assessment criteria according to which the subsidies of 1524, 1525, 1526, and 1527 were each separately assessed and collected.[7] A full key specifying both the years of the acts and the years of the payments of the taxes is given in Appendix I.

While it is clear from Table 1.1 that taxes were not granted by parliament every year during the early Tudor period, Figure 1.1 also shows that even with some multiple grants, taxes were by no means levied every year. Furthermore, it is clear that parliamentary grants of taxation were particularly frequent in the years 1487–1491, 1512–1515 and 1540–1545. Only four grants were made outside these years, namely in 1497, 1504, 1523, and 1534. It is also clear from the diagram that the incidence of parliamentary taxation was confined to roughly the same years, but sometimes with a time lag of one year. In all, out of the sixty-three years of the period, in twenty-seven years (43%) parliamentary

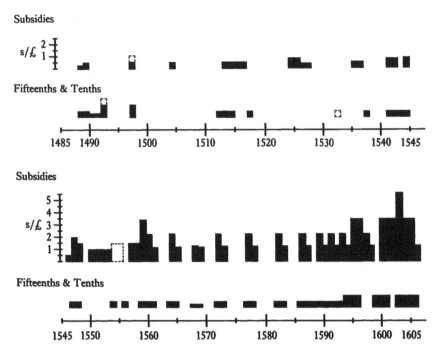

Note: The vertical scale indicates the severity of the rates in force, with a fifteenth and tenth made equivalent to a subsidy rate of 6d in the pound.
Dashed boxes indicate taxes granted, but never levied.
1487 = levied on aliens only.
Sources: See Appendix I.

Figure 1.1   Distribution of acts of parliament granting taxation and of the incidence of taxation (from Schofield, 1988). Reproduced by kind permission of Cambridge University Press.

taxes were levied, while thirty-six years (57%) remained free of tax. Of the twenty-seven years in which taxes were levied, in the majority, sixteen years, only one tax was collected, while two taxes were levied in nine years, and three taxes in only two years. But these figures do not give a true picture of the relative severity of the incidence of parliamentary taxation, for while the fifteenth and tenths were levied at a uniform rate, the directly assessed subsidies were levied at different rates and on different sections of the population.

Parliamentary Taxation and National Finance

A consideration of the years in which taxation was granted by parliament to the crown shows that, with only three exceptions, these grants were made during times of war or of imminent war. This immediately suggests that there was a close relationship between war and parliamentary lay taxation. If we now look at the one text that handles 'constitutional' relationships in the period, the '*De Dominio Regali et politico*' of Sir John Fortescue, the Chief Justice of the King's Bench from 1442, we find the following summary of the position.[8]

In the later fifteenth century the revenues and the expenditure of the crown were usually described as 'ordinary' and 'extraordinary'.[9] The former category consisted of regular receipts such as profits from crown lands and feudal incidents, and regular expenditure such as the upkeep of the royal household, the payment of royal officers and the administration of the borders.[10] 'Extraordinary' expenditures were for contingencies that could not reasonably be foreseen or estimated, such as the sending and receiving of ambassadors, the repression of rebellions and defence against sudden invasions. The 'ordinary', or private, revenue of the crown was ideally to be sufficient to cover both the 'ordinary' and 'extraordinary' expenditures.[11]

But it was also recognised that some 'extraordinary' expenditures were of such magnitude that it was unrealistic to expect the ordinary revenue of the crown to cover them. Thus, as the king was bound to defend the realm, so his subjects were equally bound to assist him in this task:

> Car mesme la ley que veut le Roy defendra son people meme la ley veut que le people grantera a luy de leur bons en aid de cel defence.[12]

This reciprocal duty on the part of the subjects to give financial assistance to the king was justified by Fortescue in terms of the king being the servant of the realm.

> For his [the King's] Realme is boundyn by Right to sustenyn hym, in everye thyng necessarye to his Astate. For as Saynt Thomas sayth, Rex datur propter Regnum et non Regnum propter Regem. Wherfor al that he dothe, owithe to be referryd to his Kyngdome. For though his Astate be the highest Astate Temporal in the Erthe, yet it ys an office, in the which he mynystrith in his Realme, Defence and Justice. And therfor he may say of hymself, as the Pope sayth of hymself and of the Church, in that he wryteth: Servus Servorum Dei. By whiche reason, right as every Servaunt owyth to have his Sustenaunce of hym that he servyth, so owght the Pope to be sustenyned by the Chirche, and the Kyng by his Realme. For 'Nemo Debet propriis expensis militare'.[13]

Fortescue preferred the king to have a large private revenue and to charge his subjects as little as possible.[14] But the expenses of wars were such that by the end of the fifteenth century they could not be waged without 'extraordinary' revenue being granted to the crown.[15]

These principles, that the king should live 'of his own', and that requests for financial aid should only be made in urgent cases and for the defence of the realm, were recognised by Edward IV when he addressed the Commons in 1467 'ore suo proprio':

> The cause why Y have called and sommoned this my present Parlement is, that Y purpose to lyve uppon my nowne, and not to charge my Subgettes but in grete and urgent causes, concernyng more the wele of theym self, and also the defence of theym and of this my Realme, rather than my nowne pleasir, as here to fore by Commons of this Londe hath been doon and born unto my Progenitours in tyme of nede.[16]

It was also recognised by the later fifteenth century that 'extraordinary' revenue should be granted to the crown by the laity in parliament and by the clergy in convocation. In 1483, an act of parliament was passed, declaring that benevolences and other non-parliamentary taxes had sometimes been levied in the past, and that they were illegal, and that they were not to be levied in the future.[17] Despite this act several non-parliamentary taxes were successfully raised during the early Tudor period, and these are discussed fully below. But here it should be noted that 'benevolences' were levied only from the richer sorts of people, who perhaps more than most needed to retain the goodwill of the crown.[18] Thus the existence of these few non-parliamentary super-taxes in no way prejudiced the principle that taxes of general incidence were only to be levied with the consent of parliament.

Parliamentary Taxation and the Redress of Grievances

In England in the early Tudor period there was no tradition that grants of taxes were to be made conditional upon, or consequent upon, the redress of grievances by the crown. As has been shown, grants of taxes by parliament were dependent upon military conditions affecting the country as a whole. Nevertheless there was in some cases at least some connection between the grant of taxation by parliament and the grant of a general pardon by the crown.

It is clear from Table 1.2 that in general there was no connection between grants of taxation by parliament and grants of general pardons by the crown in the early Tudor period, for out of seventeen grants of taxes and eleven grants of general pardon, in only six cases did these occur in the same year. And of these six cases, in only three is there any evidence that one of the grants was in any way dependent upon the other. The first case was that of the final clause of the subsidy act of 5 Henry VIII c. 17, which, as it was engrossed, contained a short statement to the effect that the king had granted a general pardon which was to be available in all courts specified by the king or the council, by obtaining letters patent, and without the need for special writs of allowance. But the relevance, and even perhaps the propriety, of this clause

Table 1.2 Grants of taxation and general grants of pardon

Year	Grant of taxes	General grant of pardon
1485	–	1 Henry VII c. 6[a]
1487	Rot. Parl., VI, 400-1	–
1487	Ibid., 401-2	–
1489	Ibid., 420-4	–
1490	Ibid., 437-9	–
1491	7 Henry VII c. 11	–
1495	–	11 Henry VII c. 1[b]
1497	12 Henry VII c. 12, 13	–
1504	19 Henry VII c. 32	C66/594 m. 27d[c]
1509	–	SP1/1/2[c]
–	–	SP1/1/3[c]
1512	3 Henry VIII c. 22	–
–	4 Henry VIII c. 19	–
1514	5 Henry VIII c. 17	by letters patent[d]
1515	6 Henry VIII c. 26	–
–	7 Henry VIII c. 9	7 Henry VIII c. 11
1523	14 & 15 Henry VIII c. 16	14 & 15 Henry VIII c. 17
1529	–	21 Henry VIII c. 1
1534	26 Henry VIII c. 19	26 Henry VIII c. 18
1540	32 Henry VIII	–
1543	34 &35 Henry VIII c. 27	35 Henry VIII c. 18[e]
1545	37 Henry VIII c. 25	–

Notes:
[a] To those who had been in Henry's army.
[b] Included pardon to those who had supported Richard III while he was king.
[c] By proclamation. Injustice had to be proved before designated arbitrators. For the significance of these pardons see Elton, *HJ* I (1958), 38; IV (1961) 4–5; and Cooper, *HJ* II (1959), 112–18.
[d] Mentioned in preamble to 7 Henry VIII c. 11.
[e] Although the calendar date of this act was 1544, it was passed by the same parliament that had granted the subsidy act of 1543.

seems to have been questioned for it was struck through, presumably during the third reading of the bill in the Lords or in the Commons.[19] On the other hand, both of the acts of general pardon of 1523 and 1544 referred in their preambles to the recent subsidies by way of justification for the grant of a general pardon. In 1523 this reference was explicit, the pardon was in recompense for a 'large and honorable subsidie'; while in 1544 the general pardon was, more vaguely, said to have been occasioned by the 'zeale and affeccion' shown to the king by his subjects in parliament. But there is no evidence that the possibility of a general pardon was raised during the debate in parliament over the grants of the taxes.

Thus, while it is possible that in these three cases, and perhaps also on the three other occasions when grants of taxes and general pardons coincided, the grant of a general pardon by the crown may have been a *quid pro quo* for the grant by parliament of taxes, this practice was in any case rare enough. At all events in no sense did it amount to a use by parliament of their power to grant taxes in order to secure a general redress of grievances from the crown. There seems to have been no occasion in the period before 1547 for parliament to use its right to grant taxes in order to secure a general redress of grievances from the crown.

2

Parliament

Taxation and the Summons of Parliament

Taxation has often been cited as one of the main reasons why the early Tudors summoned parliaments. Although there is direct evidence of a prior intention on the part of the crown to ask for grants of taxation in only three instances,[1] the very fact that all except four of the parliaments summoned during the early Tudor period granted taxes to the crown affords a *prima facie* confirmation of the traditional emphasis on the primacy of taxation in the summons of parliament.[2] But a consideration of the sessions in which taxes were granted suggests several modifications to the traditional view (see Table 2.1).

The first fact that emerges from the table is that of the sixteen parliaments summoned between 1485 and 1547, in only nine were grants of taxation made to the crown in the first session. Secondly, a distinction can be drawn between parliaments summoned before 1529 and those summoned after that date. In the earlier parliaments, taxation was always granted in the first session, or it was not granted at all. Thus it seems possible to distinguish between those parliaments summoned for the purpose of securing the grant of taxes and those summoned for other purposes. This is not to claim that a grant of taxes was the sole purpose of summoning parliament in these years, rather that it was a major purpose. Three of the eight parliaments which granted taxes to the crown before 1529 lasted for only one session, whilst of the five parliaments which were prorogued for two or three sessions, all except one made further grants to the crown.[3]

The parliaments after 1529 were of a different character, for they tended to remain in session over much longer periods of time than the earlier parliaments. Thus the need for a grant of taxation might well arise whilst parliament was in session. It is significant that no grants of taxation were made in the first sessions of the parliaments of 1529, 1539 and 1542. The 'Reformation' parliament of 1529 is a good example of this latter type of parliament. Summoned in 1529 to deal with matters quite other than taxation, it made no

9

Table 2.1 Sessions of parliament and grants of taxation

Year of first session	Sessions							
	1st	2nd	3rd	4th	5th	6th	7th	8th
1485	O	O	–	–	–	–	–	–
1487	X	–	–	–	–	–	–	–
1498	X	O	X	–	–	–	–	–
1491	X	O	–	–	–	–	–	–
1495	O	–	–	–	–	–	–	–
1497	X	–	–	–	–	–	–	–
1504	X	–	–	–	–	–	–	–
1510	O	–	–	–	–	–	–	–
1512	X	X	X	–	–	–	–	–
1515	X	X	O	–	–	–	–	–
1523	X	X	O	–	–	–	–	–
1529	O	O	X	O	O	X	O	O
1536	O	–	–	–	–	–	–	–
1539	O	O	O	X	–	–	–	–
1542	O	X	O	–	–	–	–	–
1545	X	O	–	–	–	–	–	–

Key:
X Tax granted.
O No tax granted.
– No session.
Sources:
See Appendix I, and Hall, Chronicle, pp. 655–7, 785–6.

grant of taxes until the third session, when a fifteenth and tenth was granted to the crown. The session was prorogued somewhat hurriedly because of an outbreak of the plague, and the tax, although granted, was never enacted and was allowed to 'lapse'.[4] The parliament continued through a fourth and fifth session without any taxes being granted until, in the sixth session, two subsidies and one fifteenth and tenth was granted to the crown. Parliament then continued for two further sessions, again without any grant of taxation being made to the crown. Thus, after 1529, taxation appears to take a relatively less important place in parliamentary business. The extension of parliamentary competence over many new areas meant not only that by far the majority of the sessions of parliament were concerned with matters other than taxation but also that taxation was no longer a major factor in the summons of parliament.[5]

Within each session of parliament, there had been a long tradition that money bills were passed and enacted at the end of the session.[6] This may well have originated with a desire on the part of the crown not to keep parliaments sitting longer than was necessary, and a suspicion on the part of the Commons of such intentions may well have induced them to defer granting taxation until other business had been completed. It seems unlikely, however, that such considerations were operative in the early Tudor period. Out of the seventeen sessions in which grants of taxation were made to the crown, in only eleven is there sufficient evidence by which the actual date of the grant of taxation can be established.[7] In eight of these cases, mostly occurring before 1515, parliament was prorogued or dissolved more or less immediately after taxation had been granted. In two cases, in 1523[8] and in 1543,[9] the session continued for some time afterwards. But of the eight cases in which the session was terminated immediately after the grant of taxation, in only three was this a dissolution;[10] in the other five cases parliament was recalled after a prorogation.[11]

Thus it is clear that, in general, there was no attempt by the early Tudors to use parliament merely as an assembly to be summoned for the granting of taxation and to be dissolved once this purpose had been fulfilled. Rather the tendency for money grants to be made at the end of the session was probably a ritual survival of an earlier practice, even though the original purpose of the practice was no longer relevant. It was customary for a formal ceremony to be held at the end of the session in which the Speaker of the Commons presented the instrument of grant of taxation to the king in full parliament.[12] It is significant that this ceremony was discontinued at about the same time as money grants ceased being made at the end of parliamentary sessions.[13] It is also significant that of the two cases after 1516, in which grants of taxation were made at the end of the session, one coincided with a revival of the presentation ceremony.[14]

But in three cases parliament was clearly summoned for the purpose of securing grants of taxation. In October 1496 a 'grete counsayll' granted £120,000 to the crown; but because it was considered 'not Sufficient auctoryte for the levyyng thereof', a parliament was summoned four months later which repeated the grant of the October council.[15] In March 1522 Wolsey told the Spanish ambassadors that Henry intended to summon a parliament in about two months' time in order to 'ask his subjects for the subsidies and services necessary for his great affairs'.[16] Indeed Wolsey had already sent out commissions to raise loans against the security of 'suche grauntes and contribucions as shalbe gyven and graunted to his grace at his next perliament'.[17] In the event writs for parliament were not sent out until 13 January 1523.[18] In November 1544, Paget, in a memorandum in which he surveyed the estimated expenditure in the various theatres of war, and discussed alternative ways of raising the necessary revenue, advanced detailed reasons why the summons of parliament to secure the grant of taxation should be delayed, and other devices employed in the meantime.[19] Paget's proposals were followed exactly, and when parliament was summoned a year later, it was immediately asked to grant two subsidies and two fifteenths and tenths.[20]

In two other cases, when parliament had already been summoned, and had sat and been prorogued, there was clearly an intention on the part of the crown to ask for the grant of taxation before parliament resumed sitting. In 1533, a year before parliament was asked to grant two subsidies and a fifteenth and tenth, Thomas Cromwell was compiling lists to discover the reasons for the relative effectiveness of previous subsidies,[21] and drafting a preamble for the new grant.[22] Six years later Cromwell very thoroughly prepared both the preamble and the clauses of the subsidy act in the two months before parliament was recalled.[23]

Thus although taxation was not the sole reason either for the summons of parliament or for its prolongation over many sessions, it yet featured in by far the majority of the parliaments of the early Tudor period. Also what evidence there is suggests that the ministers of the crown prepared the case for taxation and the detailed proposals for its levy some time before the demand was actually laid before parliament.

The Case for Taxation: the Preambles

When an act granting a tax to the crown was prepared it was prefaced by a preamble elucidating the circumstances which made the grant of taxation necessary. There is direct evidence of the government origin of these preambles in only three cases.[24] Nevertheless, the content of preambles is often such that it could only have been available to the ministers of the crown, that is it contained résumés of past diplomatic manoeuvres, or details of the crown's military intentions. If the preambles, as they were engrossed, were not always in the form in which they had originally been drafted by the ministers of the crown, they still represent the terms in which the crown justified to parliament its demands for the grant of taxation.

It has already been noticed that most of the grants of taxation to the crown were made in times of military activity. It has also been shown that by the end of the fifteenth century it was generally recognised that the king, in providing for the defence of the realm, was entitled to financial assistance from his subjects. Up to, and including the act of 1523, the preambles to the taxation acts justified the grant of taxation entirely in military terms. The preambles gave details of past military actions that the crown had undertaken at its own expense, or they explained that recent diplomatic manoeuvres had failed to avert war, which was now imminent, and gave some indication of the crown's military intentions. The preambles were therefore short, and in accordance with the traditional view that the proper occasion for parliamentary taxation was war undertaken in the interests of all.[25]

But from 1534 other reasons were adduced in the preambles for the grant of taxation to the crown. Indeed in 1534, when there was no pressing military crisis, other reasons had to be advanced. To justify this grant, reference was made in the preamble to some long past military expenditures, the current efforts to bring Ireland to order, some recent and intended fortifications, and the projected harbour works at Dover and Calais. These latter works and the 'reformation' of Ireland were particularly stressed because of

> the greate force strength suretie benefytt & commoditie that shall & maye ensewe to this Realme & subjectes therof.[26]

This appeal to specific civil advantages was reinforced by an extended reference to the generally beneficial nature of the king's government of the realm:

> [the king's subjects assembled in parliament] do very facylly perceyve the entier love & zeale which the kinges saide Highnes always hath borne and nowe intendeth to the conservacyon mayntenaunce & increase of the welthe estate of this Realme & the weale proffytte commoditie & quietnes of this people & subjectes of the same, And that his Highnes seketh not the same wealthe onely for his owen tyme beyng a man mortall as well as others, butt of a mere naturall zeale & ardente desyre that he hathe to provyde for the suretie & weale of this his saide Realme to conteynewe for ever hereafter, as hitherto it hate bene sagely by the highe provydence of God & the greate prudence & policye of the Prynces Kynges & Governours of the same well governed & preserved. They thynke that of verye equyte reason & good congruence they are bounde for the declaration of theyre syncerite love duetie & obedience towardes oure saide Sovereign Lorde & Kyng to shewe unto the same like correspondence of zeale gratuyte & kyndnes.[27]

Although an appeal to the military benefits of the king's government had been implicit in the preambles to previous taxation acts, the act of 1534 is revolutionary in that it is the first act that justifies parliamentary taxation primarily in terms of the civil benefits conferred on the realm by the excellence of the king's government. The grant of taxation was justified as being an equitable contribution by parliament towards the good government of the realm.

But once raised, this appeal to excellence of the king's government persisted with one exception as the major ingredient of the preambles until 1547. In the preamble to Cromwell's second subsidy of 1540, although more traditional reasons for taxation, such as the suppression of rebellions, and the preparation of the fleet against the threatened French invasions, could be cited, yet these were only mentioned. And, once again, the stress was laid on the 'innumberable benefites and goodnes' of the past thirty-one years of the king's reign.[28]

The preamble to the act of 1543 is an exception to the general trend amongst the preambles of the taxation acts after 1534. In 1543 most of the preamble was concerned with stating Henry's claim to the kingdom of

Scotland, his recent military successes, and the opportunity afforded by the death of the king of Scotland for a reassertion of his right to the Scottish throne. But the preamble of 1543 also made an unparalleled claim on the duty of parliament to support the king:

> And forasmuche as emong other consideracions and respectes the civile and politicque bodies ought to have in all common welthes, they shoulde moste principallye and speceallie regarde studye and devyse for the conservacion and increase of the royall estate honour and dignitie and estimacion of thyre chefe heade and Soveraigne Lorde by whome they be staied and governed and for the preservacion and suertie of his persone and of his succession, and with all theyre powers might and substaunce to resiste and stande againste all suche whiche by violence force fraude disceyte or otherwyse wolde attempte to decrease diminishe appaire or hurte the same, in bodie dignitie tytle or honour.[29]

This represents a considerable change both from the traditional attitude which expounded the duty of subjects to assist the king as military protector, and also from the newer doctrine which related parliamentary taxation to the general wellbeing of the realm. Here the claim is based solely upon the 'estate honour and dignitie and estimacion' of the king, which is not only to be conserved but also increased with the assistance of parliament. If pressed, such a claim might justify parliamentary taxation even for the private enrichment of the king. In fact this claim was never pressed, and indeed was never repeated in subsequent preambles. But it is an interesting commentary on the strength of the position of Henry VIII in the early 1540s that the claim could be advanced at all.[30]

The preamble to the act of 1545 reverted to the more usual practice of laying the main burden of justification for the grant of taxation upon the inestimable advantages of the king's government for the common wealth.[31] That this argument should predominate when the military case for parliamentary taxation was stronger than ever before, shows clearly how far the justification for parliamentary taxation had changed since 1485.

That additional arguments were used from 1534 to justify taxation to parliament might, *prima facie*, suggest that it was becoming more difficult to convince parliament of the necessity to grant taxes on military arguments alone. But a parallel change in the tone of the preambles in which the status of the crown was increasingly enhanced, while that of the king's subjects was increasingly abased suggests that this was not the case. References to the king in the preambles to the taxation acts had always been both respectful and humble; but from 1534 both respect and the humility became more and more abject. The climax was reached in the preamble to the act of 1545 in which the king's subjects assembled in parliament were made to praise the outstanding ability of the king to preserve them in 'tranquilitie and peace', and to declare:

[we] do yet so live out of all feare and danger as if there were no warre at all, even as the small fishes of the Sea in the most tempestuous and stormie weather doe lie quietly under the rocks or banke side, and are not mooved with the sourges of the water, nor stirred out of their quiet place, howsoever the winde bloweth; we cannot for our most bounden dueties but knowledge and confesse ourselves to have and injoy under his Highnesse, and by his most gracious and godly regiment, all that ever wee have in this world, rendring unto his Majestie next God our most humble and immortall thankes with our most humble sute and lowly prayer on our knees that may please the same to presever in studying in caring for us, who being left to ourselves are not able to continue one day in such sort as his Highnes hath preserved us almost these fortie yeeres.[32]

Accordingly they besought the king to accept 'this simple token or gift', in fact the greatest sum ever granted by parliament, 'as it pleased the great king Alexander to receive thankefully a cuppe of water of a poore man by the high way side'.[33]

The tone of these preambles does not suggest that the crown only with difficulty persuaded a reluctant parliament to grant taxes. Rather, since these preambles were acceptable to parliament, it suggests that in the 1540s the prestige and stature of the monarchy was at an unparalleled height. It also suggests that the ministers of the crown considered that an appeal to the prestige and position of the monarchy was a more compelling argument in parliament than a traditional exposition of the financial and military necessities of the moment.[34]

Parliamentary Opposition

No parliament in the early Tudor period ever opposed the grant of taxation to the crown in principle.[35] The duty of parliament to grant taxes to the crown was not disputed, thus parliamentary opposition was confined to limiting the amount of taxation granted to the crown and to imposing conditions upon the grants.

By the later part of the fifteenth century, when parliaments granted subsidies to the crown, they attempted to retain some control both over the total amount granted to the crown, and also over the way in which the taxes were levied and spent.[36] The early taxes granted to Henry VII were subject to restrictions of this kind. In 1489 a subsidy was granted specifically for the maintenance of 10,000 archers for one year. If the number of archers were diminished, then the tax granted to the crown was to be reduced, and if the archers had to be retained for longer than one year, then the tax was to be increased, always provided that no more than a certain sum was levied by taxation in any one year.[37] Again, in 1497, parts of the grants of taxation were made dependent upon the crown actually undertaking specific military expeditions.[38] The nature of these restrictions and the way in which they were gradually abandoned by parliament are discussed in detail below. Here it is only necessary to note that parliamentary opposition at the beginning of the early Tudor period was in the full tradition of fifteenth-century opposition to taxation.

But by 1512, despite disagreement by the Commons on the advisability of a personal invasion of France by the king, the main focus for parliamentary opposition was becoming increasingly the total amount to be granted to the crown by way of taxation. In 1512, William Warham, the Lord Chancellor, asked the Commons for £600,000 for the invasion of France. This was refused, and a very much smaller sum was granted.[39] Two years later parliament granted a specified sum of money; but without any conditions as to the way in which it was to be spent.[40]

Parliamentary opposition to crown demands for taxation was strongest in 1523, when Wolsey asked the Commons to grant £800,000 to the crown, leviable by a rate of 4s/£1 on goods and on income from lands, fees, offices and wages.[41] This demand was resisted on the grounds that if so great a proportion of the total wealth of the country were levied it would exhaust the stock of coin and reduce the economy to a state of exchange by barter. An attempt to persuade Wolsey to accept a lower figure met with no success, and when Wolsey tried to reason with the Commons he provoked the famous reply that 'the fashion of the nether House was, to heare and not to reason, but emong themselfes'. Wolsey then tried to show that there had been a great increase in private wealth and that the country was well able to pay the £800,000 demanded. When the Cardinal had withdrawn, the debate continued for several more days during which the crown exerted all the pressure it could on those members of the Commons over whom it had any influence.[42] This influence cannot have been very effective for finally the Commons 'passed and accorded' a series of rates, which would have yielded a sum considerably below what the crown had originally demanded.[43] When this grant was communicated to Wolsey, he rejected it out of hand, and tried to intimidate the Commons by saying that the Lords had already granted the crown's original demands. This lie was quickly exposed, for the Lords 'had graunted nothyng, but harkened all upon the Commons.'[44]

On 21 May Sir John Hussey, the Chief Butler of England,[45] and a former Master of the Wards,[46] proposed that gentlemen of £50 in lands should grant the king 1s/£1 to be levied in a third year. When this proposal was put to the vote between ten and twelve gentlemen voted in favour, while all the burgesses remained silent 'for they would not condempne, or let the gentlemen to charge themselfes'.[47] On the same day parliament was prorogued for Whitsuntide until 10 June.[48] Despite their stubborn resistance to the crown, members of the Commons were jeered as they came out into the street, for there was a popular impression that they had in fact granted Wolsey's original demands.

When parliament reassembled, the gentlemen, tricked by Hussey's proposal, and doubtless angry at the lack of support from the burgesses, proposed in turn that a rate of 1s/£1 should be levied on those with goods worth £50 and above in a fourth year. This sparked off a recriminatory debate which raged for seventeen days, after which the House divided 'so that the one yea part remained only the knightes of the shire, and the Commons stiffly affirmed that the mocioners of this demaunde, were enemies to the realme.'[49] The situation was saved by the intervention of the speaker, Thomas More, who 'after long perswadyng, and privie laboryng of frendes',[50] secured a compromise grant for the crown. But the rates finally granted were a reduction even upon those previously 'passed and accorded' by the Commons, and refused by Wolsey.[51]

The opposition of the parliament of 1523 has been described at some length because it is the only occasion for which detailed evidence is available. Several aspects of this opposition deserve to be noted. First, the opposition of the Commons throughout the two sessions was directed exclusively against the amount of money that the crown demanded. No one disputed either the desirability of hostilities against France and Scotland, or the right of the crown to ask parliament for financial assistance.[52] Such arguments as were made in support of the crown's demands were entirely concerned with demonstrating that these demands were not excessive, and would not have the deleterious economic consequences that some had imagined.[53] Secondly, the opposition of the Commons was widespread, determined and, in the end, successful. To some extent the opposition can be ascribed to a general distrust of Wolsey, who had recently levied a loan upon the basis of an assessment extracted from everyone on oath under the cover of a commission for musters.[54] But, more important, neither the crown interest in the Commons, nor the management of the House were sufficient to counteract this initial distrust of the crown's financial motives. It is not known how large the crown interest in the Commons was in 1523: but it was described by someone in the House in 1523 as being 'more part' of the House.[55] But although this interest, which was comprised of 'the knights being of the king's Counsaill, the king's servaunts and gentilmen'[56] was 'in soo long tyme ... spoken with and made to say ye; it may fortune contrarie to their hert, will and conscience',[57] the original demands of the crown were still not granted.

If the crown interest in fact comprised the majority of the House of Commons in 1523, then the success of the opposition of the Commons to the crown becomes even more significant. The failure of the crown to secure its demands must be ascribed to Wolsey's incompetent management of the House. Firstly he received the Commons deputation beseeching him to intercede with the king for a lower demand 'currishly', saying 'that he would rather have his tongue, plucked out of his hedde with a pair of pinsons, then to move the kynge, to take any lesse some.'[58] Wolsey's next move, his impetuous attempt to reason with the Commons, was even more tactless, for it reminded the Commons of their corporate entity and of their privileges. His line of argument that sumptuous buildings, apparel and feasts showed that the country was well able to afford the crown's demands, both annoyed the Commons in that the Cardinal, of all people, should grudge them good living, and provoked them into justification of the economic desirability of a high rate of consumption.[59] When, after much labouring of the crown interest, the Commons were finally induced to grant rates somewhat below those originally demanded by the crown, Wolsey not only unwisely rejected this grant out of hand, but also very foolishly alleged that the Lords had complied with the original demands. This transparent lie not only further undermined the Cardinal's reputation with the Commons, but must also have momentarily given rise to the suspicion that Wolsey was prepared to disregard what was established parliamentary procedure, namely that money bills were initiated in the Commons.

Finally, the attempt to increase the yield to the crown by the proposal put by Sir John Hussey to levy 1s/£1 on lands of £50 and above in the third year, divided the House into the 'landed menne' and the rest, and merely raised the temperature of the debate bringing home to all the undesirability of any taxation at all. The rates finally secured, although including the third and fourth year surcharges, were in total less than those granted previously and refused by Wolsey. It is, indeed, difficult to see how Wolsey's mismanagement of the Commons in 1523 could have been greater.

Thus in 1523 the crown faced the most determined opposition in the Commons that was ever shown in the early Tudor period; and most of this opposition was of its own making. It may well be that the increasingly elaborate and persuasive preambles to the taxation acts that came to be used in 1534 reflect a growing appreciation on the part of the ministers of the crown for the need to induce the Commons to agree to taxes by management and persuasion rather than by bluster and threats.[60]

In fact there is no evidence of any opposition to the grant of taxation in any of the parliaments after 1523. What evidence there is suggests that parliaments were conformable to the wishes of the crown. For example, in 1540 the Lords passed a bill granting two subsidies and four fifteenth and tenths 'nemine discrepante'.[61] In 1540, too, the ceremony of presenting the instrument of grant to the king in full parliament was revived. The presentation was made by the Speaker of the Commons who marked the occasion by a speech in which he likened the state to the human body and compared the king to the head, the Lords to the breast and the 'populus et plebs' to the remaining members.[62]

Unfortunately nothing is known of the reaction of the Commons and the Lords to the claims made on the body politic by the preamble of the act of

1543. But in 1545, the Lords again assented to a bill granting two subsidies and two fifteenths and tenths 'nemine discrepante',[63] and one observer noted a general willingness to grant the taxes.[64] It would be rash to suggest that at no time after 1523 were objections ever made in parliament to the rates of taxation demanded by the crown. But the general attitude of parliament towards the grant of taxation to the crown is clearly different from that of earlier parliaments. While the parliaments of Henry VII suspiciously imposed restrictions upon their grants of taxation, and while, until 1523, strong opposition might be voiced in parliament over the total sum to be granted to the crown, from 1534 until the end of Henry VIII's reign there was apparently no general opposition to the demands of the crown for taxation.

This general concurrence with the wishes of the crown, taken together with the large amounts of taxation granted and the attitudes expressed in the preambles to the taxation acts, argues a strong identity of interest between parliament and the crown in the 1540s.

The Evolution of a Money Bill

Drafts and amendments

It is known from independent sources that some bills granting taxation to the crown were based upon drafts prepared by ministers of the crown. The bills of 1512 (4 Henry VIII) and 1514 were drawn, written and engrossed by John Hales of Gray's Inn, who was rewarded by a payment of £10, 'by the kinges Commaundement'.[65] Also some early drafts have survived, with corrections by Cromwell, for the bills of 1534[66] and 1540.[67]

An analysis of the taxation acts, as they were passed by parliament, not only confirms that the origin of money bills lay in drafts prepared by the ministers of the crown. It also enables a distinction to be made between the original drafts and the amendments made to them in the course of parliamentary debate. If, first, we take the bills granting fifteenths and tenths to the crown, we find throughout the early Tudor period that they were short, uniform in structure, and varied little in their phraseology.[68] The first part of the bill consisted of a preamble, which changed from year to year, and which justified the grant of the taxes. The preamble was followed by a series of clauses to the effect that the fifteenth and tenth was to be levied as customary, with specified exceptions, on specified dates, and that certain persons were not to be appointed collectors, and that those who were appointed collectors were to be exempt from fees in the exchequer. While details of these clauses, such as the exceptions and dates of payment, might vary, the content and order of the clauses remained constant. To this constant corpus of clauses two types of additional clauses were attached; those favourable to the crown and those favourable to the taxpayers. Additional clauses favourable to the crown are either to be found inserted into the general corpus of clauses in the relevant place, or added at the end of the bill, after the general corpus. On the other hand, additional clauses favourable to the taxpayers are always to be found at the end of the bill and are never inserted into the general corpus of clauses.

The standard form of the bills suggests strongly that they originated in drafts prepared from previous bills and not by way of a crystallisation of random thoughts expressed in the course of a parliamentary debate. The fact that only clauses favourable to the crown are to be found inserted in the standard corpus of clauses confirms that the drafts were prepared by officers of the crown. The clauses, favourable to both the crown and to the taxpayers, which were grouped together at the end of the bills were clearly raised during the course of debate on the draft in parliament, and were not incorporated into the general corpus of the bill upon engrossment. It is significant that if any of these clauses were retained in subsequent bills, those favourable to the crown were inserted into the general corpus of clauses, whilst those favourable to the taxpayers remained in the miscellaneous section at the end. None the less, the bills granting fifteenths and tenths were short, and it is sometimes difficult to tell whether a clause was placed at the end of a bill because it was an addition to the draft, made in the course of parliamentary debate, or because that was the natural place to put it when the draft was composed.

The same difficulty does not arise with bills granting subsidies to the crown for in these the general corpus of clauses covering the rates, the dates of payment, the criteria of assessment, the appointment of commissioners, the procedure of assessment, collection, certification and account, is sufficiently large and systematic in its arrangement to make it plain whether an additional clause has been inserted in its 'proper' place, or has been attached to the end of the bill. From an analysis of the bills granting subsidies in 1489 and 1497, a clear distinction can be made between the 'body' of the bills, dealing with the levy of the subsidies, and a series of clauses which follow, concerned with laying conditions upon the size of the grant, with making certain exemptions, with clarifying assessment criteria and with improving the position of those who might be appointed collectors. Again in the development of the new form of the directly assessed subsidy in the acts of 1512 to 1515, those innovations which were designed to secure a greater efficiency in assessment and collection are to be found incorporated in the general corpus of administrative clauses, whilst those introduced to safeguard the collector and the taxpayer first appear at the end of the bills.

The case for regarding the clauses at the end of the bills as being the products of parliamentary debate is clinched by a comparison of some of these clauses with independent evidence. First, at the end of the act of 1523 there are two clauses which are concerned with the acceptance of foreign coins and plate in payment of the subsidy. We know from the evidence of Hall that the main concern of the Commons in the discussions of the bill of 1523 was that there would not be enough specie with which to pay the taxes demanded by the crown.[69] Second, towards the end of the act of 1543 there is a clause that states that a suburb of Stamford, known as Stamford Baron, shall be assessed in Lincolnshire. It is known that this clause was not attached to the bill until after the second reading by the Lords.[70] Again the acts of 1543 and 1545 contain a clause which deals with the possibility of dual liability arising, to the subsidy bill and to the subsidy of the clergy, granted by Convocation and enacted by parliament. In 1543 the clerical subsidy was given its first reading by the Lords two days after the bill for the lay subsidy had been brought up from the Commons, and both bills arrived for their third reading by the Lords simultaneously.[71] In 1545 the lay subsidy bill had at least two readings in the Lords before the bill for the clerical subsidy was brought up.[72] In both 1543 and in 1545, therefore, both the subsidy bills were thus considered by parliament roughly simultaneously, but the lay subsidy bills slightly before the clerical subsidy bills. And in both years both the lay and the clerical subsidy bills contained clauses on the question of dual liability. It is, therefore, clear that these clauses represent additions to the original drafts of the bills made in the course of parliamentary debate.[73]

Once the distinction between the clauses contained in the original draft, and the clauses added in the course of parliamentary debate, has been established, a comparison of the number of clauses inserted into the crown drafts with the number of clauses added at the end of the bills can be made. This should enable some estimate to be made of the degree to which parliamentary debate affected the final form in which the taxation bills were engrossed.

But a numerical comparison of clauses involves several difficulties. First, some decision has to be taken as to what constitutes a 'clause', for some 'clauses' are short and deal with one matter only, whilst others are lengthy and contain several separate proposals. No uniform standard can be laid down; but an attempt has been made to keep the 'clauses' as comparable as possible. Secondly, it is often difficult to determine whether a clause should be classified as favourable to the crown, or favourable to the taxpayers, for some clauses are obviously favourable to both. In such cases, for example regulations concerning legal tender, the clauses have been assigned to whichever party it appears to favour most.

Although the acts granting fifteenths and tenths were short, it is clear from Table 2.2 that not many additions were made to the standard form of the draft bills. Thus the fifteenth and tenth, as the traditional form of taxation provoked very little emendation either from the crown or from parliament.

Table 2.2   Additional clauses: fifteenths and tenths (excluding grants of exemption)

Year of grant	Total	In draft	From debate: favourable to	
			Crown	Others
1487	1	-	-	1
1490	1	-	-	1
1492	3	1	1	1
1497	1	-	-	1
1512 (3H.VIII)	-	-	-	-
1512 (4H.VIII)	-	-	-	-
1515	2	1	-	1
1534	-	-	-	-
1540	3	-	2	1
1545	1	-	1	-

Sources:
See Appendix I.

The acts granting subsidies fall into three groups. In the first of these, from 1489 to 1504, new forms of taxation were tried, and thus the whole drafts were crown innovations.[74] Thus there were no additional clauses favourable to the crown arising out of parliamentary debate; and those clauses favourable to the taxpayers were strongly limiting on the crown (see Table 2.3).[75] The second group of acts, from 1512 to 1515, contains the evolution of the new form of the directly assessed subsidy, thus the total number of new clauses is, comparatively, very high. It is clear that the new form of directly assessed subsidy was developed primarily by the ministers of the crown in the composition of the drafts before the details were discussed by parliament. But a number of amendments were made in the course of debate, many of which were subsequently incorporated by the crown into the main body of the bills.[76]

In the third group of acts, from 1523 to 1543, relatively few new clauses were introduced, and practically all of these arose out of parliamentary debate and were favourable to the taxpayers rather than to the crown.[77] These clauses tended to be on recurring subjects, such as legal tender, liability to clerical subsidies, and the status of liberties. The act of 1545 is anomalous to this third group in that five clauses tightening up the procedure of assessment and collection of the subsidy were introduced into the crown draft, and in that two retrospective clauses concerning the anticipation of a previous subsidy and the payment of a previous benevolence were introduced during the parliamentary debate.[78]

Unlike the fifteenth and tenth, the subsidy was an evolving form of taxation in the early Tudor period, and thus a great many more additional clauses were introduced both into the drafts of the bills and in the course of parliamentary debate. It is clear from Table 2.3 that although the crown was responsible for

Table 2.3 Additional clauses: subsidies (excluding grants of exemption)

Year of grant	Total	In draft	From debate: favourable to	
			Crown	Others
1489	8[a]	_[a]	–	8
1497	3[a]	_[a]	–	3
1504	2	2	–	–
1512	17	11	1	5
1514	11	9	–	2
1515(6 H.VIII)	22	19	1	2
1515(7 H.VIII)	_[b]	–	–	–
1523	6	2	–	4
1534	4	1	–	3
1540	4	–	3	1
1543	4	–	–	4
1545	12	5	3[c]	4

Notes:
[a] New form of tax, additional clauses in draft cannot be distinguished.
[b] Short act, renewing previous act with some changes.
[c] Includes two retrospective clauses concerning the anticipation of a previous subsidy, and the payment of a benevolence.
Sources:
See Appendix I.

devising the general structure of the subsidies right through the period, on every occasion some additions were made to this structure by parliament. The parliamentary additions and modifications to the crown drafts were almost entirely in favour of the taxpayer, and did not greatly increase or decrease in number over the period. This suggests that the crown drafts were diligently studied by parliament and amendments were suggested where they were deemed necessary. At no time other than in 1489, did parliament attempt to make any full-scale revision of the form of taxation proposed by the crown.

Commons and Lords

So far reference has been made to parliamentary debates without any attempt having been made to distinguish between the roles of the Commons and of the Lords in these debates. The relative importance of the two Houses in the passing of money bills is difficult to assess because there are no Commons' journals extant for the early Tudor period,[79] and what Lords' journals there are are by no means complete in their recording of the passage of bills through parliament.[80] Nevertheless, what evidence there is points to the primacy of the Commons in the passing of money bills.

First, it is known that at least on eleven occasions money bills were first debated in the Commons and then sent to the Lords.[81] Secondly, in 1523 according to the evidence of one commentator, even in the face of considerable pressure from the crown, the Lords 'graunted nothing, but harkened all upon the Commons'.[82] Thirdly, only two cases are known where the Lords amended a money bill.[83] This would suggest that the great majority of amendments, and therefore most of the discussion of the bills, took place in the Commons and not in the Lords.

The primacy of the Commons in voting taxation to the crown is reflected in the form in which grants of taxation were made. From the beginning of the fifteenth century, and right up to 1543, all grants of taxation to the crown were made by the Commons by the advice and assent of the Lords.[84] On only three occasions were separate taxes granted to the crown by the Commons and Lords, in 1404, 1472 and 1489.[85] The Commons' grants were still made 'by thadvyse and assent of the lords spirituall & temporall', while the Lords' grants were made after the Commons' grants, but not with their advice and assent.[86]

The opinion of the lawyers in the fifteenth century was that taxes were granted by the Commons and were approved by the Lords. Hody, CJ expressed this view in a case in the Exchequer Chamber in 1441:

> Et ou est dit que tiel grant prend son effect de son people; jeo dit que non, mais covient apres tiel grant eu par son people, que les seigniors du Royaulme approuvent ceo, et auxy que le roy accept.[87]

An opinion by counsel in the Abbot of Waltham's case in 1482 that a fifteenth granted without the assent of the Lords was valid,[88] is almost certainly wrong, contradicting as it does over eighty years of consistent parliamentary practice. It is perhaps significant that no suggestion was ever made that the Lords could bind the whole realm by granting taxes to the crown without the assent of the Commons.

The primacy of the Commons in the grant of taxation to the crown is again illustrated in the ceremony in which the instrument of grant was presented to the king. This ceremony was held in full parliament, with both Houses in attendance; but the actual presentation of the instrument of grant to the king was made by the Speaker of the Commons.[89] Although the Lords were not represented either in the form of the grants or in the ceremonial presentation as equal partners with the Commons in the granting of taxation to the crown, but only as advising and assenting to the grant made by the Commons, they were none the less liable to those taxes.[90] Realities were recognised in 1543, after which date taxes were granted to the crown by all those assembled in parliament.[91]

Indenture and statute: assent

From 1433 grants of parliamentary taxation was cast in the form of indentures between the Commons, acting on the advice and assent of the Lords, and the king.[92] In the early Tudor period the taxes were both said to be granted 'by this present indenture'[93] and, indeed, were engrossed in duplicate on parchment in the form of an indenture. At the beginning of the early Tudor period the contractual nature of the grant was emphasised by a ceremonial presentation to the king, of his part of the indenture, in full parliament. Although the indenture form was retained until 1533, the ceremonial presentation ceased after 1492.[94] On four occasions between 1492 and 1533 grants of taxation were made in different forms. In 1497 and in 1504 the subsidies granted to the crown were 'ordeyned establisshed & Enacted by auctoritie of this present parliament' and were not engrossed in an indentured form.[95] The grant of a subsidy in 1514, although cast in the form of an indenture, was also 'enacted', 'for the sure perfourmaunce thereof':

> Be hitt enacted by the Kyng our Sovereigne Lord and by thassent of the Lordes espirituall and temporal and the Comens in this present perlement assembled and by auctoryte of the same, That our seyd Sovereigne Lord shall have of the graunt of his seyd subgiettys the seyd somme of ClxM[1] libri.[96]

And in 1515 (7 Henry VIII) it was enacted that the king should have a second subsidy, already provisionally granted in an indenture granting a previous subsidy. But this grant too was cast in the form of an indenture.[97] Thus while the form of indenture was retained for a time, the phrase in the acts 'graunten by this present indenture' tended to be replaced by phrases about enacting, ordaining and establishing.

It is significant that at the same time fifteenths and tenths continued to be granted 'by this present indenture',[98] even when, as in 1497 and in 1515 (7 Henry VIII), they were granted together with subsidies.[99] This was probably because the grant of a fifteenth and tenth was the grant of a traditional tax, and unlike the newer subsidies, there were no new proposals for levying it to be enacted, ordained and established. Nevertheless, from 1534 the indenture form of grant was abandoned even for fifteenths and tenths.

But all money bills, especially those granting the newer subsidies possessed a dual nature. They were both grants of certain sums of money to the crown, and, in order to realise these grants, they were also a congeries of clauses specifying a whole variety of administrative actions. The indenture form was certainly an adequate form of grant; but did the clauses concerning the levying of the taxes contained in the indentures have the force of law?

By the end of the fifteenth century it was generally recognised that for a bill to be known as an act, the three-fold assent of the Commons, the Lords, and the king was necessary.[100] The precise form in which the royal assent was given does not seem to have been critical.[101] In the case of parliamentary taxation in the early Tudor period out of sixteen grants, in three cases no form of royal assent has been discovered.[102] But among the forms of assent that are known, an interesting trend can be discerned.

The first royal assent given in the early Tudor period, in 1487, was in the form of an expression of gratitude for, and an acceptance of, the grant of taxation made by the Commons:

> N'RE Sgn' le Roy remerciant a sez Comens de lour boens coers, en faisauntz les deux Grauntes suizditz, mesmes les Grauntez ad accepte, & tout le content en ambedeux l'endenturez avaunt especifie ad grauntie.[103]

For the next two grants, in 1489 and 1490, there is only record of a general expression of thanks having been given by the Lord Chancellor.[104] But in 1492 the form of acceptance was substantially the same as that of 1487.[105] In 1497 the royal assent to the grant of a subsidy took the form of the king's sign manual written at the head of the bill.[106] In 1504 the form of assent was 'Le Roye le vult',[107] and apart from the bill granting two fifteenths and tenths in 1512 (3 Henry VIII) which reverted to the 1487 form,[108] all subsequent royal assents were given in this form.[109]

Thus between 1492 and 1512 the traditional form of acceptance of money grants was superseded by the standard form of royal assent given to all acts of parliament. This change in the form of assent may well reflect the discontinuance of the ceremonial presentation of the instrument of grant to the king in full parliament, for this removed the occasion for a formal expression of thanks. When the ceremonial presentation was revived in 1540, a neat formula was devised which preserved the standard form of assent together with an abbreviated form of the earlier expressions of gratitude: 'Le Roy, remerciant ses Loyaulx Subjects, accepte leur Benevolence, et ainsi le veult'.[110]

But the discontinuance of the ceremony of presentation may itself reflect a tendency to regard taxation less as a personal grant to the crown and more as a problem in administration. Certainly both the discontinuance of the ceremonial presentation and the emergence of the 'statutory' form of assent occur at the very time when the traditional form of taxation, the fifteenth and tenth, was being superseded by the rapidly developing and far more complex directly assessed subsidy. While the administrative problems of the fifteenth and tenth were but few, and had been answered long before, those of the subsidies were new and pressing. It was the development of a whole new form of taxation which, by requiring positive administrative actions to be taken, emphasised the 'statutory' status of money bills and changed the form in which they were cast, from that of a private indenture of agreement into that of an act of parliament.

3

The Fifteenth and Tenth

It has already been shown that there were two main forms of taxation current in the early Tudor period: the fifteenth and tenth, and the directly assessed subsidy. It has also been shown that these two forms of taxation differed radically in their structure, and that while the fifteenth and tenth was the older and simpler of the two, the directly assessed subsidy was both more complex in conception, and was developed by the early Tudors to such an extent that it superseded the fifteenth and tenth as the main traditional form of taxation.

It is now necessary to examine these two forms of taxation in greater detail, to discover whom they affected, and how they were assessed and collected. The fifteenth and tenth, as the older and simpler of the two, will be discussed first. Then the evolution of the Tudor directly assessed subsidy from the fifteenth century subsidy will be described. And finally, the directly assessed subsidy will be examined in all its aspects.

The Historical Background

Throughout the fifteenth century the fifteenth and tenth was universally regarded as the normal form of parliamentary taxation. Other ways of raising taxes were tried from time to time. Several were outright failures: none were ever repeated.[1] In contrast, the fifteenth and tenth was granted again and again,[2] and more than once was called upon to replace a more experimental tax that had failed.[3]

In such a situation, just before the coverage of this book begins, in 1475, the Commons had expressed their dislike for the newer tax,

> And for asmoch as wee remembre, that the moost easy, redy and prone payment, of any charge to be born within this Reame, by the Commens of the same, is by Graunt of Xv^{es} and X^{es} all the Levie whereof amongs your people is so useuell, altho it be to them full chargeable, that noon other fourme of Levie resembleth therunto.[4]

The Commons preferred the fifteenth and tenth to other taxes not only because it was the more familiar form of taxation, but also because it was a simple tax of fixed yield, while the others were complex taxes of unknown yield and required the direct assessment of each taxpayer.

The fifteenth and tenth itself had originally been such a tax, directly assessed on moveable goods, early in the fourteenth century.[5] But widespread evasion and concealment in the assessment of the tax had soon set in, and in 1334 the king cut his losses by abandoning the direct assessment of individuals. Instead he commissioned heads of religious houses and royal officials to negotiate with local inhabitants as to how much each vill should pay. Two commissioners were allotted to each shire, one being a local prior or abbot, and the other a judge or high official of one of the king's courts.[6] If no agreement could be reached between the commissioners and the local inhabitants, the vill was to be assessed at the sum that it had paid at the previous grant of a fifteenth and tenth, in 1332.[7]

The fifteenth and tenth was never again assessed directly on the moveable goods of each taxpayer; and in all subsequent grants of fifteenths and tenths by parliament, the negotiated assessments of 1334 were taken to be the amounts due from each vill or borough. Thus the fifteenth and tenth became a fixed assessment of small geographical areas. Some changes, however, were made to the assessments of 1334: certain areas were allowed deductions for decay or natural disasters, and certain religious houses and lay communities secured letters patent of exemption. Until 1433 these allowances for decay and ruin were somewhat *ad hoc* and piecemeal; but in that year parliament deducted £4,000 for general ruin and decay in the country, to be divided between the counties and boroughs according to the proportion that each bore of the total tax burden. For the division of these sums within each county, the act of 1433 provided that commissions should be sent to a lord of each shire and to the two knights of the shire, and to a lord and the two burgesses of each borough, requiring all, or at least two of them, to apportion the decay allowance of the shire or borough amongst the different vills or wards at their discretion; and to certify the collectors of the details of their allocations.[8] Such commissions were statutorily enjoined for every fifteenth and tenth between 1433 and 1467–8, with the exception of 1463.[9] In 1446 the total allowance was raised from £4,000 to £6,000; but the methods of subdividing this sum amongst the counties and then amongst the vills remained the same.[10] There were no fresh allocations after 1467–8, and subsequent acts all referred either directly or indirectly to the allowances as established for the fifteenth and tenth of that year.[11] The only exception was the fifteenth and tenth granted in 1534. Although the act provided that the tax was to be levied in the usual manner, it was in fact levied at the rates current in 1430, thereby obtaining for the crown the £6,000 usually allowed for ruin and decay.[12]

The Levying of the Tax

Thus by 1485 the Tudors had inherited a tax that had been customarily levied in a standard form for 150 years. Little further definition was necessary in the statutes, and the Tudor acts granting fifteenths and tenths were short, making a general grant 'in manner and forme afore this tyme used' and specifying only exemptions and some additional matters of administrative detail. Indeed from the crown's point of view the administration of the fifteenth and tenth was commendably simple, for since the amounts to be paid were known and fixed, the only task was that of collection.

The appointment of the collectors

The appointment of collectors during the period from 1485 to 1587 was in the hands of the members of the Commons, who were required by statute to certify to Chancery by a specified date the names of those whom they had chosen to be collectors for their own shire or borough.[13] Default on the part of members of the Commons in this matter may well have been frequent, for in the later acts alternative arrangements to provide for such omissions were made. In 1515 the king and council, or the attorney general, were empowered to make supplementary nominations as necessary.[14] The act of 1534 enabled the king under the great seal to commission local persons to make substitute appointments,[15] and the acts of 1540 and 1545 empowered the Lord Chancellor to appoint such collectors himself. These powers were used extensively in 1541, for the collection of the second fifteenth and tenth granted by the act of 1540, when members of the Commons had certified Chancery of appointments for only six counties and three boroughs. The collectors for the remaining thirty-one counties and fourteen boroughs were nominated by the Lord Chancellor.[16] In 1540, for the first fifteenth and tenth granted by the act of that year, the Lord Chancellor sent commissions to two people in every shire and borough, stating that the members of the Commons had not nominated collectors, and requiring them to appoint sufficient collectors and to certify Chancery of their names. Although this at first appears to be the exercising of the Lord Chancellor's supplementary powers of nomination by delegation, it is not. For in this case the two people in each shire and borough to whom the commissions were sent were in fact the knights of the shires and the burgesses. The fact that these commissions were sealed in Chancery only eleven days after the dissolution of parliament suggests that for some reason the nominations to collectorship were not made, as was probably usually the case, while the Commons were sitting; and that it was therefore necessary to pursue the members back to their residence by means of letters patent.[17] Under the terms of these commissions the members of the Commons were not only to nominate sufficient collectors; but were to give them full power and authority to levy the tax. This unusual delegation of authority by Chancery removed the need for any further commissions to the collectors.[18] This is the only occasion for which it is known that this particular procedure was adopted. Yet it is quite possible that other supplementary nominations were made in other years; but this remains unknown since it was not being specified as such in the documents.

When Chancery was in possession of the names of those nominated as collectors, [19] commissions were issued under the great seal to levy and collect the customary sums, and a copy of the commission and a list of the collectors were sent to the Exchequer.[20] Table 3.1 gives the dates of these commissions and the number of collectors appointed for the shires and the boroughs. Separate commissions were sent out to every shire and to each of the three divisions of Yorkshire and Lincolnshire. Cheshire, Westmoreland, Cumberland, Northumberland and Wales were exempt from the fifteenth and tenth.[21] The commissions to the collectors of Lancashire were sent in the first instance to the Chancellor of the County Palatine. By 1485 it was also customary to send out separate commissions to sixteen cities and boroughs, namely Bath, Bristol, Canterbury, Coventry, Gloucester, Kingston upon Hull, London, Norwich, Nottingham, Oxford, Rochester, Salisbury, Southampton, Southwark, Worcester and York. From 1512 separate commissions were also sent to the collectors for Leicester, and from 1541 to the collectors for Cambridge, Derby, Exeter and Lincoln.[22] For convenience, the cities and towns which received separate commissions and which accounted separately from the counties in the Exchequer will be referred to as 'the boroughs'.

Until 1537 a number of collectors were commissioned for each shire, without any further subdivision; thus it was left entirely to the collectors themselves to decide how the work of collecting within their shire or borough was to be shared between them. But from 1541, according to statutory requirements, the collectors were appointed for specific hundreds, or groups of hundreds within the shires,[23] and were responsible only for the tax from the area assigned to them.

From the table it is also clear that, until 1541, the average number of collectors appointed for any county remained within the very narrow range of eight to ten. There were never fewer than four or five collectors in any shire, except in 1537 when one shire had three. On the other hand, the highest number of collectors appointed for any county varied widely from year to year, from thirteen in 1488, to thirty-five in 1490–1. But even when this maximum figure is at its lowest, there still remains a wide range in the number of collectors appointed for the different shires. In contrast, the number of collectors appointed for the boroughs was relatively small, and consequently the difference between the highest and lowest numbers appointed was also

Table 3.1 Commissions to collect fifteenths and tenths[a]

Fifteenth and tenth	Date of Commission	Number of commissioners						Commissions not recorded for
		Counties			Boroughs			
		Max	Min	Avg	Max	Min	Avg	
1488	7 Mar 1488	13	5	8	10	2	5	Rochester[b]
1489	20 Feb 1489[c]	14	5	8	6	2	5	Rochester
14901	1 Jul 1490	35	4	10	6	2	5	Rochester, Shrewsbury[d], Lancashire
1492 (I)	22 Feb 1492[c]	18	5	9	8	2	5	Rochester
1492(II)	28 Aug 1492[c]	19	5	9	8	2	5	Yorks, York, Shrewsbury, Nottingham
1497(I)	15 Mar 1492	27	4	9	8	2	5	Rochester, Shrewsbury
1497(II)	1 Nov 1497	28	4	9	8	2	5	Rochester, Shrewsbury
1512	7 May 1512	27	5	8	8	2	4	
1513	23 Dec 1512[e]	24	5	9	8	2	4	Rochester
1514	16 Feb 1514	25	4	10	8	2	4	Rochester, Southampton
1517	17 Jul 1517	17	4	10	8	1	4	Rutland, Salop, Hull, York, Nottingham, Southampton
1537	10 Jul 1537	20	3	10	8	2	3	(Hull, Worcester)[f]
1541	4 Aug 1540[g]	22	2	7[h]	8	1	3	
1542	26 Jul 1541	12	1	5	8	2	3	

Notes:

[a] References to the enrolments of these commissions are given in Appendix II.

[b] Rochester, nevertheless, accounted separately on all occasions. E359/39, 43, *passim.*

[c] The commissions for Lancashire were repeated on 12 Feb 1506. *CPR (1494–1509)*, pp. 458–9.

[d] Shrewsbury was granted exemption from fifteenths and tenths by letters patent dated 12 Dec 1485. *Ibid.*, p. 118.

[e] Commissions to eight counties were dated on various days in January.

[f] Missing on C60. E371 records commissions to the mayor and sheriffs of Hull, and to the bailiffs of Worcester to nominate collectors, and to return their names to the Exchequer. In the case of Worcester the two collectors originally appointed had died.

[g] On this date commissions were sent out to the knights of the shire and to the burgesses of the 'taxation boroughs' to nominate collectors and to return their names to the Exchequer by 2 November.

[h] From 1541 on, collectors were assigned to specified hundreds, or to groups of hundreds.

small. There was very little variation either in these highest and lowest numbers, or in the average number of collectors appointed for the boroughs. The innovation, in 1541, of assigning collectors to specific hundreds produced an immediate fall both in the lowest and in the average number of collectors appointed in any county, but had no effect on the number of collectors appointed for the boroughs. Unfortunately the lack of information about the collectors of the last four fifteenths and tenths of the period makes it impossible to say whether this was a permanent effect or not.

Apart from the consequences of this innovation, the general impression given by the table is that the fixed and traditional character of the fifteenth and tenth was such that by the early Tudor period, even the number of collectors appointed in the boroughs and in the counties had become standardised. In the shires the collectors were usually knights, gentlemen and yeomen; and in the boroughs, burgesses and craftsmen.[24] The acts of 1540 and 1545 imposed minimum property qualifications on collectors, land to the 'clere yerely value of x.li, or above', or goods to the value of 100 marks.[25] Thus the collectors, while not coming from the most exalted ranks of society, were substantial men and often of social importance in their localities. Both these qualifications were probably considered in the selection of the collectors, for both brought advantages to the crown. The local standing of the collectors would bring both prestige and the possibility of sanctions to ease the task of collection; whilst their substance was important not only for supporting the costs of collection, for which the official remuneration might not be sufficient, but also for providing the crown with security against the possibility of default.[26]

The commissions from Chancery to the collectors contained fairly precise instructions as to how the fifteenth and tenth was to be levied. These instructions had achieved a standard form by 1485, and did not vary throughout the period under study.[27] Upon receipt of the commission the collectors were required to go from vill to vill, or from ward to ward, and in each place to summon the 'prepositus' and two inhabitants, or in boroughs the mayor, the bailiffs and four inhabitants. The collectors were to charge these men to arrange for one or two of the richer inhabitants to levy the total sum due from the vill, 'nemini in hac parcendo' and to pay it to them without delay; or, if possible, they were to demand the tax from the 'prepositus' and the two inhabitants on the spot. Having collected the tax due from each vill or ward within their area, the collectors were to bring it to the Exchequer at Westminster before a specified date.

Such, in brief, were the duties of those appointed as collectors of a fifteenth and tenth, as contained in the commissions of appointment. But a closer consideration of these duties reveals a number of problems to which the answers are by no means straightforward.

The charges on the vills[28]

First, it is difficult to see how the collectors knew what sums were to be charged to each vill, for no details were given in the texts of the commissions, nor was any mention made of accompanying schedules containing any list of the charges.[29] It is possible that each county or borough kept a book with the 1334 assessments and the 1467–8 allowances to which the collectors referred; but it seems unlikely that the crown would have relied entirely upon the existence of such local records for the efficient levying of the tax.[30] The Exchequer had its own rolls and books of record,[31] from which the particulars of the tax charges of each vill or ward might easily have been copied and sent to the collectors; but, unfortunately, the evidence for such a procedure, although strong, is by no means conclusive.

Among the records of the Exchequer there is a class of documents known as 'particule compoti'. Each of the 'particule compoti' is headed by the names of the collectors and the tax which he was to collect, in the same form as was used in the official enrolments of the collectors' accounts in the Exchequer. There then followed a list of all the vills within the collectors' area together with the traditional charges levied upon each vill arranged in three columns.[32] The first column gave the gross sum chargeable to the vill as negotiated in 1334; the second column gave the deduction to be made for decay,[33] and the third column gave the net sum due from each vill.[34] From their form the 'particule compoti' might either have been compiled in order to inform the collectors of the sums which they were required to collect, or, alternatively, they may have been drawn up for use within the Exchequer during the accounting of the collectors. But it is difficult to see what purpose in the process of accounting these particulars could have served. Until 1541 the unit of account was the county, and since the county totals were of record in the Exchequer, there would seem to have been no need to write out all the vill totals and to add them up afresh at every account. Further, the sudden reversion in 1537 to the tax charges in 1430 meant that the sum charged on each vill changed to a figure that had been obsolete for over a hundred years. Some form of guidance must have been given to the collectors, for no suggestion of the reversion to the earlier figures was given in the commissions to the collectors, and in any case local knowledge could scarcely have been expected to extend back to 1430. Since the purpose of the reversion to the charges of 1430 was to avoid the traditional allowance of £6,000 for decay, it was only necessary in 1537 to provide the first column of figures of the 'particule compoti' giving the gross charges of 1334, and indeed the 'particule' of that year took just that form.[35]

Second, it is clear from some surviving examples that the 'particule compoti' were enclosed in leather pouches, with the names of the collectors, the county and the date of the tax written on the outside.[36] This might suggest that the 'particule compoti' were in fact sent out by messengers to the collectors. But since the form of labelling on the pouches is exactly that of the standard heading of the enrolled accounts of the collectors in the Exchequer, it might appear more probable that these pouches were intended for the storage of the 'particule compoti' within the Exchequer rather than for their despatch to the collectors in the counties. On the other hand, if the pouches were intended for the conveyance of the 'particule compoti' to the collectors, this conventional form of description of the collectors was the only means of identifying the collectors that the officers of the Exchequer could give to the messengers.

Indeed the contents of one of these pouches strongly suggests that the 'particule compoti' were in fact sent out in the pouches to the collectors, for in this pouch, labelled in the usual manner, is to be found not only a 'particule compoti', but also a commission to the collectors. If it can safely be assumed that the commission has not been stuffed into the pouch at a later date,[37] it is possible that the following procedure was adopted. First, the names of the collectors and copies of the commissions were sent to the Exchequer by the officers of Chancery. Next, the officers of the Exchequer prepared the 'particule compoti' for each commission,[38] obtaining the names of the collectors from the commissions sent from Chancery, and the sums to be levied from their own records. These two documents were then enclosed in a pouch, bearing the name and office of the collectors, which was handed to a messenger for delivery. But although such a procedure would have fulfilled the obvious need for some form of information concerning the sums to be levied from each vill to have been sent to the collectors, any temptation to conclude that such a procedure was in fact followed must be tempered by the fact that no contemporary reference has been found to this effect.

But whatever may have been the case, the collectors in many instances not only knew the detailed charges of the vills, but also were sufficiently well informed to have been able to pay exactly the right amounts to the receipt of the Exchequer.[39] On the other hand, there seems to have been some confusion as to the amounts to be allowed to the different vills for their portion of the £6,000 decay allowance. The acts of 1491 and 1512 alleged that some collectors had refused to make such allowances and had embezzled the money so obtained to their own advantage. But it is possible that some of the collectors were ignorant as to the amounts that ought to have been allowed, and were afraid of being out of pocket should the allowances prove to have been less than the inhabitants had claimed. To provide a remedy for this situation some of the earlier acts empowered justices of the peace to hear and determine complaints presented by any local officers against the collectors, and to punish the collectors at their discretion.[40] It is not known how many complaints were in fact made to the Justices of the Peace; but the omission of this clause from the acts after 1515 would suggest that these were not numerous.[41]

The delegation of powers within the vill

The second problem is the delegation of powers of collection by the collectors to the local officials or inhabitants. The commission required the collectors to summon the 'prepositus' and two inhabitants and to charge them to levy the traditional sum due from the vill,

> iungentes eisdem quod pecuniam predictam per vnium vel duos homines de singulis villis et Burgis predictis magis sufficientes in forma predicta nemini in hac parcendo vt predictum est leuari et vobis liberari faciant indilate.

Or, alternatively, the collectors were to levy the money directly from the 'prepositus' and the two inhabitants, leaving them to reimburse themselves as best they might from the pockets of their fellow inhabitants.[42] It can be said straightaway that no examples of this second alternative of an immediate levy have been found. The clear implication of the commission is that the responsibility for levying the traditional sum assessed on the vill was delegated to the 'prepositus' and two other inhabitants, and that they further appointed one or two of the more substantial inhabitants to deliver the money to the collectors.

But what of actual practice? Unfortunately no record has survived of all but a very few of these local collections; and the evidence for these is available only because, for one reason or another, disputes arose out of them that were brought before the Courts at Westminster. Thus the evidence to hand is in no sense a perfect sample. Yet the conditions which gave rise to these disputes were so heterogeneous that it is unlikely that the sample provides a grossly restricted reflection of the whole. Certainly it shows wide differences of practice in the local levying of the fifteenth and tenth, and it is useful in that it provides at least a minimum range of these differences.

However, much more caution is necessary when considering the relative frequency of different practices, for the sample may well be biased in favour of the selection of particular items and thereby gives a distorted or even wholly false picture of the true distribution of all the variations which actually occurred.[43] Since they are all the evidence that is available, such comparative figures will be given below; but it must always be remembered that they refer to that small fraction of cases that were heard before the Courts at Westminster and not to the actual practice of the inhabitants of all the vills in England from 1485 to 1547.

In the first place the collector was to order the 'prepositus' and two other inhabitants to levy the vill total. 'Prepositus' is usually translated as 'reeve'.[44] A better translation might be the more general 'head man', for this would accommodate the wide variety of practices that the documents suggest. Six cases are known in which the collectors appointed the local constable to levy the tax,[45] one in which they approached the 'Chief of that parisshe',[46] one in which they appointed the bailiffs,[47] and one where they delegated their powers to the mayor.[48]

Local assessment

The assessors

The major task of those to whom the collectors entrusted the local levy of the fifteenth and tenth was to arrange for the division of the tax charge due from the whole vill into contributions payable by the individual inhabitants. Out of the nine cases where those responsible for the local levy of the fifteenth and tenth can be identified, in six cases there is evidence that they, either alone, or with the assistance of others, assessed the inhabitants to determine the individual contributions.[49] It is perhaps significant that, although the implication of the wording of the commission is that those who were approached by the collectors were to decide how the vill quota was to be paid, no mention was made as to how this decision was to be reached.[50] In fact the evidence shows that the way in which this division of the tax charge of the vill amongst the inhabitants was effected was entirely a matter of local custom, and that the lack of precision in the wording of the commission to the collectors may well have been intended tacitly to admit this variation in local practice. Certainly the ways in which the individual contributors were assessed were of no practical importance to the crown.

Apart from assessment by those appointed by the collectors, there were three main ways in which the tax charge on the vill was divided amongst the inhabitants. First, the total charge might be traditionally apportioned on to various parcels of land within the vill. In such cases there was no need for a new assessment for every fifteenth and tenth; it was merely necessary to collect the customary sums from the current occupiers of the land.[51] Second, the size of the individual contributions might be determined proportionately to the wealth of the different inhabitants. This is certainly what was envisaged in the commission to the collectors which stated that the tax was to be levied from everyone 'pro porcione sua'.[52] In such cases a new assessment of the wealth of the inhabitants would be made for every fifteenth and tenth. Sometimes the inhabitants delegated the task of making this assessment to a few of their number,[53] on other occasions the assessment was carried out by a general meeting.[54] That this latter way of making an assessment might be cumbersome and confusing is well illustrated by a dispute which arose over the assessment and collection of a fifteenth and tenth in 1541 at Burford, Oxfordshire, and which reached such proportions that, despite the advice and assistance of both the king's steward and some local justices, it was eventually taken to Star Chamber for judgement.[55]

It is clear from the depositions in the Star Chamber files that there was a great diversity of opinion as to what rates were actually decided at the original general meeting, which was attended by over a hundred people, many of whom left before the end. The confusion over the rates to be applied led six of the inhabitants to distrust the bailiffs who were responsible for the levy of the tax. After making their own assessment of their fellow inhabitants, they were convinced that the bailiffs had managed to collect £4 more than the required sum and that they had embezzled this to their own advantage. The bailiffs claimed that in fact only 2s 10d had been collected over and above the required sum, and that this had been given to the poor. The dispute rapidly got out of hand, and the bailiffs thought that their authority as officers of the king was in danger of being subverted. But it is clear from the depositions that, even after allowances had been made for the possible existence of tension between the bailiffs and the discontented section of the inhabitants before the arrival of the collector, the raising of the town total of the fifteenth and tenth was regarded as a communal effort, and that any suspicion of attempts to manipulate the traditional procedure to private advantage aroused fierce and determined opposition.

The basis of assessment

The one thing that was not in dispute at Burford was the basis upon which the assessment was to be made; all agreed that it was to be upon the yearly rents of houses. This whole question of the basis of local assessments for the fifteenth and tenth has been much misunderstood. It is generally unknown that before 1334 the fifteenth and tenth was a tax raised by applying the rate of one fifteenth or one tenth to the assessed value of every man's moveable goods. But with the negotiated assessment of the vill totals in 1334 it has been assumed that thereafter the fifteenth and tenth became somehow based essentially on units of land or other physical, immobile, property:

> Everybody else had to pay the amount settled locally and attached to the owners of particular lands or tenements, unless excused by royal grant.[56]

> It is to be noted that the fifteenth and tenth, originally a tax on moveable goods became after 1334 a fixed tax on land ... it passes over the landless population entirely.[57]

This latter assertion that the fifteenth and tenth became a fixed tax on land and therefore passed over the landless population entirely is based on a misunderstanding of the negotiations of 1334. These negotiations fixed the amounts of tax due, not from certain lands, but from specified geographical areas, that is from vills and wards. They made no arrangements whatsoever as to how these assessments were to be raised within those areas. It is a rather simple confusion to assume that because the fifteenth and tenth became a series of fixed payments by localities, these payments were necessarily further subdivided and charged on to actual units of land.[58]

It needs to be emphasised that in theory, and to a very great extent in practice, the fifteenth and tenth after 1334 was still based on an assessment of moveable goods and chattels. The most convincing proof of the persistence of the original basis of the fifteenth and tenth into the early Tudor period is the form of a writ, preserved in a Chancery precedent book of the reign of Henry VII, annulling an assessment made on the lands of a London priest,

> Quia vero concessio predicta de bonis et rebus mobilibus prout in concessione vera continetur et non de terris et tenementis facta fuit.[59]

But if the legal basis of the fifteenth and tenth was still 'bona et catalla', it must be admitted at once that it was a very wide one. In law the term 'catalla' comprised 'all goods moveable or immoveable, except such as are in the nature of freehold, or parcel of it'.[60] The commissions to the collectors confirm that the fifteenth and tenth was to be assessed on 'bona et catalla': but add that the resultant contributions were to be proportional to the assessments and that no-one was to be spared. The fifteenth was to be levied

> Ita semper quod [secular Lords and others] pro quibuscumque bonis et catallis suis qualiacumque bona et catala illa fuerint [and priests] pro bonis prouenientibus de terris et tenementis suis [acquired since 1291] pro porcione sua cum comunitate comitatus predicti nemini in hac parcendo in forma predicta contribuant.[61]

Yet the possibility that the actual practice of assessments for the local division of the fifteenth and tenth might have strayed beyond the original basis was recognised implicitly by the acts of parliament which granted the taxes in the early Tudor period. The fifteenth and tenth was

> to be had paied taken and levied of the movable goods catalles and othre things usuelly to such Xv^{mes} and X^{mes} contributory and chargeable within the Shires Citees Burghes and Townes and othre places of this your seid realme in maner and fourme aforetyme used.[62]

The Exchequer went further and openly recognised that local assessments might be made as well on the basis of lands as on goods. When local disputes arose over assessments, the chief Baron of the Exchequer customarily directed a commission to four or five local knights or gentlemen to take the depositions of witnesses about the points at issue. In two of these commissions it was explicitly acknowledged that local assessments for the fifteenth and tenth might be based on lands.[63] However, in another dispute the Barons decided in favour of a strict interpretation of the original legal basis of the fifteenth and tenth. In 1546 the farmer of Elachynton farm in Patcham, Sussex twice petitioned the chief Baron of the Exchequer that he was customarily assessed by his neighbours for a large contribution towards the fifteenth and tenth, based not on the value of his lands or his goods but on his farm by ancient custom only.[64] He claimed that according to the laws and conscience he ought only to be charged 'according to his porcion and rate for his said goodes' and because 'your said Orator by any Order of the Comen Lawe is Lyke to be Remidiles', asked for a commission to be sent to some local gentlemen 'to here and determine the right of the premisses'.[65] The chief Baron duly issued a commission to this effect with instructions to assess all the inhabitants 'pro quantitate bonorum et catallorum suorum ... nemini in hac parcendo'.[66] Thus, when pressed, the Barons of the Exchequer upheld the literal meaning of the commissions to the collectors against an ancient local custom. But it must be emphasised that this is the only case in which the Barons sought to revise local custom, and that in the absence of a petition from an injured party they made no attempt to supervise the local assessments of the fifteenth and tenth.[67]

The continued acknowledgement of goods and chattels as the formal basis of the fifteenth and tenth is further shown by the way in which deductions were made for parcels of land that were removed, for one reason or another, from liability to the tax. The fact that deductions were granted for parcels of land in this way has been used to argue the attachment of the fifteenth and tenth to the assessed value of land. But this is true only in the most formal sense, that here it is parcels of land that are at issue. What has not been appreciated is that, with one exception, the amount to be deducted was assessed, not with reference to the area of land involved, but on the value of the 'bona et catalla' within the area.[68] Thus in 1492 information was given at an inquisition that Edward IV imparked 400 acres in Godalming, Surrey, and that this land used to support 1,000 sheep, 20 oxen, 20 cows, 20 pigs and 6 horses. The traditional local rates for assessing individual contributions towards the fifteenth and tenth were said to be 1s 8d per 100 sheep, 1d per cow, 1d per ox, ½d per pig and 2d per horse. Thus the amount to be deducted from the local tax charge was calculated at £1 1s 10d.[69] Again when three further deductions for land incorporated into royal parks were claimed by the collectors, the assessments returned by the inquisitions were formally made on the value of the goods and chattels lying within the lands in question

que quidem terre annuatim solebant pascere et depascurare tot catalla pro quibus tenentes earundem terrarum solebant dare et soluere cuilibet quintedecime et decime dicto Regi infra hundredum predictum concesse – xxijs ixd.[70]

Thus there seems to have been a general persistence in the early Tudor period of the original notion of the fifteenth and tenth as a tax on goods and chattels. This was expressed most strongly in the formal documents emanating from Chancery.[71] The statutes granting the fifteenths and tenths acknowledged that 'othre thinges' were customarily assessable for the tax and gave authority of the tax to be levied on them. This recognition of the diversity of local practice was shared by the Exchequer but under pressure the Barons enforced the literal meaning of the Chancery documents.

In view of the paucity of evidence that is available the full extent of this diversity in local practice will never be known. The three main ways in which local assessments for the fifteenth and tenth were made have already been mentioned: a fixed assignment of parts of the local charge on to parcels of land, fresh assessments on the value of lands, and fresh assessments on the value of goods. Unfortunately very little evidence indeed has survived to show the range of possibilities within these last two types of assessment; what scales of rates, sliding or otherwise, were applied, or whether or not the assessments were made on traditional items only and at traditional prices.[72] But one may safely expect the range to have been very great.

Fortunately it is possible to be a little more precise about the basis on which the assessments were made, for in forty-five cases the necessary evidence is available. These examples cover the whole period of 1485 to 1547, but they are unsatisfactory in that rather more than half of them come from the last eleven years. They are further biased in that about three-quarters of them are drawn from counties within fifty miles of London; and there are no examples at all from counties south and west of Wiltshire. It would therefore be unrealistic to expect such a sample to be representative of the country as a whole right through the period; but since they are the only evidence available, they are given in full in Table 3.2.

Within the limits of the evidence, the table shows that all three types of assessment were practised during the period under study; and that on some

Table 3.2   The basis of local assessments for fifteenths and tenths

Year	District	County	Reference
1) Assessments traditionally assigned to parcels of land:			
1537	Ilford	Essex	REQ2/2/50
1537	Denver	Norfolk	REQ2/10/44
c. 1541	Sacombe	Herts	'Plumpton Correspondence', p. 239
c. 1541–4	Luton	Beds	C1/776/36–7
c. 1541–4	Reading	Berks	C1/733/70–1
c. 1541–7	Patcham	Sussex	E111/23, 42D
c. 1546–7	Betteshanger	Kent	E159/326 Cssns. P.r–

(continued)

Table 3.2 (continued)

Year	District	County	Reference
2) Assessments according to value of land and tenements:			
1489	Beech	Staffs	E159/267 Recorda T.r.12
1497 (II)	Northmundham	Sussex	E159/274 Recorda T.r.4d
1513	Nappa	Yorks (WR)	E159/293 Recorda M.r.29
1517	Clophill	Beds	E159/297 Recorda T.r.8
1517	Sanderton	Bucks	E159/297 Recorda T.r.10d
1517	Aston	Staffs	E159/297 Recorda T.r.12d
1541	Erith & Plumstead	Kent	E368/315 SVS P.r.4
1541	Burford[a]	Oxon	St.Ch.2/7/5171
1542	Willoughby	Lincs	St.Ch.2/32/99
c. 1541–7	Hanbury	Staffs/Worcs	C1/1067/1112
c. 1546–7	Linby	Notts	ReQ2/12/118
[a] on urban rents			

3) Assessments according to value of goods and chattels:			
1488	Windsor Park	Berks	E368/262 SVC M.r.15
1488	Sunbury	Middx	E159/264 Recorda T.r.11d
1488	Godalming	Surrey	E368/265 SVC M.r.11
1492 (I)	Berwyk	Oxon	E159/270 Recorda M.r.7
1492 (II)	Cheshunt	Herts	E159/269 Recorda P.r.7d
1492 (II)	Northfleet	Kent	E159/271 Recorda M.r.13d
1492 (II)	Wonersh	Surrey	E159/270 Recorda P.r.9
1492 (II)	Compton Basset	Wilts	E159/269 Recorda H.r.13
1497 (II)	Vyntre	Sussex	E159/274 Recorda T.r.4
1512	Cinque Ports	Kent	E368/287 SVC P.r.4
1512	Otley	Yorks (WR)	E159/293 Recorda M.r.16d
1512–14	Crowchestoke	Norfolk	C1/364/32
1537	Lakenham	Norfolk	C1/1037/18–20
1541	Stoke Goldington	Bucks	E159/320 Recorda P.r.1d
1541	St Lawrence	Kent	E159/320 Recorda p.r.34
1541	Croydon	Surrey	E159/331 Recorda T.r.31
1542	Wendover	Bucks	E159/322 Recorda P.r.56
1542	Maidstone Hundred	Kent	E159/322 Recorda T.r.40
1542	Cornilo Hundred	Kent	E159/321 Recorda P.r.35
1543	Fonehope	Herefs	E159/322 Recorda P.r.55
1544	Eddesburgh	Bucks	E159/322 Recorda PH.r.43
c. 1544	Harrow	Middx	E159/323 Cssns.P.r–d
c. 1544	Boscombe	Wilts	E159/323 Cssns.H.r–
1546	Dowsthorp	Northants	E159/325 Recorda H.r.29
1547	Ampthill	Beds	E368/323 SVC M.r.5

4) Assessments according to the value both of lands and tenements and of goods and chattels:			
1512–13	Emberton	Bucks	NRO Maunsell (Thorpe Malsor) Collection M (7M)
1512–13	Islington	Middx	E159/294 Recorda M.r.25–6
c. 1541–2	Chessington	Surrey	E111/16
1542	Nursling	Hants	E111/15

occasions both lands and goods were used as a basis for assessing individual contributions to the fifteenth and tenth. There seems to be no reason for supposing that any one of the three methods of assessment was more common either in any particular region of the country or at any particular time in the period. So far as it goes, the table would appear to confirm the picture of local assessment being a matter of local custom, and therefore by no means uniform throughout the country. The apparent preponderance of assessments on goods and chattels may well hold true for south-east England; but if more evidence were available for the north and west, this might possibly alter the apparent prevalence of assessments on goods over the country as a whole.

Liability through residence

If the basis for local assessments for the fifteenth and tenth local practices were somewhat at variance with official precept, then the question of the liability to the fifteenth and tenth of those who had possessions within a vill, but were not themselves resident in it, showed a similar, but weaker, tendency towards some divergence between theory and practice. It is reasonably clear that the general legal position was that the traditional tax charged on a vill was charged on the inhabitants of that vill. This principle was clearly stated in the form of a Chancery writ of the reign on Henry VII, which ordered collectors and subcollectors not to assess some wool towards the local charges for the fifteenth and tenth, since it belonged to a merchant, resident in London:

> Ne quis sit assessatus nec taxatus alibi quam vbi moram trahit continuam ad contribuendum xvme et xe.[73]

The case for residence as a necessary qualification for local liability to the fifteenth and tenth was argued by the attorney general in an action brought before the Barons of the Exchequer in 1515. He alleged that eight inhabitants of Islington, Middlesex, had been chosen by their fellows to assess all the inhabitants of the vill to raise £6 6s 1½d, the sum traditionally charged on Islington, for the fifteenth and tenth of 1512, and again for the fifteenth and tenth of 1513. The eight elected assessors duly made their assessments and collected the £6 6s 1½d. But about five weeks later they then assessed the goods and lands lying within the vill but belonging to persons resident elsewhere, which goods the attorney general described as 'nec ibidem contributoria'. From this source the assessors collected a further £3 13s 4d which they retained in their own hands. The attorney general therefore sought the advice of the Court.[74] Although it is possible that the real reason for this action was embezzlement on the part of the eight assessors, it is significant that the attorney general saw fit to claim that the money was also wrongfully obtained by means of an illegal assessment of non-residents.

The principle of residence was implied in the various disputes that occurred from time to time between neighbouring vills as to which of them might claim the inhabitants of outlying hamlets as contributory with them. These disputes were not whether the inhabitants of the hamlets held lands or goods within their boundaries, but the larger issue of in which vill they were to be deemed to be inhabitants for the purposes of the fifteenth and tenth.[75]

But to the general principle of residence as a necessary condition for eligibility for local assessment to a fifteenth and tenth, some modification must be made in the case of those vills where there was assessment on lands. First, the place of residence of whoever held the legal title to the land was immaterial, for assessments were always made on the occupiers of the lands.[76] In those vills where parcels of land bore fixed assessments, it might well happen that the occupier was assessed, even though he was resident in some neighbouring vill.[77] But even where assessments were made anew for every fifteenth and tenth, it might still be customary to include the lands of those not resident within the vill. For example in Willoughby, in Lincolnshire, the fifteenth and tenth was assessed according to ancient custom on every

> tenaunt fermer and inhabitant within the seid towne and paryshe and every other person and persons havyng in theire propre manurance and occupaccon eny londes tenements possessions or other yerelie profyttes in fee simple, tail, life, yeres or aliter within the parishe.[78]

Even where assessments were made on the value of goods and chattels, non-residents might be charged, despite the fact that this was 'illegal'.[79] But generally the principle of residence as a necessary qualification for local liability to the fifteenth and tenth seems to have been widely observed.[80]

Local relief through bequests

But in some vills the whole procedure of assessment was obviated or reduced, because the tax charges had been offset either wholly or in part by legacies.[81] Professor Jordan in his study of philanthropy in England during the sixteenth century noted several examples of such bequests. Unfortunately most of the figures that he gives are for the wider category of 'general municipal purpose' and only in the case of Norfolk does he specify separately the amount bequeathed for relief from taxation.[82] The fifteenth and tenth was particularly suited to this form of local philanthropy since it was a tax of known amount and was charged on the community as a whole. The most common form of these bequests was the assignment of the use of certain lands to the church-wardens who were to use the profits to pay 'the taske', or the fifteenth and tenth, whenever it was levied. Under the terms of some of the bequests, in the years when there was no tax to be paid the profits from the lands bequeathed were to be used to repair the parish church or to support the poor, or for some

Table 3.3   Bequests in relief of taxation

Part I: General

Year	Locality	County	Source	Alternative uses
1473	Mendlesham	Suffolk	lands	*poor relief
1492	Burford	Oxon	lands	*_
1493	Fersfield	Norfolk	house and lands	*repair of church[a]
1493	Tibenham	Norfolk	lands	*_
c. 1485–99	Girton	Cambs	lands	*poor relief
1509	Hillington	Norfolk	lands	*_
c. 1510	Dowgate Ward	London	lands	*_[b]
c. 1500–20	Yaxley	Suffolk	lands	*repair of church
1524	Norwich	Norfolk	lands	–
1536	Castle Campes	Cambs	lands	–

Notes:
* Mendlesham, *HMC 5th Report*, 596; Burford, *HMC Various Collections*, I, 49–50; Fersfield, Jordan, *Rural Charities*, 144–5; Tibenham, *Ibid.*; Girton C1/418/6; Hillington, Jordan, *Ibid.*; Lonodn, C1/321/11; Yaxley, C1/861/623; Norwich, Jordan, *Ibid.*; Castle Campes, C1/1141/6–8.
[a] Or any other object agreed upon.
[b] Alleged by an inhabitant.

Part II: Norfolk

Decade	Value[c]
1481–90	–*
1491–1500	£39 10s 0d*
1501–10	£32 12s 0d*
1511–20	–*
1521–30	£15 10s 0d*
1531–40	£38 10s 0d*
1541–50	£1 10s 0d*

Notes:
* Jordan, *Rural Charities*, 144, n. 1.
c Annual gross yield of lands, These figures have been obtained by dividing Jordan's published figures by 20. Jordan must have obtained his capital values by multiplying the original figures for the annual value of the lands by 20. Except that in 1524 a capital sum of 200 was bequeathed with which to purchase lands to provide an annual income towards tax relief.

other charitable purpose (see Table 3.3). Jordan described Norfolk as pre-eminent amongst both counties and towns in the making of bequests in relief of taxation, and the few examples collected from other sources confirm the predominance of East Anglia in this respect.[83] The total number and the total value of bequests in relief of taxation are likely to have been very much greater than those for which evidence is available.

Local collection

Once it had been decided how the total tax charge of the vill was to be divided out amongst the inhabitants, the next task was that of collection. According to the commission to the collectors, those inhabitants whom they had appointed to levy the fifteenth and tenth in each vill were in turn to appoint one or two of the more sufficient inhabitants to collect the money due from everyone and to pay it to the collectors. But it is doubtful whether in practice this double delegation of powers was always rigidly adhered to. There are only thirteen cases in which the identities both of those who were initially approached by the collectors and of those who actually collected the money are known.[84] In all but two of these cases, those who were initially approached did not appoint one or two other persons as required by the terms of the commission to the collectors; but collected the money from the inhabitants themselves.[85] It is possible that this disregard for the second step of delegation was very widespread; for nowhere do the records distinguish between those who were authorised by the collectors to levy the fifteenth and tenth within the vill and those whom they in turn authorised to collect the money. Rather the records refer to all those concerned with the local levying of the tax, regardless of their function, as 'subcollectors'. Such a coalescence of the two stages in the local levying of the tax would have had the advantage of simplifying the question of responsibility to the collectors.

The collectors and the problems of collection

In the case of default by a vill, the collectors were empowered by their commissions to levy the sum due by way of distress. They might request the aid of the sheriff in this; but no record has survived of any such help being given. Although it was not explicitly granted in the commission the sub-collectors also exercised a power of distress against individuals who defaulted on their payments. Possibly such distresses were thought of as being levied by the collectors through the subcollectors as their deputies. The law relating to distress was very complex by the sixteenth century; but it is probable that many of the restrictions upon it were not held to apply to the king's officers.[86]

Collectors of crown revenues were, however, bound by several statutes and charters. Under Magna Carta, goods and chattels had to be seized in the first instance, and only if they proved insufficient were lands and tenements to be taken.[87] Distress by collectors of fifteenths and tenths in the early Tudor period was always on goods and chattels. Secondly, the *Estatuz del Eschekere* required that plough beasts and sheep should be spared if sufficient distress could be taken from other chattels.[88] The *Dialogus de Scaccario* enumerated a long list of goods and chattels which it considered might lawfully be distrained for the king's debts; but described as prohibited the distress of necessary foodstuffs.[89] If cattle were taken and impounded, they were not to be led off too far away.[90] The owner was to be allowed to come and feed them, and nothing was to be charged for their keep.[91] The distress was to be in reasonable proportion to the size of the debt,[92] and was not be to sold less than fifteen days after it had been taken.[93] Under the *Articuli super Cartas* distress was to be released to the debtor if he could find sufficient surety for his debts.[94] These restrictions are considerably less onerous than those placed on distress taken for private debts. The critical distinction between private and public distress was that only the latter case might the distress be sold.

Despite the possible legal complications, distress was extensively used throughout the early Tudor period both by collectors and by the relatively humble people who found themselves appointed subcollectors. Most commonly, the collectors distrained upon cattle and less often upon grain or household utensils. The main purpose of a distress was to force the defaulter to pay what he owed in order to redeem his lost possessions.[95] Probably distresses were used successfully against recalcitrant taxpayers on many occasions; but being local matters and of short duration, they have left very few traces in the records.[96] Thus it is impossible to discover how often it was necessary for the collectors to resort to distress to enforce payment of the fifteenth and tenth.

Opposition to distress: rescues

What, however, can be discovered is how often such distresses were successfully opposed, with varying degrees of violence, such that the injured collector considered it worthwhile laying information against the 'rescuers' to the Courts at Westminster.[97] But there can be no guarantee that a collector would consider it worthwhile to lay information in all such cases. First, he would have had to pay fees in the courts,[98] and second, a favourable judgement in the Exchequer, where most of the actions were brought, was not particularly advantageous to the collector.[99] Nevertheless a large number of actions were brought by collectors before the Courts.

In such actions the collector, or subcollector, would appear in person in the Exchequer and swear on a corporal oath that on a certain day and at a certain place he seized specified goods from a named person for default by him of a certain sum. He would continue either that he was prevented from taking away what he had seized by a forcible rescue, or that he had removed the goods to the 'comen pownde' from which they had been rescued subsequently. The names of those responsible for the rescue were given, usually followed by 'et alii ignoti'. The rescue was always alleged to be 'vi et armis videlicet baculis et cultellis'; but sometimes other weapons such as swords or daggers were specified.[100] The standard form of the attack was 'insultum fecerunt', and to this might be added details of the beating, wounding, or other ill-treatment of the collector. It is possible that in some cases no violence took place at all, and that the 'vi et armis' formula was used merely in order to allege a contempt of the king and a breach of the peace and thus qualify for the cognisance of the Court. But such a situation would be unlikely for it presupposes some collusion on the part of the collector; and even if this did ever occur it would be further unlikely in such a case that the collector would allege a forcible rescue in the Exchequer. It is much more probable that some violence did occur on these occasions; how much would depend upon the personalities of those concerned. Certainly the descriptions of these incidents on the Exchequer Memoranda Rolls display enough variation in detail to show that they are not just formulae, but describe within the conventions of legal terminology different degrees of danger and violence.[101]

After giving the details of his complaint, the collector 'petit auisamentum Curie'. The Barons usually decided to send a writ to the sheriff to attach[102] those complained of and to produce them in court on the next return day.[103] On seven occasions the Barons issued a writ of subpoena requiring the defendants to attend the Court on a specified day.[104] On one of these occasions the subpoena was not successful in securing the defendant's attendance and was followed by a writ of attachment to the sheriff.[105] Although the writ of attachment was the normal method of compelling appearance in the Exchequer, it will be seen from Table 3.4 that in only two cases did the sheriff actually produce the defendants in court.[106] Usually the writ was returned by the sheriff with the endorsement that those named in it 'non sunt inventi'.[107] But the writs may have had some indirect effect, for column 5 of the table shows that some 43% of the defaulters nevertheless appeared in the Exchequer.[108] Appearance by attorney was extraordinary, for only three cases have been noted,[109] and in two of these the attorneys were specially admitted 'ex gratia curie' and 'ex assensu attornati Regis'.[110] Further writs of attachment were sent out against those who did not appear; but presumably with no greater success.[111]

All those who did appear in the Exchequer were immediately committed to the prison of the Fleet. However, the proceedings were usually completed and the defaulters released on the same day, so they suffered no discomfort other than the payment of appropriate fees to the officers of the Fleet.[112] On five occasions the accused were bailed to two manucaptors and ordered to reappear in court five or ten days later, 'et sic de die in diem et termio in termium quousque etc.'[113]

Almost all those appearing before the Barons began by asserting a full defence, 'vim et iniuriam'.[114] Only five people, all accused of the same rescue, admitted their guilt at the outset, and asked to be allowed to pay a reasonable fine.[115] Generally the accused asked to hear the details of the information laid

Table 3.4 Opposition to the collection of the fifteenth and tenth

Year	1 Rescue of distresses against collectors	2 Rescue of distresses against subcollectors	3 Assaults on collectors[a]	4 Total of assaults and rescues	5 Defendants appear in Exchequer	6 Attached by the sheriff	7 Pardoned by Act of Parliament	8 Most usual fine
1488	4	1	1	6	3	–	–	3s 4d
1489	5	2	–	7	5	–	–	3s 4d
1490–1	10	0	2	12	4	–	–	6s 8d
1492 (I)	22	2	–	25	7	–	–	6s 8d
1492 (II)	15	1	–	16	9	–	–	3s 4d
1497 (I)	–	–	–	–	–	–	–	–
1497 (II)	11	2	2	15	11	–	–	6s 8d
1512	3	1	–	4	1	–	–	6s 8d
1513	1	–	–	1	–	–	–	–
1514	1	1	–	2	1	–	2	–
1517	2	2	–	4	–	–	1	–
1537	3	2	1(1)	6(1)	5	2	–	3s 4d[b]
1541	1	1(1)	(1)	2(2)	2	–	–	3s 4d[b]
1542	–	3(1)	–	3(1)	2	–	–	6s 8d[b]
1543	–	2	–	2	–	–	–	–
1544	1	–	–	1	1	–	–	7s 0d[c]
1546	1	–	(1)	1(1)	–	–	–	–
1547	2	–	–	2	–	–	2	–
Total	82	20(2)	6(3)	108(5)	51	2	5	–

Notes:
The figures are only for those cases brought before the Exchequer.
Bracketed figures in the first four columns give the number of cases brought before requests, star chamber and chancery.
[a] Including subcollectors.
[b] Only one fine recorded.
Sources: See text.

against them, and when this had been read to them, they denied that they were in any way guilty of the offences charged against them. They were prepared to 'verificare' their denials in whatever way the court might require. Most were content merely to 'petere iudicium' and be dismissed, but in nine cases the accused demanded a trial by jury.[116]

But despite these protestations of complete innocence, all those accused in the Exchequer including four of the nine who demanded trial by jury, then made what was tantamount to a technical admission of guilt.[117] They asked to be allowed to compound for a money fine on the pretext that they were withdrawing from the case for reasons of expense.[118] The Barons of the Exchequer never refused these requests and levied fines of 1s 8d, 2s 0d, 3s 4d, 5s 0d, 6s 8d, or 13s 4d on each of them. Of these six sums those of 3s 4d and 6s 8d were by far the most frequently assessed and comprise almost 75% of al the fines levied. Column 8 of Table 3.4 shows the value of the fine most frequently assessed for each fifteenth and tenth.[119] Upon payment of these fines the defendants were released from the Fleet and no further process was taken against them.[120] In five cases these fines were remitted under the terms of acts in pardon.[121]

It is remarkable that although these actions were brought by collectors or subcollectors, and involved not only physical injury to the collectors, but also financial injury in that the money for which they were answerable at the Exchequer was being withheld from them, yet the Barons of the Exchequer took no steps to award the collectors any form of compensation or damages, or even to order that the money that was being withheld should be paid to them. In this the Exchequer seems to have been acting as a revenue court, solely concerned with protecting the king's rights and punishing breaches of revenue law. In the circumstances it is difficult to see what advantage there could have been for collectors in bringing such an action in the Exchequer, other than the satisfaction of securing revenge against those who had injured them.

Certain aspects emerge clearly from Table 3.4. First, many more actions against rescues of distresses were brought by collectors during Henry VII's reign than were brought during the reign of Henry VIII. In particular, the five fifteenth and tenths from 1490 to 1497, although comprising only a little over a quarter (28%) of all fifteenths and tenths granted during the period, provided over half (62%) of all cases brought before the Courts at Westminster.[122] Of these courts, the Exchequer heard by far the greater part of the cases. Out of 104 cases only two were brought before courts other than the Exchequer: and both of these were before Star Chamber.[123] As complainants against rescues of distresses, the collectors outnumbered the subcollectors by four to one.

Very few complaints of threats or assault, other than those occurring during the rescue of a distress, were brought during the whole period. Up to

1537 all these complaints were brought before the Exchequer; and after that date before Requests and Star Chamber.[124] It is very probable that many more assaults and threats were made against the collectors than were reported to the courts.[125] The assaults, although few in number, seem more or less equally distributed between country and town; but are almost entirely confined to the south of England.

The distribution of rescues of distresses is more complex. No actions against rescue of distresses were brought from nine counties and the Isle of Wight. Five of these counties form a continuous belt from Leicestershire to Suffolk. From most counties, however, between one and five actions were brought during the period from 1485 to 1547. At the other end of the scale, over half the cases came from five counties: Shropshire (21), Staffordshire (15), Kent (11), Wiltshire (8) and Norfolk (5); and one third from Shropshire and Staffordshire alone.

Although it must always be remembered that the number of actions brought before the courts is unlikely to represent the total number of rescues of distresses actually made, yet the concentration of the reported rescues at the beginning of the period and in certain areas of the country is so pronounced, that it may well be that in fact rescue of distresses were more common in certain parts of the country than in others, and that as the civil upheavals of the fifteenth century receded further into the past, local resistance to taxes granted by parliament became less frequent.

A large proportion of the rescues against the collectors occurred when the collector was distraining for the default of the whole sum owed by a vill. On only nine occasions did the collectors distrain upon individuals for defaults in paying their own individual contributions, rather than distrain upon the subcollectors as being generally responsible for all the money due from the vill.[126] In such cases the subcollector probably evaded distraint by informing the collectors of the identity of the individual defaulters. But in seventy-three cases the collectors distrained for the default by the whole vill. In over half of these cases, numbering forty-four, the collectors distrained on the inhabitants in general, without attempting to allocate any particular responsibility for the failure of the vill to produce the tax.[127] In nine cases the collectors distrained upon the constables,[128] in one case on both the constable and other inhabitants,[129] and in nineteen cases upon one or two individuals of no specified office or position.[130] In these latter cases it may be that the distress was in fact made for a default in their own personal contributions, but that the records refer to it more generally as a default in the payment by the vill. On the other hand, it may be that these individuals were those originally delegated by the collectors to levy the tax from the vill. Or, alternatively, they may have been those who were subsequently chosen by these delegates to collect the individual contributions.

The confusion of the two groups in the records has already been explained, and the documents are no more precise here. Thus the distresses upon the constables and upon the individual inhabitants for a general default by the whole vill are of no assistance in deciding which of the two groups of local delegates and local collectors the collectors held responsible for the production of the tax due from the vill. The subcollectors, on the other hand, rarely distrained for the default by a whole vill.[131] It was their duty to collect the individual contributions, and for them to have to resort to a general distress suggests a wholesale refusal on the part of the inhabitants to pay their contributions. Generally distress by the subcollectors was on individuals for the non-payments of their personal contributions.[132]

But it must always be remembered that the figures given above are for those distresses that were rescued and reported to the Courts at Westminster. It is quite possible that they do not represent accurately the incidence of all distresses, many of which were not rescued; and many of those that were rescued may not have been reported to the Courts at Westminster.

Opposition to distress: actions at law

A distress might also be opposed at law.[133] This does not seem to have been a very popular method, for only fifteen such actions have been found for the whole period from 1485 to 1547 (see Table 3.5). This lack of popularity was probably because lawsuits involved expense and uncertainty as to the outcome. It was much simpler to effect a rescue of the distress on the spot. But where the distress had been sold, or could not be rescued, an action for some form of restitution with damages was the only form of redress available, however unsatisfactory this might be.

Most of the earlier actions against distresses were brought in the Exchequer of Pleas. Unfortunately one cannot be absolutely certain that these distresses were taken in the course of levying the fifteenth and tenth, for nowhere in the records are the causes of the distress explicitly stated. Further the collectors, by virtue of being debtors to the crown, could sue and be sued in the Exchequer of Pleas on wholly private matters.[134] But the dates of the distresses coincide with the times of the collection of the taxes, and none of the actions against the collectors which can be shown to be unconnected with their official duties involve distress in any form. Actions in the Exchequer of Pleas were brought by bill; and in every case the distress was alleged to have involved the breaking of a close.[135] In all the actions the defendants sought an adjournment, or successive adjournments, on the plea of not yet being fully informed; and in every case the enrolment breaks off before any decision was reached.[136] This may suggest either that the plaintiffs for reasons of expense or lack of confidence in the outcome dropped the suit, or that some form of settlement was reached out of court.

Table 3.5   Actions at law against distresses

Year	County	Court	Decision	Counteractions by collectors Court	Decision	Reference
1488–9	Suffolk	EP	none	–	–	E13/173/H.r.10d
1488–9	Suffolk	EP	none[a]	–	–	E13/174 T.r.3d
1488–9	Surrey	EP	none	–	–	E13/173/H.r.8d
1488–9	Worcs	EP	none	–	–	E13/174 M.r.3d
1490–1	Kent	EP	none	–	–	E13/175 T.r.14d
1492 (I)	Oxon	AO	excommunication	E	fine	E159/270 Recorda M.r.7
1513	Kent	EP	none	–	–	E13/190 M.rd
1513	Kesteven	EP	none	–	–	E13/190 T.r–d
1514	Holland	EP	none	–	–	E13/191 P.r–
1517	Essex	EP	none	–	–	E13/199 T.r–
1537	Norfolk	SCN	to plaintiff[b]	C	unknown	C1/1037/18–20
c.1537–47	Staffs	C	unknown			C1/960/3
1542	Kent	CP	unknown	E	none	E159/321 Recorda P.r.35
1542	Kent	CP	unknown	E	none	E159/322 Recorda T.r.40
1542	Kesteven	A	unknown	SC	unknown	St.Ch.2/32/99; E321/10/13

Notes:
[a] A decision for the plaintiff may be inferred. The defendant's attorney 'nihil dicit in barram et exclusionem dicte accionis', and the court commanded the sheriff to discover the amount of damages and costs by inquisition. At this point the enrolment breaks off.
[b] This was an action for debt.

Key:
A   Augmentations
AO   Archdeaconry of Oxford
C   Chancery
CP   Common Pleas
E   Exchequer
EP   Exchequer of Pleas
SC   Star Chamber
SCN   Sheriff's Court, Norwich

After 1517 no further actions were brought before the Exchequer of Pleas; instead they were referred to a number of different courts. In these actions two of the plaintiffs secured favourable verdicts, and in four cases the decision of the court is unknown. But all except one of these actions provoked counter-actions by the collectors, three in the Exchequer, one in Star Chamber and one in Chancery. One of the counteractions in the Exchequer resulted in the amerceiament of the defendant; but in the other two the enrolment breaks off before any decision was reached. The decisions of the counter-actions in Chancery and Star Chamber are not known.

The apparent lack of success of the plaintiffs in these actions is striking, for only two out of fifteen are known to have gained favourable decisions. But it is possible that this failure was not as serious as it appears, for the actions may well have induced the collectors to give satisfaction to the plaintiffs out of court. On the other hand a large proportion of the collectors who were sued in courts other than the Exchequer of Pleas not only fought the actions, but brought counter-suits in other courts.

Collective responsibility: unhelpful colleagues

Far more serious to the collectors were the difficulties caused by negligent or fraudulent colleagues. This was because several collectors were appointed for a county and they were held to be collectively responsible for the total tax due from the county. The question of collective responsibility will be discussed in greater detail below when examining the procedures in the Exchequer of Account; but one disadvantage to the individual collector may be noticed at once. Although it was customary for the collectors to divide the county between themselves, and for each to take a certain part of it, thus making the matter of collection an individual responsibility; yet when it came to accounting for the money in the Exchequer, the Barons insisted on a collective responsibility for the whole sum due from the area covered by the commission to the collectors. This meant that negligence or fraud on the part of one of the collectors would seriously embarrass the others when it came to accounting for the whole county. Further, very often not all the collectors would travel up to Westminster to the Exchequer, but those that did go accounted 'tam pro seipsos quam pro sociis suis',[137] and on their return they not unreasonably asked those who had stayed behind to contribute towards their expenses.

How serious a refusal by colleagues to reimburse money spent on their behalf might be for a collector is well illustrated by the case of a collector in Cornwall for the fifteenth and tenth of 1514. Eight collectors were commissioned for the county, and each of them collected from part of the total area. But under the pressure of process out of the Exchequer, one collector found himself constrained to pay the sum due from the whole county, and accounted for this in the upper Exchequer. Because of this the collector was some £305 out of pocket, and in addition had sustained expenses to the sum of £100. Two of his fellow collectors had died, but had left sufficient estates from which their share of the tax and costs might be recovered. Unfortunately their executors together with four other collectors refused to pay him anything; and one other collector who had given him an obligation for £140 that he would pay him £100 in 'whyte tyne', had defaulted on this payment and in addition refused to honour the obligation. Thus denied a substantial sum of money, the collector brought a suit in Chancery to force his colleagues to reimburse him.[138] On six other occasions collectors found it necessary to resort to litigation to recover money either paid by them into the Exchequer for their joint account or expended on necessary costs and not refunded to them by their colleagues.[139]

The costs of collection

The collectors of fifteenth and tenths were recompensed to a certain extent 'pro misis custibus et expensis suis circa colleccionem et leuaccionem' of the tax due from their county.[140] This payment was made by way of an allowance granted to them when they accounted at the Exchequer. Thus the collectors paid into the receipt of the Exchequer the gross sum due from their county less the allowance for their expenses. They were helped in this by the fact that by 1485 the collectors' allowances were fixed at traditional amounts.[141] From Table 3.6, it is clear that these allowances were not of a uniform rate throughout the country, but varied from 0.6% of the county charge in Kent to 2% in Cornwall. Further these variations in the allowances are not adequately explained by such additional factors as the distance of the shire from London, the size of the area to be collected from, or the number of vills included by that area. The collectors for the 17 cities and boroughs that accounted separately at the Exchequer did not usually receive any allowance for the costs of collection.[142] The total value of these allowances was but 1% of the gross yield of the fifteenth and tenth,[143] a very low proportion indeed, and much less than the 2½% allowed to the collectors of the directly assessed subsidies.[144]

In 1537, when the gross sums charged on the counties were increased by the inclusion of the £6,000 usually deducted for decayed and desolate places, the allowances to some of the collectors were increased, but the collectors of eighteen counties received the same allowances as before.[145] The increases in the allowances were granted upon petition by the collectors to the Barons of the Exchequer.[146] Thus the most likely explanation of the apparent inconsistency of the new allowances is that the collectors of the eighteen counties omitted to ask for any increase. But even amongst those allowances that were increased, no consistent principle can be discovered. Only the petition of the collectors for Nottinghamshire is recorded in full and it was evidently the test case, for once this had been decided in favour of the collectors, similar allowances were granted to other collectors in which the Nottinghamshire decision was cited by way of precedent.[147] The Nottinghamshire collectors petitioned for an allowance for the extra money that they had to collect at the same rate, 3d per £1, as their traditional allowance. The Barons granted this after consultation with the attorney general 'et aliis Domini Regis legis peritis'.[148] Unfortunately, although the increased allowances for all the other counties were expressly stated to be based on the Nottinghamshire petition and decision, yet in several cases this was manifestly not so. For example, the increased allowance granted to the collectors for Northamptonshire was arrived at neither by an extension of the old rate for the county of 2d per £1, nor by the application of the

Table 3.6 Allowances to collectors of fifteenths and tenths

County	Tax due (£ s d)			Collectors' allowance (£ s d)		
Beds	568	15	1½	5	0	0
Berks	873	5	2	6	13	4
Bucks	578	11	5	5	0	0
Cambs	826	4	1½	6	13	4
Cornwall	403	13	11	8	0	9
Derbs	390	9	8	5	0	0
Devon	803	15	9	10	0	0
Dorset	717	11	10¼	10	0	0
Essex	1,039	13	0	8	0	0
Glos	1,100	2	0	10	0	0
Hants[a]	943	13	11½	8	0	0
Isle of Wight[a]	138	4	2	2	0	0
Herefs	363	14	1½	7	0	0
Herts	513	17	0	6	13	4
Hunts	371	3	9	6	13	4
Kent	1,557	0	4	10	0	0
Lancs	318	2	4	6	0	0
Leics	616	13	11	6	0	0
Holland	560	13	8	6	13	4
Kesteven	786	7	11	10	0	0
Lindsey	1,201	7	8	10	0	0
Middlesex	286	18	6	4	0	0
Norfolk	2,757	16	10	18	0	0
Northants	976	1	7½	8	0	0
Notts	558	4	3	8	13	4
Oxon	1,102	0	5	10	0	0
Rutland	172	1	8	3	6	8
Salop	464	4	6	6	0	0
Somerset	1,131	3	0¼	10	0	0
Staffs	484	19	0	6	0	0
Suffolk	1,214	5	9½	10	0	0
Surrey	437	0	9	6	13	4
Sussex	930	14	8½	6	13	4
Warwicks	646	3	2	6	13	4
Wilts	1,280	6	0½	12	4	0
Worcs	403	16	4½	6	0	0
Yorks (ER)	817	11	11	10	0	0
Yorks (NR)	519	11	7	6	13	4
Yorks (WR)	597	15	4	8	13	4
Boroughs	Tax due (£ s d)			Collectors' allowance (£ s d)		
Bath	13	6	8	–		
Bristol	185	8	1½	–		
Canterbury	53	12	3½	–		
Coventry	62	17	5	–		

continued

Table 3.6 (continued)

Borough	Tax due (£ s d)			Collectors' allowance (£ s d)
Gloucester	98	10	1	–
Kingston upon Hull	60	9	0	–
Leicester	21	0	0	–
London	618	3	5	–
Norwich	80	6	11	–
Nottingham	37	1	0	–
Oxford	80	18	11	–
Rochester	13	13	4½	–
Salisbury	65	6	10	–
Southampton	47	9	0	–
Southwark	17	3	0	–
Worcester	17	16	0	–
York	160	10	0	–
TOTAL	31,109	15	5½	300 18 1

Note:
[a] Until 1497(I) Hants, together with the Isle of Wight, accounted jointly at £1078. 4. 9½d with an allowance of £10.
Sources: E359/39, 43, passim.

Nottinghamshire rate of 3 per £1, nor even by the application of a new rate such that the overall rate for the whole sum collected became 3d per £1.[149] It seems very doubtful whether the Barons applied any consistent principles at all in deciding the new allowances in 1537.

In 1541 the Exchequer reverted to the traditional scale of allowances.[150] Unfortunately no record of the actual expenses of the collectors of the fifteenths and tenths has survived, and so the question of whether the official allowances were sufficient or not cannot be answered. In fact it would be extremely difficult to calculate a true estimate of the cost to a collector of levying a fifteenth and tenth. The expenses of travel, of the conveyance of the specie to Westminster, and of a sojourn in London might be calculated fairly accurately. On the other hand, the costs of collecting the fifteenth and tenth within the county would depend very much on such variable factors as the degree of co-operation and efficiency shown by those to whom the collector had delegated the local collection within the vills, and upon quite incalculable factors such as the cost to the collector of the time lost to him whilst engaged upon the king's business. But it is doubtful whether many collectors found the sums allowed to them in the Exchequer to be more than sufficient to cover their expenses. It should be noted that, unlike their counterparts for the directly assessed subsidies, the local assessors and collectors of the fifteenths and tenths received no official remuneration whatsoever.[151] It is possible that some of them managed to gain some recompense for their labours by collecting somewhat more from the individuals within their area than they were required to pay to the collectors; but on the three occasions on which this is known to have happened the inhabitants brought actions against them for fraud in Star Chamber and Chancery.[152]

The time available for collection

The time allowed to the collectors in which to levy the fifteenth and tenth varied from year to year. It was determined by a statutory date for the payment of the tax into the Receipt of the Exchequer on the one hand, and by the date of receipt of the Commission to levy the fifteenth and tenth on the other. Unfortunately, there is no means of discovering when the commissions were delivered to the collectors, and so the time available to the collectors must be calculated from the date assigned to the Commission in Chancery.[153] The actual net time available to the collectors would be less by the time taken by the royal messengers in delivering the commissions, and would have been further reduced if the Commissions had been delayed in Chancery or, possibly, the Exchequer for any reason.

Apart from the exceptional figure of one week in 1497 (II), the collectors were always allowed at least six weeks in which to levy the fifteenth and tenth (see Table 3.7). On some occasions, notably in 1541 and 1542, they were

Table 3.7　The time available to the collectors for levying fifteenths and tenths.

Year	Weeks[a]
1488	15
1489	17
1490–1	19
1492 (I)	6
1492 (II)	11
1497 (I)	11
1497 (II)	1
1512	8
1513	6
1514	10
1517	18
1537	15
1541	25
1542	26
1543	date of commission unknown
1544	date of commission unknown
1546	date of commission unknown
1547	date of commission unknown

Overall average: 13½ weeks.
Notes:
[a] From the date of the commission in chancery until the statutory date of payment, see Appendices I and II.

allowed very much longer than this. The possibility of payment after the statutory date is discussed below in the chapter on the Exchequer of Account. Although the time taken to deliver the commissions, to collect the money, and to travel to London must remain conjectural, it is clear that in some years it was possible for the collectors to collect the money well in advance of the payment date. This would allow the collectors the free use of the money that they had collected for a period of several weeks. It may well be that for some the advantage of the use of a considerable sum of money free of interest more than outweighed the disadvantages of collectorship.

Unpopularity of office: limitations and exemptions

But for most the office of collector of a fifteenth and tenth was undoubtedly an onerous burden, for in addition to the problem of collecting the money and the possibility of uncooperative colleagues, the collector was liable to penalties imposed by the Exchequer should he run into arrears on his account there.[154] Thus caught between local resistance on the one hand and the inexorable demands of the Exchequer on the other, the collector was potentially in a very dangerous situation.

The disadvantages attendant upon the office of collector were recognised in the statutes. In all the acts which granted more than one fifteenth and tenth, except that of 1487, an attempt was made to mitigate the burden of collectorship by prohibiting the appointment of persons as collectors for more than one of the fifteenths and tenths.[155] Second, the acts of 1490 and 1491 attempted to stop one of the consequences of the undesirability of the office of collector, by providing for the punishment of members of the Commons who took bribes from those anxious to avoid being appointed collectors.[156] Third, in all the acts members of the Commons secured their own exemption from appointment as collectors of fifteenths and tenths.

Other individuals and groups also obtained exemption from collectorship, but by means of letters patent (see Table 3.8). Most of these exemptions were from the collectorship of all taxes, but a few were from a wide variety of other offices too. Exemptions of this kind were not numerous, but it is possible that there were more than can be discovered from the records, for if the holders of exemptions were never actually appointed collectors, they would never need to claim their exemptions, and thus no record might ever be made of them.[157]

Exemptions from Liability to the Fifteenth and Tenth

Not everyone was required to pay the fifteenth and tenth. Some may have been exempt because of their status, others were exempt because they lived in favoured localities or belonged to privileged groups. Exemptions from liability

Table 3.8 Exemptions from collectorship of fifteenths and tenths

Persons	Place	Instrument	Dated	Reference
Inhabitants	Shrewsbury	LP	12 Dec 1485	E159/265 Recorda M.r.24
Inhabitants	Shrewsbury and suburbs	LP	14 Dec 1495	E159/292 Bre. Dir. P.r.4d
Inhabitants	Wenlock	LP	29 Nov 1467	E159/322 Recorda T.r.10
Citizens	Hereford	LP	16 Oct 1457	E159/274 Recorda H.r.22
Citizens	Pontefract	LP	28 Nov 1488	E159/274 Recorda P.r.2
Burgesses	Reading	LP	4 Aug 1510	E159/297 Recorda T.r.16
John Heron[a]	Middlesex	LP	23 Jan 1511	E159/298 Recorda H.r.2
John Robinson[a]	Boston	LP	9 May 1511	E159/291 Recorda T.r.9d
William Turke	Middlesex	Bre.Dir.	10 Nov 1517	E159/296 Recorda H.r.1

Notes:
LP   Letters patent.
[a] and their heirs. This was John Heron, Treasurer of the Chamber.

to the fifteenth and tenth may be classified into five categories: persons exempt through status, areas exempt through custom, areas exempt by statute, areas exempt by petition to the Barons of the Exchequer and areas or communities exempt by letters patent.

Exemption by status

Of these four categories the most obscure is that of exemption through status. Apart from the king himself, there are three main groups which are generally considered to have been exempt from the fifteenth and tenth: the clergy, the landless and the peerage.

The question of the exemption of the landless can be quickly dismissed. This exemption is claimed by Dietz, 'it [the fifteenth and tenth] passes over the landless population entirely'.[158] It has no more solid foundation than as the corollary of his belief that after 1334 the fifteenth and tenth became a fixed tax on lands. This belief has already been shown to stem from a crass misunderstanding of the nature of the standardisation of 1334, and to be quite false. The corollary collapses with the premise. A somewhat similar exemption is alleged by Johnson:

> People who fell short of a census (of varying amount, usually stated in the instructions to the collectors) paid no contribution at all to the Fifteenths and Tenths.[159]

No evidence has ever been produced in support of this statement, and certainly there is none for the early Tudor period. Until such evidence is forthcoming, the notion of a minimum qualifying assessment for the fifteenth and tenth is best disregarded.

The case for the exemption of the clergy is most clearly stated in the Chancery precedent book of the reign of Henry VII:

> cum persone ecclesiastice in aliquibus taxacionibus ad opus nostrum leuatis inter laicos taxari temporibus retroactis non consueuerint.[160]

But as a general statement of past practice this is undoubtedly wrong. For by the end of the thirteenth century it was customary for the purposes of taxation to divide clerical wealth into the two categories of spiritual and temporal incomes, or 'spiritualia' and 'temporalia'. The former category consisted of such things as tithes, oblations, the profits from frankalmoign tenure and from the glebe land of the parish church. Temporal income was income from temporal sources such as manors, mills, markets and burgages. In the taxation of Pope Nicholas of 1291, most items of temporal income were listed as being 'annexed to sprituralities'. After 1291, tenths granted by convocation were assessed on the basis of the Taxation of Pope Nicholas; and fairly quickly parliamentary taxation was held to apply only to the temporalities of the church acquired after 1291.[161]

In the early Tudor period, although the acts were silent on the question of clerical liability to the fifteenth and tenth, the commissions to the collectors maintained the custom of the early fourteenth century by stating clearly that the fifteenth and tenth was to be levied:

aceciam de viris ecclesiasticis de bonis prouenientibus de terris et tenementis suis post annum vicesimum Domini Edwardi filii Regis Henrici quondam Regis Anglie progenitoris nostri adquisitis.[162]

The clergy were thus liable both to taxes granted by convocation and to taxes granted by parliament; but the two forms of taxation fell on different parts of their wealth. Nevertheless this dual liability provoked a few outbursts against parliamentary taxation. A vicar in Sussex drew his sword and assaulted a collector of the second fifteenth and tenth of 1497, complaining that he had already paid one subsidy granted by the convocation of Canterbury.[163] Five years earlier two priests in Oxfordshire had cited in one case the local assessors, and in the other the subcollector, in the archdeacon's court for perjury and contempt, and had secured sentences of excommunication against them.[164] Apart from these three instances nothing more is known either of friction between the clergy and those who levied the fifteenths and tenths, or of the extent to which the clergy were in fact required to contribute towards the fifteenth and tenth. But the existence of a large number of exemptions under statute and letters patent for ecclesiastical bodies suggests that clerical contributions were common. Matters were further complicated when, after the dissolution of the monasteries, lands that used to be liable only to the clerical tenth, passed into lay hands. Only one dispute over such a case has been noted; but unfortunately the decision of the court is unknown.[165]

The exemption of the peerage from liability to the fifteenth and tenth by reason of their status rests on no positive evidence, yet some modern authors have asserted its exemption. Dietz writes that the fifteenth and tenth 'did not however touch the demesne lands of peers'.[166] In this he follows Ramsay[167] and Vickers[168] who allege the exemption of the peerage in the fifteenth century, and the evidence cited by Vickers in support of this contention is also quoted by Dietz.[169] The document in question is an indenture between the collectors and commissioners of a tax granted in 1472, which recites the terms of the commission under which, *inter alia*, the demesne lands of peers were excluded from assessment. Neither Vickers nor Dietz seem to have read the document sufficiently carefully to discover that this commission was not for the collection of a fifteenth and tenth, but for the assessment and collection of a tax directly assessed on income from lands, tenements, offices and other yearly profits. The reason why the demesne lands of peers were excluded from liability to the tax was quite simply that the Commons and the Lords made two parallel, but separate, grants; and that this commission was for the levying of the Commons grant alone.[170]

Not only is the claim for the general exemption of the peerage from the fifteenth and tenth based on a simple misunderstanding of one document, but it also seems perversely opposed to all other documentary evidence. First, no exemption of the peerage existed during the early history of the fifteenth and tenth, especially at the time of the standardising of the tax in 1334.[171] Secondly, at least from 1401 onwards, the commissions to the collectors always stated that the fifteenth and tenth was to be levied from the whole lay population:

> de singulis Civitatibus Burgis et Villis ac singulis Dominis villarum ac aliis populis laicis predicti regni nostri bona et possessiones habentibus necnon aliis tam maioribus quam minoribus.[172]

Thus, formally, the peerage together with the whole lay population was liable to the fifteenth and tenth. Yet it is quite possible that Lords and other privileged groups managed, by virtue of their social position, to avoid paying their full share of the local assessments.

A tendency in this direction seems to have set in immediately after the standardisation of the fifteenth and tenth in 1334. The commission to the collectors of the next fifteenth and tenth, in 1336, threatened direct assessment by the crown of all those assessors, Lords and richer subjects who continued as before to levy the whole quota from the poorer subjects.[173]

The same suggestion, that the 'greate Estates' were not contributing to the fifteenth and tenth according to their wealth, appears at the beginning of the sixteenth century. In 1512 a subsidy was granted to supplement an earlier grant of a fifteenth and tenth. In the preamble to the act reasons were advanced why this extra money should be raised by way of a directly assessed subsidy rather than by the grant of a further fifteenth and tenth. One of these reasons was clearly the desire for an increased participation by the 'greate Estates' in bearing the burden of taxation:

> Wyllyng also the greate Estates Piers and Nobles of this Realme towarde the payment of that greater somme in suche easy maner to be charged that the same Estates Pyers and Nobles shall have benevolent courage to charge them selfe.[174]

Although there seems a reasonable likelihood that from the very moment when assessment for the fifteenth and tenth became a local matter the more powerful managed to secure for themselves some form of favoured treatment, even possibly amounting to complete exemption; yet this situation was never recognised by the crown which in the commissions to the collectors insisted right up to 1547, and possibly well beyond, that all should contribute to the fifteenth and tenth, regardless of their status, according to the rate and quantity of their goods and chattels.

Unfortunately the evidence does not exist to determine how widespread evasion by the more powerful was in the early Tudor period. The lack of evidence for the assessment of the peerage must not be taken to imply the actual exemption of the peerage from assessment, for very few records of local assessments have survived. Only one case is known in which the lands of a peer were assessed towards the fifteenth and tenth.[175] This at least belies the proposition that the peerage was altogether exempt.

Exemption by custom

Certain parts of the country were exempt by custom from liability to the fifteenth and tenth. These were Wales, Cheshire, and the northern border counties of Cumberland, Westmorland and Northumberland, including the Bishopric of Durham. Of these, Wales and Cheshire had never contributed to the standardised fifteenth and tenth, whilst the northern border counties had all done so at some stage.[176] Cheshire and Wales were regarded as exempt 'because of the mises which they paye at the change of euery prince'.[177] The northern border counties were exempt because of their liability to attend upon the wardens of the marches in all sudden raids, at their own expense;[178] and also, doubtless, because of the devastation suffered from these raids.

Exemption by statute

In the early Tudor period statutory exemptions were granted to Lincoln, Great Yarmouth and New Shoreham.[179] Cambridge was allowed a reduction in its assessment of approximately 55%.[180] In 1512 the colleges of Oxford, Cambridge, Eton and Winchester were exempted by statute,[181] and in 1515 statutory exemption was granted to all colleges, monasteries, hospitals, Charterhouses, halls, or 'other body polytike or other place corporat' that were customarily exempted by virtue of their charters or letters patent.[182]

Exemptions by petition to the Barons of the Exchequer

The Barons of the Exchequer granted exemptions for areas inundated by the sea. The vills of Tharlesthorp and Frysmerk in Yorks (ER), of Alvethely, Reynham and Wenington in Essex, and the vills of Hayling, Stoke, East Stoke, Northwood, Southwood, Mengham and Westington in Hampshire, had long been inundated and were traditionally exempted from the fifteenth and tenth by 1485. The collectors petitioned that the traditional deductions might be allowed to them. The collectors for Essex based their claim on an Inquisition held in 1453 and enrolled on the Memoranda Roll of that year, and on the accounts of the collectors of the fifteenth and tenth granted in 1467–8.[183] The collectors for Hampshire did not have to make any detailed citation of precedent to secure the traditional allowance for the Isle of Hayling.[184] On the other hand the collectors for the East Riding of Yorkshire had considerably more trouble in claiming the allowance for Tharlesthorp and Frysmerk. The collectors for both of the fifteenths and tenths granted in 1487 claimed an allowance for £2 5s 2½d out of the total assessment of £4 9s 8d, citing the accounts of the collectors of the fifteenth and tenth granted in 1443. The collectors of the first fifteenth and tenth were granted this allowance without any further trouble.[185] But for the collectors of the second fifteenth and tenth, the Barons of the Exchequer ordered a fresh inquisition to be held locally. The inquisition returned that all parts of the vill lay under water. Nevertheless the collectors were only exonerated for the £2 5s 2½d which they had originally claimed.[186] A year later other collectors claimed to be exonerated from the whole sum charged to the vill; and again a fresh inquisition was ordered, which returned as before. But this time the collectors were exonerated from the whole sum.[187] Thereafter the collectors cited the findings of this inquisition.[188]

In 1541 new claims for exoneration on account of flooding were made by the collectors for Ranesmills, Lancashire,[189] and Erith and Plumstead, Kent.[190] Both these claims were substantiated by local inquisitions, and were thereafter allowed to the collectors by the Barons of the Exchequer.

Table 3.9   Claims for exoneration for lands taken into the royal demesne

First claim for exoneration	Area	County	Reference
pre-1485	Fulbroke	Warwicks	E368/262 SVC M.r.16d
pre-1485	Cresslowe	Bucks	E368/263 SVC T.r.8
pre-1485	Weybridge-Byfleet	Surrey	Johnson, 'Surrey Returns', 169
pre-1485	Eltham	Kent	E159/267 Recorda P.r.5
1487	Godalming	Surrey	E368/265 SVC M.r.11
1487	Windsor Park	Berks	E368/262 SVC M.r.15
1541	Bedington Park[a]	Surrey	E368/331 Recorda T.r.31
1541	Nonesuch	Surrey	E368/317 SVC H.r.9
1542	Berkhamstead	Herts	E368/317 SVC P.r.1
1546	St Frideswide's College	Oxford	E368/322 SVC T.r.3
1547	Ampthill[b]	Beds	E368/323 SVC M.r.5

Notes:
[a] All collectors omitted to collect from this area; but no claim was entered until 1552.
[b] Although this land was acquired by Henry VII and never let to farm no claim was made until 1547.

Somewhat similar were the exonerations granted by the Barons to the collectors for lands taken into the royal demesne. Claims for exoneration for eleven such parcels of land were made during the period from 1485 to 1547 (see Table 3.9). As with exoneration for flooded areas, the details of the enclosed lands and their value in terms of contributions towards the fifteenth and tenth were discovered by means of local inquisitions, and on the basis of the findings of these inquisitions, the Barons exonerated the collectors.

Exemption by prerogative grant

Such exemptions were granted to both religious and lay communities either as part of the original charter of foundation or incorporation, or subsequently as a result of a petition to the crown. The exemptions were usually embodied in letters patent, either original as resulting from a petition, or by way of 'inspeximus' and confirmation of the original charter.

Secular communities

Exemptions were granted traditionally to the inhabitants of the Cinque Ports,[191] the bailiff, jurors and community of Romneymarsh,[192] the moneyers of the mint in London,[193] the inhabitants of the towns of Shrewsbury,[194] Ludlow,[195] and Queensborough.[196] In 1541 the town of Seaford, Sussex was also granted complete exemption by letters patent, but no reason was given for this exemption.[197] Reductions in assessments were granted under letters patent to Lyme Regis[198] and Melcome Regis[199] in Dorset.

The sums involved in all the exemptions and reductions allowed by statute, by decision of the Barons, and by prerogative grant to secular communities were not large. In total they comprised on average but 2% of the gross yield of the fifteenth and tenth, and of this the allowance to the inhabitants of the Cinque Ports accounted for by far the greater part.[200] From the crown's point of view, therefore, these exemptions, although numerous, did not constitute a serious loss of revenue.

Religious communities

Still more numerous, but even less serious financially, were the exemptions granted, either by charter or by letters patent, to certain religious houses from all taxes, spiritual or lay, national or local. In most cases the exemption extended to all the lands and goods of the house, and in some cases to those of the house's servants too. These grants of exemption to religious houses are confined to no one order nor to any part of the country. On the other hand the Carthusians, the Benedictine nuns and the academic colleges of Oxford are particularly well represented (see Table 3.10).

Table 3.10 Grants of exemption to religious foundations

House	Type[a]	Letters Patent	Charter	Inspeximus	Reference
Bustlesham	pA	–	3 Feb. 1399	–	E159/285 Bre.Dir. H.r.4 E368/280 Recorda P.r.9
Beauvale[b]	pC	–	–	–	E363/6, 7, 8 *passim*
Canterbury, Northgate	h	t.Ed III	–	19 Nov. 1488	E159/271 Bre.Dir. M.r.6
Canterbury, St. James[c]	h	–	–	–	E159/271 Bre.Dir. M.r. 1,5
Cotterstoke	sc	–	t.Ed IV	12 July 1488	E159/265 Bre.Dir. M.r.10d E159/274 Bre.Dir. P.r.2,7
Coventry[b]	pC	–	–	–	E363/6,7,8 *passim*
Davington[b]	pBN	t.Ed III	–	–	E363/6,7,8 *passim*
Dertford	pDN	–	–	7 Dec 1487	E159/269 Recorda H.r.37 E159/271 Bre.Dir. H.r.5
Denney[b]	aFN	–	–	–	E363/6,7,8 *passim*
Dover, Maisondieu	hAU	–	unspecified	–	E159/271 Bre.Dir. M.r.6d
Eddington	hoBO	t.Ed III	–	–	E159/263 Bre.Dir. H.r.12 E159/268 Bre.Dir. H.r.7d E159/277 Bre.Dir. T.r.1 E368/274 Recorda T.r.1
Fotheringhay	sc	t.Ed IV	–	t.H VII	E368/360 Recorda M.r.61d
Henton[b]	pC	–	–	–	E363/6,7,8 *passim*
Hull[b]	pC	–	–	–	E363/6,7,8 *passim*
Kirkby Bellars	pA	24 Jan. 1452	–	10 July 1487	E159/272 Bre.Dir. M.r.6d E368/281 Recorda M.r.34
Kilburn[b]	pBN lh	–	unspecified	4 July 1486	E363/6,7,8 *passim* E159/263 Bre.Dir. M.r.5d E159/265 Bre.Dir. H.r.12 E159/267 Bre.Dir. P.r.2d

Institution	Status				Reference
Leicester, Newark	sc	4 Dec. 1441; 12 Feb. 1461	—	1 Oct 1486	E259/264 Bre.Dir. M.r.17d; E159/264 Bre.Dir. M.r.7d; E159/265 Bre.Dir. M.r.19d
London	pC	20 Mar. 1399	—	—	E159/276 Bre.Dir. P.r.7
Maxstoke	pA	t.Ed IV	—	12 May 1500	E159/272 Bre.Dir. T.r.2
Sheen[b]	pC	—	—	5 Mar 1491	E363/6,7,8 *passim*
Syon	aBRN	24 Mar. 1465	—	17 Aug. 1486	E159/268 Bre.Dir. M.r.13d; E159/263 Recorda P.r.14; E368/262 SVC P.r.12
StratfordBow	pBN	4 Feb. 1474	unspecified	12 Mar. 1488	E159/271 Bre.Dir. M.r.9
Westminster	aB			1 Sept. 1486	E159/264/Bre.Dir. M.r.5d
Westminster, St Stephen	sc	t.Ed IV	—	20 Sept. 1485	E159/264 Bre.Dir. M.r.2; E159/268 Bre.Dir. M.r.12; E159/281 Bre.Dir. M.r.5
Winchester	ac	—	28 Sept 1395	25 Nov. 1487	E159/264 Bre.Dir. T.r.16; E159/266 Bre.Dir. H.r.4; E159/269 Bre.Dir. M.r.1; E159/272 Bre.Dir. M.r.8d
Windsor	rc	—	1 Dc. 1461	—	E159/272 Bre.Dir. P.r.6; E159/276 Bre.Dir. H.r.1; E159/281 Bre.Dir. T.r.1
Witham[b]	pC	—	—	—	E363/6,7,8 *passim*
Oxford Colleges					
All Souls	ac	—	t. H VI	10 May 1488	E159/264 Bre.Dir. T.r.17d
Magdalen	ac	14 Mar. 1336; 27 Oct. 1456	—	—	E159/265 Bre.Dir. H.r.11; E368/279 Recorda P.r.17
New	ac	—	26 Sept. 1385	—	E159/266 Bre.Dir. H.r.4
Queen's Hall	ac	—	t.Ed III	12 June 1488	E159/265 Bre.Dir. H.r.4d
Cambridge Colleges					
St Johns	ac	28 July 1520	—	—	E159/299 Bre.Dir. M.r.9

continued

Table 3.10 (continued)

House	Type[a]	Letters Patent	Charter	Inspeximus	Reference
Bourne	pA	12 Mar. 1486	–	–	E368/262 Recorda P.r.5
Chertsey	aB	–	1 Sept. 1488	–	E159/269 Bre.Dir. P.r.5d
Cheshunt	pBN	13 Jan. 1352		20 Jan. 1490	E159/280 Bre.Dir. P.r.1
Dover, St Martin	?	–	–	–	E368/269 Recorda P.r.7
		20 Mar. 1483(PS)			E368/274 Recorda H.r.11
Ludlow, St J. Bapt.	?	t. Ed IV	–	25 Nov. 1488	E368/263 Recorda H.r.14
York, St Leonard	?	–	various	4 Feb. 1487	E159/263 Bre.Dir. H.r.7d
					E159/269 Bre.Dir. M.r.1d

Six further religious houses received grants of exemption from lay taxation; but do not appear from the collectors' accounts ever to have exercised them.

Key:

t.   tempore
(PS) by writ of privy seal

Notes:

[a] See Knowles and Hadcock, *Medieval Religious Houses.*

Type of Foundation:

Order:

a	abbey	A	Augustinian
ac	academic college	AU	Austin Rule
h	hospital	B	Benedictine
ho	house	BN	Benedictine nuns
lh	lazar house	BO	Bonshommes
p	priory	BRN	Bridgettine nuns
rc	royal chapel	C	Carthusian
sc	secular college	DN	Dominican nuns
		FN	Franciscan nuns

[b] No reference to the instrument of exemption has been found.

[c] The 'breue directum baronibus' cites no previous instrument; but commands exemption 'compacientes status et indigencie Priorisse et Sororum'.

In 1489 an act was passed which nullified all prerogative grants of exemption from both the payment and collection of tenths, with the following exceptions: Ely Priory; Leicester, Newark College; Leeds, St Nicholas; Llanthony Priory; Melsa Abbey; Oxford, New College; Reading Abbey; St Albans Priory; Sheen Priory; Syon Abbey; Westminster Abbey; Westminster, St Stephen's; Winchester, Academic College; Windsor, Royal Chapel.[201] It is not clear whether this act applied to fifteenths and tenths or to clerical tenths only. The position was clarified in 1491 by a further act which established all allowances for fifteenths and tenths as they had been in the reign of Edward IV.[202] In the brief period when the 1489 act was in force, all the customary exemptions for the fifteenths and tenths continued unaffected.[203]

Again, in 1540, the act granting four fifteenths and tenths expressly declared that letters patent or other royal instruments granting exemptions from fifteenths and tenths were, for the purposes of the act, to be null and void.[204] Nevertheless, as in 1489–91, prerogative grants of exemption continued to be allowed by the Exchequer.[205] The inhabitants of Lincoln, usually statutorily exempt form fifteenths and tenths, petitioned the king that he would grant them their traditional exemption.[206] And, despite the statute, letters patent granting their release from half their charge were issued by the crown,[207] and accepted by the Exchequer.[208] On the other hand, in 1541 the Barons of the Exchequer bound the bailiffs of Shrewsbury by a recognisance to pay to the collectors the £16 8s 5d due from the town, but usually remitted by virtue of letters patent of exemption.[209]

The lack of success of these attempts to annul prerogative grants by statute is striking. On two occasions in the fifteenth century the same conflict between prerogative grants of exemption and the terms of the grant of taxation was brought before the judges in the Exchequer Chamber.[210] But these cases are not particularly helpful for they concerned grants made by convocation. While Plucknett and Chrimes are undoubtedly right in stressing the 'private law' approach of the judges to these 'public law' cases,[211] one point has been overlooked which has perhaps prevented the full force of the issues from being adequately appreciated. Granted a 'private law' approach, and leaving aside all questions of statute, there is a great difference between a grant of money by convocation, without any formal acceptance by the crown,[212] and the grant of money by parliament in the form of an indenture which the crown accepts together with all the conditions contained therein.[213] In the former case it would be difficult to show that the crown by levying the money granted by convocation thereby also bound itself to all the conditions attached to the grant, especially if these should be to the detriment of its undoubted rights. On the other hand, in the case of the parliamentary grant, the crown bound itself by its own words to accept the conditions of the grant. It would therefore have to show that its prerogative rights were somehow inalienable. It was this issue that was never taken before the judges.

But whatever decision the judges might have reached on this point had it been put to them in 1489 or in 1540, one fact plainly stands out. In contrast to earlier practice, on neither of these occasions did the crown, or any of its officers, attempt to take any advantage of the suspension of the grants of exemption.[214] This suggests that the Tudors were more concerned with safeguarding their prerogative rights than were their Lancastrian or Yorkist predecessors, even to the extent of refusing to be bound by statutes to which they themselves had assented.

Although the number of religious foundations possessing grants of exemption from fifteenths and tenths was large, the loss in revenue to the crown from these exemptions was but 1.2% of the gross yield of the tax.[215] When this figure is added to the 2% lost through exemptions of all kinds to secular groups and individuals, the total 3.2% lost in revenue from all exemptions remains a remarkably low figure.

Summary

The gross yield of the fifteenth and tenth in the early Tudor period has already been shown to have been £31,100. From this sum 1% had to be deducted for the allowances to the collectors for their collection costs; and a further 3.2% was lost by way of grants of exemption.

Hence the net yield of the fifteenth and tenth in the early Tudor period was some 4.2% less than the gross yield. Thus upon a grant by parliament of a fifteenth and tenth the expected net revenue accruing to the crown was £29,800. Whether this sum was ever collected in full is examined elsewhere,[216] but at least the maximum net yield was predictable.

It was this very predictability of the yield of the fifteenth and tenth which constituted at once both its advantage and disadvantage as a form of taxation. From the crown's point of view it could be relied upon to produce a known amount of money, certainly no more, but probably not much less; whereas a tax based on a direct assessment of wealth was subject not only to changes of economic fortune, but also to the possibility of dishonesty in the assessors. From the point of view of those granting the tax in parliament the fixed yield of the fifteenth and tenth enabled them to know precisely how much money there were giving the crown,[217] and the stereotyped nature of the tax meant that they knew what the incidence of the tax on different regions and groups of people would be.

As a tax proved in practice over 150 years, the fifteenth and tenth was attractive as the traditional form of taxation that was at the same time exceptionally easy to administer. In addition to this it had the unquestionable advantage of avoiding any inquisition by the crown into private property and wealth.[218] The question of the distribution of the tax burden within the vill, who was to pay and who was not, was left entirely to local discretion. It may well be that the continuing popularity of the fifteenth and tenth as a form of taxation owed not a little to this element of local self government.

On the other hand, the fifteenth and tenth was not without certain disadvantages, both in the eyes of the crown and of parliament. Firstly the burden of the tax was shared out according to a distribution of wealth that had prevailed in the country 150 years earlier. The economy had not remained in a state of fossilisation during the intervening years, and it was quite patent by the early sixteenth century that some parts of the country were, through prosperity, enjoying a relatively light tax burden, whilst others, less fortunate economically, were shouldering a far greater share of the total tax than could possibly have been foreseen in 1334. In 1512 the preamble to a subsidy act spoke of the necessity of devising an alternative tax:

> as well in shorter tyme as in more easy unyversall and indifferent manner to be levied then such comon tax of xv. and x. hathe or can be accordyng to the auncient Use thereof.[219]

To this discontent with the inequity of the incidence of the fifteenth and tenth was added a dissatisfaction with the possible loss of potential revenue to the crown which it entailed. Although the limited yield of the fifteenth and tenth was circumvented by recourse to multiple grants, there remained the possibility that a considerably greater overall yield could be obtained if the tax burden bore some greater resemblance to the distribution of wealth amongst the taxpayers. Certainly the point of exhaustion would not be reached so quickly.

In fact the guiding principle behind direct taxation in the early Tudor period was that the rich were better able and willing to contribute to the expenditure of the crown through taxation than were the poor. And the history of taxation in the early Tudor period was the development by the crown of a system of taxation designed to discover where the wealth of the country lay, and to tax it proportionately to its size. The poor were excluded by minimum taxable qualifications, and the rich were yet further imposed upon by benevolences and other extra-parliamentary devices.[220]

Yet while this system of taxation based upon direct assessment was being developed and expanded, fifteenths and tenths continued to be granted by parliament often in conjunction with the newer tax. The fifteenth and tenth retained its popularity as a form of taxation right through the sixteenth century, and it was regularly granted by parliament until 1623.[221]

4

The Evolution of the Directly Assessed Subsidy

The Fifteenth-Century Background

Subsidies that involved a direct assessment of an individual taxpayer's wealth by crown commissioners were seldom granted by parliament in the fifteenth century. Only seven such grants were made before 1485 (in 1404, 1411, 1427–8, 1431, 1435, 1450 and 1472),[1] and of these, two failed and had to be withdrawn (1431 and 1472).[2] Parliament regarded these subsidies as extraordinary forms of taxation, for in the acts granting three of them (1404, 1411 and 1450) it was expressly declared that they were not to be taken as precedents for the future.[3] The Common's dislike of directly assessed taxes is further illustrated by their petition, in 1432, that the abandonment of a subsidy granted the year before should be accompanied by the erasure of all traces of it from all Courts of Record.[4] In the last two grants of subsidies before 1485, parliament also attempted to withdraw the proceeds of the subsidies from direct royal control. Under the act of 1450 the subsidy was to be paid to four named servants of the crown who were to meet the military expenses of the crown directly themselves.[5] The act of 1472 went further and required that the collectors of the subsidy should deposit the money from the tax in castles, abbeys and other safe places until parliament decided to what uses it should be put. All certificates concerning the yield of the tax were to be sent to parliament and not to the Exchequer. Also in 1472 parliament made the grant of the subsidy conditional upon the crown fulfilling certain stipulated military actions. If these were not fulfilled, then no money from the subsidy was to be made available to the crown.[6] Thus it could with fairness be said that the attitude of parliament in the fifteenth century towards directly assessed subsidies was suspicious, even hostile. And towards the end of the century parliament increasingly tried to bring all aspects of this tax, including the expenditure of it, under its own control.

The one form of directly assessed taxation that was granted by parliament to the crown without any reservations was the poll tax on aliens. Five such taxes were granted in the fifteenth century before 1485 (in 1439, 1442, 1449, 1453 and 1482), and all were very similar in design. Aliens were classified either by occupation, wealth or country of origin, and each group was required to pay a fixed sum.[7]

The Poll Tax on Aliens of 1488

The first directly assessed tax to be granted to the crown in the early Tudor period, was such a poll tax on aliens, granted to Henry VII in 1487.[8] The act granting the tax was very short and merely specified the payments that each class of alien was required to make, the latest day of payment, certain exemptions, and the provision that landlords were to be held responsible for the tax due from aliens who fled after they had been assessed and before the collectors could demand the money from them.[9] As such it was a very simple tax, for the assessment only involved the discovery of aliens and the application of one of five rates to them. The rates are shown in Table 4.1. Aliens denizen, aliens engaged in husbandry, and aliens born in Ireland, Wales, Berwick, Calais and the Marches, Gascony, Guyenne, Normandy and in islands under English sovereignty, were exempt from the tax.

On 21 January 1488 letters patent were sent out commissioning between four and nine knights and gentlemen in each shire, and the mayors and sheriffs of London, York, Norwich, Lincoln, Canterbury, Gloucester, Southampton, Bristol, Hull and Nottingham and the Constable of Dover Castle and the Warden of the Cinque Ports, to assess the tax, to appoint collectors, and to return the assessments together with the names of the collectors to the Exchequer.[10]

This very simple tax has left little mark on the records.[11] But two difficulties seem to have arisen. First, several collectors appeared at the Exchequer and claimed exoneration from sums that they could not collect,

Table 4.1 The poll tax on aliens of 1488

Classification	Rate
Alien artificers, householding	6s 8d
Aliens, not householding	2s 0d
Alien brewers	20s 0d
Alien merchants, factors, or attorneys, householding or resident more than three months	40s 0d
Alien merchants, factors, or attorneys, not householding or resident less than three months	20s 0d

because the aliens on whom they had been assessed had fled out of their area.[12] The Barons of the Exchequer allowed the collectors to be exonerated from these sums and charged the defaulting aliens themselves.[13] The clause in the act laying responsibility in such cases on landlords was not invoked. Second, several private individuals came into the Exchequer and protested that they had been unjustly presented as aliens at local inquisitions, and they gave details of their parents' nationality and of the place of their birth to substantiate their claims. In all these cases the attorney general admitted their claims to be true.[14] Three collectors also brought actions in the Exchequer against rescuers of distresses. The enrolment of one of these actions is inconclusive;[15] but in the other two the defendants appeared in the Exchequer and sought to be admitted to fines rather than be tried by jury.[16]

Unfortunately there are no enrolled accounts for this tax, and so the gross yield cannot be determined accurately.[17] But so far as this can be reconstructed from the Exchequer records, it was no less than £774 4s 1d, and probably not much more than this.[18] This yield is a very low figure indeed, and no further poll taxes were levied on aliens in the early Tudor period.[19]

The Subsidy of 1489: Failure

The second directly assessed tax granted to Henry VII, in 1489, was typical of the subsidies granted to the crown earlier in the fifteenth century, in that parliament imposed numerous conditions upon the grant.[20] Indeed the grant of 1489 bears a striking resemblance to the grant of 1472.[21] On both occasions the purpose of the grant was the maintenance of an army of a specified number of archers, 10,000 in 1489, for a fixed length of time, namely one year. In 1489 the total cost of this army was estimated to be £100,000, of which parliament undertook to bear £75,000 and the Convocation of Canterbury £25,000.[22] But as in 1472, the money granted was fully appropriated to a specific military enterprise, for if the army were in any way diminished, then the king and parliament between them were to reduce the grant proportionally. Likewise if the army were to go abroad, and expenses were to rise above £100,000, then the tax was to remain in operation for a further two years, always provided that not more than £75,000 was raised in this manner in any one year.[23]

Second, parliament made quite certain that the details of private wealth discovered during the assessment of the tax should never come into the possession of the crown. The acts granting the subsidy explicitly prohibited the return of any transcripts of the inquisitions of assessment to the Exchequer or to any other Court of Record. Not even the total amount due from any area was to be certified to the Exchequer; but was to be referred to parliament.[24]

Third, the subsidy was not to be paid into the Exchequer or any other central treasury, but was to be deposited with named receivers in designated castles, towns, abbeys, and other safe keeping places, to remain until the king sent for it. This last provision marks a relaxation from the act of 1472 that established parliamentary control even over the expenditure of the money from the tax.

But, in general, the parliament of 1489 was as uncompromising in its distrust of the crown and of the Courts of Record as any of its predecessors. And like its predecessors it tried to safeguard the future, by stressing that the utter unusualness of the conditions which gave rise to the tax precluded it from being taken as a precedent for future grants.

> Also it is agreed by the said auctorite, that this Graunte in fourme aforsaid made, be never taken for example or president, nor herafter drawen in consequens; considryng that ther was never afore this any like Graunt made, but that grete necessite hath caused it at this tyme to be made, for the spede of the said payment.[25]

But, despite the protestation of parliament, the terms of the grant of 1489 were similar to those of the grant of 1472. Like the grant of 1472, that of 1489 was in fact two separate grants, one made by the Commons and the other by the Lords. The Commons granted to the crown one tenth of the annual income from all honours, castles, lordships, manors, lands and tenements, rents, fees, annuities, corrodies, pensions, fee farms, and from the temporal lands of the clergy;[26] and 1s 8d for every ten marks in the value of goods.[27] The Lords only granted a tenth of the annual income from lands and offices as above.[28] But apart from this one difference in the scope of the two grants, the Commons' and the Lords' grants were identical in all respects, and will here be treated as though they comprised one grant.

The general administration of the tax was in the hands of commissioners to be appointed by the king and commissioned by letters patent under the great seal 'as Commyssions have custumably used to be sent for the Levye of XV[es] and X[es] aforetyme granted'.[29] But the commissioners for the subsidy of 1489 were of a different kind from the fifteenth and tenth commissioners, who were only collectors, entrusted with the levy of fixed sums of money. The first task of the subsidy commissioners was to discover the value of the incomes from lands and offices, and the capital value of the goods, of everyone within their area. This they were to do 'by all manner of wayes and meanes aftir their dyscressions possible, by Examynacions, Inquerrers, or other resonable meanes.'[30]

Although the commissioners were allowed a large amount of discretion in the choice of procedure for making their assessments, they were required by the act to observe certain rules concerning the valuation of incomes and wealth for the subsidy. Income from lands and offices was to be the net current annual income, as from 1 January 1489, after all 'Rentes fees and servyces' had been deducted. All goods were to be assessed, including stocks of merchandise held by traders for sale. On the other hand, the personal apparel of the taxpayer, that of his family, the 'necessarie Utensils or Stuff of his of their Houshold', coined money and plate 'necessarie to their degree, and kept only to their use, and not to be sold', were to be exempted from assessment to the subsidy. So too were ships using the sea and their tackle.

In addition to these rules about the valuation of assessments, the act of 1489 also laid down what was to become a cardinal principle of Tudor direct assessment taxation, namely that the taxpayer was to be assessed only in the place 'where he is most conversaunt'.[31] Later this principle was to raise awkward problems of multiple assessments in the cases of those who had scattered estates or possessions; but in 1489 these complications seem neither to have been envisaged, nor to have arisen.

Once these assessments had been made, the commissioners' second task was to choose 'able and sufficient' inhabitants of the area to act as collectors.[32] These collectors were to be given indentures specifying the amount each individual taxpayer in the area was required to pay. Upon receipt of these indentures, the collectors were empowered to collect the sums contained in them, and pay them into the designated safe keeping places in castles, towns and religious houses. The collectors were to be personally chargeable for the sums contained in their indentures, and if they did not duly pay them into the designated safe keeping place, then the commissioners were to certify the relevant details to the Exchequer. The Exchequer was to recover the sums due by process against the defaulting collector, who was to be imprisoned 'till he have made Fyne in that behalfe for his seid defaute'.[33]

The assessments were to be completed before 19 April 1489, and the tax assessed on goods was to be paid into the safe keeping places before 1 May 1489. The tax assessed on lands and offices was to be collected and paid in two instalments: the first between 25 March and 1 May 1489, and the second between 29 September and 1 November 1489.[34]

Thus the subsidy of 1489 was a very different kind of tax from a fifteenth and tenth. Not only was the wealth of everyone assessed under the supervision of crown appointed commissioners according to statutory rates; but there was a clear division of function between the commissioners and the collectors. The former in no way handled the money; they were responsible in general for the administration of the subsidy act and appointed the collectors at their discretion.

The subsidy act of 1489 also differed from the acts granting fifteenths and tenths to the crown in that it was much more explicit concerning difficulties that might arise in the levying of the tax. The collectors were protected in two ways. First, the act of 1489 explicitly empowered the collectors to sell any distress if the tax due could not be levied in any other way.[35] Second, the act of 1489 allowed the collectors in the last resort to escape responsibility at the Exchequer for the defaults of others. If a person defaulted on his payment to a fifteenth and tenth and had no distrainable goods or lands, then the collector was in the unfortunate position of being charged for this sum at the Exchequer and being unable to obtain any remedy. The act of 1489 allowed the subsidy collectors to discharge themselves of responsibility in such cases by certifying to the Exchequer, together with the commissioners, the names of the defaulters and the sums assessed on them. The Barons of the Exchequer were then to order the sheriff to levy twice the sum certified directly on the defaulters themselves.[36]

The act of 1489 also protected private individuals. First, a taxpayer, with no distrainable goods or lands, but who enjoyed an income from annuities, offices, corrodies or other annual profits, was to be allowed a period of grace of up to fifteen days after the statutory payment dates in which to pay the collectors, before his name might be certified to the Exchequer. Secondly, anyone such as a tenant, suffering distress at the hands of a collector for the default of another, or anyone avoiding such a distress by making a cash payment for the default of another, was to enjoy the profits of the defaulter's lands until he had recouped the value of his distress or money payment.

Both the machinery for the assessment and collection of the subsidy and the clauses giving some measure of protection both to the collectors and to private individuals were contained in the crown proposals laid before parliament. But parliament added further clauses. Those which made the grant of the subsidy conditional upon the maintenance by the crown of the army of archers at the agreed level, and those which sought to prevent the detailed assessments of the subsidy from falling into the hands of the crown, have already been noted. But along with these clauses, parliament added others. First, the Queen, the counties of Cumberland, Westmorland, Northumberland, and the merchants of Castile, Venice, Genoa, Florence, Lucca, and the Hanse were exempted from liability to the subsidy. Second, the members of the Commons secured their own exemption from involvement with any of the administrative responsibilities of the subsidy, for no member was to be appointed commissioner, assessor, juror or collector. Third, the collectors were protected in two further ways. If any commissioner could be shown to have been influenced in his choice of collectors by bribes, he was to be imprisoned until he had paid the injured party twice the sum in question, and further until he had paid a fine to the king for the contempt. And if any receiver, in one of the designated safe keeping places, refused to take the money brought to him by the collectors, then upon certification of the facts by the commissioners to the Exchequer, the Barons were to issue process for fine against the receivers at their discretion.[37]

It is interesting that although parliament seemed determined to prevent the details of the individual assessments and of the yield of the tax from falling into the hands of the crown, when difficulties over the levy of the subsidy arose, both parliament and the crown resorted to the traditional processes of the Exchequer to coerce and punish defaulting taxpayers and officers. In general the boycott of the Exchequer was successful, for the only records to be found for the subsidy are all concerned with those very matters for which the act invoked the Exchequer's aid.[38]

On the other hand, the act was less successful in preventing the money from the subsidy from being paid to the Exchequer, for some 70% of the estimated yield of the tax was paid directly by the collectors into the Exchequer of Receipt.[39] Only two cases are known of the money having been stored in local safe keeping places, and in both cases it was in abbeys. The Cellarer of the abbey of St Edmund at Bury stored money collected from Norfolk and Suffolk and brought it up to the Exchequer.[40] The other abbey that stored money was St Mary's outside York, and of this money some was paid to military paymasters in the north; but most was delivered into the hands of the Treasurer of the Chamber.[41] Some county collectors paid the money they had collected directly to government officials. The collectors of Derbyshire paid £380 17s 5½d to the sheriff on the king's commandment,[42] the collectors of Northamptonshire paid £33 17s 2d to Richard Empson,[43] and the collectors of Cornwall and Devon paid at least £1335 9s 6d to William Hatteclif, the king's avener (provider of oats), who in turn, under the supervision of the Earl of Devon, paid it to Richard Gomersall, clerk of the king's ships.[44] A very small portion of the yield of the subsidy was assigned for the repayment of those who had lent money to the crown, and for the payment of annuities.[45]

It is interesting that although there is no trace of the collectors ever having accounted at the Exchequer,[46] yet when payments were made by the collectors to the Treasurer of the Chamber or to other royal officials, the collectors were given the official Exchequer form of receipt, namely tallies, whose sole raison d'être was that they were the only forms of receipt recognised in the upper Exchequer for accounting purposes.[47] The fact that these tallies were issued after the transactions had taken place suggests that the collectors were apprehensive that they might be called to account for the money at the Exchequer, and so petitioned for tallies to be struck as a precaution against this eventuality.[48]

Because of the lack of formal accounts the yield of the subsidy of 1489 remains somewhat obscure. Certainly, despite the provisions of the act, it was very much less than the projected £75,000. The Commons, a year later, 'as well by the Certificates by your [the king's] commissioners in that behalfe ... made, as by other resonable estimation' put the yield at not more than £27,000.[49] As far as it can be reconstructed from the records of cash received by the Exchequer of Receipt, the yield of subsidy was £20,736 12s 0d.[50] The actual yield to the crown is likely to have been less than the estimate made by the Commons on the basis of the commissioners' certificates, for they represented the gross expected yield, and probably did not take into account expenses allowed to the collectors and losses suffered through defaults in payment.[51] On the other hand, the actual yield was probably more than the figure of £20,700 reconstructed from the Exchequer records, because in view of the statutory provisions for the payment of the tax it is unlikely that all of it was paid into the Exchequer.[52]

But at whatever point between £21,500 and £27,000 the true yield of the subsidy of 1489 in fact lay, it is clear that it fell far short of the target of £75,000.[53] Contemporaries attributed this failure to the costs of collection and to the 'favour of the commmyssyoners' in setting the assessments too low.[54] There is no evidence available by which the costs of collection may be determined; but what evidence there is of the individual assessments suggests that contemporaries may well have been right in attributing the blame for the failure of the subsidy to a laxity on the part of the commissioners in supervising the assessments, for by far the majority of the assessments are on lands, and there are suspiciously few on goods.[55]

But whatever may have been the reasons for the failure of the subsidy of 1489, both the degree of the failure, and the means taken to rectify it, were typical of directly assessed subsidies in the fifteenth century. After having been twice prorogued, parliament reassembled in January 1490, and most humbly besought the king to accept in lieu of the deficit of £49,000 still owing, not another subsidy, but a fifteenth and tenth.[56] Although the crown's acceptance of this offer ensured that it would still lose some £20,000 of the original grant of £75,000, the assured yield of the fifteenth and tenth must have seemed preferable to the uncertain, and if precedent were to be followed, smaller yield of another subsidy.[57] Not only had the subsidy of 1489, like most other fifteenth-century subsidies, failed; it had even been unable to attain the yield of a fifteenth and tenth.

The Compromise Forms of 1497 and 1504

The failure of the subsidy of 1489 was so great that the crown did not attempt to levy a directly assessed subsidy for twenty-five years.[58] In 1490 and 1491 only fifteenths and tenths were granted;[59] but in 1497 it is evident that there was some dissatisfaction with a reliance upon the fifteenth and tenth as the sole form of taxation, for a grant of two fifteenths and tenths was supplemented by the grant of an 'aid'. In January 1497 parliament was asked to ratify a grant of £120,000, already made to the crown in October by a 'grete counsayll'.^{60} The usual way for £120,000 to be raised would have been by a grant of four fifteenths and tenths,^{61} and 'an aide and subsidie of as greate and large sommes of money as the seid too XVmes and X^{mes}'.^{62} This subsidy was to be in general incidence and yield exactly the same as two fifteenths and tenths, for not only was £12,000 to be deducted as for fifteenths and tenths, but every shire and borough^{63} was to pay the same total charge as it customarily did for fifteenths and tenths. Where the subsidy of 1497 differed from fifteenths and tenths was that the traditional division of the county total amongst the vills was abandoned, and consequently the size of individual contributions towards the county totals was to be determined, not by local custom within each vill, but by statutorily appointed commissioners according to the assessed value of the incomes and possessions of everyone within the whole county. Thus, within the safe framework of the fixed yield of the fifteenth and tenth, the apparatus of a direct assessment by statutorily appointed commissioners, applying universal statutorily defined criteria, was to be allowed to operate.

If contemporaries were right in attributing the disastrously low yield of the subsidy of 1489 to the favourable under-assessment permitted by the commissioners, and if it has been correctly observed that there was a tendency on the part of the richer and more powerful subjects to evade paying a just contribution to fifteenths and tenths, then this particular amalgamation, in 1497, of the directly assessed subsidy with the fifteenth and tenth provided at one blow a solution to the main defect of both forms of taxation. For not only was the yield of the tax guaranteed to the crown, regardless of the attitude of the commissioners; far more important, at last the dead hand of custom was to be lifted from local assessment towards the fifteenth and tenth, allowing, in theory, a just division of the tax burden proportionate to the wealth of each individual taxpayer.

But the arrangements of 1497 had two more positive aspects, whether these were foreseen by those responsible for them or not. Although the act of 1497 did not remove the inequities of the burden of taxation between counties, through the abolition of the fixed assessments of the vills, the tax burden was spread over each county proportionately to the distribution of wealth within that county, thereby removing many of the inequities in the incidence of the fifteenth and tenth that had arisen as a result of changes in economic fortune since 1334. Second, the arrangements of 1497 allowed commissioners to be trained in the supervision of the assessment and collection of a tax without any financial risk to the crown. If the future of parliamentary taxation as a form of revenue to the crown was to lie in directly assessed subsidies, rather than in fifteenths and tenths, as in fact it did, then it was essential that those who were to act as commissioners for these subsidies should become accustomed not only to the skills involved in the administration of this particular form of taxation, but also to the experience of working in loyalty to the crown, and against the immediate interests both of themselves and of their friends and neighbours. Otherwise the only prospect for directly assessed subsidies was that of a continuation of the débâcles of the fifteenth century. But whatever the true motives of those responsible for the subsidy of 1497 were, it is at least clear that they considered the new arrangements superior to a further grant of two fifteenths and tenths.

The details of the procedure for levying the subsidy of 1497 bear a considerable resemblance to those of the subsidy of 1489. The minimum qualifications in both lands and goods for liability to the taxes were at the same level in both subsidies; but the assessment rules of 1497 differed considerably from those of 1489. Firstly, in 1497 only profits from lands and tenements were assessable in the category of yearly profits.[64] This meant that incomes derived from offices, fees, annuities, corrodies and other annual profits were exempt from assessment towards the subsidy of 1497.[65] Also in 1497 lands liable to the Clerical tenth were explicitly exempted from the subsidy.[66] The crown proposals for the subsidy made no provision for the exemption of certain classes of goods, as had been done in 1489; but several clauses were added in parliament which exempted victuals, horses, military equipment, and household furniture and utensils, from liability to the tax, and which restricted the liability of aliens and the clergy to such of their goods and chattels as were usually liable to fifteenths and tenths. Again, the crown proposals in 1497, unlike those of 1489, made no provision for double assessment of those with property in more than one place, so a clause was added in parliament to supply the deficiency. In 1497 no one was to be charged for any goods and chattels except where they were dwelling, with the exception of 'quycke catell couchant and Levaunt', of corn growing or lying in 'the Berne Garner or in Stackis', and of stocks of merchandise held for sale. No provision was made against double assessment on lands.[67]

But assessment under the act of 1497 was of a radically different kind from that of 1489, for while the earlier subsidy assessments consisted of the direct application of statutory rates to the assessed value of income from lands or goods and chattels; in 1497 the assessments were made only as a guide towards a proportional division of a fixed sum of money due to the crown amongst a number of individuals of different wealth. Although the arithmetic was more complicated in 1497, the assessments did not have to be made nearly as accurately as in 1489. Indeed, in London, the commissioners merely grouped all those liable to the subsidy into 'iiij degress of Berers and payers'.[68]

The commissioners who were to make these assessments were nominated in a schedule attached to the foot of the act granting the subsidy.[69] Four commissioners were nominated for each shire, and four for each of thirty cities and boroughs.[70] In the shires these statutorily appointed commissioners were to be joined by the Justices of the Peace, and in the cities and boroughs by the mayors, Justices of the Peace, sheriffs, bailiffs, and 'other hed officers'.[71] Thus the administration of the subsidy was placed in the hands of men who already held public office together with a few others of some social standing.

In describing the manner in which the assessments were to be made, the act of 1497 was less specific than the act of 1489. The commissioners, calling upon the assistance of 'oder discrete persons' were simply to assess individual contributions according to the criteria laid down in the act. The commissioners had complete discretion in these assessments, and there was no appeal against their decisions. As in 1489, the commissioners, once they had made the assessments were to appoint collectors and given them lists of individual assessments; but, unlike 1489, they were to certify the collectors' names to the Exchequer, and not to parliament.[72] An important innovation was that the collectors were not to begin levying the tax until eight days had elapsed from the last day of assessment, presumably to give the taxpayers some time to find the ready money with which to pay the collector.[73]

The collectors of the subsidy of 1497 were accorded by the act all the advantages of collectors of fifteenths and tenths, namely the same allowances for costs of collection, exemption from fees in the Exchequer, exemption from appointment as collector for more than one payment of the subsidy, and assistance from local officers of the crown.[74] But the act of 1497 also granted the collectors further assistance. As in 1489 the collectors were empowered to distrain upon a defaulter's goods, and if necessary to sell them, to realise the debt, and also to distrain upon the defaulter's tenants' goods. But the act of 1497 protected the tenant to a greater degree than the act of 1489 by limiting such a distress to 'as ferre as the rent of ferme of the seid fermour or tenaunt shall severally extende unto for halfe a yere and nat further'.[75] The act of 1497 also greatly helped the collectors by allowing cases of rescues of distresses to be heard summarily before Justices of the Peace, who might commit the offenders to ward without right of bail.[76] This was obviously far more satisfactory from the collectors' point of view than the somewhat tedious process of citing the rescuer before the Barons in the Exchequer, if only because a summary imprisonment would allow the collectors to levy the distress without delay.[77]

The act of 1497 also enabled the collectors to exonerate themselves from responsibility for sums that they could not collect, and for which they could not distrain. It also provided a greater degree of protection for the defaulting taxpayers than did the act of 1489. Under the act of 1497, the collector was to make a public proclamation in the nearest market town of his intention to certify a default. After the default had been certified to the Exchequer, the defaulting taxpayer was to be allowed fifteen days' grace in which to pay, otherwise he was to answer to the Exchequer in person for double his original assessment.

In fact fifteen collectors took advantage of this provision, and certified that they could not distrain upon a total of 195 defaulting taxpayers, who owed in all £52 11s 6d.[78] None of the collectors certified the default to the Exchequer, but they appeared in person before the Barons and laid their information on oath, and in every case the Barons exonerated the collectors from the sums concerned. In fact the Barons allowed the defaulting taxpayers between fifteen days and eight weeks to pay before they doubled their assessments. Only one defaulter came and paid within the period of grace,[79] and in all other cases the Barons doubled the assessments and instructed the sheriffs to levy these sums.[80]

But although the crown had provided, in its proposals for the subsidy, a large measure of protection both for the collectors and for the individual taxpayer, several clauses were added to the subsidy act by parliament. Some of these, concerning the exemption of certain classes of goods from liability to the subsidy have already been noted;[81] but the most significant of these clauses was a proviso making the levy of the second payment of the subsidy conditional upon the crown's execution of the military expedition promised in the preamble to the act. For if Henry was to make a 'perfite peas' with the king of Scotland, and did not actually mount an expedition against him, then the second payment of the subsidy was not to be levied. And if a truce was declared, the second payment was to be suspended, only to be resumed if the expedition was mobilised before the date fixed for its collection. Thus even as late as 1497 enough of the traditional suspicion of fifteenth-century parliaments for the crown still remained for parliament to consider it necessary to appropriate half of the subsidy to the due performance of a specific military project. The second part of the subsidy was never levied, although the second fifteenth and tenth, with the same payment date, was. The main expedition against Scotland was recalled to deal with the Cornish Rebellion, part of the causes of which were protests against paying the subsidy, but two months later the Earl of Surrey led an invasion of Scotland; this had to be abandoned because of rain.[82]

Distrust of the crown is again apparent in the next subsidy, of £30,000, granted to the crown in 1504. Originally Henry had asked for two feudal aids to which he was entitled for the knighthood of his son Arthur and for the marriage of his daughter Margaret to the king of Scotland.[83] This demand by the crown was almost certainly not prompted by considerations for immediate revenue, for, as far as is known, the royal finances were at this time in a healthy state and no great expenditures were being planned.[84] As Dietz has recognised, the purpose of the demand for the feudal aids was more probably to provide an 'opportunity and legal occasion to search out all titles and tenures, and make a new record of those lands which were held directly of the crown in capite'.[85] This would have been fully in accord with the ordinary revenue policy of Henry VII which was heavily dependent upon the full exercise of prerogative tenurial rights.[86] In the event the Commons appear to have been well aware of the implications of the crown's demand for the feudal levies. They firmly declined to grant them on the ground that the uncertainty of many of the forms of the tenures would make the levy impossible to assess, and instead they offered Henry £40,000. That Henry only accepted £30,000 of the £40,000 offered to him by parliament strongly suggests that he was more interested in the tenurial revelations of a feudal levy than in the revenue it would yield to the crown.[87]

This sum of £30,000 was, conveniently, very close to the yield of a fifteenth and tenth, and was apportioned by parliament among the shires and towns so that the contributions from each area very nearly approximated to the traditional charge of the fifteenth and tenth on that area.[88] But the northern border counties were made liable to the subsidy of 1504,[89] and the fifteenth and tenth assessment of Norfolk was increased by £99.[90] On the other hand Bedfordshire, Berkshire, Buckinghamshire, Essex, Hampshire, Nottinghamshire, Oxfordshire and Somerset were granted reductions of £10 or less from their traditional fifteenth and tenth assessments. Middlesex, Wiltshire, and the town of Oxford were granted reductions of between £10 and £20, and Kent and Sussex had their assessments reduced by £169 and £69, respectively.

The procedure adopted in 1504 for the assessment and collection of these sums was nearly identical to that used for the aid and subsidy of 1497.[91] The commissioners were nominated in a schedule attached to the foot of the act, and were generally knights, esquires, and other substantial gentlemen and burgesses, including members of the Commons and some judges and other crown officials.[92] The commissioners nominated for the boroughs were to be joined by civic officials and Justices of the Peace.[93] Unlike their predecessors in 1497, the commissioners for the subsidy of 1504 were to receive the same remuneration as the collectors.[94]

Assessment was to be as in 1497, except that the minimum qualification for lands held at will for liability to assessment was raised from 20s to 28s 6d per annum, and that plough-cattle were also exempted from assessment.[95] As in 1497 the commissioners were to give the collectors lists of the assessments,[96] and were to certify the collectors' names to the Exchequer.[97] The same provisions as in 1497 were made for the benefit of the collectors and the taxpayers, except that distress by collectors on tenants for the defaults of landlords was no longer limited to the equivalent of six months' rent. Instead the tenants were permitted to deduct such losses from their subsequent rent payments, and where these losses were greater than the rent payments, they were to have an action at law for debt, in which the defendant was not to wage his law, neither have protection, nor essoin.[98]

Again in 1504, as in 1497, despite the provision for Justices of the Peace to take summary action against those who rescued distresses, several collectors brought actions against rescuers in the Exchequer. Eleven such actions were brought. In five of these the defendants compounded for a money fine;[99] in five the enrolment of the action is inconclusive,[100] and in one, involving ten defendants, two compounded for a money fine,[101] while eight elected to be tried by jury and were acquitted.[102] On the other hand, unlike 1497, none of the collectors took advantage of the clause in the act under which they could claim exoneration from sums which they could not collect, or distrain for, by certifying the names of the defaulters to the Exchequer.

But despite these differences in minor points of procedure and practice, the subsidies of 1497 and 1504 were basically similar taxes. Both were based on the fixed yields of the fifteenth and tenth, yet within the framework of these fixed yields both taxes were assessed and levied by statutorily appointed commissioners very much in the manner of directly assessed subsidies. The compromise between the two traditional forms of taxation that these two taxes represent was successful, for not only did it avoid a repetition of the failure of the subsidy of 1489, it also provided a safe basis for the development of the directly assessed, open yield, subsidy.

The Attainment of the Final Form of the Directly Assessed Subsidy

The subsidy of 1513

The evolution of the directly assessed subsidy, from the hybrid form prevalent in the later years of Henry VII to the final state achieved under the Tudors, occurred in a comparatively short space of time. The four subsidies granted in the years 1513 to 1516 contained within them practically the whole process of this evolution. Thereafter there was consolidation, notably in 1523, and some minor innovations; but the essential principles of the Tudor directly assessed subsidy, as evolved in these four years of the second decade of the century, persisted, and were embodied in taxation acts until well into the seventeenth century.[103]

The greatest step in this process was taken by those who drafted the act for the subsidy of 1513. First, the restricting framework of a fixed yield, that characterised the hybrid forms of 1497 and 1504, was abandoned, and instead a series of poll payments were granted, to be assessed on persons according to their rank and wealth.[104] The yield of the tax was unknown to parliament, and no attempt was made either to restrict it or to guarantee it at any particular sum. But with the rejection of the fixed yield, the success of the subsidy became once again entirely dependent upon the accuracy of the assessments.

However, the dangers of this situation were minimised by making the criteria of assessment very clear and simple. All that was required of the assessors was that they should assess property and income within broad limits, such as £2–£10, £10–£20, £20–£40, and so on. For each of these categories a flat payment, such as 1s 0d, 1s 8d, 3s 4d, 6s 8d, was charged, regardless of the precise position of the taxpayer's assessment within the category. Those of the rank of knight and above paid according to their status. In this way the task of assessment was made a very simple one to perform.

But the act for the subsidy of 1513 also greatly increased the incidence of directly assessed taxation by including wage earners within its scope. And in addition a poll payment of 4d was levied on everyone over fifteen years of age who received less than £1 per annum in wages. The subsidy of 1513 was thus the first major extension of the incidence of taxation since 1380.[105]

The 1513 subsidy act is also significant in that it introduced what was to become the standard procedure for the assessment and collection of directly assessed subsidies for over one hundred years. The essence of the new assessment machinery was that in the first instance the individual assessments were made by local officers and inhabitants in writing, under the general supervision of nationally appointed commissioners. The commissioners, if they saw fit, might examine both the assessors and those who had been assessed, and amend the assessments accordingly. The commissioners were to calculate the tax due from every individual at the statutory rates, on the basis of these assessments. The 1513 act also introduced the principle that every person, even though he might be liable to assessment under more than one category (i.e. for his income from lands, his income from wages, and the capital value of his possessions), was only to be charged according to one of these assessments, namely the one that would yield the largest amount of tax to the crown.

The essence of the new machinery of collection was that it was a two-tier arrangement, again supervised by the commissioners. The commissioners were to choose local officers and substantial local inhabitants as 'petty' or local collectors, and give them lists of the sums to be charged against every person within a small area, usually a parish or a township. The commissioners were also to appoint 'certayne sufficient and able persones' to be 'high' collectors, for larger areas, usually a hundred, and give them lists of the 'petty' collectors within their area together with the sums for which they were responsible. The task of the high collectors was to collect the tax money from the petty collectors and to convey it to the Exchequer at Westminster. Although some of the elements of this form of assessment and collection had been present in earlier forms of taxation, the particular combination of these elements as introduced in 1513 was unprecedented.[106]

The new form of the subsidy was accompanied by an increase in the number of commissioners, from an average of ten per shire for a fifteenth and tenth and the subsidy of 1504, to an average of thirty-five. The commissioners were also given far wider powers of discretion and summary jurisdiction than had ever been granted to commissioners for taxes before, even to the extent of being enabled to fine local officers of the crown who had refused to cooperate in the levying of the subsidy.[107]

Most of the innovations of this act, and certainly the overall conception of its design can be ascribed to the original crown draft laid before parliament.[108] The clauses that appear to have resulted from debate in parliament are concerned with supplementing the provisions of the original draft. Two of these, concerning the powers of commissioners, and double assessment, have been noted already. Others exempted members of the Commons from appointment as collectors, collectors from fees in the Exchequer, and spiritual persons and certain academic colleges from liability to the subsidy.[109] Another provided for the remuneration of the collectors and the commissioners out of the yield of the subsidy at 2d/£ for each high collector, and 2d/£ for each group of commissioners.[110] Finally, parliament required that a copy of the 'wrytyng triplicate' given by the commissioners to the high collectors and containing the sums for which they were responsible, was to be given to the knights and burgesses to bring with them to the next parliament. Thus, although parliament in 1512 made no restriction on the yield of the subsidy, they still arranged to be kept informed of its size.

The subsidies of 1514, 1515 and 1516

After the innovations of the act for the subsidy of 1513, the next subsidy granted to the crown in 1514 appears somewhat retrogressive, for parliament granted a named sum of £160,000.[111] But this was in no sense a reversion to the fixed grants of 1489 and 1472, for there was no attempt to prevent the crown from enjoying the yield of the subsidy should it prove to be greater than £160,000; rather any surplus that might accrue from the subsidy was explicitly granted to the crown. Nor was the £160,000 appropriated to any specific military project, rather the sum of £160,000 was regarded as a minimum grant.[112]

It was proposed to raise this sum by levying a rate of 6d/£ on the value of income from lands, offices, and wages, and on the capital value of goods. It is difficult to see on what basis it was decided that this rate would be sufficient to raise the £160,000, for there was no survey of wealth to hand, and the rates of 1513 were cast in so radically different a form that no deductions from them could possibly have been drawn. In fact the subsidy, despite its novelty, only produced a gross yield of just over £50,000.[113]

However the rate of 6d/£ was arrived at, its levy entailed the assessment to the nearest pound of the value of moveable goods, and of income from lands, offices and wages of every person over fifteen years of age, and thus demanded from the assessors and commissioners a far greater precision in assessment than had ever been required of them before.[114] The procedure of assessment introduced by the act for the subsidy of 1513 was retained, but with two important modifications. First, the assessments were to be made on oath, rather than by way of simple declaration. Second, an attempt was made to provide relief for those who were assessed before several groups of commissioners. Commissioners, upon request, were to provide a certificate of assessment which might be shown to commissioners in other counties and thereby inhibit a double assessment, but if a further assessment had already been made, then the larger was to be taken and the smaller annulled.[115] The collection of the subsidy of 1514 was to be as that of the subsidy of 1513, except that the petty collectors were to be remunerated for their expenses at 2d/£.[116] This was the first time that local collectors had ever received an official reward for their labours.[117]

Although the innovations in the procedure of assessment and collection of the subsidy act of 1514 are relatively minor, the act is significant in that it marks the complete return to a directly assessed subsidy raised by the application of a statutory rate per pound on the assessed value of the wealth of the individual taxpayer. But the subsidy act of 1514 is also interesting for two further reasons. First, most of the miscellaneous clauses which appeared at the end of the act for the subsidy of 1513, supplementing the proposals of the crown draft, were integrated into the main body of the text of the act of 1514,[118] and very few miscellaneous clauses remained at the end of the act.[119] This suggests that the act of 1514, as engrossed, was almost entirely contained in the crown draft laid before the Commons, which was in effect a rearranged version of the act for the subsidy of 1513. In fact the same man, John Hales, of Gray's Inn, drew up both of these acts.

The second interesting feature of the act of 1514 is a clause empowering the Commons or, if the Commons were not in session, a committee of the Commons and some royal officials, to exercise an over-riding control over the administration of the subsidy.[120] To this committee or to the Commons, the commissioners were required by the act to send certificates of the names of those whom they had appointed high collectors together with the sums for which they were responsible.[121] The committee, or the Commons, were empowered to fine defaulting commissioners,[122] to appoint commissioners for those areas for which none had been assigned, and to determine all questions arising out of the subsidy with the force of law.[123] The committee, or the Commons, were also to calculate the yield of the subsidy, and if it all fell short of £160,000, they were to estimate a series of rates sufficient to make good the deficit and institute a second subsidy which was to be levied in the same form as before.[124]

But despite these apparently comprehensive powers granted to the Commons, or the committee, in order to guarantee the grant of £160,000 to the crown; in 1515, when the yield of the subsidy of 1514 was clearly seen to be insufficient,[125] it was considered that neither the committee nor the Commons had sufficient authority to institute a second subsidy.[126] Instead the second subsidy was granted by a fresh act of parliament.

The first subsidy act of 1515 was, in fact, almost identical to the subsidy act of 1514. The most important innovation in the crown draft was the provision of a standard form of oath to be taken in connection with the making of the assessments. And again the crown draft comprised almost the whole of the act,[127] and few clauses were added during the course of parliamentary debate.[128] Provision was also made in this act for a committee to exercise control over the commissioners and to take steps to institute further taxation should the overall yield to the crown still be less than £160,000. But the composition of this committee was much more heavily weighted with royal officials than was the earlier committee,[129] and the powers were confined exclusively to this committee and were not transferred to the Commons if they were in session. The powers of control over the commissioners granted to the 1515 committee were much the same as those granted to the committee of 1514.[130] But the 1515 committee was given more precise instructions as to how the deficit, if any, should be made good. If the deficit were to be more than £30,000, then a second subsidy identical to the first was to be initiated;[131] but if the deficit were to be less than £30,000, then the committee was to divide this up amongst the counties and boroughs at its discretion.[132]

Once again, the second subsidy was necessary,[133] and once again this was levied not on the authority of the committee, but by a fresh act of parliament. Thus in the second session of 1515, parliament briefly granted, together with a fifteenth and tenth, a second subsidy identical to the one just levied.[134] But since it was now certain that the original grant of £160,000 would be attained,[135] the control of the commissioners by a committee of parliament and royal officers was abandoned in favour of control by the Exchequer through its traditional forms of process.[136]

Thus by 1515 the subsidy act had reached the form that was to remain virtually unchanged throughout the early Tudor period. But the evolution of this form, from the hybrid forms of 1497 and 1504, although occurring within the short space of four years, was brought about in three distinct stages. In the first stage, that of the act for the subsidy of 1513, the principle of an open yield was re-introduced; but the basis of assessment was a graduated poll tax rather than a rate per pound. But at this stage too the fundamental principles of assessment and collection were stated in the crown draft, while several additions and modifications to them were made in the course of parliamentary debate. In the second stage of the evolution of the directly assessed subsidy, represented by the act of 1514, not only were these general principles of assessment and collection retained, but the additions and modifications of 1513 were incorporated into the crown proposals for the subsidy. But also in 1514 the basis of assessment was changed to that of a rate per pound on the assessed value of incomes and of the capital value of goods. This marks the return to the directly assessed subsidy, but on a far more complex basis than anything before in the history of taxation. It is perhaps significant that the two key acts in the development of the Tudor directly assessed subsidy were drafted, written and engrossed by John Hales, of Gray's Inn, who later became one of the Barons of the Exchequer.[137] The third stage of the development, the acts of 1515, is altogether less important. The main principles and forms of the act of 1514 were retained, with but minor modifications from the crown and from parliament.

The subsidy act of 1523 and after

The act of 1523 was very largely concerned with consolidating the provisions of the acts for the subsidies of 1512–16, in some places repeating the clauses verbatim, while in others improving on them both in precision and in comprehensiveness.[138] The success of the draughtsmanship of this act may be gauged from the fact that subsequent subsidy acts, with the exception of 1534, retained almost unchanged the wording of 1523. But three important innovations were made in the crown draft for this subsidy. First, the assessment of everyone of the rank of Baron or Baroness was taken out of the hands of the commissioners and put under the supervision of the Lord Chancellor and other senior royal officials.[139] This must certainly be construed as an attempt to secure a stricter assessment of the aristocracy rather than to allow them a more lenient one. Both Wolsey's own personal efforts to raise money by all kinds of taxes and loans at this time, and the thoroughness with which the aristocracy were actually assessed point to this interpretation.[140] Second, the law of distress in default of payment of taxes was defined so that the defaulter was allowed eight days' grace in which to pay the tax due, before his goods were sold.[141] And third, the position of the collectors was made easier by a clause that allowed them to be exonerated in their account at the Exchequer from sums that they had been unable either to collect, or to levy by way of distress, because the defaulters had died or fled.[142] Again, in 1523, the crown draft was so comprehensive in its proposals that few additional clauses are to be found at the end of the act. Apart from exemptions, and the liability of tenants and lessees, these were mainly concerned with the acceptance of foreign coins and plate in payment for this subsidy.[143]

But if the act of 1523 marked a consolidation of the new form of the directly assessed subsidy, the act granting the next subsidy, in 1534, disregarded it. The clauses throughout the act bore little resemblance to those of the 1523 act, and were in general far less comprehensive and precise in their construction. Much of this act, notably the crucial sections concerning the procedure of assessment, were very deficiently drafted, omitting the entire apparatus of the forms of oath and other safeguards.[144] On the other hand the act of 1534 removed the last vestige of parliamentary control over the administration of the directly assessed subsidy. Up to this date the commissioners had been appointed by parliament; in 1534 and thereafter they were appointed entirely by the crown.[145]

The last three acts of the period reverted to the form of the act of 1523. The acts of 1540 and 1543 introduced only minor modifications into the general scheme of taxation;[146] but the five new clauses in the crown proposals for the act of 1545 suggest a tightening up in the administration of the subsidy.[147] First, whereas previously assessments had always been made only to the nearest pound, under this act assessments were not to be so rounded, and the tax charges were to be calculated on fractions of a pound. Secondly, certain minimum qualifications of personal wealth were required for those who were appointed high collectors,[148] and as additional security the high collectors were required to enter into recognisances, to the value of twice the tax money for which they were responsible, that they would pay all that they had collected to the Exchequer by the statutory payment date, and the balance of their charge within one month thereafter.[149] A further clause reinforced the prohibition upon the officers of the Exchequer from charging the collectors any fees, by imposing a fine of twenty times the value of any such fine together with imprisonment at the king's pleasure for any such offence.

Finally, the act of 1545 required two or three commissioners from each shire, at the crown's nomination, along with the Peerage, to be assessed before the Lord Chancellor, the Lord Treasurer and the Lord President of the Council. At the same time these commissioners were to take an oath promising to assess their fellow commissioners impartially when they returned to their counties. The crown clearly suspected that the fact that the commissioners usually assessed each other either had, or might, lead to a collusive under-assessment; and they sought to prevent this by introducing assessment from outside on the assumption that those who had been heavily assessed by the Lord Chancellor and his two colleagues would be less willing to see their fellow commissioners escape lightly.

But with the exception of these five clauses in the act of 1545, the crown proposals for subsidy acts after 1523 introduced no major change in the form of taxation as evolved in the acts of 1512, 1514 and 1515. The very comprehensiveness of the crown drafts tended to reduce the number of clauses added to the bills during the course of parliamentary debate. These were usually concerned with exemptions from liability to the subsidies, the definition of legal tender, and the question of dual liability to lay and clerical taxation. Only once did parliament pass a clause directly limiting the powers of the crown. In 1540 a clause was affixed to the subsidy bill in the Commons by which all prerogative grants of exemption from taxation were declared null and void for the purposes of the taxes granted in the bill.[150] But in general there was no attempt, either by parliament or by the crown, to alter radically the form of subsidy as it was evolved in the second decade of the century.

5

Directly Assessed Subsidies 1513–47

The final form of the early Tudor subsidy was developed very quickly by the acts of 1512 and 1514, and all subsequent subsidy acts retained this form, although elaborating on it, and modifying it, in several directions. The seventeen subsidies levied between 1513 and 1547 were therefore basically of the same kind. This chapter will provide a general analysis of this form of taxation, while at the same time noting the individual variations of each of these subsidies.[1]

The General Administration of the Subsidies

The general administration of directly assessed subsidies in the early Tudor period was in the hands of commissioners who supervised both the assessment and collection of the taxes. For the earlier subsidies before 1534 these commissioners were appointed by parliament and their names were written in a schedule attached to the foot of the subsidy acts.[2] In addition, provision was made by the subsidy acts for the appointment of commissioners for those areas for which parliament omitted to designate commissioners. For the subsidy of 1513 these supplementary appointments were to be made by the king in Council, and for the subsidies of 1514, 1515–16 and 1524–7, by the king in council or by the attorney general. For the subsidies of 1535–6 the commissioners were to be appointed in the first instance by the king. But for the remaining subsidies of 1541–7, appointments were to be made by the Lord Chancellor, the Lord Treasurer, the Lord Privy Seal and the Lord President of the Council, or any two of them, of whom for the subsidies of 1544–7 the Lord Chancellor was to be one.

The commissions were sent out from Chancery in the form of Letters Patent under the Great Seal, and were generally enrolled on the Fine Rolls.[3] The form of the commission together with the names of the commissioners was sent to the Exchequer by way of the Original Rolls.[4] A copy of the subsidy act was also usually sent to the Exchequer accompanied by a writ commanding the Barons to administer the act and issue process if necessary 'secundum legem & consuetudinem Anglie'.[5]

The form of the commission was quite short, formally appointing those named in it as commissioners and requiring them to levy the subsidy according to the provisions of the act, as contained in a transcript enclosed with the commission.[6] Indeed all the subsidy acts required that one or more copies of the act should be sent with each commission. For the subsidies of 1513, 1514, 1515–16, and 1535–6 only one copy was necessary; but for the subsidies of 1524–7 eight copies were required, and for the later subsidies of 1541–7 ten copies. It is known that the copies of the act for the subsidies of 1535–6 were printed,[7] and very probably they were printed in other years also. For all the subsidies after 1524, except those of 1535–6, the subsidy acts required the commissions to be delivered to the commissioners some two to three weeks before the first day of assessment.[8]

Generally one commission was sent to each shire. Yorkshire and Lincolnshire were divided into their three traditional parts, and the Isle of Wight was separated from Hampshire.[9] All counties in England, and from 1544 all counties in Wales, were liable to assessment under the subsidy acts with the exception of those listed in Table 5.1. Thus, apart from the inclusion at various dates of Cheshire, Wales, and aliens in the northern counties, commissions for the subsidies were sent to the same counties as commissions for the fifteenths and tenths.[10]

Table 5.1   Counties statutorily exempt from liability to subsidies

Subsidy	Northern border counties[a]	Cheshire	Wales	Overseas possessions[b]
1513	[X]	[X]	[X]	[X]
1514	[X]	[X]	[X]	[X]
1515–16	X	X	[X]	[X]
1524–7	X(A)	X	X[c]	X
1535–6	X(A)	-	X	X
1541–2	X(A)	-	X	X
1544–6 ('43)	X(A)	-	-	X
1546 ('45)–7	X(A)	-	-	X[d]

Notes:
(A): Exemption did not extend to aliens.
[X]: No exemption in the statute; but no commission sent.
[a] Westmorland, Cumberland, Northumberland, Bishopric of Durham.
[b] Ireland, Calais and the marches, Guisnes, Hammes, Guernsey, Jersey.
[c] Inhabitants of, property in, and fees from were exempt.
[d] 'Bolloigne and the Countie of the same' added.
Sources: As Appendix I.

Table 5.2 Cities and towns receiving separate commissions

Subsidy	Statutes XV & X towns[a]	plus	Commissions as enrolled omit	add
1513	X	–	Shrewsbury	New Windsor
1514	X	–	–	–
1515–16	X	–	Bath	Bishop's Lynn, Winchester
1524	X	Chichester, Colchester, Derby, Exeter Hereford, Ipswich, Northampton, New Windsor, Yarmouth	–	–
1525	X	ditto	3 towns[b]	–
1526–7	X	ditto	–	–
1535	–	at king's discretion	–[c]	–
1536	–	at king's discretion	–[c]	–
1541	X	as 1524: Chester in place of Chichester	–	Newcastle
1542	X	ditto	–	Newcastle, Cambridge, Westminster, Winchester
1544	–	'everye Citie and Towne being a Countie in itself'[d]	to all towns as 1542, except Newcastle	–
1545–6 ('43)	–	ditto	–	–
1546 ('45)–7	–	ditto	–	–

Notes:
[a] Bath, Bristol, Canterbury, Coventry, Gloucester, Kingston upon Hull, Leicester, Lincoln, London, Norwich, Nottingham, Oxford, Rochester, Salisbury, Southampton, Shrewsbury, Southwark, Worcester, York.
[b] Commissioners for Southampton, Southwark and New Windsor appear amongst the county commissioners. The enrollment of commissioners is incomplete, for it extends to thirty-two counties only.
[c] Strictly this might be held to designate only those cities and towns possessing their own sheriffs; that is, Bristol, Canterbury, Chester, Coventry, Gloucester, Kingston upon Hull, Lincoln, London, Newcastle, Norwich, Nottingham, Southampton, Worcester, York.
[d] From the table it is clear that the commissions were not always sent out in accordance with the provisions of the statutes.

Sources:
Statutes – Appendix I; Commissions – Appendix II.

Separate commissions were also sent to several cities and towns. These towns were always specified in the subsidy acts, except in the act for the subsidies of 1535–6, which committed the matter entirely to the king's discretion. These cities and towns were basically those which received separate commissions for the levying of fifteenths and tenths together with a few additional towns, as shown in Table 5.2.

In addition to these separate commissions to certain cities and towns, the subsidy acts, with the exception of the act for the subsidies of 1535–6, provided for the appointment of between six and two 'auxiliary' commissioners for other towns.[11] These 'auxiliary' commissioners' names were to be included in the commissions to the shires, but they were to act only within the town limits, and only in conjunction with at least two of the full commissioners for the shire. Further, the 'auxiliary' commissioners were to receive no fees for their pains and might be fined by at least four of the full shire commissioners if they proved recalcitrant or if they exceeded their powers in any way.

It is difficult to tell how many of these 'auxiliary' commissioners were actually appointed, for apart from the subsidies of 1524 and 1525, they are not clearly designated as such in the county commissions. It is reasonably certain that local officers named in the county commissions were in fact 'auxiliary' commissioners. For the earlier subsidies, towards the end of the list of commissioners for certain counties, the names of towns are often appended to the names of commissioners. It seems a reasonable inference that these commissioners and those whose names appear immediately after them were also 'auxiliary' commissioners.[12] For the subsidies of 1541, 1542 and 1544 only the officers of certain towns are specified, without their names, and they are widely scattered throughout the county lists. The number of names in between these entries is far too large for all of them to have been 'auxiliary' commissioners, and it has been assumed that for these subsidies only local officers were so designated. Thus, despite the unsatisfactory nature of the evidence, it seems sufficiently clear that 'auxiliary' commissioners were widely appointed for all subsidies up to 1525 and that from 1536 very few 'auxiliary' commissioners were appointed at all (see Table 5.3).

The number of commissioners appointed for any shire or town was not fixed; indeed for some counties and towns very many more commissioners were appointed than were for others. It seems likely that the number of commissioners appointed bore some relation to the size of the area and of the population of the county or town concerned.[13] But in general both the range and the average number of commissioners appointed both for counties and towns remained the same over the whole period, except that the greatest number of commissioners appointed for any town tended to decline (see Table 5.4).

The commissioners were appointed from the leading men in the shires and boroughs, and a list of subsidy commissioners are substantially the same as

Table 5.3   Number of 'auxiliary' commissioners

Subsidy	Towns	Total no. of 'auxiliary' commissioners	Plus unspecified no. of 'auxiliary' commissioners
1513	37	159	–
1514	19	81	–
1515–16	21	91	–
1524	40	208	aldermen, bailiffs
1525	42	207	aldermen, bailiffs
1526–35	–ᵃ	–	–
1536	5ᵇ	1 mayor	bailiffs in 4 towns
1541	7	1 mayor	bailiffs in 6 towns
1542	7	–	bailiffs in 7 towns
1544	15ᶜ	7 mayors	bailiffs in 8 towns
1545–7	–ᵃ	–	–

Notes:
ᵃ For these subsidies no lists of commissioners have survived.
ᵇ For this subsidy no provision for 'auxiliary' commissioners was made in the act.
ᶜ Wales became liable to assessment.
Sources: As Appendix II.

lists of Justices of the Peace.[14] That is the commissioners in the shires were predominantly Lords, knights and gentlemen together with Bishops and Judges, and in the boroughs, leading merchants and craftsmen. It is interesting that for the subsidies of 1524 and 1525 no peers were appointed as commissioners.[15] Apart from these two subsidies there was very little change in the names of those appointed as commissioners from one subsidy to the

Table 5.4   Number of commissioners appointed

Subsidy	Counties		Towns		Households	
	Range	Average	Range	Average	Range	Average
1513	66–8	33	24–4	11		
1514	81–7	31	27–2	10		11ᵃ
1515–16	72–6	31	25–3	11		18ᵃ
1524	58–6	28	23–4	9	11–4	6
1525	58–6	27	23–6	9	11–4	5
1526–35	–	–	–	–	–	–
1536	56–8	22ᵇ	–	–	–	–
1541	67–8	25	16–4	8	8–4	5
1542	65–8	27	15–4	8	7–4	5
1544	74–12	34ᶜ	17–4	10	9–4	5
1545–7	–	–	–	–	–	–

Notes:
ᵃ One combined commission for the King's and Queen's Households.
ᵇ Names of commissioners are available for only thirty-two counties.
ᶜ Excluding the counties of Wales, with a range of 23–8, and an average of 12.
Sources: As Appendix II.

next. In some counties a few names were added to the commission, in others a few subtracted, and in others no change at all was made. When additions and subtractions were made to the numbers of commissioners, it was the lesser gentry that were affected.[16]

The social standing of the commissioners reflects the responsibility that the subsidy acts laid upon them, for the commissioners were in full control of every aspect of the administration of the subsidy acts and were given wide powers of discretion and compulsion to secure their implementation, even to the extent of being able to command and punish the traditional local officers of the crown, namely constables, bailiffs and sheriffs.

Special commissions

The acts for all the subsidies, except that for the subsidies of 1535–6, also required that commissions should be sent to the head officers of certain royal and other households to assess and levy the subsidies on the members of those households. But once again more commissions were issued than were specified in the subsidy acts (see Table 5.5).

The practice of issuing separate commissions for royal and other households led to a large number of individuals being assessed twice, once in their home counties and again in one of the households. The problems of double assessment are discussed later; but here it might be noted that over the whole period one third of all double assessments involved the households.[17]

For the subsidy of 1524 and for all subsequent subsidies a separate commission was issued for the assessment of the peerage. For the subsidies of 1524–7 most of the peers were assessed by Wolsey in Middlesex, and by the Bishop of London and the Prior of the Order of St John, in Essex. Peers resident far from London were assessed by local bishops, abbots and officers of the crown.[18] For all subsequent subsidies the acts named the Lord Chancellor, the Lord Treasurer and the Lord Privy Seal as commissioners for the peerage; but allowed the king full discretion to appoint further commissioners either in addition to, or in place of, these three officers. The commissions for the assessment of the peerage do not appear in the Chancery Enrolments; but so far as can be gauged from the collectors' accounts, in practice the assessment of the peerage was undertaken almost entirely by the three officers mentioned in the subsidy acts.[19] Unfortunately very little can be discovered about the way in which these commissioners actually assessed the peerage; for example, whether they deputed local officers to assess those peers resident far from London or not.[20] The tax money due from the peerage was collected by special collectors, usually servants of the Lord Chancellor, and not by the ordinary collectors in the shires.[21]

Table 5.5 Commissions to royal and other households

Subsidy	Statutes[a]	Commissions issued[b]	Returns from	References for returns: E359/
1513	K Q	K Q	–	38/4HVIII
1514	K Q	K Q	K Q	38/5HVIII, 2d, 4d
1515	K Q	K Q	K Q Cd	38/6HVIII, 5d, 8d
1516	K Q	K Q	K Q Mn	38/7HVIII, 3d, 12d
1524	K Q Ps FQ Cd	K Q Ps FQ Cd	K Q Ps FQ Cd	41/1st payment, 2, 2d, 14
1525	K Q Ps FQ Cd	K Q Ps FQ Cd	K Q Ps FQ Cd	41/2nd payment, 4, 13, 13d, 14d
1526	K Q Ps FQ Cd	–	K Q Cd	41/3rd payment, 2d, 5d
1527	K Q Ps FQ Cd	–	K Q Cd	41/4th payment, 3, 5d, 6d
1535	–	–	K Q	44/26 HVIII, 1st payment, 13d
1536	–	–	K Q	Ibid., 2nd payment, 7, 10d, 11d
1541	K Q Pr	K Q Pr Cl	K Q Pr Cl	44/32 HVIII, 1st payment. 9, 11d, 14, 18d
1542	K Q Pr	K Q Pr Cl	K Q Pr Cl	Ibid., 2nd payment, 6, 15d
1544	K Q Pr	K Q Pr Cl	K Q Pr Cl	42/43&35 HVIII, 1st payment, 6, 7d, 18
1545	K Q Pr	.	K Q Pr Cl	Ibid., 2nd payment, 6d, 9, 17d, 18
1546 ('43)	K Q Pr	–	K Q Pr Cl	Ibid., 3rd payment, 10d, 11d, 14, 14d
1546 ('45)	K Q Pr	–	K Q Pr	42/37 HVIII, 1st payment, 14d, 15d; E179/69/44,55
1547	K Q Pr	–	K Q Cl[c]	Ibid., 2nd payment, 2, 15; E179/69/44, 47, 55

Notes:
K King's Household (including chamber).
Q Queen's Household (including chamber).
Cd Cardinal's Household.
Mn 'Hospicium ministrorum infra hospicium regis'.
Ps Princess' Household.
FQ Dowager Queen of France's Household
Pr Prince's Household.
Cl Anne of Cleves' Household.
Sources: [a] See Appendix I. [b] See Appendix II. [c] The king died twelve days after the 1st assessment day.

Exemption and division

There were two circumstances in which commissioners might claim exemption from service. The first was that under all the later subsidy acts no-one was to be appointed a commissioner outside the shire in which he was resident. It is remarkable that only three claims for exemption were made under this head during the whole period. Two of these claims were made in 1524,[22] and one in 1527,[23] and all appear to have been successful.

Second, a commissioner might claim exemption from service if he could show that he had received no notice of his appointment as a commissioner. This claim was permitted under an early fifteenth-century statute, which required the commissioner to make his claim on corporal oath, either in the Exchequer or before a Judge, by writ of 'dedimus potestatem'.[24] Twenty-four claims for exemption were made under this head, and all of these were for the subsidies of 1524–7 and 1535 (Table 5.6). One third of these claims were made by heirs or executors of commissioners, and a quarter by commissioners for the peerage. The success rate of these claims as recorded on the Memoranda Rolls appears to be very low; but as the enrolment generally breaks off before any conclusion is reached, the actual success of these claims may well have been much higher.

But the majority of the commissioners, who did not claim exemption from service, once they had received their commission, were permitted by the subsidy acts to divide themselves according to hundreds, parishes or wards, or however they might find most convenient. However, there always had to be at least two commissioners, and for the subsidies of 1544–7, three commis-

Table 5.6   Claims for exemption from service as a commissioner on account of insufficient notice

Subsidy	Total no. of claims	By heirs, executors	By peerage commissioners	Dedimus potestatem	Success	Reference
1524	6	2	3	1	2	A
1525	2	1	1	0	0	B
1526	2	0	2	1	0	C
1527	13	5	0	7	5	D
1535	1	0	0	1	1	E
Total	24	8	6	10	8	

Sources:
A   E159/308 Recorda M.r.35d; /309 Recorda P.r.22, 22d, T.r.18; /310 Recorda P.r.33d; /313 Recorda M.r.52.
B   E159/309 Recorda P.r.22d; /311 Recorda M.r.39.
C   E159/309 Recorda P.r.22d; /313 Recorda T.r.14.
D   E149/313 Recorda P.r.27d, 31; /314 Recorda H.r.39, 39d, 40, 40d, 43, 44, 44d, 45; /315 Recorda T.r.25d.
E   E159/315 Recorda H.r.21.

sioners, assigned to each division. From 1523, the subsidy acts accorded members of the Commons the privilege of not being assigned to any subdivision outside the hundred in which they were resident.[25] In practice, the commissioners divided the area of their commission so that a small group of commissioners was responsible for each hundred or group of hundreds.[26] The ultimate unit of administration of the early Tudor subsidy was therefore very small, and the administration of the subsidy acts was thus a local matter undertaken by the social leaders of the locality. Thus in the absence of a large trained civil service the enforcement of the subsidy acts relied entirely upon the local influence of the social leaders of the country. In the early Tudor period the effectiveness of this influence was undoubted; but ultimately the success of the subsidies was dependent upon the loyalty of these social leaders to the interests of the crown.

Ministerial control over the commissioners

Once the commissioners had been appointed they were completely autonomous under the subsidy acts within the limits of their commission, and in fact there was very little intervention by ministers of the crown in the administration of the subsidy acts. Only two attempts were made to supervise the collection of the subsidy, when Wolsey and Cromwell were concerned with the size of the London assessments. On the other hand, the Privy Council in 1540 exercised a fair degree of control over the appointment of the commissioners for the subsidy of 1541. The Privy Council appointed the commissioners for London,[27] and also commanded the Lord Chancellor to withdraw three commissions, already issued, and to re-issue them with certain other names included.[28] The Privy Council also dealt with the French and Imperial ambassadors' objections to the assessment of their fellow-countrymen as aliens towards this subsidy,[29] and even issued a letter to the Lord Mayor of London commanding him to forbear levying the subsidy on four Spaniards.[30]

Otherwise the only other interventions by the Privy Council in subsidy matters concerned the subsidy of 1546 ('45). For this subsidy the Privy Council demanded a copy of the names of all the commissioners from the Lord Chancellor, and revoked one commission in order to substitute one commissioner in place of another.[31] The Privy Council also commanded the collectors in Yorkshire to pay the subsidy money directly to John Uvedale, Treasurer of the garrisons on the Scottish border.[32]

Thus, apart from a few further interventions in subsidy matters arising from their judicial functions,[33] the Privy Council and other ministers of the crown seem to have exercised very little control over the commissioners and their administration of the subsidy acts. The task of levying the subsidies was therefore entrusted entirely to the commissioners under the sanctions of the traditional processes of the court of the Exchequer.[34] But this lack of official control by the ministers of the crown over the commissioners should occasion no surprise, for the ministers themselves, together with all other senior servants of the crown, were appointed as commissioners in their home counties, and were therefore in any case in direct control of the levying of the subsidies.

The task entrusted to the commissioners by the subsidy acts was threefold. They were to secure the correct assessment of everyone within their area, they were to arrange for the collection of the tax money and for its transportation to Westminster, and they were to certify to the Exchequer the amount of tax due from their area and the names of those whom they had appointed collectors. Every aspect of the commissioners' work was minutely regulated by each subsidy act, which required the commissioners faithfully to execute its provisions without 'omyssyon favour affeccyon fere drede or malice'.[35]

Assessment

The first task that the commissioners had to perform was the correct assessment of everyone within their area according to the rates and criteria laid down in the subsidy acts. This assessment involved the application of statutory rates to the assessed value of two categories of income and to one category of possessions.

What was assessed?

The first category of taxable incomes was defined as:

> for every pownde yerely that the same person or eny other to his use hath in fee symple fee tayll terme of lyfe, terme of yeres execusyon by ward by Copy of Courtrolle or at Wyll in eny londis tenementis rentys services hereditamentis annuyties fees corrodies or other yerely profettes.[36]

The first category of assessable incomes therefore comprised any income from any source provided it was received yearly. Thus wages were included in this category if they were paid by the year, but not if they were paid by the day, week or month.[37] The scope of this category must be clearly emphasised because there is a misleading tendency to regard it as having been confined to income from lands alone.[38]

In practice, however, by far the greater number of assessments made under this category were on income from lands; but it must be admitted that it is not clear from the wording of the subsidy acts precisely what incomes derived from lands were included in this category and what were not. It has already been said that the basis of this category was that all the incomes were received by the year. If this principle was applied to income from lands it would have resulted in the assessment only of those lands which were let to farm for a fixed annual sum, and in the exclusion from assessment of all other profits derived from the immediate cultivation of lands, whether these profits were gained by a tenant or lessee, or by a freeholder cultivating his own demesne.[39] It is, however, possible that a notional 'yearly' value was assigned to lands not let to farm for a fixed annual payment, rather in the manner that similar values were assigned to demesne lands by escheators, and that by this means directly worked land became liable to assessment for the subsidies. Unfortunately there is no direct evidence by which this difficulty might be resolved; but the universality of this practice of assigning virtual annual values to all manner of lands in the sixteenth century makes it very probable that directly farmed lands were in fact assessed towards the subsidies.[40]

It should also be noted that these assessments were probably made on the net, rather than the gross value of incomes. Certainly this should have been so for the subsidies of 1524–6 and 1535–42, because the acts specified that assessments were to be made on 'the clere yerely value' of incomes. But despite the lack of any explicit instructions in the acts for the other subsidies, it seems very likely that assessments were made on the net value of incomes for them also, for the fact that the acts for the earlier subsidies of 1489, 1497 and 1504 had included such a specific requirement suggests that it was general practice in the early Tudor period in assessing annual incomes to take the net rather than the gross value.

If assessments of yearly incomes were in fact made on net rather than on gross values, then those liable to assessment on such incomes would have been able to claim deductions for annuities attached and charged to parcels of land, or in the case of incomes from offices, for their expenses in providing the wages of a deputy. Thus the values of annual incomes as given by the subsidy assessments, being subject to certain conditions imposed by the subsidy acts, may very well differ from other contemporary valuations of the same incomes.

The second category of assessable incomes was defined as 'wages and other profittes for wages'.[41] This category was restricted for the subsidies of 1514, 1515 and 1516 to wages received 'by the yere'; but for the subsidies of 1513, 1524 and 1525 all wages, however received, were liable to assessment. After 1525 this category was no longer included in the subsidy acts, and thereafter wages were liable to assessment only under the first category of 'yerely profettes'.[42]

The third category of assessable wealth comprised, broadly, all 'goodes or catalles moveable'.[43] For the subsidy of 1514 this category was further defined as:

for every pownde in Coyne and the valewe of every pownde that eny such person hath in plate household stok of marchaundyse or other goodys or Catallys moveables both within the Realm and without.[44]

For the subsidies of 1515 and 1516 this definition was extended to include

household blades of Cornes ... and of all such sommes of money that to hym [the taxpayer] is owyng wherof he trustis in his conscience suerly to be paid, except and of the premisses deducted such sommes of monay as he owys and in his conscience truly entendys to pay.[45]

But for these subsidies, and for all subsequent subsidies, the acts retained the words 'and all other goodes and catalles moveable', and thus effectively rendered all moveable property liable to the assessment. But for the subsidy of 1524 and for later subsidies, personal clothing, other than certain jewels, were exempted from liability to assessment.[46]

The extension of liability to assessment to money loaned to others, and all subsequent subsidy acts, also retained the converse exemption of debts owed to others. This aspect of the assessment of moveable property is very important because in certain circumstances it might produce assessments apparently incommensurate with the tangible wealth of the taxpayer. Thus, as with assessments on annual incomes, there should be no surprise if assessments on moveable goods do not tally exactly with other contemporary estimates, such as inventories, which were not compiled according to the same criteria.[47]

For some of the subsidies a poll tax was also levied on certain classes of persons. In 1513 the entire subsidy was of the nature of a poll tax. For the subsidies of 1524 and 1525 a poll payment was levied on those 'beyng of the value of xls. in goodes' or receiving wages to the value of one pound per annum or above.[48] But in all other subsidies the poll payments were designed to be levied on aliens who were not otherwise eligible for assessment. Only in 1514 was such a poll tax levied on everyone who was otherwise not liable to pay the subsidy.

Minimum qualifications

But liability to assessment both under the three main categories, and for the poll taxes, was further limited by the provision in all the subsidy acts of certain minimum qualifications. For the three main categories this limitation took the form of minimum assessments below which no tax was payable, and for the poll taxes minimum age limits were specified.[49] These minimum qualifications are given in Table 5.7. It is clear from the table that the minimum qualifications remained at much the same level throughout the period, with the exception of the subsidies of 1526–7 and 1535–6, which had very high minimum assessments.

The effect of the minimum assessments was to exclude a large proportion of the population from liability to the subsidies. It has been estimated that even with the very low minimum assessments of 1524 some 33% to 48% of the assessable adult population in three towns were not assessed for the subsidy.[50] Again in the West Riding of Yorkshire, for which the assessable population in the 1540s probably numbered about 25,000 adults, only 15,000 persons were actually assessed towards the subsidy of 1545. And when, in the following year, assessments were made under a new act for which the minimum assessment for moveable goods was raised from £1 to £5, the total number of people assessed towards the new subsidy was only 4,600.[51] Thus the raising of the minimum assessment by £4 in one county reduced the total number of people liable to pay the subsidy by 70%. It is clear, therefore, that the subsidies of 1526–7 and 1535–6, with their very high minimum assessments, can have concerned only a very small percentage of the total population.

Even more striking is the picture provided by the next subsidy of 1546 ('45), in the West Riding. Here only 7.3% of those who paid the subsidy were assessed at £20 or above in annual incomes or in goods; while only 0.3% were assessed at £50 or above in goods, and only 0.8% at £50 or above in annual incomes. If it is assumed that the distribution of wealth was roughly similar over the rest of the country in the preceding twenty years, and if it is further assumed that about 40% of the assessable population was generally too poor to be assessed, then the proportion of the adult population that was assessed for the subsidies of 1535 and 1536 was probably of the order of 1.4%, while the corresponding proportions for the subsidies of 1526 and 1527 were probably 0.15% and 0.06%. Although both assumptions are probably open to considerable adjustment on account of regional differences and the effects of inflation, the difference in magnitude between the proportions calculated as probably assessed towards the restricted subsidies, and the proportion of 52–67% found assessed towards the 'unrestricted' subsidy of 1524, is dramatic enough.

Rates of payment

For the subsidy of 1513 the rates were flat payments levied on each category of assessed values; but for all other subsidies the rates were expressed by the subsidy acts as so many pennies or shillings to be levied on every pound of the assessed value of incomes and moveable property. Usually the subsidy acts specified a simple rate per pound for each category of assessment; but in the last few subsidies of the period higher rates were imposed on the higher assessments. At the beginning of the period the rates for each of the three categories of assessment were the same; but in the 1540s the rates levied on assessments on moveable goods were lower than those levied on assessments on annual incomes.

Table 5.7 Rates of payment and minimum assessments 1513–47

Subsidy	Moveable Goods		Annual Incomes		Wages		Polls	
	Range (£)	Payment	Range (£)	Payment	Range (£)	Payment	Min. Class Age	Payment
1513	2–10	1s 0d	2–10	2s	1	4d[a]	Duke	£6 13s 4d
	10–20	1s 8d	10–20	5s	1–2	8d		
	20–40	3s 4d	20–40	10s	2	1s 0d	Marquess, Erle, Marques & Countesse	£4
	40–100	6s 8d	40	20s				
	100–200	13s 4d						
	200–400	26s 8d					Baron, Baronett & Baronesse,	£2
	400–800	40s 0d						
	800–	53s 4d					Knights, not being lords of parliament	30s
		Rate/£		Rate/£		Rate/£		
1514	2–	6d	1–	6d	1–	6d	everyone n.o.l.	15s 4d
1515	2–	6d	1–	6d	1–	6d	aliens n.o.l.	15s 8d
1516	2–	6d	1–	6d	1–	6d	aliens n.o.l.	15s 8d
1524	2–	6d	(1)–	1s 0d			goods at £2, or wages at £1–	16s 4d
							aliens n.o.l.	16s 8d
1525	20–	1s 0d as 1524						

Year	Band	Rate	Band	Rate	aliens n.o.l.	
1526			50–	1s 0d		
1527	50–	1s 0d	20	6d		
	20–					
1535		6d				
1536		6d				
1541	20– (aliens £1)	6d	20– (aliens 1)	1s	aliens n.o.l.	12s 4d
1542	20– (aliens £1)	6d	20– (aliens 1)	1s	aliens n.o.l.	12s 4d
1544	1–5	2d	1–5	4d		
	5–10	4d	5–10	8d		
	10–20	8d	10–20	8d (aliens 2s 0d)		
	20–	8d	20–	8d (aliens 3s 0d)		
		(aliens 2s 0d)				
1545	1–5	1d	1–5	2d	aliens n.o.l.	16s 4d
	5–10	2d	5–10	4d		
	10–20	4d	10–20	8d (aliens 1s 0d)		
		8d	20–	1s 0d (aliens 1s 6d)		
		(aliens 1s 0d)				
1546 ('43)	(as 1545)					
1546 ('45)	5–10	8d	1–	2s 0d[b]		
	10–20	1s 0d				
	20–	1s 4d				
1547	as 1546 ('45)					

Notes:

x–y means £x and up to, but not including, £y.

n.o.l. Not otherwise liable to payment

[a] subject to a minimum age qualification of 15 years.

[b] wages received by servants not liable unless more than £2 per annum.

Except where special rates given, and except for the subsidies of 1546 ('45) and 1547, aliens pay at double rates.

Sources: See Appendix I.

It should be noted that the rates were for 'every pownde' of the value of the assessments, and that therefore until the subsidy of 1546 ('45) all assessments were rounded down to the nearest pound. The act for the last two subsidies of the period, in contrast, required the rates of payment to be applied to precise assessments, involving, if necessary, fractions of a pound.

Increased rates of payment

For all subsidies except those of 1546 ('45) and 1547, aliens not denizen were required to pay double rates of payment. For the subsidies of 1535–46 ('43) double rates were also levied on gilds, brotherhoods, fraternities and other associations 'corporatte or not corporate'. For the subsidies of 1541 and 1542 goods held 'to the use of any other person within age or of full age', that is held by trustees, were also to be charged double rates of payment.

Exemptions from liability to the subsidies

Married women were almost certainly not assessed towards the subsidies. Although they were explicitly exempted by the subsidy acts only for the subsidies of 1513 and 1514, the fact that they were unable under the common law to own in their own right either lands or goods makes it very likely that assessments would have been made on their husbands alone.[52] The subsidy rolls bear this out, for the number of women appearing as having been assessed is very small, and many of these are described as widows.[53]

The position of infants is not so clear. Under the common law they might acquire and own property,[54] and there were no minimum age qualifications in the subsidy acts concerning assessment for annual incomes, wages or moveable property.[55] But normal practice in the early Tudor period seems to have been for the property of children to have been assessed on the head of the family. Where there was no head of the family, as with orphans, the assessment was made in the name of the child, or sometimes its guardian. Orphans, however, were exempted from liability to the subsidies of 1541 and 1542. For the subsidies of 1546 ('45) and 1547 orphans under twenty-one years of age and possessing less than £20 worth of goods were also exempted from liability. Additionally, property temporarily in the king's hands, such as the lands of minors held of the crown *in capite*, and property forfeited to the crown, such as the goods of felons and traitors, were naturally exempt from liability to the subsidies.[56]

Apart from the cases mentioned above, and apart from those parts of the country which were totally exempted under the subsidy acts, very few persons or groups of persons were exempted from liability to the subsidies. The group most consistently receiving statutory exemption from liability to the subsidies was the inhabitants of the Cinque Ports, who were specifically exempted by every subsidy.[57] The inhabitants of Brighton were exempted from the subsidies of 1515, 1516 and 1524–7, but on no other occasion. The act granting the subsidies of 1524–7 also granted exemption to the Wardens of Rochester Bridge, to the inhabitants of Ludlow, and to everyone who had been an inhabitant of Westborne in Sussex at the time of the recent fire. These exemptions were therefore temporary and usually granted by way of relief for some hardship.

Personal exemptions were only granted by two of the subsidy acts. The act granting the subsidies of 1524–7 exempted the queen from liability, and the act granting the subsidies of 1535–6 exempted both the Queen (who now was Anne Boleyn) and Catherine of Aragon.[58] Exemptions were also granted under the subsidy acts to certain academic colleges and religious houses. The Colleges of Oxford, Cambridge, Eton and Winchester were exempted from all subsidies up to 1527. Exemption was also extended to the Charterhouses and Syon for the subsidy of 1513, to the same houses and Dertford for the subsidy of 1514, to these houses and 'Menresse denny and Brosyard'[59] for the subsidies of 1515–16,[60] and to all these, together with New College, Newark, for the subsidies of 1524–7. No exemptions were allowed to academic colleges or to religious houses by the subsidy acts after this date.

However, some form of exemption of clerical property was granted by all the subsidy acts. Generally church furniture – chattels and ornaments 'ordeyned for the honour and service of Almighty God' – was exempted from liability to the subsidies,[61] and in general lands that were liable to the clerical tenth, or disme, were also exempt.[62] But when a clerical subsidy was granted at the same time as a lay subsidy, problems of dual liability arose. The acts for the lay subsidies of 1513 and 1514 deemed that all clergy who were liable to the clerical subsidies should be exempted entirely from the provisions of the lay subsidies; while, in contrast, the acts for the subsidies of 1515 and 1516 required the full assessment to the lay subsidies of the lands of the clergy, unless they were dismable, and of their 'catalles and blades of Cornys'.[63] For the remaining subsidies, in general only the temporal lands of the clergy were to be assessed, but there were some conditions in which even these might be exempted.[64] For the subsidies of 1524–7 these lands were to be assessed both for the clerical and for the lay subsidies; but they were to be taxed only by whichever of the two would yield the most revenue to the crown. For the subsidies of 1535–6 the act granted a wide exemption to all clergy who paid first fruits or tenths to the crown; but for the subsidies of 1541 and 1542 the temporal lands of the clergy were again fully liable to assessment under the lay subsidy act. The acts granting the last five subsidies of 1544–7 provided a somewhat complex formula the meaning of which appears to be that persons liable under the lay act for their annual incomes from lands, or for their

Table 5.8 Claims against wrongful assessment of spiritual persons

Subsidy	No. of persons	Total sum £ s d	E359
1536	2	7 13 4	/44 26 HVIII, 2nd payment, 4d
1541	10	42 3 0	/44 32 HVIII, 1st payment, 7d, 8, 12d, 14, 14d, 17, 17d, 18, 18d
1542	2	2 13 4	Ibid., 2nd payment, 11d, 19, 19d
1544	1	2 10 0	/42 34 & 35 HVIII, 1st payment, 17d
1545	2	4 0 0	Ibid., 2nd payment, 16d, 17d
1546 ('45)	25	21 3 8	/42 37 HVIII, 1st payment, 1d, 5d, 8

moveable possessions, or for both, and under the clerical subsidy act for their spiritual possessions, were to be assessed only under the lay act for their annual incomes from lands, including spiritual possessions, or for their goods.[65] Nevertheless, despite the provisions of the lay subsidy acts, several spiritual persons were wrongfully assessed towards the lay subsidy and had to claim exoneration from these assessments (see Table 5.8).[66]

But apart from the exemptions mentioned above, which were specifically allowed by the subsidy acts, liability to the subsidies in the early Tudor period was universal. Accordingly the subsidy acts overruled all prerogative grants of franchises liberties or any other form of discharge from taxation, and explicitly declared such grants for the purposes of the subsidies to be void and of no effect.[67] This annulment of prerogative grants should not be construed as a parliamentary attack on the royal prerogative, for the position of the clauses containing this annulment in the subsidy acts shows that it was introduced in the crown drafts of the subsidy bills, and not in the course of parliamentary debate.[68] Indeed the suspension of these grants of exemption was very much to the financial advantage of the crown.

Assessment rules

Assessment for the subsidies was subject to three cardinal rules laid down in the subsidy acts. The first rule was simply that all assessments were to be made according to current values. This rule was enjoined by all the subsidy acts, except the act granting the subsidies of 1535–6, and if it were properly applied, it would have constituted the main safeguard of the yield of the subsidies in what became an age of rapid inflation.

The second rule was stated by all the subsidy acts. It was that no-one was to be 'double chardged neither sett for ij causes',[69] but that the category under which a person was taxed was to be determined so that 'the greatest and moost somme accordyng to his substaunce by reason of this acte ought or may be set and taxed.'[70] Thus where a person was liable to assessment under more than one category, he was to pay only under that category which produced the highest tax charge on him. Some cases must have been obvious from the start; but in others, especially with the differential rates of payment for the subsidies in the 1540s, a full calculation for every category of assessment may well have been necessary. How far such a procedure was in fact necessary cannot be discovered, for none of the original assessment documents, which were superseded by the final lists of assessments and tax charges drawn up by the commissioners, have survived.

The third rule was that everyone was to be taxed only where they were 'moste conversaunte abydyng or recynte' and that no one was to be 'double charged ne sett at severall places by reasone of this acte'.[71] Those who were abroad at the time of the assessment were to be assessed where their property was situated, or where their factor or attorney was resident. The assessment was to be made on the evidence of the factor or attorney or in default of these on the evidence of neighbours and local inhabitants.[72]

But those who were resident in more than one shire or hundred might still find that they had been assessed twice. In such cases the subsidy acts allowed anyone who had been assessed by one group of commissioners to present a certificate of assessment, drawn up by these commissioners, to other groups of commissioners who he suspected were about to assess him. This certificate of assessment was to be sufficient to prevent all other groups of commissioners from proceeding with their assessments. If, however, a further assessment had been made before a certificate of assessment could be presented, then the lesser of the two assessments was to be cancelled upon the due presentation to the commissioners responsible for it of a certificate testifying to the other, greater, assessment. For the subsidy of 1514 this claim against the lesser of the two assessments had to be made before the lists of tax charges were given to the petty collectors. For the subsidies of 1515 and 1516 this period was extended until certification day. For the subsidy of 1524 and for all subsequent subsidies no time limit was specified by the subsidy acts for the cancellation of lesser assessments. Instead the taxpayer was to pay the greater sum only, and the collector's receipt for his sum together with a certificate of assessment from the commissioners was to be sufficient to discharge him from all claims for equal or smaller sums from other collectors. If, however, another collector demanded a larger sum, then the taxpayer was to pay the balance to him over and above what he had already paid.

This system meant that many assessments were certified to the Exchequer that could not be collected, because the taxpayer had paid on a higher assessment elsewhere. Thus from 1524 the collectors had to petition for exoneration from such sums when they accounted in the Exchequer. In this way a record has survived of all double assessments not inhibited by a certificate of assessment before the certification day.

Table 5.9   Claims against double assessments

Subsidy	Total No.	Lesser assessment paid first	Involving Households	Reference: E359
1515	2	–	50%	/38HVIII r. 8d[a]
1516	19	–	100%	–[b]
1524	59	–	91%	/41 1st payment, *passim*[c]
1525	28	–	57%	/41 2nd payment, *passim*
1526	2	–	0%	/41 3rd payment, 2d, 7d
1527	3	–	67%	/41 4th payment, 6d, 7d
1535	65	–	83%	/44 26HVIII, 1st payment, *passim*
1536	61	–	57%	/44 26HVIII, 2nd payment, *passim*
1541	394	4%	42%	/44 32HVIII, 1st payment, *passim*[d]
1542	388	4%	16%	/44 32HVIII, 2nd payment, *passim*[d]
1544	665	23%	22%	/42 34 & 35 HVIII, 1st payment, *passim*[e]
1545	574	14%	13%	/42 34 & 35 HVIII, 2nd payment, *passim*[e]
1546 ('43)	256	6%	47%	/42 34 & 35 HVIII, 3rd payment, *passim*[e]
1546 ('45)	541	4%	38%	/42 37HVIII, 1st payment, *passim*[f]
1547	433	6%	54%	/42 37HVIII, 2nd payment, *passim*[g]
TOTAL	3490	9%	34%	

Sources: Additional references as follows:
[a] E404/90/7 HVIII/8.
[b] E404/92/11 HVIII/-.
[c] 372/375 Ad. Res. Norfolk; /376 Res. Kanc.
[d] See Table 5.11; E372/389 Res. London.
[e] See Table 5.11; E372/390 Ad.It. Kanc. E404/104/36 HVIII/-.
[f] See Table 5.11.
[g] See Table 5.11; E372/394 Ebor., Ad. It. London; /395 Cornub., Cantab/Hunt. Res. Lincs, Monmouth, It. Sussex.

Although Table 5.9 shows clearly that a large number of people were in fact assessed twice, it does not show all those who might have been liable to assessment in two places. This can never be discovered, for those who successfully prevented a second assessment from being made by a prompt presentation of commissioners' certificates before the statutory certification date ensured that no documentary trace of their liability to the second assessment would be made.[73] Again, the figures for the total number of cancelled double assessments would be more significant, if it were known what proportion of the total number of assessments they represented. For example, although the total number of cancelled second assessments for the subsidies of 1535–6 was about one-sixth of the number of cancelled assessments for the subsidies of 1541–2, the total number of people actually assessed towards the earlier subsidies might very well have been only one fortieth of the total number of people assessed towards the subsidies of 1541–2.[74] But since the total number of assessments can now never be known, the proportion of double assessments must also remain in obscurity.

Nevertheless, the absolute increase in the number of double assessments is dramatic enough. Much of this increase may well be explained by the increase in the number of people liable to assessment produced by inflation. It is significant that where total taxable population is known to have fallen, as between the subsidies of 1544 and 1546 ('45), the number of double assessments falls too.[75] But another interesting trend can be discerned from Table 5.9. Where subsidies were granted by the same subsidy set and were levied in consecutive years, such as in 1524–5, 1535–6, 1541–2, 1544–6 and 1546–7, the number of double assessments tends to fall in the second and third years. This probably reflects not so much an actual decline in the numbers of people liable to double assessment; but rather that the taxpayer, made aware of this liability in the first year, made efforts in the following years to present a certificate of assessment from the first group of commissioners who had assessed him, to the other groups of commissioners and thus prevent further assessments from being made and returned to the Exchequer.

But the question of double assessment introduces one of the problems of the early Tudor subsidies, namely whether the assessments, made as they were within small administrative areas of hundreds, or groups of hundreds, were intended to reflect the total wealth of the individual taxpayer wherever it might happen to be, or only that part of his total wealth that was situated within the assessment area. There is no direct answer to this problem for the subsidy acts are not explicit on this point, and no dispute arose for decision. But the question is plainly of crucial importance for the correct interpretation of the subsidy assessments for the purposes of biographical or social history. Fortunately the existence of the large number of double assessments listed in Table 5.9 enables some kind of answer to be given.

It is clear that if the hypothesis that assessments were made only on that part of the wealth of the taxpayer that was situated within the assessment were correct, then the chances of finding two identical assessments of the same person, made in different parts of the country, would be very small indeed. On the other hand, if the alternative hypothesis, that assessments were based on the total wealth of the individual, wherever it happened to be situated, were correct, then all double assessments might be expected to be identical.

Table 5.10 shows the proportion of double assessments that were found to be identical. From this table, we can see that about one out of every three double assessments was found to have involved identical figures. This is a remarkably high proportion, and since the probability of such a result is so small, the hypothesis that assessments were based solely on the part of the taxpayer's wealth that was situated within the assessment area must clearly be discarded.

Table 5.10   Proportion of double assessments found to be identical

Subsidy	Double assessments	Identical	% Identical
1515	2	–	0
1516	19	–	0
1524	59	2	3
1525	28	10	36
1526	2	1	50
1527	3	1	33
1535	65	12	18
1536	61	10	16
1541	394	90	23
1542	388	140	36
1544	665	161	24
1545	574	217	38
1546 ('43)	256	97	38
1646 ('45)	541	245	45
1547	433	198	46
Total	3490	1184	34

Source: As for Table 5.9.

But even if the alternative hypothesis that assessments were theoretically made on the basis of the total wealth of the taxpayer, regardless of where it was situated, is to be preferred, it is clear that in the majority of cases when two assessments of the same person were made in different places, different figures were arrived at. Unfortunately in all but a few of these cases the difference between the size of the two assessments has not been recorded. However in these few cases the individual taxpayers came into the Exchequer themselves and petitioned for a complete exoneration from one of the assessments on the grounds that they should not have been so assessed in the first place, because they were not resident within that area. All these petitions are for exoneration from higher assessments, so it appears that when taxpayers were assessed in areas where they were not resident at lower figures, they did not trouble to challenge the legitimacy of the assessment, but relied upon the double residence rule which automatically annulled lesser assessments. But when claims were made in the Exchequer for exoneration from higher assessments, full details both of residence and of the value of both assessments had to be given. From these claims some idea can be gained of the possible discrepancies both in the value and in the basis of double assessments (see Table 5.11).

Thus in these cases the double assessments might not only differ considerably in size, in some cases the larger assessment being several times greater than the smaller; but also in the category on which the assessment was based. One example will show how widely discrepant such a double

Table 5.11 Discrepancies between 'illegal' double assessments

Subsidy	No. of claims	No. changing basis[a]	Average discrepancy[b]	Loss of revenue	References
1541	2	0	75%	£35	A
1542	7	3	371%	£38	B
1544	12	9	53%	£68	C
1545	17	11	98%	£116	D
1546 ('43)	1	1	-	£3	E
1546 ('45)	14	5	102%	£147	F
1547	25	11	170%	£260	G
TOTAL	78	40	145%	£697	

Notes:
[a] That is one assessment on annual incomes, the other on moveable goods, or vice versa.
[b] Of double assessments not changing basis of assessment, expressed as a percentage of the lower assessment.
Sources:
A   E159/320 Recorda P.r.61, 68.
B   E159/321 Recorda P.r.48, T.r.24, 25, M.r.68, 69; E159/322 Recorda H.r.45; E159/326 Recorda P.r.32.
C   E159/323 Recorda P.r.23-2936, 43, 44, T.r.24, 25; E368/330 Recorda M.r.48.
D   E159/321 Recorda P.r.11; E159/323 Recorda H.r.51-63, 70-75; E159/324 Recorda P.r.30, 44, M.r.52.
E   E159/324 Recorda H.r.56.
F   E159/325 Recorda P.r.69-74, 78, 79; E368/324 Recorda H.r.33, P.r.25, M.r.50.
G   E159/326 Recorda T.r.40, 42-52, 55-9, M.r.24-8, 32d, 143; E159/328 Recorda M.r.9.

assessment might be. In 1547 Christopher Alen was assessed in London, where he was not resident, at £1,000 in moveable property, for which he was required to pay £66 13s 4d to the subsidy. But he was also assessed in Buckinghamshire where he resided, for an annual income from lands worth £80, for which the tax payable was only £8.[76]

But the discrepancies revealed by the table are not sufficient to change the conclusion that subsidy assessments were generally made on the overall total of a taxpayer's wealth. First, the number of these widely discrepant cases is relatively small, compared to the total number of double assessments recorded, and second, almost all these cases are of a somewhat special nature in that they concern high assessments in London on persons not resident in the city.

The most reasonable conclusion from the available evidence would seem to be that in theory subsidy assessments were made on the total wealth of the individual wherever he was situated; but in practice it happened more often than not that assessors were insufficiently informed of wealth accruing to those whom they were assessing from outside the assessment area. Indeed, unless the commissioners put the taxpayer on oath, there was no means provided by the subsidy acts by which an assessor in one part of the country could discover the wealth of the taxpayer outside the assessment area, especially if the taxpayer himself was unforthcoming or evasive on this point.

To this extent, therefore, the procedure of assessment of the early Tudor subsidies was unsatisfactory, although the loss of revenue thereby entailed was not very great. And to this extent also the third rule of assessment favoured the small minority of taxpayers whose wealth was scattered in many places.

The third rule of assessment has been discussed at some length because it entails some of the most crucial questions concerning assessment towards the early Tudor subsidies. The converse of the third rule of assessment was the prohibition by all the subsidy acts, except the act for the subsidy of 1513, of wilful removal from one residence to another with the intent of escaping assessment altogether.[77] Such removals were to be punished by the imposition of a fine equal to, and in addition to, the best available assessments of the defaulters. Any two commissioners could impose such fines, by two Justices of the Peace, or by the Barons of the Exchequer. Only one case of fraudulent removal has been discovered; but this case is not clear cut because the alleged defaulter claimed that he was too poor to be assessed in the first place.[78] Other cases may well have occurred; but owing to the deficiencies of the original commissioners' returns it is unlikely that they can ever completely be reconstructed.[79]

The procedure of assessment

For the subsidies of 1513–16 the commissioners were to embark upon the procedure for assessment as soon as they received their commission. For all subsequent subsidies the assessment was to start on a date specified in the subsidy acts.[80] The first step in the procedure of assessment was for the commissioners to summon before them at least two, or more at their discretion, inhabitants or local officials, such as constables, to a preliminary meeting.[81] The commissioners were empowered by the subsidy acts to fine anyone summoned and not attending £1, unless a reasonable excuse, such as sickness, could be substantiated by 'twoo credible personees'.[82] At this meeting those who had been summoned, known as 'assessors' or 'presentors' were required to take an oath promising that they would make honest assessments.[83] No precise form of oath was specified for the subsidy of 1514; but the assessors of all subsequent subsidies were required to take the following form of oath:[84]

> I shall truely inquire wyth my felowis that shalbe sworne wyth me of the hundred Wapentake Ward town or other place of the best and most value and substaunce of every persone duellyng or abydyng wythin the lymytes of the places that I and my felowys shalbe charged wyth, or wyche shall have his or their most resort unto any of the same places and chargeable wyth any somme of money by the act of the seid subsidie and of all other articles that I shalbe charged wyth touchyng the seid act and accordyng to thentent of the same, and thereuppon as nere as

shall comme to my knowliche truely present and certifie before you the names and surnames the substaunce and values of every of them aswell of Landes Tenements or other hereditamentes and possessions recyted in the seid act, as of goodes and catalles and also of wagis and profyttes for wages of the seid persones and every of them chargeable by the seid act, wythout concelment favour love affeccion dred fere or malice so God me help and all the Seyntes and by this booke.[85]

Refusal to take this oath was to be punished by a fine of £1.[86]

The commissioners were then to explain to the assessors the rates of payment, the minimum assessments, and other criteria specified by the subsidy acts. For the subsidies of 1513, 1514 and 1536, no provision was made by the acts for this preliminary explanation of the terms of assessment; while for the subsidies of 1545 and 1547, the commissioners were required by a royal letter accompanying the commission to associate with their explanation of the rates and criteria of the subsidy a general exhortation as to its political and financial necessity.[87] The assessors were then told to go away, to assess everyone as they had promised in their oaths, and to return on a specified day with their assessments in writing.[88]

This preliminary assessment of the subsidies by local assessors is the crucial stage in the whole procedure of levying the early Tudor subsidies. Unfortunately, because these preliminary assessments were superseded by the revised lists of assessments prepared by the commissioners, none of these documents have survived. Thus it cannot be discovered whether the assessments were made by direct inspection, by interrogation, by estimation, or on the basis of records such as rentals or inventories. Nor can it ever be discovered what items of income from lands were included in the assessments and what were not. Further, the disappearance of the original assessors' lists also makes it impossible to discover how many people the assessors saw fit to assess under more than one head, and also how many of the total number of assessments the commissioners saw fit to revise. This serious lack of documentary evidence makes it very difficult to decide how accurate early Tudor subsidy assessments really were.

All those assessors who did not bring in their written assessments on the pre-arranged day were to be fined £1.[89] The commissioners were to 'pleynly and diligently overloke all the same certificates',[90] and, if necessary, to question the assessors about them. If the commissioners were still dissatisfied with the assessments they might summon those who had been assessed to be examined in person.[91] The summonses were to be delivered by local officials 'at their mansions or to their persones or by opyn proclamacions at their parisshe churches or otherwyse'.[92]

Those who, after due warning, failed to appear before the commissioners were to be rated at double the highest available assessment, or more at the commissioners discretion.[93] Reasonable excuses for absence were to be accepted, provided that two credible witnesses substantiated them. The commissioners were to examine those who had been summoned upon oath, which, with the exception of the subsidies of 1513–14, and 1535–6, was to be taken in the following form:

> I shall feithfully truely and pleynly accordyng to my knowliche shewe unto you the Kynges Comyssioners and to other by you assigned the best and grettest value or above [sic] of all my yerely profyttes in Londes Tenementes rentes or such like possessions, wages, yerely profyttes for wages and the best and grettest value of all my goodes and catalles and summes of money to me owen accordyng to the graunt of this acte of subsidie, and truely answer to that I shall be examyned of, touchyng the premisses wythout Covyn or dysceyte so God me help and all the Seyntes.[94]

On the other hand, anyone might volunteer to give evidence on oath before the commissioners if he wished to challenge the original assessment made on him.[95] The same form of oath was used, and until 1544 the commissioners were bound to accept such testimony. But for the subsidies of 1544–7, the commissioners were permitted to use their discretion.[96] For these subsidies also if it was proved within a year that anyone had sworn a false assessment, then a fine of four times the assessment was to be levied on the guilty party.[97]

The commissioners assessed each other, and for this a minimum of two commissioners as assessors was usually required. For the subsidies of 1513 and 1514 this assessment was to be by oath, certificate, or otherwise; and for the subsidies of 1515–16 by oath or otherwise. For the subsidy of 1524 and for all subsequent subsidies no oath was required and the commissioners merely examined each other. For the subsidies of 1544–46 ('43) this might be done by any number of commissioners or even by their appointees.

For the subsidies of 1546 ('45) and 1547 a rather different procedure was adopted. Two or three commissioners from each commission were to be nominated by the king for assessment with the peers. After being assessed they were to take an oath before the Lord Chancellor, the Lord Treasurer and the Lord President of the Council, or any two of them, that they would assess their fellow commissioners impartially. They were then to return to their counties and boroughs and make these assessments.

From the information derived form the original written assessments submitted by the assessors, and from their examinations both of the assessors and of those who had been assessed, the commissioners were to draw up a list of the tax due from everyone. This would have involved first calculating the tax charge for all the categories under which the individual had been assessed at whatever rates were applicable, and then discarding all the charges other than that which yielded the most revenue to the crown.

Thus although the main task of assessment was performed by local assessors, the main responsibility both for the accuracy of the assessments and for the correct calculation of the tax charges lay entirely with the commissioners.

The timing of the assessments

The assessments for all the subsidies had to be completed before a date specified by each of the subsidy acts.[98] For the subsidy of 1524 and for all subsequent subsidies the acts also specified the earliest date on which assessment might begin. These dates are given in Table 5.18 below. From this table it is clear that with the exception of the four subsidies of 1513, 1514, 1546 ('45) and 1547, assessments were always made in the weeks around Michaelmas.[99] This was clearly the most sensible time of the year for the assessment of annual incomes, for Michaelmas was the main season for the payment of rents and other yearly profits. It was also probably the best season, from the crown's point of view, for the assessment of moveable goods, for the harvest was gathered in and not yet consumed. Altogether the weeks around Michaelmas probably saw the greatest transference of incomes in the year, and were therefore best suited for assessment to taxation, for not only would debts be at a minimum, but the value of receipts and expenditures would still be fresh in the mind.

For those subsidies for which both the beginning and the end of the assessment period were limited by the subsidy acts it is possible to determine the time allowed for assessment. This time was remarkably constant. For the subsidies of 1524–7, six weeks were allowed for assessment, for the subsidies of 1544–6 ('43) seven weeks, and for the subsidies of 1546 ('45)–7 only four weeks.[100]

Collection of the Money

Once the assessments had been made, the commissioners' next task was to arrange for the local collection of the money due from everyone assessed towards the subsidies, and for its safe transport to the Exchequer, or to wherever it was directed to be paid.[101]

Local collection: the petty collectors

First of all the commissioners were to appoint petty collectors and to assign them to districts as they found convenient. The petty collectors were to be given lists of the tax due from everyone within their collecting area. The subsidy acts required these lists to be cast in the form of an indenture and to be handed to the petty collectors before a specified day, which might be anything up to three weeks after the last assessment day.[102] The petty collectors were to be appointed from among local inhabitants and officers, and therefore may or may not have been the same people who were appointed as assessors.

Upon receipt of their lists the petty collectors had power to levy the sums contained in them, and in default of payment to distrain upon the goods and chattels of the defaulter. As from 1524 this distress was subject to certain statutory conditions, namely that the goods distrained had to be held for eight days before they might be sold. They were to be held at the defaulter's cost, and were to be sold only after they had been 'appreysed' by between two and four local inhabitants. Any surplus cash accruing from this sale, over and above the original debt and the costs of the distress, was to be returned to the defaulter.

The high collectors

In addition to the petty collectors the commissioners were required to appoint high collectors, usually one for every hundred, or group of hundreds, whose task was to receive the money from the petty collectors and to convey it to the Exchequer, or wherever it was directed to be paid.[103] Members of the Commons and the commissioners themselves were exempted by the subsidy acts from appointment as high collectors, and the office tended to be filled by gentlemen, yeomen or 'generosi', and, more rarely, knights.[104] For the subsidies of 1524, and for all subsequent subsidies, the subsidy acts prohibited anyone from being appointed a high collector for more than one of the subsidies granted by each act.[105] Also for the subsidy of 1524 and for all subsequent subsidies no one who was resident in a corporate town was to be compelled to act as a high collector outside that town.[106] And for the subsidies of 1546 ('45) and 1547 the subsidy acts required that the high collectors should be worth £10 a year in lands or a hundred marks in goods.[107] For these subsidies the commissioners were also required to take recognisances from the high collectors to the value of two times the sum that they were to collect.[108] These recognisances were to be voidable upon the due payment of the tax money to the Exchequer by a certain date.[109] Refusal by the high collectors to subscribe to such a recognisance, or failure on the part of a commissioner to certify a recognisance to the Exchequer, entailed a fine of £10.[110]

For all the subsidies the commissioners were to make an indenture with the high collectors, under their own seals, containing a list of the petty collectors together with the sums due from each of them. These lists were to be written on parchment and were to be evenly agreable & concordaunt with the hoole some comprised in the seid endenture as is beforeseid to be delyverd unto the seid officers and inhabitauntes.[111]

For the subsidies of 1513–16 these lists were to be given to the high collectors not later than one month after the last assessment date, and for the subsidies of 1524–6 ('43) not later than three weeks after the last assessment date.[112]

Immediately upon receipt of these lists the high collectors were empowered to start collecting from the petty collectors. They were to arrange with the petty collectors suitable times and places for the handing over of the money, and at this payment the high collectors were to allow the petty collectors 2d in the pound as their collecting fee.[113] In the case of non-payment the high collectors had the same powers of distress over the petty collectors as the petty collectors had over individual taxpayers.

The main task of the high collectors was the conveyance of the tax money from their area to the Exchequer at Westminster.[114] In the Exchequer they were exempted by the subsidy acts from all fees,[115] and on their account they were to be allowed 6d in the pound to reimburse their costs of collection. Out of this 6d they had already allowed 2d to the petty collectors for their costs, and on their return they were required by the subsidy acts to pay a further 2d in the pound to the commissioners, to be divided amongst them according to how much work and expense each of them had borne. If the high collectors refused to pay this money, the commissioners were to have an action at law for debt, in which the defendant was not to wage his law, nor have protection or essoin.

Thus the early Tudor subsidies cost only 6d in the £, or 2½%, of the gross assessed yield, to collect, and this sum was divided evenly between the commissioners, the petty collectors and the high collectors. The only group receiving no remuneration was the assessors, except in so far as they were also appointed petty collectors.

The time allowed for collection

The time allowed by the subsidy acts for the collection of the subsidies does not follow any general rule. The first problem is the length of time allowed to the petty collectors in which to make their collection. This depended entirely upon the speed with which the commissioners gave them, and later the high collectors, their indentures. The interval between the latest days specified by the subsidy acts for handing these indentures to the petty collectors and to the high collectors varied greatly from subsidy to subsidy (see Table 5.12).

The time available to the petty collectors would have been increased if the commissioners had handed them their indentures before the dates specified in

Table 5.12   Interval between latest date for handing indentures to the petty and to the high collectors

Subsidy	Interval
1513	3 weeks
1514	2 weeks
1515–16	4 weeks
1524–7	same day
1535–6	uncertain[a]
1541–2	same day
1544–6 ('43)	3 weeks
1546 ('45)–7	4 weeks[b]

Notes:
[a] Latest date for petty collectors' indentures not precisely specified.
[b] Thus in statute. Indentures to petty collectors before 31 March; indentures to high collectors before 28 February.
Sources: As Appendix I.

the subsidy acts, or if they had handed the indentures to the high collectors after the statutory dates. Similarly the time available to the petty collectors would have been decreased if the commissioners were slow in handing them their indentures, but prompt, or early in handing the indentures to the high collectors. Since the actual dates on which these indentures were handed over to the petty collectors cannot now be discovered,[116] it is impossible to calculate the time actually available to the petty collectors in which to make their collection. The time allowed by the subsidy acts to the high collectors, that is the interval between the latest date specified in the subsidy acts for the handing to them of their indentures and the latest date for the payment of their money into the Exchequer, also varied greatly, from three to twelve-and-a-half weeks (see Table 5.13).

Table 5.13   Interval between receipt of indentures by high collectors and latest date of payment

Years	Weeks
1513	7½
1514	6½
1515–16	3
1524a	4
1524–7	9
15641–2	12½
1544–6 ('43)	12½
1546 ('45)–7	4

Notes:
1524a The anticipation of the subsidy of 1524.
Sources: As Appendix I.

It is difficult to say whether these times allowed to the high collectors in which to make their collection were in fact sufficient, for so much would have depended upon the co-operation of the petty collectors and of the individual taxpayers. Certainly, with the exception of the subsidies of 1541–6 ('43), the time was probably too short for any profitable use of the tax money by the collectors to their own advantage.[117]

Legal tender

The subsidy acts also laid down regulations as to the currency in which the subsidies might be paid. In general, all silver coins, irrespective of size or condition, were to be acceptable as payment for the subsidies. The one exception to this rule was that 'spurred pennies' were to pass for half-pennies.[118] For the subsidy of 1524 and for all subsequent subsidies the list of coins acceptable for payment was extended to include 'goldes grotes halfgrotes or pens or any of them'.

Refusal of cracked or clipped coins was especially prohibited by the subsidy acts. All the acts, except the act for the subsidy of 1513, provided that if it could be proved either before the Barons of the Exchequer, or the Justices of either Bench, or before any Justice of the Peace, sheriff, mayor, bailiff, or 'other hed officers' that a collector or officer of the Exchequer of Receipt had refused to accept a coin designated as current by the subsidy acts, then the tenderer of the coin was to quit of his debt, and the refuser was not only to be burdened with finding the debt himself, but also might be imprisoned or otherwise punished at the discretion of the Judge, magistrate, or head officer. In the event, no such cases have been found.

For the subsidy of 1524, and for all subsequent subsidies, payment might be made in foreign coins, and the subsidy acts specified the rates of exchange at which these coins were to be accepted.[119] The act for the subsidies of 1524–7 also allowed payment to the collectors to be made in plate, and specified the price per ounce for each type of plate. The officers of the mint were to give the collectors coins in return for the plate, and were not to charge them either for coinage or for wastage.[120] If the officers of the mint refused to exchange plate, then the collectors were to have an action at law for debt with double damages, in which action the defendant was not to wage his law, nor have protection or essoin. The experiment of accepting plate in payment for the subsidy arose entirely from the Commons' anxiety in 1523 that the stock of coins in the realm would be insufficient to meet the demands of the subsidies without severe damage to the economy, and was not repeated.[121]

Very little evidence has survived concerning the currency in which the subsidies were paid, but for the short period from autumn 1544 to summer 1546 the rough book of one of the Tellers in the Exchequer of Receipt notes the coins which the collectors of the subsidies of 1545, 1546 ('43) and 1546 ('45), and the collectors of the fifteenth and tenth of 1546 brought to the Exchequer.[122] Most collectors paid in a variety of coins, sovereigns, angles, crowns, roses, nobles, royals,[123] testoons, groats, half-groats, pennies, half-pennies and farthings.[124] Of these, sovereigns, angels, groats, half-groats and pennies were by far the most common. The most common coin of all was the groat, and some collectors paid in large sums of money entirely in groats. Foreign coins were very rare. Most common amongst them was the French crown of the sun;[125] but otherwise only a few 'Dukattes' and 'Double Dukatates' were brought by the collectors to the Exchequer.

Transferred liability to payment

The subsidy acts also laid down certain rules concerning the transfer of liability to payment from one person to another. These rules were of two kinds. The first specified cases in which liability rested entirely upon persons other than those who had been assessed *ab initio*, while the second set of rules concerned the transfer of liability upon default of payment by the person originally assessed.

Liability *ab initio*

Masters, both secular and ecclesiastical, were required by the subsidy acts to pay all taxes assessed on their servants for their wages, and in default of payment were liable to distress at the hands of the collectors. In their turn masters were empowered by the subsidy acts to recover these subsidy payments by retaining them from subsequent wage payments.[126] For all the subsidies, except those of 1513 and 1514, all persons such as trustees or officials of corporations, holding or administering property not their own, were held personally liable for the payment of the tax assessed on this property; but they were entitled under the acts to recoup their losses upon handing over the property, or upon expiry of their term of office.[127] Landlords of aliens assessed for the poll payments of the subsidies of 1541–6 ('43) were also liable for the payment of the tax assessed upon their tenants.[128]

For the subsidies of 1524–7 and 1535–6 the subsidy acts clearly exempted tenants and lessees from liability for payment of tax assessed on their holdings, despite any agreements to the contrary, and transferred this liability entirely to the landlords.[129] If, nevertheless, the tenants or lessees were distrained upon by the collectors, then they were entitled by the subsidy acts to retain the value of this distress from their next rent payments. If they were unable to do this, they were entitled to bring an action at law for debt with treble damages against the landlord, in which action the defendant was to be allowed neither protection nor essoin.[130]

Liability transferred upon default

Default in payment by an individual taxpayer, or by a petty collector, set in motion a series of liabilities. It has been shown that in the first instance a collector was empowered by the subsidy acts to distrain upon the defaulter's goods. As from 1515 the subsidy acts provided for further action to be taken upon the authority of a certificate from at least two commissioners, based in turn upon the sworn testimony of a high collector.

Thus if the defaulting party died, or departed out of the collector's area, so that no distrainable goods could be found, the commissioners might authorise the collectors, or any officer anywhere in the county,[131] to levy the sum due by way of distress either upon the property of the defaulter himself, or upon the property of anyone owing him fees, annuities, rents, debts, or holding any property to his use or in trust for him, or if he had died, upon the property of his heirs, executors or administrators.[132] This distress might extend to lands and tenements, and was thus wider in scope than the distress allowed to the collectors in the first instance which was confined to moveable goods only.[133] Those suffering this second form of distress for the default of others were entitled by the subsidy acts to deduct the value of the distress from their subsequent payments of rents, fees, annuities or debts, or when they returned the defaulter's property to him. The special form of action for debt, as described for tenants and lessees, was only available to them for the subsidies of 1524–7.

Officers making these distresses outside their own jurisdiction were to be remunerated out of the profits of the distress at the rate of 2d for every mile that they had travelled. If, however, because of the death, flight or fraud of the defaulter no distrainable property could be found, or if property that had been distrained could not be sold, the commissioners might request any officer to arrest the defaulter, or his heirs, executors, administrators, trustees, tenants or debtors, and to imprison them 'without bayle or maynprize' until the sum due was paid, together with a fee of 1s 9d to the officer who made the arrest.[134] Should such persons escape from prison, then the gaoler, if convicted of negligence, was to pay double the tax in question to the collectors, twice the arresting fee to the officer in question, and a fine of £2 to the king. For the subsidy of 1524, and for all subsequent subsidies, the commissioners were required to certify to the Exchequer by the 'terme next folowing' all actions that they had authorised to be taken outside the area of their commission. In the event, no such certificates have been found.

Difficulties arising during the collection

As from 1524, in all the above situations, if recovery of the sums due proved impossible before the payment date, then upon the evidence of a certificate from at least two commissioners, the responsibility for the collection of outstanding debts was to be transferred from the high collectors to the Exchequer, which was to issue its traditional forms of process.[135] But this appeal to the powers of the Exchequer was only to be made in the last resort when all other means had failed. The subsidy acts, by outlining a set of procedures, by specifying a series of liabilities to payment, and by endowing the commissioners with wide discretionary powers, sought to secure the settlement of difficulties in the localities before the payment date, after which they became the inevitable concern of the Exchequer.

Nevertheless, despite the provisions of the subsidy acts, a large number of claims were made by collectors for sums that they had been unable to levy. All these claims were supported by certificates from the commissioners.[136] The claims were of two kinds, for sums that could not be collected because the taxpayer had departed out of the collector's area, and for sums that could not be collected because no distrainable goods could be found. In claims of the former kind most of the defaulters were said to have departed 'ad loca ignota', but in several cases the new abode of the defaulter was certified to the Exchequer. This information was of great value to the officers of the Exchequer, for the only way in which they could try to recover these sums was by a writ of 'fieri facias' addressed to a sheriff, by the King's Remembrancer, or by means of the Summons of the Pipe.[137] If they did not know to which county a defaulter had fled, they had no alternative but to address the writ to the sheriff of the county from which the certificate attesting the flight had originated. This, as might be expected, was not a very successful procedure, but without the necessary information as to the whereabouts of the defaulter, it was the only one open to them.

It is clear from Table 5.14 that claims for exoneration because of the flight of defaulters were both more numerous and involved larger sums of money than claims based on a lack of distrainable goods. But although both the numbers and the values of both sorts of claim fluctuated from one subsidy to another, they were altogether very much larger in the 1540s than in earlier years. The reason for this increase in the number of exemptions claimed by the collectors may lie partly in an increased awareness on the part of the collectors of their privileges under the subsidy acts, and partly in the unsettled conditions during the wars of the 1540s.[138] The proportion of claims for taxpayers leaving the collecting area that were made by the London collectors is especially high and may well reflect a greater mobility of population in the capital relative to the rest of the country.

But these figures only represent those cases for which the local procedures specified in the subsidy acts did not suffice, and which had to be referred to the Exchequer. Unfortunately no record has survived of those cases which were dealt with at once by the commissioners under the powers granted to them by the subsidy acts, and thus a large part of the work of the commissioners and collectors must remain unknown.

Table 5.14   Claims for exoneration by collectors from illeviable sums

Subsidy	Flight			Distress impossible		Both
	No. defaulters	London	Amount £ s d	No. defaulters	Amount	% of yield 'lost'[a]
1516	4	0%	11 18 0	–	–	0.03
1524	63	97%	25 16 6	7	9 17 8	0.06
1525	26	19%	7 11 4	14	18 18 9½	0.04
1526–7	–	–	–	–	–	–
1535	38	58%	49 9 10	–	–	0.20
1536	18	39%	16 15 0	–	–	0.07
1541	22	23%	24 0 0	–	–	0.05
1542	95	64%	74 5 0	5	46 18 8	0.25
1544	117	86%	343 15 4	21	29 8 0	0.47
1545	248	68%	318 3 8	91	41 6 0	0.61
1546 ('43)	93	27%	45 6 8	63	23 5 3	0.12
1546 ('45)	104	81%	453 17 0	79	334 3 10	0.69
1547	147	96%	840 16 6	52	124 9 8	0.94
Total	975	68%	2211 14 10	331	628 7 10½	

Note:
[a] of gross certified yield; see table 40, column 1.
Sources: E359/38 7VIII, 12d; E359/41 passim; E359/42 passim; E359/44 passim.

The only other aspect of the problem of defaulters for which evidence has survived is that of the rescue of distresses. Complaints against such rescue were brought before the Barons of the Exchequer by both high and petty collectors, in the same way as similar complaints were brought by collectors of fifteenths and tenths. But the subsidy collectors brought far fewer complaints than did the collectors of fifteenths and tenths. Only eight cases were brought during the entire period, four by high collectors against petty collectors, and four by petty collectors against individual taxpayers. These actions in the Exchequer were not very successful, for in only two cases were the defendants successfully brought before the Exchequer.

The smallness of the number of complaints brought by the subsidy collectors before the Exchequer, together with the small number of similar complaints brought in the same period by collectors of fifteenths and tenths, suggests that resistance to distress was not a major problem for collectors of taxes during the reign of Henry VIII (see Table 5.15).

It has been shown that in the course of administering the provisions of the subsidy acts the commissioners were given wide powers of control both over private individuals and over officers of the crown. In addition to the specific powers discussed above, the commissioners were given the general power to punish any officer of the crown whom they considered had defaulted on, or negligently executed, their precepts by a fine of £1. The commissioners were

Table 5.15   Complaints against rescues of distresses

Subsidy	Total no. of complaints	By high collectors	By petty collectors	Means of summons	Appear in Exchequer	Fine	Act of Pardon
1524	3	2	1	A	0		
1525	1	1	0	A	0		
1527	1	0	1	S	1	2s 0d	
1535	2	1	1	S	1		
1647	1	0	1				1
Total	8	4	4	2A/2S	2	1	1

Key:
A   By writ of attachment
S   By writ of subpoena
Sources:
1524: Salop. E159/303 Recorda H.r.13d; Staffs: /304 Recorda H.r.17d; Soms: /311 Recorda T.r.14.
1525: Yorks (WR). E159/306 Recorda H.r.3. 1527: Derbs. E159/307 Recorda H.r.2. 1535: Salop:
E159/316 Recorda P.r.22, T.r.3. 1547: Surrey: E159/326 Recorda P.r.23.

also given a general power to fine anyone hindering the operation of the subsidy acts, or imprison or punish them in any other way at their discretion.[139] The commissioners were also required by the subsidy acts to certify details of all fines that they had imposed on defaulters to the Exchequer. Most fines were to be certified together with the assessments, and were to be levied by the collectors together with the tax charges. But for the subsidies of 1513 and 1514 fines assessed on 'auxiliary' commissioners and fines assessed on uncooperative officers of the crown; and for the subsidy of 1535–6 fines assessed on uncooperative officers and individuals were to be levied by process out of the Exchequer.

No record has been found of any process out of the Exchequer to levy these fines. Of the fines certified by the commissioners with the subsidy assessments and collected by the collectors, only two examples have been noted.[140] It is possible that a complete inspection of all the surviving certificates of assessments would reveal more such fines; but it is very unlikely that it would alter the impression gained from a fair number of these certificates that the imposition of fines by the commissioners was a rare occurrence. The task of the commissioners was therefore not merely administrative, for in the course of their supervision of the assessment and collection of the subsidies they were required by the acts to assume powers of a distinctly judicial nature.

Certification

But the commissioners were by no means free agents, for ultimately they were accountable for their actions before the Exchequer. Their main obligation

Table 5.16   Interval, in weeks, between last day of assessment, certification and payment

Subsidy	Assessment to certification	Certification to payment
1513	11	1
1514	9	2
1515–16	2	5
1524–7	9	4
1535–6	–ᵃ	3½
1541–2	4	11½
1544–6 ('43)	4	11½
1546 ('45)–7	4	3

Notes:
ᵃ No last day for assessment specified in the act.
Sources: See Table 5.18 and Appendix I.

towards the Exchequer was the certification of all assessments and fines before a date specified in the subsidy acts. This certification was essential for the preparation of the collectors' accounts, and, in cases of difficulty, for the ultimate recovery of the tax; for all Exchequer processes were, perforce, based upon the commissioners' certificates.

The latest date for the return of certificates of assessment to the Exchequer as specified by the subsidy acts fell somewhere between the last date for assessment and the last date for the payment of the subsidies. The intervals between these three dates are shown in Table 5.16.[141] Thus for many of the subsidies the commissioners were not required by the subsidy acts to send their certificates to the Exchequer until a very short time before, according to the subsidy acts, the collectors should have been in a position to open their accounts at the Exchequer. This would have placed a great burden upon the officers of the Exchequer concerned with the preparation and audit of accounts; and it is interesting that for the later subsidies, for which the certificates were much more detailed, the certification date was moved further away from the last payment date.[142]

Generally the commissioners were required to send their certificates to the Exchequer; but for five of the earlier subsidies they were also required to send duplicate commissions elsewhere (see Table 5.17). The circumstances that required the duplicate certificates for the first three subsidies have already been discussed. Certificates were sent both to the Exchequer and to the Treasurer of the Chamber in 1535 and 1536 because the collectors were required by the subsidy acts to pay the money from the subsidies to the Treasurer of the Chamber while still accounting at the Exchequer. It is more difficult to understand why duplicate certificates were to be sent to the Treasurer of the Chamber for the subsidies of 1524–7, for the collectors both paid and accounted for the subsidies at the Exchequer. The Treasurer of the

Table 5.17   Recipients of duplicates of commissioners' certificates

Subsidy	Recipients
1513	Knights and burgesses, to take to the Commons
1514	Committee of the 'Cheker Chamber',[a] or to the Commons
1515	Committee of the 'Cheker Chamber'[b]
1524–7	Treasurer of the Chamber
1535–6	Treasurer of the Chamber

Notes:
[a] For this committee, see p. 88.
[b] For this, different, committee, see p. 89.
Sources: As Appendix I.

Chamber only received the Anticipation of the subsidy of 1524; but this was levied under a different commission and on the basis of an independent assessment.[143] Possibly the provision for duplicate copies of the commissioners' certificates to be sent to the Treasurer of the Chamber was a device to obtain certificates of assessment for the immediate use of ministers of the crown.[144]

The contents of the certificates grew more detailed as the subsidy acts required more and more information to be certified to the Exchequer. For the subsidy of 1513 the commissioners were required to send a joint certificate to the Exchequer containing the names of all the high collectors within the commission area together with the 'hole summes' charged upon them, as contained in the indenture made between them and the commissioners. For the subsidy of 1514 the commissioners were to make a similar certificate; but might either charge the whole sum due from the commission area to all the high collectors collectively, or might indicate for which part of the total sum each high collector was to be held responsible. The acts granting the subsidies of 1515 and 1516 were somewhat anomalous in that they omitted to require the commissioners to certify the names of the high collectors.[145] But under these acts the commissioners were permitted for the first time to return separate certificates if they were unable to make a joint certificate for the whole commission area. In this case one of the certificates, in addition to specifying the usual information concerning assessments and fines, was to contain a list showing which commissioners were responsible for the other parts of the commission area. This 'key' certificate was to be sent to the Exchequer before the statutory date; while the certificates from the other parts of the commission area were allowed a period of four days grace in which to be returned.[146]

The act granting the subsidies of 1524–7 corrected the omission of the collectors' names; but stressed that it was to be made abundantly clear in the commissioners' certificates what sums each high collector was to be held responsible for, so that the collectors were not inadvertently double charged when they accounted at the Exchequer. The commissioners were also required to hold a meeting to pool their assessments and fines. The purpose of such a meeting was probably twofold. First, it would have ensured that all the commissioners were mobilised simultaneously, instead of each group of commissioners taking its own time over the preparation of the certificates. Second, through the comparison of the different assessment lists, it would have helped to eliminate double assessments from being made within the same commission area.

The act granting the subsidies of 1524–7 also made a most important innovation in that it required that the 'key' certificates were to contain not only the gross sums to be charged to each high collector, but also the particular sums levied on each individual taxpayer. Thus an anomaly arose between the requirements of the 'key' certificates and those of the other, separate, certificates, for the subsidy act only required for these latter certificates the certification of the gross sums chargeable to the high collectors. The terms of this act were repeated by all subsequent subsidy acts, without any attempt to remove this anomaly. Nevertheless, in practice, both for the subsidies of 1524–7 and for all subsequent subsidies, the commissioners' certificates all contained details of the particular sums levied on each individual taxpayer.[147]

For all the subsidies the minimum number of commissioners who could make a certificate returnable to the Exchequer was two. From 1515, if a commissioner died, the subsidy acts charged his heirs, executors or administrators with the responsibility for all his obligations under the subsidy acts. Further, the death of any commissioner or collector was not to make any order or instruction given under the terms of the subsidy acts null or void. In default of certification, the Exchequer was to issue process against the commissioners until proper certificates were forthcoming.[148]

The Time Allowed for Levy of the Subsidies

The times allowed by the subsidy acts for the assessment and collection of the subsidies are given in Table 5.18. It is clear from the table that where a subsidy act granted more than one subsidy the dates for each of the stages in the levying of the subsidies remained the same, and the subsidies were spaced out at yearly intervals. This was probably the simplest and most convenient way in which to arrange for several consecutive levies. In the first place it retained the seasonal advantage of having the assessments in the autumn, and secondly, because the subsidies took on an average five months to levy, it avoided the confusion that might be occasioned by simultaneous or overlapping levies.

Table 5.18 The statutory dates for the levy of the subsidies

Approx. date of enactment[a]	Commission to be delivered by	Assessment from	Assessment to	Lists to petty collectors before	Lists to high collectors before	Certification to Exchequer before	Payment to Exchequer before	Enactment – Payment	Assessment – Payment
20 Dec 1513	–	–	10 Apr 1513	8 days	1 month	14 June 1513	1 July 1513	6½ months	12 weeks[c]
4 Mar 1514	–	–	16 Apr 1514	14 days	1 month	18 June 1514[b]	1 July 1514	4 months	11 weeks[c]
5 Apr 1515	–	–	29 Sept 1515	0 days	1 month	15 Oct 1515	21 Nov 1515	7 months	7 weeks[c]
22 Dec 1515	–	–	29 Sept 1516	0 days	1 month	15 Oct 1516	21 Nov 1516	11 months	7 weeks
early July 1523	16 Sept 1523–6	29 Sept 1523–6	11 Nov 1523–6	3 weeks	3 weeks	14 Jan 1524–7	9 Feb 1524–7	7 months	19 weeks
Dec 1534	–	–	–	convenient time	3 weeks	13 Oct 1535–6	6 Nov 1535–6	11 months	–
24 July 1540	6 Aug 1540–1	1 Sept 1540–1	20 Oct 1540–1	3 weeks	3 weeks	16 Nov 1540–1	6 Feb 1541–2[d]	6½ months	22½ weeks
late March 1543	6 Aug 1543–5	1 Sept 1543–5	20 Oct 1543–5	0 days	3 weeks	16 Nov 1543–5	6 Feb 1544–6	10½ months	22½ weeks
24 Dec 1545	4 Jan 1546–7	16 Jan 1546–7	12 Feb 1546–7	31 Mar 1546–7	28 Feb 1546–7	10 Mar 1546–7	1 Apr 1546–7	3½ months	11 weeks

Notes:
[a] This is taken, as far as possible, to be the date of the third reading by the Lords, or the presentation of the instrument of grant to the crown. See pp. 23–4.
[b] Certificates to the committee in the 'Cheker chamber' by 1 July 1514.
[c] Since no commencement date for assessment is given in the acts this interval is calculated from the last date from assessment. The actual time taken by assessment and collection would therefore be somewhat longer.
[d] Payment date for 4d poll on aliens: 8 Feb 1541–2.
Sources: See Appendix I.

The table also shows that the overall time from the grant of the subsidy to its payment was very long. In four cases this interval was almost a year, in three cases it was about six months, and in only two cases was about three months. But this interval was by no means entirely taken up with the assessment and collection of the subsidies. The actual levying of the subsidies took in general only about five months.[149] The variation in length of the interval, therefore, between the grant and the payment of the subsidies depended mainly on the time that was allowed to elapse before the assessment began. In two cases the subsidy acts arranged for the assessment to begin within a month of the date of the grant of the subsidies, and a further two arranged for the grants to begin within one or two months. These subsidy acts, of 1540, 1545, and of 1514 and 1523, were all passed in times of military necessity. But the acts of 1512 and 1543 were also passed under such circumstances; but they did not require the assessments to begin until some four or five months later. However, of the two acts which specified the longest intervals before assessments were to begin, that of 1534 was passed in peacetime, with no urgent military necessity, and that of 1515 (7 Henry VIII) was granted while the previous subsidy was still being paid, and had the effect of extending that subsidy for a further year.[150]

Nevertheless, if an interval of five months is taken as the average time necessary for the levy of a subsidy, and if a further interval of one or two months is taken as a reasonable time for the appointment of the commissioners and the preparation of the copies of the subsidy acts, it is clear that the directly assessed subsidy was a somewhat slow means of raising revenue necessitated by urgent military expenditures.[151]

Anticipations

The length of time needed to levy a subsidy led the crown on two occasions, in 1523 and in 1545, to anticipate the statutory payment date. On 2 November 1523, while the assessment for the subsidy of 1524 was still in progress, commissions were sent to between six and eleven of the chief commissioners, together with certain Lords, in each shire except Yorkshire and Lancashire,[152] and to the head officers,[153] and between three and six commissioners in twenty-four towns,[154] to 'practise' with everyone possessing annual incomes and moveable goods worth £40 and above to pay the subsidy of 1524 immediately instead of at the date specified in the subsidy act.[155] The commissioners were given lists of all those worth the minimum £40, which were taken from the assessments made eighteen months earlier by the commissioners for musters.[156] Two of the commissioners for the Anticipation were nominated as collectors and they were to pay the Anticipation money to the Treasurer of the Chamber, not the Exchequer, before 30 November.[157]

Since the subsidy was not payable to the Exchequer until 9 February, the Anticipation meant a saving of ten weeks.

For the second Anticipation, in 1545, a somewhat different procedure was adopted. Some time in June 1545,[158] instructions were sent to some of those who had been commissioners for the subsidy levied in the previous year to approach all those who had been assessed towards that subsidy at £10 in moveable goods or at £5 in annual incomes to persuade them to pay the new subsidy at once and on the basis of their assessments to the previous subsidy, instead of waiting for the new assessments to be made in the following September and October. If they chose to do this, any higher assessment that might be made on them during September and October was to be disregarded. The offer was to remain open until Michaelmas; but the commissioners were to try to extract payment before 1 July, and they were to appoint sufficient collectors to pay it to the Exchequer before 15 July.[159] Since the statutory payment date for the subsidy was not until 6 February 1546, the Anticipation gained some seven months for the crown. The crown, indeed, was desperately in need of money at this date, as the agonised memoranda of the councillors well show.[160] Later, on 11 May 1545 Trinity Term was adjourned until 6 October for all courts except the Exchequer and First Fruits and Tenths, and all justices and commissioners were to return home and see that all money due to the crown from whatever source was to be brought to the Exchequer at once.[161] In order to persuade the taxpayers to agree more readily to the Anticipation of 1545, the commissioners were instructed to explain how the defence of 'them ther wyffes and childern' was costing almost £40,000 a month and that the king was not only spending his own money and selling his lands, but was working night and day for the safety of the country. To impart a sense of urgency to the occasion the commissioners were also instructed to allege that a Franco–Scottish invasion was imminent.[162]

Another effort to accelerate the payment of a subsidy, but not by Anticipation, had been made the year before, when a signet letter, dated 9 November 1544, that is some three weeks after the last assessment date and some twelve-and-a-half weeks before the statutory payment date, was addressed to the commissioners ordering them to summon the high collectors and command them to levy the subsidy and pay it to the Exchequer without delay.[163] This attempt to speed up the assessment affected everyone liable to pay the subsidy. But on both occasions when time was gained by the levy of a separate Anticipation in place of the regular payment, it was only the richer taxpayers that were approached by the crown.

The Efficiency of the Administration of the Subsidies

Very little record has survived of the actual administration of the subsidy acts by the commissioners, for much of their activity was never committed to writing. However, some light can be thrown on some aspects of their practice. First, the dates on which the commissioners handed the indentures containing the sums due from the petty collectors to the high collectors can be compared with the dates specified for its procedure in the subsidy acts. The actual dates of the indentures are to be found from the copies of these indentures that the commissioners were required to certify to the Exchequer. These certificates are conveniently collected together for the subsidies of 1513, 1514 and 1515. For the subsidy of 1513 the act required the commissioners to hand the indentures to the high collectors before 10 May. The file of certificates shows that in fact most of these indentures were made in June.[164] Again for the subsidy of 1514 none of the indentures was made before the date specified in the subsidy act; most were made within one month after this date, and some even later.[165] But for the subsidy of 1515 all the indentures except two were made before the date specified in the subsidy act.[166] This was probably because the subsidy act required the commissioners to certify a copy of the indenture to the Exchequer two weeks before the latest date for handing the indenture to the high collectors.[167]

Unfortunately, for all the subsequent subsidies the commissioners' practice of sending several separate certificates for each part of the commission area resulted in a profusion of the number of certificates together with their subsequent dispersal, and somewhat uncertain survival, amongst the records of the Exchequer.[168] Thus, in the absence of any evidence to the contrary, it is tentatively suggested that the majority of the commissioners for the later subsidies handed over the indentures to the high collectors within a few weeks of the dates specified in the subsidy acts.[169]

Another, more general, means of assessing the efficiency of the commissioners in administering the subsidy acts, is to consider the number of complaints brought against the commissioners by taxpayers and by collectors. While these clearly may not represent the total number of the failings and misdemeanours of the commissioners, the machinery of the subsidy acts was such that serious lapses on the part of the commissioners would either have been detected by the Exchequer or would have had serious consequences for the collectors who might reasonably be expected to have sought relief by way of complaint to the Barons of the Exchequer.

In fact the number of complaints brought against the commissioners was very small. Over the whole period only four complaints were made, two by collectors, one by an individual taxpayer, and one by an anonymous informer. In addition, the officers of the Exchequer discovered two cases of fraud perpetrated by the commissioners. The two complaints brought by the high collectors against the commissioners in the Exchequer were both for failure by the commissioners to deliver to them the indentures containing the sums that they were to collect from the petty collectors. In default of these certificates the high collectors were unable to collect any of the tax, yet because their names had been certified to the Exchequer, they were subject to the rigours of process out of that court. In one of these cases it was discovered that a commissioner had not only collected the tax money himself, but had also collected £24 more than the sum that he had certified to the Exchequer as being due from that area.[170]

The two cases of fraud discovered by the officers of the Exchequer were both perpetrated by two commissioners in the North Riding of Yorkshire who returned fictitious names as collectors for the Wapentake of Hallikeld for the subsidies of 1524 and 1525.[171] On both occasions the commissioners were summoned to account for the money due from the Wapentake themselves.[172]

The two complaints, one brought by an anonymous informer, and the other by an individual taxpayer, were both against Sir Anthony Cope, a commissioner in Oxfordshire. The anonymous informer told the Barons of the Exchequer that in the returns for the subsidy of 1536 Cope had omitted to include his own name in the certificate of assessment and had thereby escaped taxation. This allegation was checked against the certificates of assessment and found to be true. Cope was discovered in the Exchequer and was assessed by the Barons on the basis of his own declaration of his wealth, but at twice the statutory rate by way of a fine for his offence.[173] Some six years later a husbandman alleged in Chancery that Cope and another commissioner, when he visited them to ask them the value of his subsidy assessment, robbed him, unlawfully imprisoned him, evicted his wife and children, threatened him with torture, and forced him to sign a document the contents of which he did not know. The husbandman believed that these actions were taken in reprisal for his refusal to bribe Cope and the other commissioner to reduce his assessment.[174] Unfortunately neither Cope's answer to the charge, nor the decision of Chancery, is known, so it cannot be determined how much truth there was in these allegations.

But in general, despite the insufficiency of the evidence, it would seem that in consideration of the numbers involved, the commissioners administered much of the machinery of the subsidy acts with a fair degree of efficiency. Failings there certainly were, but not many were of a sufficient degree of seriousness to make much mark upon the records. But efficiency on the part of the commissioners in operating the machinery of the subsidy acts was of limited advantage to the crown if two more vital aspects of the commissioners' work were performed inadequately. The success of the early Tudor subsidies depended more than anything else upon the accuracy of the assessments and upon the efficiency of the commissioners in certifying these assessments to the Exchequer.

Efficiency in the certification of assessments

Unfortunately the evidence necessary for assessing the efficiency of the commissioners in certifying assessments to the Exchequer is unsatisfactory except for two of the subsidies. For the subsidies of 1514 and 1515 the commissioners certificates were collected together on a single file and each certificate was endorsed with the date of its receipt at the Exchequer. For the subsidy of 1514, 80% of all the certificates were delivered to the Exchequer by one of the commissioners between two and four weeks after the latest date specified for certification in the subsidy act.[175] But for the subsidy of 1515, 7% of the certificates were actually delivered by the commissioners before the statutory date, while 45% were delivered within two weeks after this date, and a further 28% between two and four weeks after the statutory date.[176] For both these subsidies about 20% of the certificates due from the commissioners are missing from the files and probably arrived in the Exchequer very much later.[177] Nevertheless the promptitude of the commissioners in delivering the certificates for the subsidy of 1515 shows a considerable improvement over that of the commissioners for the subsidy of 1514.

Unfortunately comparable information for the other subsidies is not readily obtainable. Most of the certificates for the subsidy of 1513 are not filed, and very few of those that are filed are endorsed with the date of their receipt at the Exchequer.[178] The certificates for the subsidy of 1516 are neither filed nor, generally, dated.[179] For the subsidies of 1524 and for all subsequent subsidies, when even more separate certificates were returned by different groups of commissioners within the same commission area, many hundreds of certificates were made for each subsidy.[180] These certificates are at present scattered throughout the class E179 in the National Archives, and the immense labour required to collate all these certificates would be of limited value since very many of the certificates have not survived, and of those that remain by no means all were endorsed with the date of their receipt at the Exchequer.

Other evidence for the efficiency of the commissioners in returning the certificates of assessment to the Exchequer is scarcely more promising. It was the practice of the Exchequer to issue writs to the sheriffs to distrain upon the commissioners in order to encourage them to send in their certificates.[181] Unfortunately the enrolment of the issue of these writs was somewhat haphazard, and there is no record at all for the issue of these writs for the subsidies of 1526–7, 1536 and 1545–7. For the subsidy of 1524 these writs were sent out against all the commissioners except those for Southwark and Worcester some three months after the date specified in the subsidy act for the return of the certificates.[182] But for this subsidy the commissioners were instructed to revise their assessments, after they had been certified to the Exchequer, so the date of the writs to the sheriffs can scarcely be used as an indication of the promptitude of the original certification.[183] For the subsidy of 1525, however, writs were sent out in May against the commissioners for four counties who were thus clearly late in returning their certificates to the Exchequer.[184] Annotations to the enrolment of writs directed against the commissioners for the subsidy of 1541 show that all the commissioners, except those for the four northern border shires had certified before the date on which the writs were returnable by the sheriffs.[185] This date was some two months after the statutory certification date; but it is quite possible that many of the commissioners in fact sent in their certificates well before this date, and possibly also before the statutory date. For the two remaining subsidies for which evidence survives the results are even more disappointing. For the subsidy of 1542 there are no annotations to the enrolment of the writs against the commissioners, showing whether the commissioners had certified or not,[186] and for the subsidy of 1544 the annotations do not extend beyond the first rotulus of the enrolment.[187]

This plainly unsatisfactory evidence might be supplemented by a consideration of the number of issues forfeited by the commissioners during this process of distress by the sheriff. A certain number of these forfeitures have been noted amongst the records of the Exchequer;[188] but in insufficient numbers to form any general picture of the inefficiency of the commissioners. Thus because of the insufficiency of the evidence no clear answer can be given to the question of whether the commissioners were prompt in certifying assessments to the Exchequer or not. What evidence there is suggests that most commissioners returned their certificates fairly soon after the dates specified in the subsidy acts. An exception, though, must be made for the commissioners of the peerage. This commission was not included in the Chancery enrolments of subsidy commissions, and the commissioners were, therefore, not normally subject to distress on the authority of writs from the Exchequer. Wolsey, in fact, attempted to both have his cake and eat it by delivering the names of the commissioners for the subsidies of 1524–7 to the Exchequer, and writs of 'distringas' were sent out against them, but very late.[189]

The accuracy of the assessments

The accuracy of the assessments is the crucial question in determining the success of the subsidies of 1513–47. The directly assessed subsidies were designed to improve upon the fixed yield of the fifteenths and tenths by making their yield a proportion of the wealth of the country. In an age of increasing inflation this was plainly a sensible approach to direct taxation, but it made the yield of the subsidies entirely dependent upon the accuracy of the assessments of the taxpayers' wealth. It is known that in the fifteenth century and again in the latter half of the sixteenth century these assessments were very far from being true valuations of the wealth of the taxpayers.[190] But was the position any different in the latter part of Henry VIII's reign? We shall postpone an answer to the crucial question of the accuracy of the assessments until the final pages of this study. Meanwhile, we must calculate the actual yield of each subsidy and the speed with which it was received by the crown. But before this can be done something must first be said of the way in which the money from the taxes was received and accounted for by the Exchequer.

6

The Procedure and the Records
of the Exchequer

At the outset a distinction must be made between the Upper Exchequer, or
Exchequer of Account or audit, and the Lower Exchequer, or the Exchequer of
Receipt. The names of these two divisions of the Exchequer suggest their
differing functions. The Exchequer of Receipt was concerned with
administering and recording the receipt and issue of the king's money, either
in specie or by way of some monetary instrument. The Upper Exchequer was
exclusively a department of audit, equipped to record, and enforce, the full
payment of all revenues due to the crown, other than those which had been
specifically excepted from its purview, regardless where or how the money had
actually been paid. While the Exchequer of Receipt was a court and produced
records valid in a court of law, it differed essentially from the Upper
Exchequer in that it was not a full 'court of record', for it had neither the
means nor the powers either to summon or to punish.[1] The Upper Exchequer,
on the other hand, possessed very wide powers of this kind, for not only could
it command the arrest of a defaulter together with the seizure of all his
possessions, it also had the power to convict and imprison or fine anyone who
impeded the collection of the king's revenues.[2]

Thus the records of the Exchequer of Receipt may be expected to yield
information as to the amount of revenue received by the crown from taxation,
together with details of the date of its receipt and of the form in which it was
paid. On the other hand, the records of the Upper Exchequer may be expected
to provide comprehensive statements of the account of each collector together
with full details of any defaults, delays, excuses or claims that may have
arisen. Since each series of records in both divisions of the Exchequer were
compiled for specific purposes in relation to the administration of revenue,
there is no reason to expect amongst the records of the Exchequer any consolidated account of the total yield of any of the taxes granted by parliament.[3]
In order to arrive at such a total figure it is necessary to collate several

different types of record, where possible using each to cover deficiencies in other sources. Anything less than a full collation of all the available Exchequer material can only produce results that are at best misleading, and at worst, grossly inaccurate.

The Exchequer of Receipt

With a very few exceptions, the collectors of taxes granted by parliament were required by statute to pay the money that they had collected directly to the Exchequer of Receipt.[4] Once they had made this payment they were committed to the 'ancient course' of the Exchequer, by which they received tallies as tokens of receipt for the money which they had paid to the Tellers in the Receipt, for exhibition to the auditors in the Upper Exchequer as proof of their payment so that they might obtain their final acquittance or discharge. But before the collectors could proceed to their account in the Upper Exchequer, they had to pass through the machinery for the recording and authentication of tallies that comprised the main business of the Exchequer of Receipt.

The first stage in this process was the noting of the amount paid, together with the name of the payer, the nature of the revenue, and the date, term and year of the payment, by the Teller in his book. These entries were later written up on the Tellers' Rolls. The Teller then wrote out a bill, a long thin piece of parchment duplicating the details which he had just entered in his book. This bill was sent down to the 'court sitting' below, possibly down a trunk. The court consisted of six or seven officers, of whom the first to come into play was the Cutter of the Tallies who, upon receipt of the Teller's bill cut a tally into the required shape. The writer of the tallies then wrote the particulars contained in the Teller's bill on the face of the tally, while the clerk of the pells and the two Chamberlains' deputies recorded these same details on three separate Receipt Rolls. When the ink on the tally had dried, the tally was struck longitudinally down the narrow side, but slicing off to one side before the end was reached to form a stock and foil, so that both contained both the marks and the writing denoting the details expressed in the Teller's Bill. The officers then compared their different entries to ensure their complete agreement. The stock was handed to the collector as his receipt, while the foil was kept by the Chamberlains' Deputies under three locks and keys, unless the 'Chamberlaynes Deputies on the otherside or one of them' were present and took custody of the foil at once.[5] This is by no means all that was required before the tally was acceptable in the Upper Exchequer as proof of payment to the crown; but the rest of the procedure took place in the Upper Exchequer, and it too will be discussed in due course.

In the Exchequer of Receipt several series of records were produced by the 'ancient course', namely the Tellers' Books,[6] the Tellers' Rolls,[7] the Tellers' Bills,[8] the three Receipt Rolls[9] and the tallies themselves.[10] Of these records the tallies are generally not available, and only a very few of the Tellers' Books and Bills have survived. There remain the Tellers' Rolls and the three Receipt Rolls as the main sources for the Exchequer of Receipt. But two serious objections can be made against the Tellers' Rolls. In the first place they are far from complete for much of Henry VII's reign.[11] Secondly, they only record cash payments made to the Tellers, and cash payments made by the Tellers; that is they do not record any money received or paid by monetary instrument. On the other hand, the Receipt Rolls are not open to this objection, for they record all Receipts, whether in cash or by monetary instrument; and for this reason they have been used as the main source for the receipt of money from taxation at the Exchequer of Receipt.[12]

The Receipt Rolls form an almost continuous series between 1485 and 1547, and for only twelve years have no rolls at all survived.[13] For all but two-and-a-half of these years it has proved possible to use the Tellers' Rolls to recover payments made in cash to the Exchequer of Receipt. But it would be unwise to rely upon the Receipt Rolls as either complete, or trustworthy, records of the procedures and actions which they purport to describe, for an inspection of the warrants for issues soon shows that the most innocent and plain entry on the Receipt Rolls, may, in fact, be totally fictitious.

Warrants for issues were letters addressed to the Treasurer and Chamberlains of the Exchequer, ostensibly to request them to make payments to specified people, but often to require an adjustment of the records in order to accommodate some past irregularity, or informality, of procedure in the handling of the crown's finances.[14] Two examples of the importance of these warrants must suffice. On 16 October 1489 a warrant under the Privy Seal was sent to the Treasurer and Chamberlains of the Exchequer. It explained that when the collector for Hampshire of the fifteenth and tenth of 1488 was bringing the money which he had collected to Westminster, he had been robbed of £20 of this money,

the which twenty poundes ye our said Tresourer and Chamberlains chargied yourself by taille levied at our said Receipt the furst day of December the fourth yere of your Reigne as money by you receyued of the said xvme.

The collector had, in fact been given a tally witnessing the receipt of this £20 when, in fact, it had not been paid; but to cover themselves, the officers of the Exchequer had demanded a bond from the collector that he would pay them the £20 before the following Easter. This he was unable to do, and hence his suit to the king. The Privy Seal warrant continued by commanding the

Treasurer and Chamberlains to hand back the bond to the collector without requiring him to pay them the £20; and

> in the Recordes of our said Receipt called the pele of Issue doo make unto the said John Bartlot late Collectour an issue of twenty poundes as money by you paied vnto him of our Rewarde for the sustentacion of his said loss, without prest or othre charge to be sette vpon him for the same.[15]

This example shows clearly that a tally had been struck and entries had been made in the Tellers' Rolls and in the Receipt Rolls to the effect that £20 had been paid to the Exchequer, when in fact no such payment had been made. Without the warrant it would have been impossible to discover the fictitious nature of the entries in the records, for the Issue Rolls for this date have not survived.

The second example shows that an entry on the Receipt Rolls of a simple cash payment into the Exchequer may, in fact, conceal several informal and unrecorded transactions. A Privy Seal warrant, dated 20 August 1489, explained that the collectors of the subsidy of 1489 in Yorkshire had delivered, 'by our special commaundment', £551 4s 2½d from the money which they had collected to the safe keeping of the abbey of St Mary beside York. This money the abbot had been commanded to pay to William Beverley, Dean of Middleham and a roving paymaster in the north. Beverley had in turn paid about half of the sum to four separate people in the north, and had handed over the balance to the Treasurer of the Chamber.[16] Neither the abbot, nor William Beverley, nor the collectors of the subsidy had had any acquittances for this money. The Treasurer and Chamberlains of the Exchequer were therefore ordered to provide acquittances for them.[17] This, in fact, was done by recording a plain tally of Receipt for £551 4s 2½d from the collectors in Yorkshire on both the Receipt and the Tellers' Rolls.[18] From these entries it would normally have been concluded that the collectors had brought this money to the Exchequer in person and had paid it to the Tellers.

From these two examples it is clear that a concentration on any one of the records to the exclusion of all others may well result in an incomplete understanding of the role of the Exchequer of Receipt in the administration of the revenues of the crown, and is almost certain to lead to inaccuracies in the calculation of total amounts of revenue received.

Payment by assignment

It has already been noticed that money from taxes granted by parliament might be paid elsewhere and yet appear in the records of the Exchequer of Receipt. Indeed by 1485 there was a regular procedure by which revenues due to the crown were short-circuited and assigned to be paid directly to others to whom the crown owed money, without either party coming to the Exchequer of Receipt.[19] These transactions were performed and regulated by means of the assigned tally. Assigned tallies were, in essence, the same as normal tallies given to those who paid money to the Tellers, that is they were forms of receipt. But, in the classic case, they were struck before any payment was made to the Exchequer, upon a warrant directed to the Treasurer and Chamberlains, and they were handed as a form of payment to the party to whom the crown owed money. The assigned tallies went through the same form of controlment in the Exchequer of Receipt as did the ordinary tallies, and like them the details contained on the tallies were enrolled on the Receipt Rolls. However, in the case of assigned tallies the enrolment on the Receipt Rolls contained in the right-hand margin the name of the person in whose favour the tally had been struck together with the name of the person to whom the tally had actually been handed. This was usually enrolled in the form 'pro AB per manus CD', or 'pro AB per manus proprias'.

The holder of the assigned tally had now to seek out the collector of crown revenues specified on the face of the tally and demand from him the sum specified by the tally. With luck he would be paid, and as a form of receipt he would hand over his assigned tally. The collector would now have paid his money to someone other than the crown, but in return he would possess a tally of the same form as if he had paid his money to a Teller and had gone through all the controlment of the Exchequer of Receipt.[20]

But if the tally was 'bad', that is if the collector was unable for any reason to pay the holder of the tally; then the holder would bring the tally back to the Exchequer of Receipt where he would be given a new one. On the Receipt Rolls this entailed crossing out the entry of the previous tally, and entering the sum in question immediately below as a 'mutuum per talliam', or fictitious loan, for by this time the membrane, or day, total had been cast and the original entry had been included in it, as though the sum had actually been received. In fact it had not been received, and so it had to be entered as a 'loan' from the creditor together with a reference as to where a new tally of assignment might be enrolled.[21]

In the early Tudor period no 'mutua per talliam', concerning revenue from parliamentary taxation, have been found on the Receipt Rolls, and, *prima facie*, it would appear that no collector of taxes defaulted on the claims of those holding assigned tallies.[22] But two suits concerning such defaults have been found on the Plea Rolls of the Exchequer of Pleas. One was brought by a creditor of the wardrobe against the collectors of the fifteenth and tenth of 1492 (II) in Kent, because they had only paid him part of the value of the assigned tally. The enrolment breaks off before the case ends, and since no 'mutuum per talliam' is recorded on the Receipt Roll, it is probable that the action in the Exchequer of Pleas was sufficient to enforce full payment by the collectors.[23] The other case was brought by the King's Remembrancer against the sheriff for Gloucestershire for default upon two tallies assigned upon seizures that the sheriff had made of the collectors' goods and upon a fine levied upon the sheriff for an insufficient return to a writ. In this case the King's Remembrancer secured judgement in his favour together with 10s costs. It is not known whether he was successful in realising this decision.[24]

In the reign of Henry VII assigned tallies of this kind, anticipating payment to the Exchequer of Receipt, were mainly given to military paymasters in the north; but they were also given to officers of the Exchequer for their wages, to the Cofferer of the Household, to various people in payment of annuities, and to certain people in repayment of loans previously made by them to the crown. It is possible that in the case of assigned tallies given to the officers of the Exchequer, no anticipated payment took place, but the collectors paid them the money when they arrived at the Exchequer in the normal course of their business. The sums assigned in this way for each of the taxes are given in Table 6.1.

But assigned tallies were also used to regularise payments that had already taken place. The procedure for striking these tallies was very much the same as that already described; but instead of the tallies being struck before any payment of money had been made, in this case they were struck after, often some time after, the payment of money, and they were handed directly to the collectors themselves. The chief use of this procedure was when the collectors, on the authority of a royal warrant, had made a direct payment to a military paymaster or to some other officer of the crown before they had brought their money to the Exchequer.[25] Although the collectors almost certainly had a form of receipt from those to whom they had paid the money, together with the original warrant authorising the payment, in practice these documents do not seem to have been of sufficient authority to secure an allowance for the sums in question upon the collectors' accounts at the Exchequer.

There were two ways in which such an allowance might be obtained. Either the collectors might obtain from chancery a 'breue directum Thesaurario et Baronibus' rehearsing the circumstances and requesting that a suitable allowance should be made in their accounts,[26] or they might obtain a writ under the privy seal, again rehearsing the circumstances, but addressed to the Treasurer and Chamberlains, in the Exchequer of Receipt, and requesting them to strike a tally recording the receipt of the money from the collectors as if it had been assigned to those to whom it had actually been paid.[27] The collectors now possessed a tally which was automatically allowed to them together with all other tallies upon their account in the Upper Exchequer, just as if the payment had originally been made according to the normal procedure of assignment.[28] Assigned tallies were also used to secure the exoneration for the collectors for sums with which they had been charged on their accounts

Table 6.1 Revenue from parliamentary taxation levied by way of assigned tally

(a) Fifteenths and Tenths

Year	'Anticipated' payment (£)	Assigned by way of book keeping (£)	Write-off/ reward (£)	Total (£)	Approx. net yield of tax (£)
1488	80	103	–	184	29,700
1489	926	615	–	1,541	29,600
1490–1	9,483	392	–	9,875	29,800
1492 (I)	320	WA	–	WA + 320	29,900
1492 (II)	3,108	1,496	13	5,617	27,700
1497 (I)	–	WA + 1729	–	WA + 1729	29,900
1497 (II)	11	821	–	832	29,900
1512	–	–	–	–	29,600
1513	–	600	15	675	29,600
1514	–	–	–	–	29,600
1517	–	–	–	–	29,600
1537	–	–	–	–	35,800
1541	–	–	–	–	30,100
1542	–	–	–	–	30,200
1543	–	–	–	–	28,900
1544	–	–	–	–	30,100
1546	–	–	–	–	29,800
1547	–	–	–	–	29,800

but which the crown had decided to remit.[29] This use of assigned tallies was rare in the early Tudor period.

In these last two cases it is difficult to see why recourse was had to the procedure of striking an assigned tally rather than to the more simple procedure of obtaining a 'breue directum' commanding the Barons to make an allowance in favour of the collectors upon their account. The explanation may lie in the fact that while the 'breue directum' was usually issued under the Great Seal, the warrant to strike an assigned tally was usually issued under the Privy Seal, and was therefore probably cheaper for the collectors to procure.[30] From Table 6.1, it is clear that although there was a considerable variation in the proportion of each tax that was paid by each of the three forms of assignment, assignment in general was most common on the fifteenths and tenths before 1500, and became increasingly rare during the reign of Henry VIII. This is consonant with the general trend towards the near complete disappearance of assignment during the early Tudor period.[31]

However, on five occasions a very large proportion of the yield of the taxes appears as having been assigned to one person. Indeed on these occasions the collectors had been ordered, either by statute or by subsequent royal warrants,

Table 6.1   *(continued)*

(b) Subsidies

Year	'Anticipated' payment (£)	Assigned by way of book keeping (£)	Write-off/ reward (£)	Total (£)	Approx. net yield of tax (£)
1488	326	–	–	326	700
1489	250	–	–	250	27,000
1497	–	WA + 804	–	WA + 804	30,700
1504	–	WA (ar)	–	WA (ar)	30,900
1513	–	1,479	–	1,479	32,600
1514	–	–	–	–	49,700
1515	–	7	19	26	44,900
1516	–	4	75	79	44,900
1524	–	4,433	–	4,433	56,600
1524a	–	–	412	412	15,700
1525	–	–	–	–	64,800
1526	–	–	–	–	5,700
1527	–	–	–	–	9,100
1535	–	WA	–	WA	21,700
1536	–	WA	–	WA	23,400
1541	–	–	–	–	46,600
1542	–	–	–	–	48,200
1544	–	10	–	10	76,600
1545	–	–	–	–	57,400
1546 ('43)	–	–	–	–	55,000
1546 ('45)	–	–	–	–	109,800
1547	–	–	–	–	97,800

Notes:
WA   Wholesale assignment to a specified treasurer.
WA(t) Wholesale assignment to Treasurer of the Chamber after receipt by the tellers.
1524a Actually levied by anticipation.
[1] Approximate net yield from Table 7.1, column 5.
Sources:
E401/975-1181; E404/79-104; BM (microfilm) Salisbury MSS, 212/2,9.

to pay the taxes to these other persons. But the collectors were still expected to account at the Exchequer, and the difference between the place of payment and the place of account was bridged by means of assigned tallies.

On 5 April 1492 a writ under the Privy Seal was sent to the Treasurer and Chamberlains of the Exchequer informing them that the king had 'deputed and assigned' Sir Reynold Bray to be 'tresourer of our werres' against France, in which capacity he was 'to haue the hoole Receipte aswele of the said xvme as of the Disme'.[32] The Treasurer and Chamberlains were to strike 'somany and asmany tailles in due form ... vpon either of the said xvme and xme as either of them shall amounte vnto' and were to give these tallies to Bray or to his deputies.[33] The Receipt Rolls show that such tallies were indeed struck in the form 'pro Bray' but were handed to the Under-Treasurer, who was the head officer of the Exchequer of Receipt, and later to three of the Tellers. These tallies were recorded in groups of about a dozen, from the fifteenth and tenth and from the Canterbury tenth indiscriminately, from various counties, and for all sorts of amounts. The entries were bracketed together and marked as assigned to Bray 'per manus' of the Under-Treasurer or one of the Tellers.[34] The scatter of the counties, the randomness of the sums for which the tallies were struck, and the late date of their enrolment on the Receipt Rolls, suggest that they were not struck for presentation to the collectors in the counties. Rather it is more likely that Bray used the officials of the Exchequer of Receipt as his deputies, just because they were the most strategically placed to receive the money with the least additional effort. The Tellers would retain the money informally in their possession and hand it over to Bray. Meanwhile they would obtain assigned tallies from the 'court' sitting below, and hand them to the collectors. The actual procedure of payment was thus in effect very similar to the usual payment into the Exchequer of Receipt. The only difference was that the tallies were marked as assigned 'pro Bray', because the Privy Seal writ, and the enrolment specified the Tellers rather than the collectors as the persons to whom the tallies had been handed as a means of controlment upon the Tellers.

It is difficult to see what advantages this somewhat unusual procedure had over the more usual practice of a plain payment into the Exchequer of Receipt, together with a 'dormant' warrant in favour of Bray. It saved the Tellers the labour of making entries on their Rolls both with regard to Receipt and Issue; but on the other hand they must have had to keep some form of informal record of their Receipts. In the 'court' sitting below, there was no saving of work.

Five years later another writ under the Privy Seal was sent to the Treasurer and Chamberlains informing them that the king had appointed Sir Robert Lytton, Under-Treasurer of England,[35] to be Treasurer of the Wars against Scotland, and directing them that all money from the first fifteenth and tenth and from the first subsidy payable in 1497, together with the proceeds of various clerical taxes, benevolences, and loans were to be paid to him.[36] The character of the enrolments on the Receipt Rolls is in all respects similar to that of the enrolments of five years earlier;[37] and the conclusion seems to follow that once more the money was in fact paid to the Tellers in the Exchequer of Receipt, who were again used by the Treasurer of the Wars as his deputies because of their advantageous position for receiving the money.[38]

Seven years later assigned tallies were used in yet another way. Although the subsidy of 1504 was to be paid by the collectors into the Exchequer, the officers of the Exchequer were required by a writ under the Privy Seal to pay it immediately to the Treasurer of the Chamber. In their records they were to enter this as an Issue made to the Chamber by the hands of John Heron.[39] In fact only about one eighth of the subsidy is recorded on the Receipt Rolls as assigned to the Chamber 'per manus' John Heron.[40] Since it is known that all the yield of this subsidy was initially paid into the Receipt,[41] it would appear that there was some uncertainty as to how the subsequent payment to the Chamber was to be entered in the records.

On the other hand, there was one notable occasion when assigned tallies were not used to bridge the gap between the place of payment of a tax and the place of account. In 1523 those who had been commissioned to levy part of the subsidy of 1524 by way of anticipation were directed to pay the money which they had collected to the Treasurer of the Chamber;[42] but on 15 November 1524 a writ under the Privy Seal was sent to the Barons of the Exchequer instructing them to call the collectors of the anticipation to account. But the Barons were required to accept the bills of Receipt of the Treasurer of the Chamber as valid evidence of payment by the collectors to the crown.[43]

But on the next occasion when the whole of a tax was paid to the Treasurer of the Chamber, the subsidy of 1535, the Treasurer of the Chamber's bills of receipt were not admitted by the Upper Exchequer as sufficient evidence of payment to the crown. That some difficulty arose over this point seems clear from the fact that although the subsidy was due to be paid to the Treasurer of the Chamber before 6 November 1535, no account was heard in the Upper Exchequer before the Easter term of 1536.[44] Indeed the issue was resolved a few weeks earlier by a writ under the Privy Seal, dated 27 March 1536, which recalled that the subsidy act had made no mention of the validity of the Treasurer of the Chamber's bills of receipt for the purposes of accounting in the Exchequer. Accordingly upon presentation by the collectors of these bills, the officers of the Exchequer of Receipt were to strike tallies for like amounts, in the form 'pro Camera Regis', and hand them to the collectors without charge.[45] The writ is endorsed as having been 'deliberatum per Barones in Receptam Scaccarij xviij^{mo} die maij a° xxviij Regis Henrici viij°', and ten days later the first of several large batches of tallies assigned to the Chamber were struck in the Exchequer of Receipt.[46]

The fact that the writ was delivered to the officers of the Receipt by the Barons suggests that the decision to strike tallies duplicating the Treasurer of the Chamber's bills was procured at their suit. Certainly neither the Treasurer of the Chamber, nor the collectors, nor the officers of the Exchequer of Receipt had anything to gain from this decision; indeed the latter two had much to lose, for both were put to considerable trouble and expense by it.[47] The difficulty experienced by the Barons in admitting the Treasurer of the Chamber's bills as evidence of payment may appear somewhat unreal, especially since the solution of striking tallies duplicating the bills would seem equally to admit their validity as evidence of payment to the crown. The obstinacy of the Barons probably arose in the first place from a jealousy of the

Chamber as a rival financial department, and secondly from an unyielding insistence on the ancient procedures of the Exchequer.

This dispute highlights the position of the tally as the sole form of Receipt, other than a special writ addressed to the Treasurer and Barons under the Great Seal that was acceptable in the Upper Exchequer for the purposes of accounting. Although the usual form of assignment, by way of an 'anticipated' payment, disappeared as far as revenue from taxation was concerned during the early Tudor period, the assigned tally continued to be used to adjust a variety of situations to the exigencies of the procedure of accounting in the Upper Exchequer.

Exchequer terms and payment dates

But most of the collectors for most of the taxes during the early Tudor period brought cash to the Exchequer of Receipt in person, and received in exchange for it plain tallies, which they then took to the Upper Exchequer in order to be discharged of their account. The Receipt Rolls show that the Exchequer of Receipt kept two extended terms, Michaelmas and Easter, as opposed to the four shorter terms of the Upper Exchequer and the courts of law.[48] These longer terms opened around the traditional opening dates for the corresponding terms in the Upper Exchequer, and continued, with a short break during the vacation times before Hillary and Trinity, until late February, and late in July.[49] But although the Exchequer of Receipt was thus open for the greater part of the year, entries on the Receipt Rolls recording the striking of tallies are by no means to be found for every day. But there seems to be no pattern in the distribution of these entries, so it may be reasonable to conclude that the entries on the Rolls reflect the fluctuations in the actual payments to the Tellers, and that there were many days on which no money at all was paid into the Exchequer of Receipt.[50]

The bulk of payments into the Exchequer of Receipt, other than those made by collectors of parliamentary taxes, were made by officers of the crown such as sheriffs, bailiffs, escheators and collectors of the customs and subsidies.[51] These officers were usually called upon to account at the beginning of the Michaelmas term, and in some cases at the beginning of the Easter term too.[52] As a result the pressure of payments in the Exchequer of Receipt was heaviest at the beginning of the Michaelmas and Easter terms. It is interesting that the dates of payment for parliamentary taxes, as specified in the statutes, appear to have been deliberately chosen to avoid these two periods, and to fall, with a few exceptions, as shown in Table 6.2, in the middle or at the end of the Exchequer terms.[53]

In theory, therefore, the business concerning the payment of taxes in the Exchequer of Receipt should have been concentrated in the days immediately

Table 6.2   Dates of payment of parliamentary taxes

Subsidy	Fifteenth and tenth	Payment date
	1488–9	24 June, 11 Nov
1488		1 May
1489		1 May, 1 Nov[1]
	1490–1	11 Nov
	1492	1 April, 11 Nov
	1497	31 May, 8 Nov
1497		31 May, [8 Nov][2]
1504		1 Dec
	1512	1 July
	1513	2 Feb
1513		1 July
1514		24 June
	1514	30 April
1515–6	1517	21 Nov
1524–7		2 Feb[3]
1535–6		6 Nov[4]
	1537	1 Nov
	1541–4	4 Feb
1541–2		6 Feb
1544–6 ('43)		6 Feb
1546 ('45)–7		1 April
	1546–7	30 June

Notes:
[1] Payable to designated receivers in the counties.
[2] Never levied.
[3] Anticipation payable to Treasurer of the Chamber, by 30 Nov.
[4] Payable to treasurer of the chamber.
Sources: See Appendix I.

preceding the statutory payment dates, and the collectors should then have been ready to proceed to their account in the Upper Exchequer where, by this time too, the pressure of business should have eased. But before the question of whether in fact the collectors did pay the money into the Exchequer of Receipt by the dates specified in the statutes can be examined, it is necessary to follow the collectors into the Upper Exchequer.

The Exchequer of Account

The summons to account

The officers of the Upper Exchequer did not leave the collectors to appear at the Exchequer in their own time. Rather a series of writs were despatched summoning the collectors to appear, and the commissioners of subsidies to send in their certificates, before certain dates. This task was entrusted to the King's Remembrancer who had in his possession all the necessary information, that is the names of the Commissioners and the collectors,[54] and the dates specified by the statutes for the certification and payment of the taxes.[55]

In the first place writs were sent to the sheriffs instructing them to distrain upon the commissioners to send in their certificates, and upon the collectors to appear and account at the Exchequer, and commanding them to return the writs to the Exchequer endorsed with the value of the distress which they had levied.[56] This distress was usually only a small sum,[57] and was taken by way of a precautionary bond which was to be forfeited only if the party did not certify, or account, by the day fixed for the return of the writ to the Exchequer.[58]

The first of these writs of distress were almost invariably sent out just before the statutory date for certification or payment,[59] so that the return day for the writs, and so the last day for the commissioners to certify or for the collectors to appear, without forfeiting the distress, was the first return day falling after the statutory date (see Table 6.3). It is clear from the table that the general issue of writs of distress was by no means always recorded on the Memoranda Rolls, and that consequently, for many of the taxes information concerning the despatch of such writs must be derived from isolated enrolments of individual cases.[60] Nevertheless for most of the taxes the earliest writ

Table 6.3 Earliest writs of distress requiring certification or appearance at the Exchequer

(a) Fifteenths and tenths

Year	For first return day, or otherwise	Reference (E159/)
1488	X	264 Recorda T.r.22
1489	X	265 Recorda T.r.11
1490–1	X	267 Dies dati H.r.
1492 (I)	X	268 Recorda P.r.20
1492 (II)	X	269 Dies dati H.r-
1497 (I)	X	273 Fines T.r-
1497 (II)	4 months	274 Dies dati H.r-
1512	X	291 Dies dati T.r-
1513	X	292 Dies dati P.r-
1514	?[1]	–
1517	GX[2]	296 Bre. Ret. M.r-
1537	G 5 months	316 Bre. Ret. H.r-
1541	GX	319 Bre. Ret. H.r-
1542	X	321 Fines P.r-
1543	GX	321 Bre. Ret. H.r-
1544	GX	322 Bre. Ret. H.r-
1546	?	–
1547	?	–

Table 6.3   (*continued*)

(b) Subsidies

Year	Commissioners to certify		Commissioners to appear	
	For first return day, or otherwise	Reference (E159)	For first return day, or otherwise	Reference (E159)
1488	_³	–	X	264 Fines T. r-
1489	_³	–	_⁴	–
1497	_³	–	X	273 Recorda T.r.14d
1504	_³	–	?	–
1513	?	–	?	–
1514	?	–	X	293 Dies dati M.r-
1515	?	–	?	–
1516	?	–	?	–
1524a	?	–	2½ years	305 Recorda T.r.16
1524	G 6 months	303 Bre. Ret. Pr-	?	–
1525	GX	303 Bre. Ret. M.r-	4 months	304 Recorda T.r.1
1526	?	–	4 months	305 Recorda T.r.3
1527	?	–	X	306 Recorda P.r.25d
1535	9 months	315 Bre. Ret. T.r-	9 months	315 Dies dati T.r-
1536	G 9 months	316 Bre. Ret. T.r-	1 year	316 Dies dati H.r-
1541	GX	319 Bre. Ret. M.r-	X	320 Fines P.r-d
1542	GX	320 Bre. Ret. M.r-	X	321 Dies dati P.r-
1544	GX	322 Bre. Ret. H.r-	?	–
1545	?	–	?	–
1546 ('43)	?	–	?	–
1546 ('45)	?	–	?	–
1547	?	–	9 months	327 Dies dati H.r-

Notes:
G   Enrolment of a general issue of writs to all commissions or groups of collectors.
X   Earliest noted writ returnable on first return day after statutory date.
1524a   The Anticipation of part of the subsidy of 1524.
[1] One writ noted for Lancashire, returnable 8½ years later. But Lancashire is a special case. E159/302 Recorda M.r.18.
[2] Only for 20 counties.
[3] No certification required from the commissioners.
[4] No account to reach any court of record.

that has been found was returnable on the first return day after the statutory certification or payment date. And for almost all the cases in which there seems to have been some delay in despatching the first writs of distress, this can be attributed to special circumstances.[61] It should be noted that for the fifteenths and tenths of 1488, 1489 and 1490–1, for which two payment dates were specified,[62] the writs of distress were sent out for the first date to call the collectors to a preliminary 'view' of account, after which the collectors were granted adjournments until the second payment date.

If the commissioners did not send in their certificates or if the collectors failed to appear to account by the return date of the writ of distress, then the distress returned as levied on them by the sheriff was declared to be forfeit to the crown, and the sheriff was charged with this sum on his account.[63] The writ of distress was then renewed, in the same terms as before; but returnable by the sheriff at the beginning of the subsequent term. But after a certain time, if the collectors still did not appear at the Exchequer, a very much stronger process was used to summon them to account.[64] A writ was sent to the sheriff to attach the collectors to produce them before the Barons in the Exchequer on the next return day.[65] Meanwhile the sheriff was to seize all the collectors' lands and possessions into the king's hands, so that if the collectors did not appear in the Exchequer by the return day of the writ, they might be held as forfeit to the crown.[66]

Thoroughly executed, this was a drastic enough form of summons; but before it was put into effect the collectors were allowed a certain period of time during which they were only liable to the simple writ of distress. The period that was allowed to elapse before the writs of attachment were sent out appears to have varied somewhat not only between one tax and another, but also between different groups of collectors for the same tax. Table 6.4 shows these varying intervals between the first writs of distress and attachment. It

Table 6.4   Intervals between issue of first writs of distress and first writs of attachment

(a) **Fifteenths and tenths**

Year	Interval in terms[1] Maximum	Minimum	References E159/
1488	3	–	265 Recorda T.r.26
1489	5	5	267 Recorda M.r.24d; 272 Recorda M.r.14
1490–1	6	7	268 Recorda P.r.15; M.r.21
1492 (I)	3	3	268 Recorda P.r.20; 269 Recorda H.r.34
1492 (II)	2	12	269 Recorda P.r.6d; 274 Recorda T.r.14
1497 (I)	5	–	274 Recorda M.r.2a3
1497 (II)	2	10	275 Recorda M.r.28; 276 Recorda T.r.19d
1512	3	–	291 Recorda H.r.5d
1513	4	–	293 Recorda P.r.10
1514	2^2	18^2	293 Recorda H.r.18; 297 Recorda H.r.12
1517	4	10	297 Recorda H.r.11; 299 Recorda T.r.9d
1537	3	–	317 Recorda H.r.39
1541	–	–	–
1542	–	–	–
1543	–	–	–
1544	–	–	–
1546	–	–	–
1547	–	–	–

also shows that there was a tendency for the stronger process of attachment, together with a full seizure of lands and possessions, to have been withheld until at least two or three terms had elapsed after the issue of the first writ of distress. But, although most writs of attachment and seizure were issued at about this time, in some cases several terms, or even years, appear to have elapsed before resort was finally had to the stronger process.

If the collectors failed to appear in the Exchequer by the return date of the writ, their lands and possessions which had been seized by the sheriffs were forfeit to the crown. The possessions were forfeit forever, and the issues from the lands were forfeit until the collectors had completed their account at the Exchequer.[67] As far as can be discovered these forfeitures were true penalties,

Table 6.4   (continued)

(b) Subsidies

| Year | Interval in terms[1] | | References E159/ |
	Maximum	Minimum	
1488	–	–	–
1489	$-^3$	$-^3$	–
1497	2	13	274 Recorda H.r.13; 277 Recorda M.r.7
1504	2^2	11^2	283 Recorda T.r.30; 285 Recorda M.r.50
1513	2^2	6	293 Recorda P.r.15; 294 Recorda P.r.14
1514	3	4	294 Recorda T.r.12; T.r.24
1515	3^2	12^2	295 Recorda T.r.34; 297 Recorda H.r.18
1516	8	32	297 Recorda H.r.4d; 303 Recorda H.r.17d
1524a	–	–	–
1524	3^2	11^2	303 Recorda H.r.23d; 306 Fines M.r-
1525	2	7	304 Recorda H.r.18; 306 Recorda P.r.21
1526	3	17	306 Recorda P.r.25; 310 Recorda M.r.87
1527	2	7	306 Recorda H.r.37; 308 Dies dati P.r-
1535	2	7	315 Recorda H.r.12; 316 Recorda P.r.30
1536	1	5	317 Recorda P.r.37; 318 Recorda P.r.10d
1541	–	–	–
1542	3	–	321 Recorda M.r.93
1544	–	–	–
1545	2^2	–	324 Recorda M.r.112
1546('43)	–	–	–
1546('45)	–	–	–
1547	$2^{2,4}$	–	326 Recorda M.r.142

Notes:
1524a   The anticipation of the first part of the subsidy of 1524.
–   No information available.
[1] Half-terminal returns are rare and have been ignored.
[2] No date for first writ of distress available; the calculation assumes that it was returnable on the first return day after statutory payment date.
[3] No account to reach any court of record.
[4] Only one writ of distress recorded; but returnable 1 term after writ of attachment.

for the collectors were not allowed to offset them against the total sum that they owed to the crown.[68] The sheriffs were formally charged with paying these forfeited sums to the crown, and were required to account for them at the Exchequer.[69]

But even when the collectors had appeared at the Exchequer and had begun their account, it not infrequently happened that they withdrew from the Exchequer without permission from the Barons.[70] In such cases fresh process was begun to summon them back for the completion of their accounts. If the collectors had withdrawn before their account had been heard in the full Exchequer, a '*compoto non audito*' process was issued by the King's Remembrancer in the same form as has already been described, but starting immediately with a writ of attachment and seizure of possessions. If, on the other hand, the collectors had withdrawn after their account had been heard in the full Exchequer, '*compoto audito*', but before they had been granted their final acquittance, a slightly different form of process was issued against them by the Lord Treasurer's Remembrancer. In such cases a writ was sent to the sheriff requiring him to attach the collectors and to produce them in the Exchequer on the return date of the writ; but meanwhile to levy the sum that the collectors still owed to the crown from their lands and possessions.[71] Since the purpose of this process was as much the recovery of the debt outstanding on the collectors' account as a means of recalling the collectors, the sums seized by the sheriffs, in contrast to the position under process issued by the King's Remembrancer, were taken in payment of the collectors' debt to the crown.[72] Since, also, the size of the sum to be levied was always specified, because by this stage it had been determined, the seizures tended to be taken in goods, the value of which could be realised immediately through sale, rather than in lands, the payment of the issues of which took at least until the subsequent Michaelmas to realise. As before, the sheriffs were charged with these seizures on the Pipe Rolls.[73]

When writs of attachment were issued against the collectors, they were held to have committed a 'contempt' against the crown, and upon their appearance in the Exchequer, regardless of whether they had been produced by the sheriff or whether they had arrived there voluntarily, they were immediately committed by the Barons to the prison of the Fleet.[74] But this committal may well have been more technical than real, for in most cases the collectors were admitted to account on the same day.[75] In some cases the collectors were allowed to be bailed to at least two persons, initially for periods ranging from two days up to a term; but the bail could always be extended.[76] On completion of their account the collectors were released from the Fleet upon payment of a fine.[77] In some cases this fine was remitted by an act of general pardon,[78] while in others the officers of the Exchequer apparently omitted to levy the fine, and fresh process of attachment and seizure was commenced to summon the collectors back to the Exchequer.[79]

Table 6.5   Fines upon collectors for absence from their accounts at the Exchequer

Value of fine	Number of instances
4d	1
1s 0d	43
1s 8d	150
2s 0d	339
3s 0d	1
3s 4d	97
4s 0d	2
5s 0d	17
6s 8d	42
10s 0d	10
13s 4d	4
20s 0d	4
40s 0d	1
TOTAL	709

Sources:
Unless otherwise stated all references are to the 'Fines' section of the Rolls. This section bears no numeration.
E159/: 266 M; 267T; 268 P; 269 P, T; 270 M,H,T; 271 M, P, T; 272 H,P,T; 273 M,H,T; 274 M, H, P T; 275 M, H, P, T; 276 M, H, P, T; 277 H, P, T; 280 M; 281 H; 283 M, H, T; 284 M, H, P, T; 285 M, H, P, T; 286 M, H; 287 M; 291 H; 292 P; 293 P; 294 T; 295 T; 297 H; 299 H; 303 T, M, H; 304 P, T, M, H; 305 P, T, M, H; 306 P, T, M, ; 307 P, T, M, H; 309 M; 310 M; 312 M; 315 T, M, H; 316 P, M, H; /317 P, M; 320 P, T, H; 321 P, H; 322 P, T, M, H; 323 T, M E368/: 266 SVC H, r. 7, T; 267 H; 279 H, P; 281 M, H; 282 M; 300 T; 301 T; 306 P.

The fines levied for these 'contempts' varied considerably in size. Sometimes the variations can be attributed to the gravity of the 'contempt', but on other occasions they appear to bear no relation to any other relevant factors. It is clear from Table 6.5 that the most common fine was 2s 0d and that it comprised almost 50% of the instances recorded. It is also clear that the smaller fines were much more frequently imposed than were the larger ones. Although the distribution given in the table is for the period as a whole, at no time during the period was the distribution any different. The revenue accruing to the crown from these fines was, comparatively, very small, and totalled only £96 4s 0d over the entire period.[80]

The death of a collector

If a collector died during the course of any of these processes, the fact was usually notified to the Exchequer by the sheriff when he returned the writ of attachment to the Exchequer. Sometimes the sheriff was commanded merely to distrain the heirs, executors or administrators to appear at the Exchequer in place of the dead collector;[81] but more often the officers of the Exchequer sent out a more comprehensive writ to the sheriff commanding him to hold an inquisition post mortem to discover the date of the death of the collector, the value of his lands and goods on the day of his death, their present owners, the names of the deceased's heirs, executors or administrators, and to certify this information to the Exchequer. The sheriff was further to distrain the heirs, executors or administrators to appear at the Exchequer to account, and meanwhile was to seize all the lands and goods of the deceased into the hands of the king.[82] The seizure of lands of deceased collectors for their debts to the crown provoked several of the descendants of the collectors into disputing before the Barons of the Exchequer as to whether the lands might lawfully be seized or not. The arguments used in these disputes are obscure; but in most cases the issue appears to have turned upon the nature of the tenure of the lands.[83]

Appearance at the Exchequer: attornies

Although, under the ordinances of 5 Richard II, all accountants at the Exchequer might appear by attorney,[84] in fact few collectors of parliamentary taxes employed professional attornies in their dealings with the Exchequer. When several collectors were appointed collectively for one area, as for the fifteenths and tenths before 1541 and for the subsidies before 1514–16, it was usual for the collectors to send only a few of their number up to the Exchequer where they registered themselves as attornies for their colleagues.[85] This arrangement presupposed a fair degree of co-operation amongst the collectors. The difficulties that arose when this co-operation was lacking have already been discussed; but it might be noted that for the fifteenths and tenths of 1517 and 1537 some of the collectors who had duly appeared for their account at the Exchequer, instead of registering themselves as attornies for their colleagues, rather petitioned the Barons that process should be issued against them to prevent them from continuing to detain the money which they had collected, and to force them to come to account.[86] But these difficulties were removed when a single collector was appointed for each area, and when this became common practice, few collectors appeared by attorney in the Exchequer.

The procedure of account

Immediately upon arrival at the Exchequer the collectors, or their attornies, were required to take an oath that they would account faithfully.[87] They were then assigned by the Marshall of the Exchequer to one of the six auditors.[88] The auditors' task was to draw up the charge on the collectors.[89] For the fifteenths and tenths this was readily obtainable from the books of record in the Exchequer,[90] while for the subsidies the charge had to be calculated from the commissioners' certificates,[91] adjusted, as necessary, to allow for claims against illeviable sums, and to eliminate double assessments, provided these could be based upon further certificates from the commissioners. The charge, as drawn up by the auditors, ended with the 'summa onerabilis', or the gross sum to be charged upon the collector.[92] The task of balancing the collectors' credits and allowances against the charge prepared by the auditors belonged to the Barons of the Exchequer.[93] The account was therefore, formally, divided into two distinct stages, the preparation of the charge and the granting of allowances, and each stage was performed by a different set of officers in the Exchequer.[94]

The audit of the account by the Barons, and their decisions on the credits and allowances claimed by the collectors, were recorded by the Lord Treasurer's Remembrancer on his Memoranda Roll, in the section '*status et visus compotorum*'.[95] In these enrolments the collectors, '*audito compoto*', were said to owe a certain sum. This sum was the '*summa onerabilis*' as prepared by the auditor. The enrolments continued that the collectors, '*factis allocacionibus in dicto compoto ingrossato quieti sunt ibidem*', or alternatively, 'debent' some smaller sum.[96] In some cases the collectors then went on to make further claims for allowances which were considered by the Barons, and enrolled in full on the Memoranda Rolls. From the form of these enrolments two inferences may be drawn. Firstly the perfunctory record of most of the allowances, and the detailed enrolment of a few, may have reflected a procedure by which the more routine allowances were considered in advance, and that the decisions reached then were merely endorsed by all the Barons in full Exchequer. Thus it was only the more unusual claims for allowances that were heard in full by all the Barons. On the other hand, it may well have been that the abbreviated record of most of the allowances was only a clerical convention to save the labour of writing out all the allowances in full, and that all allowances were in fact made in full Exchequer.[97]

But if the more routine claims by the collectors for allowances were heard before the account was brought before the Barons in full Exchequer, it is unlikely that this would have been done by the auditors, for, without exception, the auditors' accounts ended with the '*summa onerabilis*', and no allowances other than those based on the commissioners' certificates, were ever made by the auditors.[98] But it is clear from a heading on the auditors' accounts that one of the three junior Barons was always associated with each auditor.[99] If any preliminary allowances were made, it is more likely that they were made by the Barons and that the clerical work of preparing the charge against the collectors and their claims for allowances was undertaken by the auditors.[100] If this was in fact the case, it would only have been those claims about which the Baron wished to consult his colleagues that would have been heard in detail by the full court of the Exchequer and enrolled *in extenso* by the Lord Treasurer's Remembrancer, while in the great majority of cases the court would merely have endorsed the auditing Baron's routine allowances.

But despite the likelihood of such a procedure, especially in view of the pressure of the large number of accounts on the Barons' time, it is equally possible that the junior Barons, acting alone, in fact exercised nothing more than their customary supervision over the auditors in the preparation of the charges against the collectors; and that the granting of allowances was reserved for the decision of all the Barons in full Exchequer.[101]

The first allowance that a collector would claim would be for the tallies, which he had received in return for his payments to the Exchequer of Receipt. But in order to secure recognition of the stock of the tally that was handed to him in the Exchequer of Receipt, the collector had first to get it joined to the foil in the Upper Exchequer. It has already been shown that the foils of the tallies had been delivered to the Chamberlains' Deputies in the Upper Exchequer. These officers daily sorted the tallies they had received from the Exchequer of Receipt 'by the Sheires moneths and yeares', and made them up into bundles which were stored in cupboards until the accountant came and asked for the stock and foil to be joined. The foil would then be searched out, laid alongside the stock in the accountant's possession, and if the two agreed, the details would be entered in a 'controlment Booke'. The stock and foil, joined together, were then marked 'with an Iron Instrument' in a particular way 'like to a halfe moone'. The Secondary of the Pipe then examined the entry in the Chamberlains' Deputies' book and the joined tally to ensure their agreement, and endorsed the entry in the book with the date. The Secondary of the Pipe took custody of the stock, and the foils remained with the Chamberlains' Deputies, until the accountant came to claim allowance for the tally on his account.[102] The stock, or possibly both the stock and the foil, would then be shown to the Baron auditing the account, who, if everything was in order, would allow them to the collector on his account.[103]

The collectors would also claim allowance for the costs of collection. For the fifteenths and tenths these allowances were fixed at traditional sums and were recorded in the Exchequer,[104] while for the subsidies they were specified by statute at 6d/£.[105] The collectors would also claim other allowances as might be necessary, such as for exemptions claimed by religious houses and secular groups and individuals within their area, or for payments which they had made on the basis of royal warrants. In making these claims the collectors had to produce sufficient authority. This could either take the form of a citation of the record of a previous occasion on which the same claim had been granted by the Barons,[106] or if the claim were new, by the submission of a 'breue directum Thesaurario et Baronibus', rehearsing the original royal warrant to the collectors prohibiting them from levying the tax on certain persons, or commanding them to make extraordinary payments, and requesting the Barons make due allowance to the collectors upon their account.[107] If the circumstances concerning the basis of the claim for an allowance were in doubt, the Barons would commission local gentlemen to enquire into the facts and to certify their findings to the Exchequer.

All these allowances were then totalled, and if they equalled the gross charge on the collectors, as prepared by the auditor, then the collectors were quit of their account, or 'quieti sunt'. If, however, the total of the allowances did not reach the total charged upon them, further process was taken to levy the debt outstanding. If, more rarely, the total of the allowances was greater than the total charged to the collectors, then it was recorded in the collectors' accounts that they had a 'superplusagium' of so much. Usually such balances were very small and were remitted to the king.[108] But on a few occasions they were worth a few pounds, and upon petition to the Barons could be assigned by the collectors to the use and advantage of others in their account at the Exchequer.[109] No case has been noted in which such balances were refunded to the collectors.

The only exceptions to this procedure of account occurred for the early fifteenths and tenths of 1488, 1489, and 1490–1. These taxes were payable in two distinct halves, yet on all three occasions the collectors were summoned to account immediately after the payment of the first half was due. But instead of a full account being taken, the collectors underwent a 'view of account' for the first half of the tax.[110] This 'view' was drawn up by an Exchequer auditor in the same form as a full account; but, unlike the full account, it continued past the statement of the gross charge due from the collectors and gave details of allowances made to them. This preliminary view appears to have been regarded as a somewhat informal procedure and was left very much to the auditor, for in several cases no Baron is mentioned as being concerned with the account.[111] In due course the collectors were subjected to the full procedure of account in the usual manner.

At any time after taking the oath of faithful accounting the collectors, or their attornies, could petition for an adjournment until the next term.[112] This seems always to have been granted to the collectors, and providing they appeared every term, no restriction seems to have been imposed on the total number of such adjournments that might be granted.[113] But if the collectors failed at any time to appear at the Exchequer they immediately became liable to the process of summons by way of attachment issued by one of the two Remembrancers.

Debts upon accounts

In many cases a certain proportion of the sum charged to the collectors was still owed after their account had been heard in the Exchequer. In order to secure the due payment of these sums the officers of the Exchequer followed one of three courses. First, they might take recognisances from the collectors, or from others willing to stand as surety for them.[114] These recognisances were usually for a somewhat larger sum than the amount owed by the collectors to the crown and were voidable if the collectors fulfilled certain conditions contained in them before a specified date. The condition might simply be that the collectors were to close their account before a certain date;[115] but more often the collectors were required to pay what they owed on their account, either before a certain date, or, more usually, in a series of instalments spread over various periods of time and with various intervals between each instalment.[116]

It is clear from Table 6.6 that the practice of taking recognisances from the collectors for the debts outstanding upon their accounts was by no means universal in the early Tudor period. Indeed it was only for the fifteenths and tenths of 1537 and 1542 and for the subsidies of 1524 and 1525 that the number of recognisances reached any significant proportion.[117] But for the subsidies of 1546 ('45) and 1547, and for the fifteenths and tenths of 1546 and 1547, recognisances were demanded in accordance with the subsidy act from all collectors upon their appointment.[118] These recognisances were for twice the value of the sums which the collectors were to collect and were voidable if the

Table 6.6   Recognisances taken by the officers of the Exchequer from the collectors

(a) Fifteenths and tenths

Year	No.	References
1488	1	E368/262 SVC H.r.7
1489	2	E159/267 Recogn. T.r-, Recorda T.r.23
1490–1	1	E159/272 Recogn. M.r.1
1492 (I)	0	–
1492 (II)	0	–
1497 (I)	1	E368/272 SVC M.r.15
1497 (II)	2	E368/271 SVC P.r.9, T.r.6d
1512	1	E159/291 Recorda H.r.5d
1513	3	E159/307 Recogn. P.r-, P.r-d, M.r-d
1514	1	E159/304 Recogn. P.r-.
1517	3	E159/304 Recogn. H.r-; /300 Recogn. M.r.5
1537	12(a)	E159/317 Recogn. M.r-, H.r-, H.r-d; /318 Recogn. T.r-, H.r-; /320 Recogn. H.r-d; /321 Recogn. T.r-d
1541	4	E159/320 Recogn. H.r-; /321 Recogn. M.r-d; /322 Recogn. T.r-d; /325 Recogn. T.r-d
1542	13(b)	E159/321 Recogn. P.r-, P.r-d, T.r-, T.r-d, M.r-d, H.r-; /324 H.r-, H.r-d
1543	2	E159/322 Recogn. T.r-d, M.r-d
1544	1	E159/323 Recogn. T.r-d
1546	0	-
1547	1	E159/326 Recogn. T.r-

collectors paid all the cash that they had in hand on the statutory payment dates, and the balance due from their area within one month thereafter.[119]

If a collector did not fulfil the conditions of a recognisance, a writ of 'scire facias' was sent to the sheriff commanding him to inform the collector that he

Table 6.6   Recognisances taken by the officers of the Exchequer from the collectors

(b) Subsidies

Year	No.	References
1488	0	–
1489	0	–
1497	3	E159/274 Recorda H.r.26d, 27; E368/271 SVC P.r.12d
1504	0	–
1513	0	–
1514	2	E159/274 Recorda H.r.26d, 27; E368/271 SVC P.r.12d
1515	0	–
1516	7	E159/297 Recorda H.r.4d; /299 Recorda T.r.9; /301 Recogn. M.r-, /304 Recogn. M.r.4d; Recorda T.r.8d; /308 Scr. Recogn. P.r-; E368/297 Recorda T.r.8
1524a	0	–
1524	13	E159/303 Recogn. H.r.1, 1d, 2, 2d, 12d; /304 Recogn. P.r.1; /310 Recogn. M.r-d, Recorda P.r.38; E368/301 Recogn. P.r.1
1525	18	E159/304 Recogn. P.r.1, 1d, H.r-; /305 Recogn. M.r.4, 4d, H.r-; /306 Recogn. T.r-, H.r-; /308 Recogn. P.r-, T.r-; /318 Recogn. T.r-
1526	3	E159/306 Recogn. P.r-, M.r-d; /310 Recogn. H.r-d
1527	7	E159/308 Recogn. T.r-d, H.r-d; /309 Recogn. P.r-d, H.r-d; /313 Recogn. H.r-d; /320 Recogn. P.r-
1535	1	E159/321 Recogn. H.r-d
1536	5(c)	E159/317 Recogn. M.r-; /318 Recogn. T.r-d; /320 Recogn. T.r-d, M.r-d; /326 Recogn. H.r-
1541	2	E159/320 Recogn. H.r-; /321 Recogn. T.r-d;
1542	1	E159/322 Recogn. P.r-d
1544	2	E159/323 Recogn. M.r-d, H.r-d
1545	3(d)	E159/324 Recogn. T.r-d; /326 Recogn. H.r-; /327 Recogn. H.r-d
1546 ('43)	4	E159/324 Recogn. M.r-, H.r-, H.r-d; /327 Recogn. H.r-d
1546 ('45)	0	-
1547	1	E159/327 Recogn. H.r-

Notes:
[1] And one recognisance from an individual to the Barons to pay the amount assessed on him by them for his contribution to the fifteenth and tenth. E159/324 Recogn. M.r-
[2] Including one recognisance from a collector that he would pay the sheriff the value of lands seized by him and a fine levied on the sheriff by the Barons.
[3] Including one recognisance from an individual to pay the collectors, and another from an individual to pay direct to the Exchequer.
[4] Including one recognisance from a commissioner to appear in the Exchequer, and another from an individual to pay direct to the Exchequer.
1524a   The Anticipation of the first part of the subsidy of 1524.
Sources: As specified in the Reference column.

was to appear in the Exchequer on a specified date to show cause why the forfeiture specified by the recognisance should not be levied. If the collector did not appear, or failed to show sufficient reason for the cancellation of the recognisance, the sheriff was charged with levying the value of the recognisance by way of the Summons of the Pipe. Only two cases of the enforcement of forfeited recognisances have been noted throughout the entire period.[120] Unless the enrolment of this process is wholly unreliable, this would suggest that the taking of recognisances was an effective way of securing the payment of debts outstanding upon the collectors' accounts.

But it was far more usual for the officers of the Exchequer to turn over the debt at once to the sheriffs to levy by way of distress. In a very few cases this was done by way of a writ of 'fieri facias' to the sheriff issued by the Lord Treasurer's Remembrancer.[121] But usually the debts were put in the Summons of the Pipe and the sheriffs were charged with them in the Pipe Roll at their 'apposal' in the Exchequer at the following Michaelmas. In some cases the collectors paid in the money to the Exchequer of Receipt themselves, and this was noted on the Pipe Rolls. Thus, although the collectors were still ultimately responsible for the full payment of the taxes, the immediate responsibility for these sums to the Exchequer was transferred to the sheriffs.[122]

The sheriffs were also made responsible for levying sums due from certain individuals or groups, such as religious houses, but for which the collectors had secured exoneration from their accounts. In general, when a collector secured exoneration from sums on the basis of royal writs, no further action was taken by the Exchequer. But in some cases, notably for the very large number of claims for exemption from fifteenths and tenths made by the collectors for religious houses and secular communities on the basis of prerogative grants, and for the claims made by the collectors for the subsidies for exoneration from sums assessed on individuals which for various reasons they could not collect, the Barons exonerated the collectors, but instead charged the individuals and the religious and secular communities with answering for these sums. The sums were estreted from the collectors' accounts, some straight to the Exannual Rolls, but most were transferred to the Pipe Rolls.[123] Those sums estreted to the Exannual Rolls were virtually written off, while those transferred to the Pipe Roll were entrusted to the sheriff to levy by way of the Summons of the Pipe.[124] But by 1485 almost all the claims for exemption from fifteenths and tenths by virtue of prerogative grant were of long standing, and their allowance in the Exchequer should have been automatic.[125] It is difficult, therefore, to see why for every fifteenth and tenth during the early Tudor period the officers of the Exchequer, by ordering the sheriffs to levy the sums, should have insisted on requiring the parties claiming the exemption to appear in the Exchequer merely to duplicate the claim already made by the collectors.[126] But whatever were the reasons behind this procedure, the practical result was that a considerable amount of the 'tail-end' of the taxes was left to the sheriffs to levy. Thus in order to calculate the total net yield of the taxes to the crown it has proved necessary to follow through several decades on the Pipe Rolls the fortunes of many hundreds of small sums due from the collectors, from defaulting individuals, and from communities claiming exemption from the taxes.

Enrolment of debts on the Pipe Rolls

These sums were always enrolled separately on the Pipe Rolls, that is they were not in the first instance included in the sheriffs' consolidated accounts. But although the entries are easy enough to recognise, the significance of the answers of the sheriffs on being charged with these sums, or of the notes of the clerk of the Pipe, is by no means always clear. In the simplest cases, the comments to the entries charging the sheriffs followed immediately upon the entries in the main text of the Roll, and were in the same form as similar entries on the collectors' enrolled accounts. These comments would record either the allowance of further tallies brought by the collectors,[127] or the allowance of claims made by the collectors for remuneration, or of claims made on behalf of, or by, others, such as religious houses, for exemption from the taxes.[128] In such cases the active agents in reducing or clearing the charge against the sheriffs were clearly the collectors or other parties concerned and not the sheriffs themselves.[129] But these entries are comparatively rare and it would seem that in the great majority of cases the collectors did nothing, and that the whole onus of securing payment to the crown fell entirely upon the sheriff.

But in some cases the marginal annotations on the Pipe Roll show that the debt had been temporarily taken out of the charge of the Summons of the Pipe. The annotation 'Recognicio inde' meant that the debt was to be levied by the alternative method of taking a recognisance from the collector. The motif 'rus',[130] followed by the name of a county, meant that the debt had been transferred to another sheriff, and the mark 'ex' signified that the debt had been transferred to the Exannual Rolls. Further annotations such as 'diem clausit extremum' and 'fieri facias' signified that the debt was still charged to the sheriff but by way of direct process from the Lord Treasurer's Remembrancer rather than on the Summons of the Pipe.[131]

But in most cases the sheriffs were apposed on their account for these sums and their answers to each of the debts were recorded by the Clerk of the Pipe in the left-hand margin of the Pipe. First, the sheriff might claim 'non in summonicionem', that is that the debt had been omitted from the Summons of the Pipe. In this case the debt was transferred to the sheriff for the following year. Second, the sheriff might answer 'nichil', that is that the debtor had no possessions on which he might levy the debt. This answer was usually accompanied by the note 'fiat commissio', which referred to the procedure, available under the Statute of Rutland, by which commissions of enquiry were appointed to investigate the truth of such a claim and to report their findings back to the Exchequer.[132] If the commissioners substantiated the sheriff's claim, the debt was transferred out of his charge on to the Exannual Roll.[133]

On the other hand, the sheriff might answer that he had levied the sum. If the whole debt had been levied the sheriff would answer 'tot' and the mark 'T' was set opposite the enrolment of the debt in the left-hand margin of the Pipe Roll.[134] If only a part of the debt had been levied the amount was written in the left-hand margin, prefixed by the letter 'O', presumably standing for 'oneratur'. In both cases the sums concerned are generally to be found specified in the sheriffs' consolidated accounts.[135]

But the fact that the sheriff had levied the debt by no means meant that it was necessarily paid to the crown. Indeed because of its inclusion in the sheriff's consolidated account, the tax debt lost its identity, and the question of its eventual payment to the crown became subject to the fortune of the sheriff's account as a whole. Since in the early Tudor period these accounts were of great complexity, involving petitions for exemptions on many different items, it has not proved practicable to trace them over the sixty-three years of the period under study.[136] This means that for the purposes of calculating the actual sums received by the crown from each tax, it has proved impossible to determine whether the debts levied by the sheriffs were ever in fact paid to the crown.

There remain two further marginal annotations on the Pipe Rolls, which need to be discussed: 'On^i T', and its variant 'On^i Exo^a in R seq. T'. The basic part of the annotation, 'On^{i}' means 'oneratur nisi habet [vicecomes] sufficientem exoneracionem', and it has been differently interpreted by writers on the sheriffs' accounts. Coke thought that 'On^{i}' was on the normal mark upon the sheriffs' accounts for 'issues ameriaments and mean profits' and that this mark made him a debtor to the crown.[137] On the other hand, Gilbert, writing considerably later, considered that 'On^{i}' was a form of discharge, signifying that the sheriff claimed exoneration either because the party had paid in the debt himself, or because of some order of the Exchequer, or because of a royal warrant discharging the debt.[138] For the early Tudor period Coke's account is clearly inadequate since he is apparently unaware of the plain 'T' or 'tot', mark which was the usual form of charge on the sheriffs. Gilbert's account is equally unsatisfactory since the situations which he describes as being pertinent to 'On^{i}' are all covered by the alternative annotations, 'In Thesauro', 'ex' and 'Sed non debent'.

Nevertheless, it is clear from the invariable conjunction of 'On^{i}' with 'T' in the composite form 'On^i T' in the early Tudor period that 'On^i T' was some form of provisional charge on the sheriffs, perhaps not so emphatic as 'T' alone.[139] Vernon, writing in the first part of the seventeenth century, says that items marked 'T' and 'On^i' were to be included in the total sum due from the sheriff, 'except onely there shall be some good cause of discharge by matter of Record, or other to be made in open Court'.[140] No items bearing the mark 'On^i t' have been found detailed in the consolidated charge on the sheriffs; but it is quite possible that they were included in the general total of charge without being separately specified.[141] It is therefore suggested, that in the early Tudor period 'T' and 'On^i T' were the two charge marks made on the sheriffs; but that while the mark 'T' designated that the sheriff admitted having levied a debt, the mark 'On^i T' signified that the sheriff had not levied the debt, but rather had given notice that he intended to claim exoneration from the sum; and that in the meantime, until he could make good his claim, the officers of the Exchequer held him responsible for the debt.

The additional annotation of 'Exo^a in R seq.', or 'exoneratur in Rotulo sequente', that is in the Pipe Roll for a subsequent year,[142] is often to be found appended to 'On^i T' in the early Tudor period. But since debts bearing this annotation may reappear in subsequent years either together with the same annotation,[143] or even noted as having been paid into the Exchequer,[144] it is clear that 'Exo^a in R seq.' refers only to the exoneration of the debt from the account of a particular sheriff and not to a general remission of the debt.[145] Since sheriffs might secure exoneration from debts for reasons quite unconnected with the nature of the debt, such as by way of reward from the king,[146] this annotation is plainly of little use in determining whether the debt itself was ever paid to the crown or not.

Thus, for the purposes of calculating the net yield to the crown of the taxes, it is clear that the only annotations on the Pipe Rolls that admit of no ambiguity are 'ex', 'in Thesauro', and 'Sed non debent'. All the other marks refer to the levy of the debts by the sheriffs; and since the uncertainty of whether these debts were actually ever paid to the crown is so great, it has been thought more prudent to consider them as uncollected. It is, however, quite possible that some of these debts were in fact levied and duly paid by the sheriffs to the Exchequer, and thus the figures for the net yields of the taxes to the crown given in the following chapter may well underestimate the sums received by the crown from the taxes and at the same time exaggerate the proportion of the gross yield of the taxes that remained uncollected. However, the upshot of this discussion is that the proportions of each of the taxes that are therefore in doubt are never sufficiently large to modify significantly the figures given for the net yield of each for each of the taxes levied for the king.

7

The Yields of the Taxes

The approximate yields of the taxes in the early Tudor period have been known for some time. The traditional yield of the fifteenth and tenth has been general knowledge since at least 1888,[1] and figures for the yields of the subsidies have been given by Dietz.[2] But the figures that have been available so far are unsatisfactory for two reasons. First, they are only the gross total yields, that is, the nominal yield of the taxes, and they do not show either how much money the crown should have received, or how much in fact was received by the crown. Second, some of the figures given by Dietz for the fifteenths and tenths, the yields of which are known, are so eccentric as to cast doubt on the validity of his figures as a whole.[3]

It was therefore considered desirable to examine the yield of the taxes in the early Tudor period in some detail. First, the gross, or nominal, yield of each tax has to be known. This figure represents the total of the sums charged by the auditors to each collector, either on the basis of the traditional charges for the fifteenths and tenths, or from the commissioners' certificates for the subsidies. From this gross sum have to be deducted first the amounts allowed to the collectors by way of remuneration, secondly exemptions granted by the crown, and thirdly double-entries and other book-keeping devices. The totals for each tax of each of these three categories are interesting in their own right. Once these deductions have been made a figure can be obtained for the net expected yield of each tax to the crown. This, for the purposes of government finance, is a far more significant figure than the gross yield, which in one sense represents the actual yield of the taxes to the crown. Second, the net yields have been examined to discover what proportion of them was actually paid to the crown, and how much remained uncollected.

In order to obtain this information it has been necessary to refer to the enrolled accounts of the individual collectors.[4] For each tax this has required the examination of between fifty-three and three hundred and ninety-five accounts.[5] Although most of these accounts gave all the details that were required, they were cast in paragraph form and had to be transcribed and separated into tabular form to enable totals to be cast. In several cases, where the remainders of the collectors' accounts were transferred to the sheriff to levy, it has been necessary to pursue the search on the Pipe Rolls. This has been a particularly difficult task, especially with regard to the hundreds of individual debts outstanding from the aristocracy and the inhabitants of London on the subsidies of the 1540s.

It was also necessary to ensure that every hundred in the country was represented in the collectors' accounts. If an area appeared to be missing, it sometimes happened that it was in fact covered by an account for another hundred; but not declared as such on the account. This could only be discovered if the original commissioners' returns or the 'particule compotorum' were extant.[6] If, however, it was clear that there was no enrolled account for a particular area, recourse was had first to the summary of accounts on the 'status et visus compotorum' on the Lord Treasurer's Remembrancer Memoranda Rolls.[7] This summary gave the gross charge on the collectors, and the outcome of the account, together with details of any unusual claims for exoneration. If the summary noted that the collectors had been acquitted of their account, then the collectors' remuneration could be calculated and the amount paid in to the Exchequer interpolated.[8] But in some cases no summary of the collectors' account was given on the 'status et visus compotorum', and it was necessary to refer to the original auditor's account by which the collectors were charged.[9] If this account were extant, the gross charge against the collectors was known, and the sum allowed for their remuneration might be calculated. The only way to determine how much was paid in to the Exchequer was to search the Receipt Rolls.[10]

Several areas for which there were no enrolled accounts have been recovered in this way; but for others the necessary documents have not been available, and these have had to be accounted as missing. These areas, for which there is no information, are listed for each tax in Table 7.1. Thus by piecing together all the available fragments of information, a well-nigh complete account can be rendered for each of the taxes in the early Tudor period. The totals of each of the different aspects of these taxes are summarised in Table 7.1.[11]

So that the table may be properly understood, something should be said of the nature of each of the columns.

(1) Gross yield

This is the sum of the figures drawn up by the auditors and charged to the collectors. For the fifteenths and tenths these figures were based on the books of record in the Exchequer,[12] and for the subsidies on the commissioners' certificates of assessment corrected as necessary by the commissioners' certificates for double assessment.[13]

Table 7.1 Yields of the taxes (£ ± 0.5)

(a) Fifteenths and tenths

Year	Gross yield (1)	Collectors' remuneration (2)	Deduc-tions (3)	'Debent res-pondere' (4)	Net yield (1) less (2), (3) and (4) (5)	Received (6)	Levied by sheriff (7)	(7) as a % of (5)[a] (8)	Uncollected (9)	(9) as a % of (5)[a] (10)	Error (11)	Dietz (12)	Missing areas (No. of hundreds) (13)
1488	31,171	302	731	468	29,670	29,072	22	—	690	2	+14	61,560	
1489	31,127	301	752	449	29,625	29,405	24	—	195	1	−1	20,830	Rochester
1490–1	31,106	301	553	491	29,761	28,861	515	2	381	1	−4		Rochester
1492 (I)	31,120	301	558	397	29,864	29,300	32	—	531	2	+1	53,360	
1492 (II)	28,964	276	563	390	27,735	27,011	6	—	741	3	+23		Yorkshire ER, NR and WR, Hull, York
1497 (I)	31,110	301	542	393	29,874	29,266	34		575	2	+1	55,104	Rochester
1497 (II)	31,110	301	554	396	29,859	29,252	178		435	1	+6		Rochester
1512	31,063	301	769	420	29,573	29,501	14		70		+11	28,878	
1513	31,142	301	766	490	29,587	29,563	—		10		−14	27,769	
1514	31,110	301	906	350	29,553	29,319	22		212			29,408	
1517	31,123	301	901	342	29,579	29,553	28						
1537	36,923	341	370	389	35,823	35,669	24		131		+1	33,270	b
1541	30,996	302	397	166	30,131	30,130	23		17		+39	29,558	Herts (1)
1542	31,025	244	372	133	30,226	30,151	24		52		+1	29,507	Salop (1)
1543	29,783	293	380	165	28,945	28,940	20				+15	29,827	Beds (1), Dorset (1), Glos (1), Norf (7), Salop (1), Yorks NR (1)
1544	30,994	292	417	150	30,135	30,130	2				−3	29,125	Dors (2), Glos (1), Salop (1), Yorks NR (1)
1546	30,684	296	364	197	29,827	29,824	3		9		+9	29,539	Sussex (1 rape), Exeter, Norwich
1547	30,746	296	392	208	29,850	28,831	14		3		−2	29,156	Glos (1), Salop (1), Exeter London (3 wards), Norwich

(b) Subsidies

Year	Gross yield (1)	Collectors' remuneration (2)	Deductions (3)	'Debent respondere' (4)	Net yield (1) less (2), (3) and (4) (5)	Received (6)	Levied by sheriff (7)	(7) as a % of (5)[a] (8)	Uncollected (9)	(9) as a % of (5)[a] (10)	Error (11)	Dietz (12)	Missing areas (No. of hundreds) (13)
1488	744[c]	?	95		679	571							d
1489	27,000[c]	?				18,300						27,000	d
1497	31,648	301	302		30,735	30,088	13		631		−3	29,850	Rochester
1504	31,659	640			30,929	30,873	26		55	2	+25	31,800	
1513	33,430	547	326		32,557	32,563	4				+10	32,814	King's household, Queen's household
1514	50,905	1,234			49,671	49,422	15		237		+3	48,085	Cornwall (1)
1515	46,007	1,116			44,891	44,819			74		+2	45,637	Yorks WR (1)[e]
1516	45,523	1,088			44,435	44,074	246		117		+2	41,663	Berks (1), Glos (1), Lancs (1)
1524	73,793	1,434	15,714		56,645	56,445	21		180		+1	71,778	Salop (1)
1524a	(15,943)	264	18		15,661	15,616	37		12		+4		Cornwall, Derbs, Hants, Herefs, Staffs, Warwicks, Worcs, Coventry, Canterbury, Derby, Nottingham, Salisbury, Shrewsbury, Southampton, Winchester[f]
1525	66,464	1,657			64,807	64,517	116	2	173		−1	66,064	Hunts (1), Kent (4), Salop (1), Lords (1)
1526	5,889	146	75		5,667	5,521	121		26		+1	4,686	d
1527	9,372	235			9,137	9,116	13		7		−1	9,031	d
1535	22,321	549	62		21,710	21,621	46		55		+12	21,280	Kent (3), Salop (3)
1536	24,052	595	17		23,440	23,094	157		188		−1	22,526	Hants (1), Herts (1), Kent (6), Lancs (1), Lincs (4), Middx (1), Norf (2), Oxon (3), Yorks WR (1), Lincoln, Shrewsbury
1541	48,172	1,209	344		46,619	46,595	26		25		+27	46,413	Kent (1), Cumbs (aliens)
1542	49,535	1,230	31		48,274	48,119	41		117		+10	48,047	Cumbs, Westmland, N'humb, Durham (aliens)

Table 7.1 (continued)

Year	Gross yield (1)	Collectors' remuneration (2)	Deductions (3)	'Debent respondere' (4)	Net yield (1) less (2), (3) and (4) (5)	Received (6)	Levied by sheriff (7)	(7) as a % of (5)[a] (8)	Uncollected (9)	(9) as a % of (5)[a] (10)	Error (11)	Dietz (12)	Missing areas (No. of hundreds) (13)
1544	78,703	1,949	148		76,606	76,113	253		250		+10	75,080	N'humb, Westmland (aliens)
1545	59,181	1,451	318		57,412	56,789	279		348		+4	56,052	Hants (1), Lancs (1), Norf (3), N'humb, Westmland (aliens)
1546 ('43)	56,423	1,377	87		54,959	54,170	411		378			52,139	Norf (4), Durham, Westmland (aliens)
1546 ('45)	14,050	2,816	1,396		109,838	105,967	1,552	1	2,322	2	+3	105,766	Durham (aliens)
1547	100,285	2,479	851		96,955	90,486	2,327	2	4,145	4	+3	91,244	N'humb, Westmland (aliens)

Notes:

1524a The anticipation of the first payment of the subsidy of 1524.
[a] Percentages are given to the nearest whole figure. No percentages less than 1% are supplied.
[b] Dietz notes that the second fifteenth and tenth is not on the subsidy roll. In fact no second fifteenth and tenth was ever granted.
[c] By reconstruction and estimation from very incomplete evidence.
[d] The number of counties which should have sent contributions is not known.
[e] Not assessed because of the plague. E179/279/3/96, 101.
[f] These areas, except for Hants, Warwicks, Worcs, Canterbury, Southampton, Winchester, were exonerated because the money was paid to the collectors for the subsidy. E159/305 Recorda T.r.1619, M.r.27, 31; /306 Recorda P.r.30; /308 Recorda M.r.16. No commissions to levy the anticipation were sent to Yorkshire or Lancashire, LP, III, 3504.

Sources:

E359/38, 39, 4144, passim, supplemented by E368/259325, SVC, passim, E372/331395, passim; E401/9751181, passim, and E179, passim.

(2) Collectors' remuneration

For the fifteenths and tenths, these figures were the traditional values contained in the books of record in the Exchequer. The remuneration for the collectors of the subsidies of 1497 and 1504 was based on these figures.[14] For the subsidy of 1513 the collectors were remunerated at the rate of 4d/£, and for all subsequent subsidies at 6d/£.[15] The collectors of the Anticipation of the subsidy of 1524 were remunerated at 4d/£,[16] and the collectors of the subsidy at 6d/£ on the yield of the subsidy net of the Anticipation. For all other subsidies the rate was calculated on the gross yield of the tax.

(3) Deductions

For the fifteenths and tenths these were usually for exempted areas and communities, such as the Cinque Ports. For the subsidies this class comprised claims for exemption, virtual exemptions on the authority of the Barons if the sheriff could not levy, and various bookkeeping devices.

(4) 'Debent respondere'

Claims for exemption made especially by religious houses to the collectors. The collectors were exonerated from these sums by the Barons, but the religious communities themselves were charged with proving their title to exemption or answering for the sums concerned.

(5) Net yield

The total amount of money that should have been paid to the crown.

(6) Received

The total amount of money known to have been paid to the crown.

(7) Levied by sheriff

From the entries on the Pipe Rolls it is uncertain whether this money was ever paid to the crown or not.

(8) (7) as a percentage of (5)

A percentage of the expected cash yield of each tax.

(9) Uncollected

The amount which is shown by the records to have been neither levied nor remitted by the crown.

(10) (9) as a percentage of (5)

A percentage of the expected cash yield of each tax.

(11) Error

The error found upon summing all the different items in each class. This may be produced either by overpayment of small sums by the collectors, or by clerical error on the part of the Exchequer clerks. Considering both the size and number of the figures involved the errors are remarkably low.

(12) Dietz

The figures given for the yields of the taxes given in Dietz, *English Government finance*, appendix table VII. Dietz does not indicate whether these represent the gross yields, the net yields, or the sums actually collected.

(13) Missing areas

Areas for which no information is available. In some cases this is because no commissions to levy the taxes were sent to these areas,[17] and in others because there may have been no one liable to taxation there.[18]

Several facts emerge from the table. First, the figures given by Dietz for the yields of the taxes are by no means fully in agreement with the figures given by the table. In some cases Dietz's figures are nearer to the gross yields of the table, while in others they are closer to the net yields, or to the sums actually received by the crown. In general Dietz's figures are of the order of 10% less than the gross yields as given in the table; but on some occasions, notably for the fifteenth and tenth of 1490–1, the disparity can be much more serious.[19]

Second, the figures for the gross yields of the fifteenths and tenths confirm the traditional reputation of the fifteenth and tenth as a fixed yield tax. The gross yield in the early Tudor period was of the order of £31,100, and the major deviations from this figure can be explained by special circumstances.[20] Nevertheless, there was some variation, usually not more than £60 above or below £31,000, which cannot be accounted for, and which, in view of the fact that the charges against the collectors were based on books of record in the Exchequer, is somewhat surprising.

The figures of the gross yields of the subsidies from 1513, when direct assessment was first introduced, naturally vary considerably. A comparison of the gross yields with the rates at which each of the taxes were levied, as given in Table 5.7, shows that the variation in the size of the yields of the subsidies is directly correlated with the variation in the rates of levy and the variation in the specification of the assessable population. Thus it is impossible to compare the subsidy of 1514 with the subsidy of 1523, for they were levied at different rates and on different populations. Unfortunately, no adjustment to allow for the differences in rates and population can be made, because the differences applied only to a part of each subsidy, and it cannot be determined what proportion of the whole this part comprised.[21] In no cases do the rates of any two subsidies stand in a simple proportional relationship, such as one being twice the other. This being so, the only general comment that can be made concerning the gross yields of the taxes in the early Tudor period is that an increase in the rates of the taxes, and increases in the geographical area liable to taxation,[22] both invariably brought about a greater or lesser increase in the gross yield of the taxes, while increases in the minimum assessments for the taxes considerably reduced their yields.[23]

But the impossibility of identifying the proportion of any increase in the gross yields of the taxes that might be attributed to an increase in the rates or extent of taxation has the unfortunate effect of precluding two possible uses of the figures for the gross yields. First, it would have been interesting to observe the effects of inflation on the gross assessed yields of the subsidies. Since inflation is known to have occurred in the first fifty years of the sixteenth century,[24] and since the yields of the subsidies were directly linked to the money value of rents and possessions, the rise in the subsidy yields might also have been expected to rise. But since it is impossible to distinguish the effects of the rise in the rates of taxation from the effects of the increase in the scope of taxation, and the effects of inflation, the most that can be said is that the gross yields of the subsidies were probably increased as a result of the inflation of the money values of the wealth assessed. But this enhancement of the money value of the gross yields of the taxes was probably of little value to the crown since the money price of the goods and services that were purchased with the taxation money were also enhanced by inflation.[25]

Thus the only comparisons that can be made for the gross yields of the taxes are between those subsidies for which the rates of taxation were the same. These subsidies were almost always granted by the same statute and were always levied with one year's interval between them.[26] The shortness of time between the levy of the subsidies means that the effects of inflation and of movements in the assessable gross national product would have been reduced to a minimum. It is therefore probably reasonable to regard the variations in the gross yields between these comparable subsidies as reflecting primarily the accuracy of the assessments. Four groups of two subsidies and one group of three subsidies are thus comparable, and the variations of the gross yields within these groups both confirm and supplement the conclusions already reached on the accuracy of subsidy assessments.

However, if the gross yields of the subsidies were dependent upon a number of factors and varied considerably in size, other aspects of the yields of the subsidies showed a greater degree of uniformity. As has already been explained the sums allowed to the collectors of fifteenths and tenths and subsidies by way of remuneration were fixed, and this is borne out by the figures given in the table. But in the figures given for the deductions made from the gross yields there is a greater degree of variability. For the fifteenths and tenths the figures largely comprised the deductions allowed to the inhabitants of the Cinque Ports. This figure was reduced after the fifteenth and tenth of 1489, and diminished even further after the subsidy of 1517.[27] The great increase in the sums allowed by way of deduction for the fifteenths and tenths of 1512 to 1517 is explained by the statutory exemptions granted to certain academic colleges and religious houses. For the subsidies the sums allowed by way of deduction varied greatly, for they were dependent upon unforeseen contingencies such as the 'illegal' assessment of spiritual persons, mistakes in double charging of collectors, and the writing off of illeviable assessments. The sums charged upon religious communities claim in exemption under the head 'debent respondere' varied little, except for the fall in the total number of such claims produced by the dissolution of the monasteries. Nevertheless, that there was any variation at all shows that all religious communities holding prerogative grants of exemption did not exercise them on every occasion.

When all these sums have been deducted from the gross yields, the net yield, or the amount expected to be paid to the crown, is obtained. For the fifteenths and tenths, where these deductions were fairly constant, the net yield was usually about £1,300 less than the gross yield, or about £29,800. For the subsidies the relationship between the gross and net yields was not so uniform, for the miscellaneous deductions varied considerably. But the net yields were always at least 2½ per cent less than the gross yields, which was the amount allowed to the collectors for their remuneration; but if the miscellaneous deductions were numerous the net yield might be very much less than this.

The success of each tax may very simply be gauged by considering how much of the net expected yield was in fact collected. It is clear from the figures given for the total amounts received by the crown for each tax that in most cases less than 1 per cent of the net yield remained uncollected. Thus in general in the early Tudor period between 99 per cent and 100 per cent of the money due to the crown by way of parliamentary taxation was in fact duly paid to the crown. The only exceptions are the fifteenths and tenths of the early part of the reign of Henry VII, where between 1 per cent and 4 per cent of the net yield remained uncollected, and the subsidies of 1546 ('45) and 1547 where between 3 per cent and 6 per cent appears to have been lost to the crown. But since part of this 'wastage' comprised sums which were levied by the sheriff, and for which it is uncertain whether they were paid to the crown or not, it may well be that the actual loss was even smaller than this.

But even if the most pessimistic view is taken, it is clear that ultimately the crown in the early Tudor period was spectacularly successful in securing the due payment of money accruing by way of parliamentary taxation. But important as the full payment of the taxes was, the fact that most of the taxes were granted in time of military necessity meant that it was equally essential that the taxes should be paid quickly. The speed of the payment of the taxes, and the effectiveness of the means taken to coerce defaulters, are examined in the next chapter; but here it might be noted that both the tardiness of the collectors and the ineffectiveness of the sheriffs suggests strongly that the ultimate success of the crown in securing the full payment of the taxes is to be attributed primarily to the inexorability of the forms of process issued by the officers of the Exchequer.

8

The Efficiency of the Collection of the Taxes

Speed of Payment

Since almost all the taxes in the early Tudor period were granted in times of war, clearly the speed with which they were paid into the Exchequer was of vital importance to the crown.[1] It has already been shown that several months elapsed between the decision by parliament to grant the taxes and the statutory date by which the taxes were to be paid to the Exchequer. But it could also happen that the taxes came in slowly and were not in fact paid by the dates in the statutes. In order to discover how soon the crown actually did receive the money from parliamentary taxes, the entries on the Tellers' and Receipt Rolls recording the receipt of the money from the collectors have been classified by date into five groups. The first group comprises the payments that were made for each tax before the statutory payment date, the second group the payments made between the payment date and one month thereafter, the third group the payments made between one month and six months, the fourth group the payments between six months and one year, and the fifth group the payments made later than one year after the statutory payment date. For the purpose of comparison the total sums in each group for each tax have been expressed as percentages of the total sum of money known to have been received from the tax by the crown, and these are given in Table 8.1. For some of the taxes a proportion of the yield was paid by assignment, but since the date of the enrolment of the assigned tally does not necessarily correspond with the date of the effective use of the money by the crown, the proportion so assigned has been expressed separately.[2]

First, it is necessary to disregard those taxes for which the percentage of the yield that cannot be found on the rolls of the Exchequer is high. This means that the fifteenths and tenths of 1488, 1492 (I), and 1497 (II), and the subsidies of 1497 and 1504 must be excluded from consideration.

Table 8.1 Speed of payment of the taxes (£ ± 0.5; % ± 0.5)

(a) Fifteenths and tenths

Year	(1) Total Received (£)	(2) Before payment (%)	(3) Payment date −1 month later (%)	(4) 1 months– 6 months (%)	(5) 6 months– 1 year (%)	(6) After 1 year (%)	(7) Assigned (%)	(8) Unaccounted (%)
1488	29,072	14	–	17	26	0	–	43
1489	29,405	0	31	38	16	1	5	9
1490–1	28,861	4	4	25	2	24	34	7
1492 (I)	29,300	0	0	0	6	3	1	90
1492 (II)	27,011	0	0	46	15	9	21	9
1497 (I)	29,266	7	38	37	4	3	6	5
1497 (II)	29,252	6	0	28	0	4	3	49
1512	29,501	3	64	27	4	2	–	–
1513	29,563	5	38	49	4	2	2	–
1514	29,319	0	52	36	6	7	–	–
1517	29,553	4	2	45	20	24	–	5
1537	35,669	0	8	6	50	36	–	–
1541	30,130	3	11	65	10	7	–	4
1542	30,151	4	11	62	13	7	–	3
1543	28,940	3	10	73	12	7	–	+5
1544	30,130	10	29	57	1	–	–	3
1546	29,824	57	26	13	5	0	–	–
1547	28,831	40	23	27	12	0[a]	–	+1[a]
Average[e]		9	23	40	12	9	4	(3)

Table 8.1 (*continued*)

(b) Subsidies

Year	(1) Total Received (£)	(2) Before payment (%)	(3) Payment date −1 month later (%)	(4) 1 months– 6 months (%)	(5) 6 months– 1 year (%)	(6) After 1 year (%)	(7) Assigned (%)	(8) Unaccounted (%)
1488	571	22	0	16	1	3	57	–
1489	18,300	0	0	48	38	12	1	–
1497	30,088	0	1	54	12	4	3	26
1504	30,873	15	0	30	20	6	–	29
1513	32,563	9	29	47	13	6	2	–
1514	49,422	0	12	62	13	12	–	–
1515	44,819	4	9	57	13	4	–	13
1516	44,074	0	2	52	27	20	–	–
1524	56,445	18	29	19	20	5	8	–
1524a	15,616	5	69	21	0	5	–	–
1525	64,517	0	19	65	5	11	–	–
1526	5,521	0	3	37	24	33	–	3
1527	9,116	0	4	37	23	36	–	–

		b						
1535–6	44,715	b	—	—	—	—	—	—
1541	46,595	7	44	30	8	8	—	3
1542	48,119	16	7	59	10	3	—	5
1544	76,113	12	38	49	0	0	—	—
1545	56,789	?[c]	[84][c]	9	3	4	—	—
1546 ('43)	54,170	78[d]	11	5	0	1	—	5
1546 ('45)	105,967	44	32	23	1	0	—	—
1547	90,486	0	2	87	9	19[a]	—	—[a]
Average[e]		14	21	40	11	10	4	—

Notes:

1524a   The Anticipation of the subsidy of 1524.

[a] No Receipt Rolls were examined after Easter 1548.

[b] Receipt books of the Treasurer of the Chamber have not survived.

[c] Neither the Tellers nor the receipt rolls for Michaelmas 1545 have survived.

[d] 62% was paid before the payment date for the Anticipation.

[e] Disregarding those taxes with figures greater than 25% in column 8.

Sources:

Column 1: Table 7.1, Column 6.

Columns 2–6: E401/975–1181, *passim*; E405/75–116, *passim*.

Column 7: Table 6.1.

If, first of all, the average figures for the distribution of the payment of the fifteenths and tenths and of the subsidies in each of the five groups are considered, it is clear that in general in the early Tudor period, only about 10% of the money received by the crown reached the Exchequer before the statutory payment dates. Within one month after the payment dates a further 22% was paid in, between one month and six months a further 40%, between six months and one year a further 12%, and after one year after the payment dates a further 10%. Thus, in general, most of the yield of the taxes was paid to the crown in the period between one and six months after the statutory payment dates, by which date only 20% of the taxes remained to be paid in. In aggregate this means that the crown could expect to receive one tenth of the yield of the taxes before the payment dates, one third within one month thereafter, three-quarters within six months, four-fifths within a year, and the balance some time later.

But these are average figures and it is clear that the distribution of payments for each of the individual taxes differed somewhat from this. With regard to the payment date, very few taxes achieved the average figure of 10 per cent. The only taxes for which a sizeable proportion was paid to the crown before the statutory payment date were the fifteenths and tenths of 1546 and 1547, and the subsidies of 1546 ('43) and 1546 ('45). The collectors of these two fifteenths and tenths, and the subsidy of 1546 ('45), were for the first time bound by recognisances upon their appointment to pay in all the cash which they had on hand by the payment date and the balance within one month thereafter.[3] This device seems to have been successful in securing an earlier payment of a very large proportion of the taxes. The collectors of the subsidy of 1547 were also bound by similar recognisances; but the tax appears in the table as having been paid to the Exchequer somewhat later than these other taxes. The tardiness of the payments was due not to the inefficiency of the collectors but to the fact that the whole machinery for levying the subsidy was delayed, presumably by the death of the king on 28 January 1547.[4] In the event, the commissioners and the collectors were informed by a proclamation of the dates by which they were required to certify the assessments, or to pay in the tax collected. In the case of the commissioners they were given an extra nine weeks to certify after the statutory certification date, and the collectors were allowed some thirteen weeks after the statutory payment date.[5] In fact 68% of the yield of the subsidy was paid before this revised payment date, and a further 13% within one month thereafter.[6]

The high figure for the portion of the subsidy of 1546 ('43) that was paid before the statutory date reflects the fact that part of the subsidy was levied by way of Anticipation. In fact, 62% of the yield of this subsidy was paid to the Exchequer before the last day fixed for the payment of the Anticipation; and the Anticipation may therefore be said to have been extraordinarily successful.[7] The Anticipation of the subsidy of 1524, on the other hand, was not so successful for only 5% of the Anticipation was paid in before the required date. Although a further 69% of the Anticipation was paid within one month from this date, this sum only represented 16% of the yield of the subsidy, and the subsidy itself was due to be paid only one month later. Clearly, therefore, the Anticipation of 1524 was of little effect.[8]

The taxes for which a high proportion of the yield was paid between the payment date and one month later are scattered all over the period. Apart from a slight preponderance of the later taxes over the earlier ones in this group, the chief tendency is for the first in a consecutive series of taxes to have a greater proportion paid in within this period than was the case for the subsequent taxes. This suggests that a form of 'fatigue' set in during periods of sustained taxation.

As with the average for all the taxes, for most of the taxes the period between one and six months after the payment date saw the payment of the highest proportion of the yields of the taxes. The only exceptions to this are the fifteenths and tenths of 1512, 1514 and 1537, and the subsidies of 1524, 1541 and the Anticipation of the subsidy of 1524, and the subsidies and fifteenths and tenths of the later 1540s. The proportions of the taxes that were paid in during the period from six months to one year after the payment date were usually the inverse of the proportions that were paid in during the period from the payment date until one month thereafter. For the period later than one year after the payment date the proportions are in general as low as for the period immediately before the payment date. But it is interesting that all the taxes for which a relatively high proportion of the yield was delivered to the Exchequer during this period were the last of a series of taxes. This again suggests that 'fatigue' set in during periods of sustained taxation.

If the collectors had not paid in the money by two years after the payment date, unless a recognisance had been taken from them stalling the debt, there was little chance of it ever being paid to the crown. Such situations were, however, rare, and only involved sums of any size with the collectors for Hampshire, Shropshire, Staffordshire, and the West Riding of Yorkshire, for some of the taxes in the reign of Henry VII. These collectors still owed large sums of money well into the reign of Henry VIII, and sooner or later obtained a royal pardon for them.[9]

But in order to assess the efficiency of the collectors in paying in the money derived from parliamentary taxation, some account must be taken of the time available to the collectors in which to make their collection. For the fifteenths and tenths this is very difficult to estimate; but it would appear from Table 3.7 that least time was allowed to the collectors of the fifteenths and tenths from 1492 until 1514, that between half as much again and twice this time was allowed to the collectors of the fifteenths and tenths before 1492, and of 1517 and 1537, and that about two and a half times as much time at least was allowed to the collectors of the fifteenths and tenths of 1541 and 1542, and probably also to the other collectors in the 1540s. But when these times available to the collectors are compared with the actual performance of the collectors in paying in the money, it appears that the length of time available does not, in fact, seem to have been connected with the efficiency of the collectors. The collectors for some of the fifteenths and tenths for which the least time for collection was allowed were among the most successful in making prompt payment; and the outstanding performance of the collectors of the fifteenths and tenths of 1546 and 1547, standing in marked contrast to the performance of other collectors in the 1540s, is more probably to be attributed to the recognisances taken from these collectors than to the increased time allowed to all the collectors in the 1540s.

The times allowed to the collectors of the subsidies in which to make their collection were given in Table 5.13. This does, indeed, appear to have had some effect on the speed with which the subsidies were paid to the crown. The restricted time allowed for the collection of the subsidies of 1515 and 1516 was accompanied by a reduction in the aggregate sums paid in by one month after the payment date,[10] and the increase in the time allowed for the collection of the subsidies in the 1540s coincided with an improvement in the speed with which those subsidies were collected. But these improvements in performance are very small when compared to the changes brought about by the Anticipation of 1546 ('43) and the recognisances taken for the subsidies of 1546 ('45) and 1547. Indeed although the time allowed for the collection of these last two subsidies was considerably less than the time allowed for previous subsidies in the 1540s, they were nevertheless paid in far more quickly.

In general, therefore, there seems to have been no overall trend during the early Tudor period either towards an improvement, or towards deterioration, in the speed with which the taxes were collected. The only general observation that can be made is that when several taxes were levied in succession, the speed of collection tended to decline.

Speed of Account at the Exchequer

While the speed of payment of the taxes was of prime importance for the crown, it was also desirable that the collectors should come at once and clear their accounts at the Exchequer, for otherwise much time and expense might be wasted in issuing the full weight of process against them. The number of groups of collectors for each tax and proportion that accounted at various intervals before and after the payment dates are given in Table 8.2.

Table 8.2 Number of groups of collectors and their speed of accounting at the Exchequer

Year	Total number of groups	In term before payment date (%)	In term of payment date (%)	1–3 terms thereafter (%)	4 terms and more thereafter (%)	Unknown (%)
(a) Fifteenths and tenths						
1488	54	0	54	21	20	6
1489	53	0	28	42	28	3
14901	56	0	25	38	32	5
1492(I)	53	0	32	46	21	2
1492 (II)	53	0	0	40	47	13
1497(I)	56	0	61	23	14	2
1497 (II)	54	0	1	63	32	4
1512	58	0	28	46	17	9
1513	56	0	25	45	30	0
1514	56	0	34	34	30	2
1517	55	0	0	20	80	0
1537	54	0	0	20	80	0
1541	256	0	4	65	28	2
1542	210	0	9	69	20	2
1543	190	0	10	78	10	1
1544	193	0	23	72	5	1
1546	168	0	50	43	4	2
1547	166	0	40	52	6	2
(b) Subsidies						
1488	28	0	18	57	25	0
1489	—[a]					
1497	77	0	4	59	31	5
1504	58	0	5	37	46	11
1513	67	0	18	44	37	1
1514	155	0	1	13	84	2
1515	261	0	18	51	29	2
1516	288	0	3	51	45	1
1524a	45[b]	0[c]	2	51	44	2
1524	384	0	0	62	36	2
1525	395	0	12	54	33	2
1526	169	0	3	53	43	1
1527	185	0	3	47	46	4
1535	258	0	0	45	55	1
1536	245	0	0	20	80	0
1541	267	0	34	53	11	1
1542	266	0	20	68	11	1
1544	339	0	33	62	4	1
1545	318	0	57	37	4	1
1546 ('43)	288	2[d]	85	11	2	0
1546 ('45)	298	45	31	19	3	1
1547	273	0	27	63	9	2

Notes:
% All figures are ±0.5%
1524a The Anticipation of the subsidy of 1524
[a] No accounts for this subsidy were to reach any court of record.
[b] A further ten groups of collectors did not account because the money was levied by the subsidy collectors. E159/305 Recorda T.r.16–19, M.r.27, 31; /306 Recorda P.r.30; /308 Recorda M.r.16.
[c] Calculated from 'payment date' at Trinity 18 Henry VIII, because although the exchequer was instructed to distrain the collectors to account in Michaelmas 16 Henry VIII, no such writs of distress were issued until Trinity 18 Henry VIII. E159/303 Recorda M.r.1; /305 Recorda T.r.16–19.
[d] Part of this subsidy was levied by way of Anticipation. See pp. 133–4.
Sources: E359/38, 39, 4144, *passim*.

First, it is clear from the table that the number of groups of collectors who accounted separately increased fourfold during the early Tudor period. For the fifteenths and tenths, this increase took place in 1541 when, for the first time, the collectors were assigned to hundreds or groups of hundreds.[11] It is interesting that thereafter the number of groups of collectors appointed for fifteenths and tenths declined, which means that the collectors were being given larger areas to cover. For the subsidies, until 1525 the increase in the number of groups of collectors appointed follows the changes in the statutory regulations governing the appointment of high collectors, while the figures of the subsidies of 1526–36 reflect the small number of people who were liable to those subsidies.[12] There was some variation in the numbers of groups of collectors appointed for the subsidies in the 1540s, but in general these numbers were lower than those for the subsidies of 1524 and 1525.

For the Exchequer the effect of this increase in the number of groups of collectors appointed was a corresponding increase in the volume of work involved in their accounts. But the burden of the administration of the parliamentary taxes on the Exchequer also depended on the speed with which the collectors accounted. The table shows that very few collectors accounted before the term in which the statutory payment dates fell, and that these were almost entirely the collectors for the subsidy of 1546 ('45).[13] If, however, an adjustment is made for the late levy of the subsidy of 1547, 28% of the collectors for this subsidy accounted in the term before the revised payment date.

Ideally, the collectors should have accounted, at the latest, in the same term as the payment date, and those collectors who did so avoided any form of process issued against them out of the Exchequer. For some of the taxes quite a high proportion of the collectors accounted this early, and this must have entailed a considerable saving in the work of the King's Remembrancer and his clerks. It is interesting that until 1520 the collectors of fifteenths and tenths were in general much quicker to account than were the collectors of subsidies; but after 1540 the position was reversed. Since the term in which the payment date fell usually extended for some time after the payment date, nearly all those collectors who are shown in Table 8.1 as having paid in their money not later than one month after the payment date, also accounted in the same term as the payment date.[14]

It was, however, quite possible for the collectors to appear at the Exchequer, enter upon their account before an auditor, and depart with the permission of the Barons for any number of terms before their account was heard formally by the Barons. Since, unless the collectors subsequently failed to reappear at the Exchequer, this procedure is nowhere recorded amongst the Exchequer documents, it is impossible to tell when, and how often, this practice occurred. Thus also the proportion of the collectors who are shown in the table as having accounted between one and three terms after the payment date were *prima facie* liable to writs of distress 'ad computandum', it may well be that they had in fact appeared at the Exchequer earlier than this, and had been granted an adjournment, or a series of adjournments, so that no process was actually issued against them. This may also be true of those collectors who accounted even later, after three terms after the payment dates, and who were therefore *prima facie* subject to writs of attachment. Indeed the fact that there were more people who were thus liable to attachment was greater than the number of attachments that have been recorded, suggests strongly that this was in fact the case.

At all events, a high proportion of the collectors for most of the taxes did not have their account heard until at least four terms after the term of the payment dates of the taxes. The most notable exceptions were the collectors for the subsidies in the 1540s and for the fifteenths and tenths from 1543. But, in general, it is clear from the table that while about 75% of the yield of both the subsidies and the fifteenths and tenths might have been expected to have been paid to the Exchequer within six months after the payment date, it was not until the 1540s that a comparable number of collectors had had their accounts heard in the Exchequer even nine months after the payment dates. Additionally, while only a few taxes resulted in a considerable sum to be paid after one year after the payment dates, until the 1540s a high proportion of the collectors for most of the taxes had not accounted by then.

Defaults by the Collectors

The contrast between the 1540s and the rest of the period is shown even more clearly when the nature of the defaults by the collectors is considered. As has already been explained, the three main defaults by the collectors on their accounts: refusal to appear for account, withdrawal before their account had been heard by the Barons, and withdrawal after their account had been heard, but before they had been formally acquitted, all incurred the issue of writs of attachment. Table 8.3 shows how many groups of collectors incurred process of attachment for each of the three kinds of default.

If the total number of attachments are expressed as percentages of the total number of groups of collectors appointed, it is clear that in the years 1541–7 they reduce to a zero frequency. Second, with the exception of the subsidies of 1497 and 1504, which were based on their incidence on the fifteenth and tenth, the collectors of subsidies committed in general fewer defaults than did the collectors of fifteenths and tenths.

If the nature of these defaults is now considered, it will be seen that the most common default of the collectors of subsidies lay in their failure to come

Table 8.3 Number of groups of collectors subject to writs of attachment

Year	Reason for writ				
	To account	Withdrawal before account	Withdrawal after account	Total	Total as % of total no. of collectors % (±0.5)
(a) Fifteenths and tenths					
1488	2	3	2	7	13
1489	5	2	5	12	23
1490–1	4	6	2	12	21
1492 (I)	2	3	3	8	15
1492 (II)	3	8	0	11	19
1497 (I)	1	2	11	14	25
1497 (II)	5	1	8	14	26
1512	1	5	0	6	10
1513	2	2	1	5	9
1514	4	5	0	9	16
1517	5	4[a]	3	12	22
1537	1	6[b]	2	9	17
1541	0	32[c]	0	32	12
1542	0	19	0	19	9
1543	0	14	0	14	7
15447	0	0	0	0	0
Total	34	110	37	181	–
(b) Subsidies					
1488–9	0	0	0	0	0
1497	6	4	15	25	33
1504	5	13	2	20	35
1513	4	2	1	7	10
1514	3	4	2	9	6
1515	3	3	0	6	2
1516	6	10	3	19	7
1524a	0	1	0	1	2
1524	38	4	1	43	11
1525	42	8	0	50	13
1526	16	6	3	25	15
1527	14	12	0	26	14
1535	16	6	0	22	9
1536	7	4	0	11	4
1541	0	5	0	5	2
1542	1	22	0	23	9
1544	0	2	0	2	0
1545	1	0	0	1	0
1546	0	0	0	0	0
1547	1	1	0	2	0
Total	163	107	27	297	–

Notes:
1524a The Anticipation of the subsidy of 1524.
1 That is, of the total number of groups of collectors.
[a] In one case, the collectors petitioned for process of attachment to be issued against their colleagues.

ᵇ In five cases, the collectors petitioned for process of attachment to be issued against their colleagues.
ᶜ In two cases, the collectors petitioned for process of attachment to be issued against their colleagues.
Sources:
Last column calculated on column 1 of Table 8.2. Otherwise as sources for Table 8.5; but omitting
references marked (X). Also: ('Recorda' unless otherwise stated).
Fifteenths and tenths
1488   E159/264 Dies dati M.rd; E368/265 P.r.19.
          (F) E159/268 P.r.17d.
1489   (F) E368/263 T.r.7d.
1490–1   E159/268 M.r.22; E368/265 SVC H.r.8.
          (F) E159/267 dies dati H.r; /268 T.r.8; E368/267 H.r.7.
1492 (I) E368/266 SVC H.r.7; /269 SVC M.r.9.
          (F) E368/267 T.r.13d; /279 H.r.27.
1492 (II) E159/269 Dies dati H.r, T.r; /270 M.r.15d, P.r.15d.
          (A) E159/269 H.r.36, P.r.6d, T.r.11d; /274 T.r.14.
1497 (I) (F) E368/271 T.r.6d, SVC M.r.12; /277 T.r.12d.
          (A) (F) E159/274 M.r.23.
1497 (II) E159/274 Dies dati T.r; /275 M.r.28; E368/271 SVC P.r.9.
1512   E159/291 Dies dati H.r.
          (A) Ibid., T.r.
1513   E159/299 Bre.Ret. H.r.4d.
1514   E159/304 P.r.16d.
1517   E159/303 H.r.12, 18, 24d; E368/293 SVC P.r.8d.
          (A) E159/299 T.r.9d.
1537   E159/317 Fines P.r, M.r.
          (A) E368/314 M.r.17, H.r.3.
1541   E159/320 Fines P.rd; /322 Fines P.r, P.rd, T.r, M.r.
1542   E159/321 Fines H.r; /322 Fines P.r, P.rd, T.rd, M.r, H.rd; /323 Fines T.r.
1543   E159/322 Fines T.r, M.rd, H.r, H.rd.
Subsidies
1497   E159/273 T.r.13d, Dies dati T.r; /274 M.r.29d, H.r.13, Dies dati H.r; /282 H.r.9;
          E368/271 SVC H.r.8d; /272 SVC P.r.9; /278 Bre.Ret. H.r.5d, 10d.
          (A) E159/274 Dies dati M.r.
          (F) E368/271 SVC H.r.8; /277 P.r.14.
1504   E159/283 T.r.37, 39; /284 M.r.2, 49, 54, 54d, H.r.19d.
          (A) E159/284 M.r.51, H.r.31, 39.
          (A) (F) E159/283 T.r.29.
1514   E159/303 H.r.18d; E368/298 SVC H.r.14; /303 Bre.REt. H.r.4.
1515   E159/295 M.r.28; /305 Fines P.r, M.rd.
1516   E159/297 H.r.12d, 13, 19, /299 M.r.17; E368/299 P.r.3d.
          (A) E159/297 H.r.4d; /299 T.r.9.
          (F) E368/299 SVC T.r.6.
1524a   (F) E159/305 Dies dati T.r.
1524   E159/305 P.r.8d, H.r.18, Dies dati P.r; /305 Fines P.r; /306 Fines M.r;
          E368/310 Bre.Ret.H.r.2.
          (A) E159/303 H.r.19d.
1525   159/304 Dies dati T.r, H.r; /305 Fines M.rd, H.r; /306 M.r.42.
          (A) E159/305 Dies dati T.r; /306 M.r.28d, Fines P.r, M.r; /308 M.r.25d; /310 M.r.87
1526   E159/305 Dies dati T.r; /306 M.r.28d, Fines P.r, M.r; /308 M.r.25d; /310 M.r.87.
1527   E159/306 H.r.37, Fines T.r; /307 P.r.20d, H.r.24, Dies dati P.r, T.r, M.r, H.r;
          /308 Dies dati P.r.
1535   E159/305 H.r.12d, Dies dati T.rd; /316 M.r.47.
          (F) E159/316 P.r.12.
1536   E159/317 H.r.40; /322 Fines P.r.
          (A) E159/318 P.r.10d.
1541   E159/320 Fines P.rd; /322 Fines P.r, P.rd.
1542   E159/321 Fines H.r; /322 Fines P.r, P.rd, T.rd.
1544   E159/323 Fines T.r, M.r.

to account, while the most frequent default of collectors of fifteenths and tenths was their tendency to withdraw from the Exchequer before their account had been heard by the Barons. For the collectors of the fifteenths and tenths, withdrawal after their accounts had been heard by the Barons was as frequent a default as was their failure to come to account in the first place, while for the collectors of the subsidies this former default was by far the least frequent of the three.

Defaults by the collectors were far more frequent during the reign of Henry VII than during the reign of Henry VIII. Indeed during the latter reign it was only for the fifteenths and tenths of 1514, 1517 and 1537, and for the subsidies of 1524–7 that more than 10 per cent of the groups of collectors incurred processes of attachment. And by the end of Henry VIII's reign, attachment for these defaults had almost ceased altogether.

There are two main reasons which may explain this improvement in the performance of the collectors. Either the conditions facing the collectors improved during the early Tudor period, or the conditions remained the same and the improvement was rather the result of an increased efficacy of the forms of process against the collectors.

The Efficacy of the Forms of Process out of the Exchequer

It is, unfortunately, impossible to determine the efficacy of the preliminary writs of distress 'ad computandum' issued by the Exchequer. First, the sheriffs' returns to these writs are difficult to collate,[15] and second, even if such a collation were practicable, there is no means of determining whether the appearance of the collectors at the Exchequer was due to these writs or to quite other reasons. But far more important was the question of the efficacy of the writs of attachment and total seizure of lands and goods which were resorted to when it became clear that the collectors were not prepared to account of their own accord. The first question that arises is how many of the collectors were actually attached by the sheriffs in response to these writs. Table 8.4 gives the number of collectors that the sheriffs attached and produced at the Exchequer, the number that they attached, but which were subsequently rescued, and the number that were attached but who could not be produced, because they were too old or too sick to travel to Westminster.

It is immediately apparent that the number of attachments made by the sheriffs compared with the number of groups of collectors subject to attachment is very low indeed. And when it is remembered that in the earlier part of the period each group contained several collectors, and that at all times several writs were sent out against each group, the number of attachments actually made by the sheriffs appears almost negligible. The sheriffs in fact

Table 8.4 Number of collectors attached by the sheriffs

Year	Number of groups to be attached	Number of collectors attached		
		Produced	Sick	Rescued
(a) Fifteenths and tenths				
1488	7	–	–	–
1489	12	–	–	–
1490–1	12	–	–	–
1492 (I)	8	–	–	–
1492 (II)	11	1	–	2
1497 (I)	14	–	2	1
1497 (II)	14	–	–	2
1512	5	1	–	–
1513	5	3	–	–
1514	9	–	–	–
1517	12	14	–	–
1537	9	15	5	5
1541	32	5	–	–
1542	19	–	–	–
1543	14	–	–	–
1544–7	–	–	–	–
(b) Subsidies				
1488–9	–	–	–	–
1497	25	7	1	5
1504	20	36	1	5
1513	7	–	–	–
1514	9	1	–	1
1515	6	–	–	–
1516	19	7	1	1
1524a	1	–	–	–
1524	43	1	–	–
1525	50	7	1	–
1526	25	–	1	–
1527	26	2	2	–
1535	22	1	2	–
1536	11	1	–	–
1541	5	–	–	–
1542	23	–	–	–
1544	2	–	–	–
1545	1	–	–	–
1546 ('43)	–	–	–	–
1546 ('45)	–	–	–	–
1547	2	–	–	–
Total	378	104	16	22

Notes:
1524a   The Anticipation of the subsidy of 1524
Sources:
Column 1: Total column of Table 8.3. Other columns: see sources for Tables 8.3, 8.5, references preceded by (A). Also E159/274 Recorda H.r.27; E368/301 Recorda T.r.25d.

returned the vast majority of the writs with the endorsement 'non sunt inuenti', that is that they could not find the collectors.[16] Thus it is clear, first, that the writ of attachment was singularly unsuccessful in securing the presence of the collectors in the Exchequer, and, second, that the fault lay entirely with the sheriffs, who appear to have performed their office with as much, if not a greater, regard to local loyalties and interests as to those of the crown.

But the writs of attachment also commanded the sheriffs to seize all the lands and goods of the collectors.[17] The annual values of the lands and the capital values of the goods seized by the sheriffs are shown in Table 8.5. The table shows that for most of the taxes, seizures of lands were more common than seizures of goods. But for the three taxes of 1497, seizures in goods vastly outweighed seizures in lands. But from the column of the table which gives the average value of the seizures from each group of collectors subject to writs of attachment, it is clear that in no sense did the sheriffs actually seize all the collectors' lands and possessions. Indeed, the sheriffs often returned the writs endorsed 'nulla habent bona', or if some seizures had been made 'nulla habent plura bona'. Nevertheless, even when sufficient deductions are made for seizures allowed to the collectors upon their account and for seizures released by royal pardon, the total value of the seizures over the whole period still amounted to a considerable sum. However, it is clear that if the sheriffs had executed these writs properly this sum would have been very many times greater. That the sheriffs were failing in the duties of their office was recognised in the sixteenth century. The commission on the Courts of Revenue reported in 1553:

> Also the king taketh much losse by reason that the processse of Thexchequer and of all other Courts is not well served by the Sheriffs specially upon Extents and Attachment wherein is daily used much Corrupcion and Affeccion and therefore worthy of Reformacion.[18]

An anonymous writer on the Exchequer in the reign of Henry VIII was also aware of the deficiencies of the sheriffs:

> Also much processe by writte is made owte of the said Exchequire agaynst collectors of tayles & other subsedeis & other officers Accomptaunte, and other the kinges dettors, which processe many tymis is full evill executed aswell by Shirreiffes for that that [sic] many of the said persons be of little or noe substaunce as for fauour to many of them shewed by the saide Shirreifes.[19]

But the Barons of the Exchequer were equally well aware of the sheriffs' failings, for if they found reason to suspect the veracity of any of the returns of the writs,[20] they fined the sheriffs more or less severely, presumably according to the circumstances of the case. These fines, which were also imposed for

Table 8.5   Sheriffs' returns of seizures (£ ± 0.5)

Year	Lands (£)	Goods (£)	Average value per attachment (£)	Allowed towards debt (£)	Deduct Pardoned (£)	Net gain (£)
(a) Fifteenths and tenths						
1488	106	5	16	–	105	6
1489	51	80	11	60	52	19
1490–1	60	20	7	13	–	67
1492 (I)	56	2	7	–	–	58
1492 (II)	44	11	5	–	–	55
1497 (I)	20	286	22	9	–	297
1497 (II)	20	249	19	8	–	262
1512	37	–	6	–	–	37
1513	14	–	3	–	–	14
1514	61	–	7	–	–	61
1517	91	29	10	27	–	93
1537	43	2	5	–	–	45
1541	55	60	4	–	–	115
1542	55	31	4	–	–	86
1543	–	17	1	–	–	17
1544	–	–	–	–	–	–
1546	–	–	–	–	–	–
1547	–	–	–	–	–	–
Total	724	792		117	157	1232
(b) Subsidies						
1488	–	–	–	–	–	–
1489	–	–	–	–	–	–
1497	25	567	24	544	12	36
1504	144	29	87	4	–	169
1513	46	8	8	7	–	47
1514	31	12	5	–	–	43
1515	8	–	1	–	–	8
1516	49	16	3	16	–	49
1524a	–	–	–	–	–	–
1524	130	–	3	–	–	130
1525	86	21	2	–	–	107
1526	22	22	2	8	–	36
1527	10	1	0.5	–	–	11
1535	43	27	3	–	–	70
1536	14	–	1	–	–	14
1541	–	–	–	–	–	–
1542	36	14	2	–	–	50
1544	50[a]	–	–	–	–	50[a]
1545	7	–	7	–	–	7
1546 ('43)	–	–	–	–	–	–
1546 ('45)	–	–	–	–	–	–
1547	5	3	4	6	–	8
Total	706	720		579	12	845
Grand total	*1430*	*1512*		*696*	*169*	*2077*

Notes:
1524a   The anticipation of the subsidy of 1524.
[a] Derived from the sale by the barons of a lease of lands belonging to a collector who died without having closed his account. E368/319 Recorda M.r.35.

continued

Table 8.5   (*continued*)

Sources for Table 8.5:
Unless otherwise stated all references are to the 'Recorda'.
Fifteenths and tenths:
1488   E159/265 T.r.6d.
         (F) E159/265 M.r.24, T.r.26.
1489   E159/266 Dies dati M.r–; /267 M.r.32; /272 M.r.14; E368/264 H.r.6, 6d; /281 M.r.6d.
         (F) E159/267 M.r.24, 24d, 33.
1490–1   E159/267 Dies dati H.r–; /268 M.r.21, P.r.15; E368/267 M.r.21.
         (F) E159/267 Dies dati H.r–; /268 T.r.10, Dies dati H.r–
1492 (I)   E159/268 Dies dati P.r–;
         (F) E159/268 H.r.35; P.r.20; /269 H.r.34.
1492 (II)   E159/269 Dies dati H.r–; /270 P.r.15; E368/268 SVC H.r.7; E379/42/9–16HVII(X).
1497 (I)   E159/273 Dies dati T.r–; E368/2270 SVC H.r.6d, T.r.7d (X); /271 SVC M.r.12, H.r.5;
         /272 SVC M.r.15; /278 T.r.21 (X).
         (F) E159/273 T.r.12d; E368/271 SVC M.r.12, H.r.5.
1497 (II)   E159/276 P.r.2, 21, T.r.19d; E368/271 SVC T.r.6d; /272 SVC M.r.14, 14d;
         /282 H.r.18 (X); /283 H.r.26d (X); /284 M.r.38 (X).
         (F) E159/274 H.r.24; E368/271 SVC P.r.9, T.r.6d (X); /272 SVC M.r.14, H.r.9.
         (A) (F) E368/272 SVC T.r.2.
1512   E159/291 Dies dati T.r–.
         (F) E159/291 M.r.28d, H.r.5d.
1513   E159/292 Dies dati P.r–.
         (A) E159/293 P.r.10
         (F) E159/292 T.r.18d, 19.
1514   E159/293 H.r.18; /294 P.r.13, 14d, 15; /295 T.r.36; /297 H.r.12; /299 H.r.23
         (F) E159/294 P.r.18.
1517   E159/297 H.r.4, 11; /305 Fines T.r–d; E368/202 P.r.36.
         (A) E159/296 Dies dati H.r–; /297 H.r.23; /299 P.r.6.
         (F) E159/297 H.r.11d.
1537   E159/317 P.r.36d, Dies dati M.r–;
         (A) E159/317 H.r.39.
         (F) E159/317 M.r.58.
1541   E159/319 Fines H.r–; /320 Fines P.r–, P.rd, T.r–.
1542   E159/321 P.r.72, Fines P.r–, P.r–d.
1543   E159/322 Fines M.r–.

Subsidies
1497   E159/277 M.r.7; E368/271 SVC M.r.13; /272 SVC P.r.9; /273 SVC M.r.11;
         /274 M.r.16 (X); /278 M.r.30 (x); /279 H.r.16d (X); E379/116/21–22HVIII, Salop (X).
         (A) E159/275 H.r.25.
         (A) (F) E368/271 SVC M.r.8, P.r.12d
         (F) E159/275 H.r.23; E368/271 SVC H.r.7, P.r.12; /279 M.r.31.
1504   E159/283 T.r.38; /284 M.r.60; /285 M.r.50; E368/282 SVC M.r.4.
         (A) E159/283 T.r.30; /284 M.r.53.
         (A) (F) E159/284 M.r.49.
1513   E159/289 M.r.31d; /293 P.r.15, 15d; /294 P.r.12, 14; /295 M.r.29.
         (F) E159/293 H.r.14d.
1514   E159/293 Dies dati M.r–; /294 T.r.12d, 24; /303 T.r.12.
         (A) E159/294 M.r.41, P.r.15d.
1515   E159/295 T.r.34; /296 P.r.10.
         (F) E159/297 H.r.18.
1516   E159/297 H.r.15d, 18d, P.r.12; /298 M.r.34d, H.r.14; /300 H.r.36; /301 T.r.14;
         /303 M.r.13d, H.r.17d; E368/299 SVC T.r.6.
         (A) E159/297 H.r.16d.
1524   E159/303 H.r.19, 20, 23d, Dies dati M.r–; /304 Fines P.r–, T.r–.
         (F) E159/303 H.r.22d.

Table 8.5 *(continued)*

Sources to Table 8.5 continued
1525   E159/304 H.r.18, 18d, Dies dati H.r–, Fines P.r–; /305 P.r.21, M.r.28, Fines P.r–, P.r–d,
        T.r–; /306 P.r.21.
        (A) E159/304 Dies dati H.r–.
1526   E159/305 Dies dati H.r–; /306 P.r.25, M.r.40, Fines P.r–d, T.r–; /307 Dies dati M.r–;
        /309 M.r.30; E368/301 P.r.1.
        (A) E159/306 P.r.21d; /307 M.r.45.
1527   E159/306 Fines T.r–d; 307 P.r.32, H.r.5, 21, Dies dati P.r–; /310 Dies dati H.r–.
        (A) E159/306 Fines H.r–; /307 H.r.18, 18d; /309 Fines M.r–.
1535   E159/315 H.r.12, 18, Dies dati T.r–; /316 M.r.45, 48, 48d.
        (A) E159/315 H.r.15.
1536   E159/316 Dies dati H.r–; /317 P.r.34, M.r.61, 63
1542   E159/321 M.r.93; Dies dati P.r–, P.r–d.
1544   E159/319 M.r.35.
1545   E159/324 M.r.112.
1547   E159/326 M.r.142; /327 Dies dati H.r–.

failure to return writs,[21] or for blank returns,[22] varied in severity from 6s 8d to £10.[23] Table 8.6 gives for each tax the total number of fines levied on sheriffs, together with their total and average values. Taking the two parts of the table together, it appears that in general the number of fines levied on the sheriffs was greatest during the reign of Henry VII, and that, except for 1525, relatively few fines were levied during the reign of Henry VIII. There is no immediately apparent trend with regard to the size of the fines imposed on the sheriffs and these may therefore be taken to have depended entirely upon the circumstances of each case. The total sum accruing to the crown from these fines was not large.

But it is clear that the sheriffs were not fined every time that they made a false return to a writ, otherwise the volume of fines would have been very much larger than it was. The considerations which prompted the Barons to fine a sheriff or to allow the return are not apparent from the evidence of the records. It is possible that under the pressure of business only the more flagrant cases, for which the necessary evidence was forthcoming, were singled out for punishment.

But regardless of the severity, or lack of severity, with which the sheriffs were fined by the Barons of the Exchequer, it is plain that throughout the early Tudor period process out of the Exchequer was indeed 'full evill executed ... by Shirreiffes'.[24] Since this process was entirely dependent upon the sheriffs for its execution, the result was that the efficacy of the traditional methods of compelling the collectors to account was reduced almost to vanishing point. And yet many even of the most consistently offending collectors in most cases appeared sooner or later to account. It may therefore well be that what process out of the Exchequer lacked in strength it more than compensated for by its unrelenting regularity. But there was clearly no increase in the efficiency of the sheriffs' execution of the writs sufficient to account for the improvement in the

Table 8.6 Fines levied upon sheriffs for insufficient execution of exchequer writs (£ ± 0.5)

Year	Number	Total value (£ ± 0.5)	Average value (£)
(a) Fifteenths and tenths			
1488	4	6	1.5
1489	19	27	1.4
1490–1	12	31	2.6
1492 (I)	5	6	1.2
1492 (II)	13	23	1.8
1497 (I)	20	30	1.5
1497 (II)	16	21	1.3
1512	9	32	3.6
1513	6	16	2.7
1514	3	12	4.0
1517	1	5	5.0
1537	1	1	1.0
1541	1	2	2.0
1542	8	32	4.0
1543	1	1	1.0
1544–7	–	–	–
Total		245	
(b) Subsidies			
1488–9	–	–	–
1497	27	42	1.6
1504	2	17	8.5
1513	1	7	7.0
1514	1	1	1.0
1515	–	–	–
1516	2	5	2.5
1524a	1	6s 8d	6s 8d
1524	2	7	3.5
1525	19	24	1.3
1526	3	8	2.7
1527	3	7	2.3
1535	3	7	2.3
1536	3	7	2.3
1541	–	–	–
1542	3	14	4.7
1544	1	5	5.0
1545	2	10	5.0
1546–7	–	–	–
Total		161	

Notes:
1524a   The Anticipation of the subsidy of 1524.
Sources:
See sources for Tables 8.3, 8.55, references preceded by (F). Also ('Recorda' unless otherwise stated).

Table 8.6   *(continued)*

Sources to Table 8.6 continued
Fifteenths and tenths
1488	E159/265 T.r.13
1489	*Ibid.*, T.r.11–13d, 27d.
1490–1	E368/268 H.r.11d; /279 H.r.26d, 27; /282 H.r.1.
1492 (I)	E368/279 H.r.27.
1497 (I)	E159/273T.r.14, Fines T.r–; E368/277 P.r.8d; /281 H.r.4, 23; /282 H.r.16; /286 M.r.16, T.r.7.
1497 (II)	E368/273 H.r.17; /275 P.r.6d; /279 P.r.3d, 9; /281 M.r.3d; /283 M.r.25d, H.r.26d; /290 P.r.16.
1513	E159/295 M.r.16d.
1514	E159/302 M.r.8.
1541	E159/320 Fines T.r–.

Subsidies
1497	E159/273 T.r.14d, Dies dati T.r–; Fines T.r–; /279 P.r.10; E368/273 H.r.17; /274 SVC P.r.12; /275 P.r.21; /278 M.r.24d; /279 P.r.9d, H.r.26d; /283 M.r.59d.
1516	E159/304 T.r.11.
1524	E159/305 M.r.30.
1525	E159/304 T.r.1, 9–12, H.r.11, Dies dati T.r.1d, M.r.3d; /305 Fines P.r–, P.r–d; /308 H.r.15.
1526	E159/305 T.r.3.
1527	E159/306 P.r.25d; /308 M.r.6, 30d.
1535	E159/315 H.r.13.
1536	E159/317 P.r.37; /318 M.r– [i.e. penultimate].
1542	E159/323 P.r.46.
1545	E159/324 M.r.112.

collectors' promptitude and regularity upon their accounts. The alternative hypothesis that there was an improvement in the conditions in which the collectors made their collections will now be examined.

Popular Opposition to Parliamentary Taxation

Popular opposition to parliamentary taxation might take any form between the two extremes of the stealthy rescue of a distress from the common pound to the full-scale rebellion aimed at no less than the punishment of the king's evil councillors. Opposition on this latter scale was rare in the early Tudor period. On only two occasions when there was a general recourse to arms was the burden of taxation the sole, or even the major cause of discontent. In 1489 the commons in Yorkshire assembled at Topcliffe. Polydore Vergil and the Great Chronicle of London lay sympathy with the Yorkist cause to the rebels' credit;[25] but other contemporary commentators ascribed the rising entirely to their antipathy to the subsidy of 1489.[26] The Earl of Northumberland called together the gentry and their supporters and advanced against the rebels.[27] The Earl was slain and the revolt thereby assumed a more serious character, the rebels adopting the somewhat imprecise but stirring purpose:

to geynstonde suche persons as is abowtward for to dystroy oure suffereyn Lorde the Kynge and the Comowns of Engelond, for suche unlawfull poyntes as Seynt Thomas of Cauntyrbery dyed for.[28]

The rebellion was quickly crushed by an expedition under the Earl of Surrey.[29] The second rebellion against taxation broke out eight years later at the other end of the country, in Cornwall. Contemporary sources are unanimous in ascribing the cause of this rebellion to the taxes of 1497.[30] Once more the object of the rebellion was expressed as the necessary punishment of the evil councillors of the king, and once again the rebellion was defeated.[31] On the third occasion when there was a general recourse to arms, in rebellions in Lincolnshire and Yorkshire in 1536, although taxation was one of the grievances of the rebels, it was by no means the only or even the most important one.[32] Nevertheless, despite the existence of other reasons for these risings, part of the opposition was directed against the parliamentary taxes that were being levied at that time.[33]

Although rebellions against taxation were rare in the early Tudor period, it would be a mistake to belittle their importance. Nevertheless, it should be remembered that only two rebellions were directed solely against taxation and that these both occurred at the beginning of the early Tudor period in unstable times, and were confined to very small regions. Second, it may be significant that these rebellions all occurred when a subsidy was being levied. This at first appears surprising because the subsidy did not touch the 'commons' nearly so much as did the fifteenth and tenth. But it is suggested that this confirms the point already made that it was the fifteenth and tenth that was considered to be the traditional and acceptable form of taxation, and that the subsidies, because of their infrequency during the fifteenth century, were regarded with suspicion by much of the population.[34] The removal of this attitude and acceptance of the subsidy as a 'proper' form of taxation was by no means the least of the achievements of the Tudors.

Second, parliamentary taxation in the early Tudor period might provoke a passive resistance against making any form of contribution to the crown. As far as is known, this occurred on any considerable scale on only one occasion, in 1513 in the wapentakes of Staincliffe and Ewcross in the north-west of the West Riding of Yorkshire. The opposition first broke out in Richmondshire in the North Riding;[35] but it seems to have been effective only in Staincliffe and Ewcross.[36] About nineteen towns refused either to pay the fifteenth and tenth or to be assessed towards the subsidy.[37] The crown capitulated over the fifteenth and tenth and remitted the sum due from the area;[38] but the commissioners for the subsidy managed after two years to get all but two of the towns to agree to be assessed, and the money from this subsidy was certainly collected because the collector accounted four years later.[39]

But the most frequent form of resistance to parliamentary taxation in the early Tudor period was the unpremeditated outburst of violence by an individual against a collector. And it is the distribution of these sporadic attacks, conceived in the heat of the moment that provides the most sustained and coherent picture of the attitude of the taxpayers to taxation throughout the early Tudor period. This opposition occurred in two essentially different situations. Either it was occasioned by the seizure of the goods of the taxpayer by the collector in default of payment, or there was no ostensible cause for the violence other than the fact that the collector was collecting money for the king. The former attacks were 'rescues of distresses', while the latter were assaults. Unfortunately, all information about these attacks is derived entirely from complaints brought by the collectors either to the Exchequer or to Chancery or to one of the conciliar courts, and thus very many more such incidents may have taken place than have been recorded. However, there is no reason to suppose that the collectors from any one area were any more diligent either than the collectors from any other area, or at any one time rather than at another, in bringing these complaints; and thus the geographical and chronological distribution of these complaints should not grossly distort the actual distribution of the incidents themselves throughout England in the early Tudor period.

The assaults are concentrated heavily in a small area around London and along the south coast. This is in marked contrast to the distribution of rescues of distresses over half of which occurred in the two counties of Salop and Staffordshire alone. The only other counties in which a relatively large number of rescues took place were Kent and Wiltshire; otherwise, apart form a belt of counties from Leicestershire to Suffolk for which no rescue have been recorded, the distribution of rescues of distress was fairly evenly spread throughout the country.[40]

The distribution of assaults and rescues over the period is given in Table 8.7. Only eleven assaults against collectors have been recorded for the whole period, and ten of these were against collectors of fifteenths and tenths. Similarly, by far the majority of the rescues of distresses were directed against the collectors of fifteenths and tenths. Although this might appear to throw some doubt upon the contention that the fifteenth and tenth was the more acceptable of the two forms of taxation, it is indeed more probable that the greater incidence of violence against the collectors of fifteenths and tenths reflects rather the lower social and economic status of those who were called upon to pay those taxes.

It is clear from the table that by far the majority of the rescues took place in the early years of Henry VII's reign, and that by the end of the period such rescues were relatively infrequent. The assaults, although more evenly spaced over the period, were so few in number that they hardly affect the obvious

Table 8.7 Complaints of rescues of distresses and of assaults against the collectors

Year	Rescues	Assaults
(a) Fifteenths and tenths		
1488	5	1
1489	7	0
1490–1	10	2
1492 (I)	24	0
1492 (II)	16	0
1497 (I)	0	0
1497 (II)	13	2
1512	4	1
1513	1	0
1514	2	0
1517	4	0
1537	5	2
1541	3	1
1542	4	0
1543	2	0
1544	1	0
1546	1	1
1547	2	0
Total	104	10
(b) Subsidies		
1488–1513	–	–
1514	–	1
1515–16	–	–
1524	3	–
1525	1	–
1526	–	–
1527	1	–
1535	2	–
1536–46	–	–
1547	1	–
Total	8	1

Sources: As Tables 3.4 and 5.15. Also E159/293 Recorda T.r.15d.

conclusion that opposition towards collectors of parliamentary taxes declined dramatically during the early Tudor period, so that by the end of Henry VIII's reign it was but a shadow of what it had been at the start of the Tudor dynasty.

9

Taxation and the Political Limits of the Tudor State

Taxation occupies a sensitive position in the nexus of constitutional, political and social relationships, for it is through taxation that economic resources are mobilised for political ends. But societies differ not only in the ends which they deem proper to be attained by taxation, but they are also constrained in the kinds of tax they can levy by the nature of their economic resources, and by their level of administrative skill. Moreover, since taxes entail compulsion, the ways in which they are authorised and organised are essentially political matters. A study of taxation, therefore, should throw light not only on the social and economic characteristics, but also on its political and administrative structure and its constitutional concepts of obligation and consent.[1] The early Tudor period furnishes a particularly interesting episode in the history of taxation in England for it was under Henry VIII that taxation based on the direct assessment of each individual was revived after having been abandoned as unworkable in the fourteenth century.[2] Direct assessment was to be abandoned again in the mid-seventeenth century after decades of complaint over evasion and under-assessment, and would not be revived again until the very end of the eighteenth century.[3] In the long run, therefore, the Tudor experiment in taxation failed, but an examination of that experiment, and of the timing and causes of its failure, may throw some light on the changing political limits of the Tudor state.

In Tudor England taxation was levied within an agreed theory of public finance which reflected conventional notions abut the rights and duties of king, parliament and people. The king, as chief magistrate of the realm, was charged with the provision of defence and justice. Accordingly, the crown should be endowed with sufficient regular revenues, ideally in the form of income from landed estates, to enable it to meet both the ordinary expenses of government, and immediate emergencies such as rebellion or invasion. However, it was evident that prolonged military campaigns were, in practice, too expensive to be met from any surpluses on the ordinary account. Constitutional theory matched the duty of the king to defend the realm with a reciprocal duty on the part of his subjects to grant him financial aid in providing for this defence. By the later fifteenth century, it was generally accepted that a gracious aid fulfilling this obligation could only be asked for in parliament, where the crown had to demonstrate the existence of a state of emergency threatening the safety of the realm, and where it was the commons which determined the size of the grant.[4]

In theory, therefore, national taxes were expected to be episodic rather than permanent. They could be levied only with the consent of parliament, though parliament could not withhold consent if the crown's claim that a state of emergency existed was correct. In practice and with few exceptions, both crown and parliament in the Tudor period respected these reciprocal obligations. The case for taxation was made in parliament largely in terms of military expenditures, or of financial need arising directly from past military expenditures, as in the case of the Antwerp debt.[5] The Commons debated the size of the sum to be granted, occasionally disagreeing with the crown's military plans, as shown by their opposition to Henry VIII's plans to invade France in 1512, but they did not deny the crown taxation in a state of emergency.[6]

The crown, on its side, did not attempt to levy general taxation without securing parliamentary approval. Apparent exceptions, such as the notorious 'forced loans' and benevolences, turn out on closer inspection to underpin the principle of parliamentary consent.[7] First, the loans were not taxes; they were repaid usually within a year from the revenue accruing from parliamentary taxation.[8] Second, both loans and benevolences which were not repaid were levied only in times of military emergency, and were levied from a very restricted and wealthy section of the population, the size of the payments being negotiated on an individual basis. Moreover, the crown took great care to justify the necessity for loans and benevolences in precisely the same terms of national emergency as were used in justifying the necessity of taxation in parliament, and used persuasion, not compulsion to secure compliance.[9] Third, when the crown needed to enforce the payment of an agreed sum by way of a benevolence, or to renege on an agreement to repay a loan, it obtained a parliamentary sanction in the form of a special statute.[10] Finally, the Amicable Grant of 1525, which was the only occasion on which the crown attempted to levy a compulsory benevolence from a wide section of the population at standard rates, provoked universal, uncompromising and successful opposition on the constitutional ground that it was 'not by an ordre of the law', and its promoter, Wolsey, was held to be a 'subversor of the Lawes and Libertie of England'.[11] Far from superseding parliamentary grants, loans and benevolences, respectively, were devices for anticipating, or supplementing, the collection of duly authorised taxes from a small number of wealthy subjects. They were necessary because military exigencies could not wait upon the lengthy process of the summons of parliament, the passage of legislation, and the setting into operation of the whole complex machinery of Tudor taxation.

The manner in which taxes were authorised testifies to a mutual understanding of the constitutional position, and to a practical political co-operation between the crown and parliament in Tudor England. However, the granting of taxes in a time of emergency was one thing, ensuring that individual subjects actually paid in accordance with their ability to contribute to the defence of the realm was quite another. To study this, the provisions of the subsidy acts concerning assessments need to be examined to judge whether they were enforced or not.

On this issue the Tudor subsidies have certainly had a bad press, for historians have had little difficulty in finding contemporary comments alleging substantial, and widespread, undervaluation. Perhaps the most celebrated example is Sir Walter Raleigh's statement in the 1601 parliament that 'our estates that be 30l or 40l in the Queen's Books, are not the hundred part of our wealth'.[12] However, almost all of the comments in this genre date from the second half of the reign of Elizabeth; it is much more difficult to find contemporary allegations of serious undervaluation earlier in the Tudor period, though it is true that the period lacks the detailed records of parliamentary debates, which provided so much of the later evidence of publicly acknowledged undervaluation.[13] Apart from an improbable allegation by the French ambassador in 1541,[14] there are two indications of official suspicion of undervaluation earlier in the century: remarks to this effect in Cromwell's remembrances in connection with the subsidies of 1535–6,[15] and Wolsey's threat in 1516 that the mayor and aldermen of London were 'to be sworn of and vppon the true value of their substaunce within the sum of C markes'.[16]

The most systematic continuing source of comment on the adequacy of the subsidy assessments in the period is the correspondence from the crown, or Privy Council, to the subsidy commissioners, of which several examples have survived, beginning in 1524. In the year after which the individual assessments had been received by the Exchequer, the crown informed the commissioners in some parts of the country that, in some cases, the individual assessments appeared to have been made erroneously 'partly by inadvertence and misexposicion of the said act and partly percaas by favour', and instructed the commissioners to revise them.[17] Thereafter, correspondence was usually confined to letters accompanying the subsidy commission, in which the crown encouraged the commissioners to be diligent in discharging their duties. A modern edition of two subsidy rolls for the City of London in 1541 and 1582, finds that undervaluation was rife at these dates.[18] It was only in the late 1550s that these letters show that the crown was aware of serious and systematic undervaluation, and evidently suspected that the rot was beginning at the top.[19] Writing in 1558 to the subsidy commissioners the queen enjoined them first to assess themselves

> ... according to the juste valewe of your landes or goodes with out the whiche ye cannot haue auctorie [sic] to call earnestly vpon others to do the same.[20]

In a parallel letter to an inner group of trusted commissioners of exceptionally high status the queen admitted that the assessments of commissioners had been 'farre vnder the Some of that they all knowe you have whiche wee haue heretofore felt to our grete losse'.[21]

During Elizabeth's reign, the Privy Council continued to reproach the commissioners for favouring themselves and their friends, and accused them of a growing catalogue of malpractices, all of which undermined the accuracy of the assessments and the yield of the subsidies to the crown. In 1576 the council accused the commissioners of conniving in a general basis in the assessments in favour of the rich whereby

> ... heretofore persons of very great possessions and wealthe haue ben assessed at very meane sommes, and persons of the meaner sorte haue ben enhanced to paye after the vttermost value of their substance ...[22]

In 1593 this accusation was made publicly by the Lord Keeper in an address to parliament, in which he claimed that the queen herself attributed the low yield of the subsidy to the fact that

> ... the wealthier sort of men turn this charge upon the weaker, and upon those of worst ability, for that one dischargeth himself, and the other is not able to satisfie what he is charged withal.[23]

By 1589 the council had apparently abandoned the notion that the assessments should be realistic valuations of the wealth of individual taxpayers, assuring the commissioners that

> ... although we meane not herby to have anie men of wealth assessed comparablie to their livings, but with some mediocrity according to their callings.[24]

By 1601 the extent of the retreat from any expectation that the assessment provisions of the subsidy act would be implemented was painfully clear:

> ... for allthoughe her Majestie dothe not expect from yow that accordinge to the purporte of this guifte and graunte from the high Courte of Parliament all men shal be taxed at their iust and true valewes eiether of their landes or goodes nevertheless ... there ought good regard to be had to assess men in some farr better proporcion then heretofore hathe bene done.[25]

Indeed by the 1590s the degree of undervaluation had become so notorious that the council was reduced to attempting to ensure that Justices of the Peace were at least assessed at the minimum statutory qualification for office (£20 income from lands) by threatening to put anyone assessed at a lower sum out of the commission.[26] Finally, in 1598 the Privy Council complained of a further abuse, namely that in some parishes a few poor persons were assessed 'and the whole paryshe dothe contrybute to the payment of the same'.[27] Forty years later this was described as normal assessment practice in an East Riding village.[28]

Thus the council's correspondence with the commissioners confirms the allegations of contemporary commentators that substantial undervaluation was rife in the later years of Elizabeth's reign. If these sources can be taken at face value, undervaluation would appear to have been unremarkable earlier in the Tudor period, and only to have become sufficiently serious to be worthy of comment some time in the middle of the century. However, arguments *ex silentio* are notoriously unsafe. A proper answer to the question of the adequacy of the enforcement of the assessment clauses of the Tudor subsidy acts requires a direct check of the accuracy of the subsidy assessments against independent valuations of taxpayers' wealth.

Helen Miller has already made such a check for the peerage.[29] Peers were assessed on a national basis by a special commission, so their assessments should not have been affected by the undervaluation arising from the local collusion amongst the commissioners complained of by the crown and Privy Council. Yet despite substantial inflation, the average assessment of the peers fell from £800–900 in Henry VIII's reign to reach about £300 in the late 1580s, at which level it remained for the rest of Elizabeth's reign.[30] A significant feature of this decline was a drastic reduction in the assessments of the richest peers: in Henry VIII's reign the highest annual incomes were about £3,000, while from the 1580s they were a little over £1,000. Indeed from the late 1580s only two peers were assessed at more than £1,000 (only one from 1593), yet almost a third of the peers were assessed at this level in the years before 1560.[31]

The annual income of the peers, therefore, would seem to have been ludicrously undervalued in the later sixteenth century, and this inference is confirmed in those cases in which the subsidy assessments can be compared with independent evidence. For example, the Earl of Oxford was independently estimated as worth £12,000 per annum in the 1570s, yet he was assessed at £1,000 in the subsidies of 1571 and 1576, £200 in 1581 and £100 thereafter.[32] On the other hand, when the subsidy assessments of the peers made in the reign of Henry VIII were checked against independent evidence, they 'were more than mere formal assessments'; that considerable efforts were made by the subsidy commissioners to reach a genuine assessment; and that on the whole they were not unsuccessful.[33] In the case of the peerage, therefore, there appears to have been a marked decline in the rigour with which the clauses of the subsidy act were enforced. But the peerage constituted a very small minority of taxpayers, subject to special assessment procedures. Before we can make any general statements about the enforcement of the subsidy acts, we need to discover whether other taxpayers were also tolerably accurately assessed in Henry VIII's reign, and whether they too succeeded in getting their assessments reduced to a fraction of their true worth by the final decades of the century.

In order to test the accuracy of the subsidy assessments, we need to find independent valuations of individuals' incomes, or wealth. For the comparison to be fair, the independent valuations should have been made within a short period of time of the subsidy assessments, and they should provide sufficient detail to enable a comparable tax assessment to be made, taking account of the assessment rules in the subsidy acts. For example, the tax on annual incomes was on the 'clear yearly value', so charges such as management expenses, annuities payable to others, and the wages of deputies in office need to be identified and excluded.[34] And in the case of goods, items such as personal clothing and debts owed by the taxpayer were exempt and thus need to be identified, so that the valuation can be adjusted accordingly. These are demanding conditions, but two sources were found which, though far from ideal, provided information in sufficient detail to enable a comparison with the subsidy assessments to be made. They were the engrossed feodaries' surveys kept by the Court of Wards and Liveries, for annual incomes; and probate inventories, for moveable goods.

The feodaries' surveys contain valuations for all the estates of persons dying seized of any parcel of land held by knight service in chief of the crown, and the engrossed accounts consolidate valuations from several counties as a matter of convenient record for the Court.[35] The documents not only list the income yields of estates, but note enfeoffments to use, as well as annuities and other charges on revenue. Although the surveys cover landed income in exceptional detail, the values contained in the surveys are not necessarily correct. In principle the feodaries were supposed to make an independent, and more realistic, valuation of lands than the suspiciously low figures certified by the escheators, but it is far from clear how far they achieved that aim.[36] Moreover, since the feodaries confined their attention to lands, omitting incomes from other sources such as fees and offices, their surveys do not provide a full record of the clear yearly value of the annual incomes of the deceased. Thus, in comparing the subsidy assessments with the feodaries' surveys, it is important to bear in mind that although the latter offer an independent estimate of annual incomes, the information they provide is both stylised and incomplete.

The books of engrossed surveys were searched for individuals who had died a reasonable interval after being assessed for a subsidy, and whose assessments had survived amongst the records of the Exchequer. Forty-nine cases were found spanning the years 1524 to 1560.[37] In ten cases the feodaries' surveys produced clear yearly values which were less than the subsidy assessments. Since this outcome probably indicates that the individuals concerned had substantial incomes from sources other than land, these cases have been disregarded. Amongst the remaining thirty-nine cases, which included four knights, and three peers, a clear pattern emerged. First, amongst the thirty-three cases dating from Henry VIII's reign, the subsidy assessments showed no tendency towards any great or lesser accuracy during the course of the reign: at all dates they were spread fairly evenly across a range of between 47 and 96% of the landed income as assessed by the feodaries.[38] On average the subsidy assessments of these rich landowners were about two-thirds (68%) of the independent valuations. In principle, the absence of any information in the feodaries' surveys about annual incomes from sources other than land results in too low a target valuation, and so gives the subsidy assessments an unfair advantage in the comparison. In practice, however, this is unlikely to have been a serious source of error, since for most members of the social class investigated here, land provided the overwhelming bulk of annual incomes assessable under the subsidy acts. In Henry VIII's reign, therefore, the subsidy assessments on annual incomes would appear to have been tolerably realistic, a far cry from the openly acknowledged farce they had become towards the end of Elizabeth's reign.

Second, among the remaining six cases dating from the years 1556 to 1560, the level of assessment was clearly inferior, ranging from 25 to 51% of the independent valuations.[39] The average subsidy assessment was only 38% of the survey valuation, much lower than the 68% achieved under Henry VIII. Although six cases may appear to be rather few on which to base any conclusion, the contrast with the thirty-three Henrician cases is so great that the quality of assessment may be presumed to have worsened markedly after Henry VIII's death.[40]

Fortunately, the independent valuations of taxpayers' goods contained in the probate inventories have survived in greater numbers, and so provide a better basis for investigating changes in the accuracy of assessment over time. Inventories of the goods of deceased persons were required by canon law, and by the statute of 21 Henry VIII c. 5, as a safeguard against fraud on the part of executors and administrators.[41] Moreover, it was in the interests of the latter to have the inventory made because their liability to meet the legacies and debts of the deceased was limited to the value of the inventory.[42] However, by the same token, it was in the interest of executors and administrators to obtain as low a valuation as possible; and it was to prevent this that 21 Henry VIII c. 5, s. 2 required them to make the inventory in the presence of two creditors or beneficiaries of the estate, if any, otherwise in the presence of two honest persons, preferably next-of-kin. According to this section of the act the inventory was to contain 'all the goodes catells wares marchaundyses as well movable as nott movable whatsoever' of the deceased. Furthermore, the church courts required the goods of the deceased to

> be particularly valued and praised by some honest and skilfull persons, to be the iust value thereof in their iudgements and consciences, that is to say, at such price as the same may be solde for at that time.[43]

In principle, therefore, probate inventories should provide a fair valuation of a person's goods in current prices. The position with regard to debts was more complicated: canon law required debts owing to the deceased to be included in the inventory, but not debts owed by the deceased. However, it was in the interests of executors or administrators to include them, since that registered a debt on the estate and limited their liability.[44] Provided the inventories specify all debts, and provided they give enough detail for tax-exempt categories such as personal clothing, and non-moveable goods such as crops in the fields, to be identified, they would appear to furnish a basis for comparison with the subsidy assessments on moveable goods.

There can, of course, be no guarantee either that inventories were complete or that the valuations were realistic. While some inventories were immensely detailed, others, generally those of poor people, were summary in the extreme. There is little evidence on the reliability of the valuations, though it is encouraging that an investigation of probate values of grain in East Anglian inventories in the period 1660–1735 found that they were only 15% below current market prices, and fluctuated closely in sympathy with them.[45] As in the case of the feodaries' surveys, it must be remembered that the subsidy assessments are being compared with valuations that are independent, but not necessarily accurate.

A search was made of diocesan record offices to locate all inventories made a few months after a subsidy assessment, and for which there was a matching subsidy assessment for the individual concerned amongst the records of the Exchequer. The search was confined to the period before 1575, and the conditions of access prevailing in the archives at the time of the search, together with the ravages of time since the sixteenth century, combined to limit both the temporal and the geographical coverage of the investigation.[46] In the event only 580 cases could be found in which a direct comparison could be made between a probate valuation and a recent subsidy assessment.[47]

The data are drawn from twenty-one counties and cover the period from 1524 to 1578. However, as Table 9.1 shows, the cases are very unevenly distributed across time and space. Only twenty cases were available before 1543, compared with 307 for the last five years of Henry VIII's reign, 121 for Edward and Mary, and 132 for the first half of Elizabeth's reign. Lincolnshire

Table 9.1 Probate inventory/subsidy assessment comparisons: number of cases by area and period[a]

Area	Period 1524–42	1543–5	1546–7	1549–56	1559–68	1571–2	Total	(%)
Yorks (13) / Lancs (7)	2	5	3	4	*1*	5	20	(3)
Staffs (46) / Salop (10)	6	22	17	9	*1*	*1*	56	(10)
Derbs (32) / Notts (3)	*0*	21	5	6	*0*	3	35	(60)
Lincs	8	77	45	*18*	8	28	184	(32)
Leics (33) / Rutland (1) / Cambs (2) / Suffolk (2) / Essex (1)	2	12	11	5	*1*	8	39	(7)
Warwks (79) / Worcs (35)	*0*	38	28	17	**16**	15	114	(20)
Berks (43) / Wilts (8) / Bucks (2)	2	*2*	16	15	**13**	5	53	(9)
Hants	*0*	*0*	5	**47**	*0*	**27**	79	(14)
All	20	177	130	121	40	92	580	(100)
(%)	(3)	(31)	(22)	(21)	(7)	(16)	(100)	

Notes:
[a] Figures which are less than half the frequency that would be expected with a uniform distribution across time and space are printed in *italic* type; figures which are more than double the expected are printed in **bold** type.

Sources:
Subsidy assessments: E179.
Probate inventories, loose or filed with original wills and administration, usually unnumbered, from the following repositories and courts:
Yorks: Borthwick Institute, York: Dean and Chapter of York; Dean of York. Leeds City Libraries Dept: Archdeaconry of Richmond (Eastern Deaneries).
Lancs: Lancashire County RO, Preston: Chester Consistory; Archdeaconry of Richmond (Western Deaneries).
Salop, Staffs, Derbs: Lichfield Joint RO: Lichfield Consistory.
Notts: P. A. Kennedy, ed., *Nottingham Household Inventories* (Thoroton Society Record Series, XXII, 1962).
Lincs: Lincolnshire Archives Office, Lincoln: Lincoln Consistory.
Leics: Leicestershire County RO: Archdeaconry of Leicester.
Rutland, Essex: PRO: Prerogative Court of Canterbury.
Cambs: University Library, Cambridge: Chancellor of Cambridge University.
Suffolk: Suffolk RO, Ipswich: Archdeaconry of Suffolk.
Warwks, Worcs: Worcestershire County RO: Worcester Consistory.
Berks: Bodleian Library, Oxford: Archdeaconry of Berks.
Wilts: Wiltshire County RO, Trowbridge: Archdeaconry of Sarum.
Bucks: Buckinghamshire County RO, Aylesbury: Archdeaconry of Buckingham.
Hants: Hampshire County RO, Winchester: Winchester Consistory, and unclassified wills.

provides almost a third of all the cases, and Warwickshire and Worcestershire a further third.

These counties, together with Staffordshire, Derbyshire, Leicestershire, Berkshire and Hampshire contribute 531 (92%) of the cases. The remaining forty-nine come from a further thirteen, mainly neighbouring, counties; consequently, large tracts of the country are entirely unrepresented. One reason why only 580 cases could be found is that inventories were accepted only if the appraisal was within a reasonable time of the subsidy assessment. In the event, the average interval between the two valuations was 4.8 months; in a quarter of the cases it was under four months, and in three-quarters less than 7 months (see Table 9.2).[48]

A comparison of probate valuations and subsidy assessments on the scale attempted here is bound to be subject to some error. First, the documents were linked on the basis of matching names, and in the case of common names it is possible that documents relating to two separate individuals have been improperly linked and compared.[49] Second, the fact that the two valuations were not drawn up at the same time, means that some of the discrepancies in wealth may have been genuine, though we may well be suspicious if the subsidy valuation is always the lower of the two. Third, the summary nature of some of the inventories, and the uncertainty over the degree to which they reveal the true debt position of individuals, will in some cases have defeated the attempt to apply the subsidy assessment rules to the information on wealth contained in the inventory.[50] Thus a comparison of the valuations in the two sets of documents can only be an approximate exercise. But so too must have been the original subsidy assessments, for it is unlikely that the assessors

Table 9.2   Intervals between subsidy assessments and probate valuations

Months	No.	Per cent	Cumulative per cent
Under 1	22	3.8	3.8
1	40	6.9	10.7
2	46	7.9	18.6
3	59	10.2	28.8
4	146	25.2	54.0
5	54	9.3	63.3
6	67	11.6	74.8
7	55	9.5	84.3
8	35	6.0	90.3
9	24	4.1	94.5
10	15	2.6	97.1
11	17	2.9	100.0
Total	580	100.0	

Sources: See Table 9.1.

would have had either the time, or the courage, to make a full visual appraisal of everyone's moveable possessions, as at the making of a probate inventory, and some items, such as debts, would have been invisible to them.

In the circumstances, therefore, it is scarcely surprising that the outcome of the comparison is that the subsidy assessments on goods comprised a much lower percentage of the probate valuations than did the assessments on lands of the valuations of the feodaries' surveys. Even after deducting from the inventories those items which were not liable to be taxed, notably personal clothing and crops in the field, the subsidy assessments averaged only 30% of the valuations, compared to the overall figure of 63% for annual incomes. This result may partly reflect the greater difficulty in making a fair comparison between the sources in the case of moveable goods, but it is likely that the task of assessing annual incomes was intrinsically less prone to error. A high proportion of annual income was derived from land, and since land was visible and its value per acre usually a matter of local knowledge, the subsidy assessors would probably have been able to make a reasonable estimate of its net annual value.

Although on average the subsidy assessments amounted to only 30% of the matching probate valuation, there is a considerable variation around this figure with individual subsidy assessments ranging from 2 to 100% of the probate valuations. Table 9.3 shows that most of the subsidy assessments – nearly 60% – lay in a range from between 10 to 40% of the probate valuations. However, 17% of the assessments were apparently highly deficient, at less than 10% of the matching probate valuation, while at the other extreme 16% of the assessments amounted to between 50 and 100% of the probate valuations.

Was this variation from case to case wholly fortuitous, reflecting individual circumstances that we can no longer recover? Or do the data contain patterns of variation that will enable us to identify the factors that were systematically associated with the accuracy of assessment under the subsidy acts? There are six factors whose influence on the accuracy of the assessments can be tested on the data. First there are two factors which may have intervened to complicate the comparison between the probate valuations and the subsidy assessments. They are variations in the interval of time that elapsed between the valuation and the assessment, and variations in the complexity and visibility of the wealth to be assessed. A second pair of factors relates to aspects of the assessment process. Since the number of individuals eligible for assessment varied considerably from subsidy to subsidy according to the minimum exemption limits in force, we can use variations in the latter to investigate whether the accuracy of the assessments was affected by the magnitude of the administrative burden imposed on the assessors and the commissioners. We can also take into account the wealth of the taxpayers to test whether the

Table 9.3   Subsidy assessments as a percentage of probate valuations

Percentage of probate valuation	Number of cases	Per cent of cases
Under 10	96	16.6
10–9	155	26.7
20–9	121	20.9
30–9	69	11.9
40–9	44	7.6
50–9	29	5.0
60–9	21	3.6
70–9	10	1.7
80–9	11	1.9
90–9	4	0.7
100–	20	3.4
Total	580	100.0

Sources: See Table 9.1.

commissioners were guilty of systematically favouring the rich with more lenient assessments than they allowed the poor, as alleged by the Elizabethan Privy Council. Finally, we can examine whether there were any systematic variations in the patterns of underassessment over time or across space. Did the commissioners in some parts of the country consistently implement the subsidy acts with greater rigour than their counterparts elsewhere? And did the accuracy of the subsidy assessment of moveable goods decline substantially during the Tudor period, as was the case with assessments of annual income?

Since there are several possible factors that could have influenced the accuracy of each subsidy assessment, we shall need to find a way of estimating the relative importance of each factor net of the effect of the others. This is important, because some of the factors are interconnected in ways which make it difficult to disentangle their separate effects, and which may lead us into drawing false conclusions. For example, Table 9.1 shows that the geographical distribution of the data for some of the subsidies, notably those levied in 1543 and between 1559 and 1568, was most unusual. Conversely, the data for some of the areas, notably Hampshire and Staffordshire/Salop, were drawn far more heavily from some periods than others. If we were simply to tabulate the accuracy of the assessments by period, we would not know whether any patterns we found reflected genuine changes over time, or whether they were spurious, having been produced by changes in the mix of areas, which themselves differed in the accuracy of the assessments. And if we were to tabulate by area, we should be in the same dilemma: the geographical patterns might be genuine, or merely reflect the fact that the data for each area were drawn unevenly from time periods which differed in the accuracy of the assessments.

Thus, in seeking to explain the variation in the accuracy of the subsidy assessments we need to find a form of analysis which takes account of the interconnections between the various explanatory factors, such as time period and area, and corrects for the unavoidable unevenness in the historical data. There are several ways of achieving this result by statistical methods, and Table 9.4 reports the results of a technique known as multiple classification analysis.[51] This form of analysis estimates the magnitude of the *independent* influence of each of the six explanatory factors outlined above, eliminating the effects of any interconnections between then which otherwise would improperly distort the results.[52]

Each has been divided into a number of categories. For example, 'Region' comprises eight groups of counties, and six time periods are distinguished. The table shows for each category of each factor the number of cases (column 1), the percentage of the probate valuation which the subsidy assessments in that category on average attained (column 2), and the amount by which the figure for that column deviated above, or below, the overall mean figure of 29.7% (column 3). If the accuracy of the subsidy assessment were strongly associated with a particular factor, we should find marked and systematic differences in the deviations for each category within the factor. For example, a decline in the accuracy of the assessments over time would appear in the table as a regular progression from large positive deviations above the average in the early periods to large negative deviations in the later period. Small or disorderly differences between the deviations for each category indicate that the factor is not systematically related to the variation in the accuracy of the subsidy assessments.

The coherence of the relationship is measured formally by calculating the statistical significance of the effect of each factor, and the results are indicated by means of asterisks attached to the figures in the final column of the table, labelled 'beta'. Factors without asterisks are unlikely to be systematically related to variations in the accuracy of the subsidy assessments. The beta figures themselves are summary measures of the relative importance of each factor in accounting for the variation in the accuracy of the subsidy assessments.[53] The factors have been listed in the table in ascending order of importance and it is immediately apparent from their very low beta values that the first two factors, namely the complexity of wealth being valued and the interval between the two valuation dates, had no systematic influence on the accuracy of the assessments. While each of the remaining four factors included in the analysis appears to have been associated in a consistent manner with variations in the accuracy of the subsidy assessments, in the case of the next two factors listed in the table there is some doubt about the strength of the association.

Both the latter factors, the geographical region where the assessments was made and the level of the exemption limit in force, have respectable beta

Table 9.4 Independent net effects of six factors on the accuracy of subsidy assessments[a]

Factor	No. of cases	Percentage of probate valuations	Deviation from mean (29.7%)	Beta
	(1)	(2)	(3)	(4)
Complexity of wealth[b]				0.03
0–4	204	28.9	−0.8	
5–14	177	29.8	0.1	
15–	199	29.0	0.7	
Interval (subsidy − probate)				0.05
0–2 months	108	27.7	−2.0	
3–5 months	259	29.6	−0.13	
6–8 months	157	28.0	1.7	
9–11 months	56	29.0	−0.7	
Region				0.13*
Yorks/Lancs	20	33.3	3.6	
Salop/Staffs	56	23.6	−6.1	
Derbs/Notts	35	22.8	−6.9	
Lincs	184	30.1	0.4	
Leics etc.[c]	39	31.0	1.3	
Warw/Worcs	114	29.4	0.3	
Berks/Bucks/Wilts	53	32.1	2.4	
Hants	79	32.4	2.7	
Exemption limit				0.18
£1–2	179	25.1	−4.6	
£3	108	28.0	−1.7	
£5	155	30.1	0.4	
£10	138	36.5	6.8	
Period				0.24**
1524–42	20	48.7	19.0	
1543–45	177	33.1	3.4	
1546–47	130	32.2	2.5	
1549–57	121	27.6	−2.1	
1559–68	40	21.2	−8.5	
1571–72	92	22.1	−7.6	
Net wealth				0.66**
£0–9	83	59.0	29.3	
£10–9	99	39.4	9.7	
£20–9	76	35.4	5.7	
£30–59	122	23.7	−6.0	
£60–99	138	16.2	−13.5	
£100–	62	9.9	−19.8	
Multiple R^2	0.48			

Notes:
[a] Adjusted for the effects of other factors.
[b] Percentage of wealth in probate valuation exempt from assessment to the subsidy.
[c] Includes Rutland (1), Cambs (2), Suffolk (2), Essex (1).
* statistically significant at the 5 per cent level.
** statistically significant at the 1 per cent level.
Sources: See Table 9.1.

scores (0.13 and 0.18, respectively), and the figures in column 3 of the table show a coherent pattern of systematic deviation from the average for the accuracy of assessment associated with the various categories of each factor. It would seem that subsidy assessments were made a little more realistically than average in the north and in a central southern region, and somewhat less realistically than average in a belt of North Midland counties running from Shropshire to Nottinghamshire. And it would also appear from the systematic progression in the deviations from average for the various levels of the minimum exemption limit that the accuracy of the assessments was indeed consistently reduced by any increase in the number of taxpayers to be assessed. However, despite appearances, the exemption limit factor failed to attain statistical significance, indicating that overall its effect was weak when measured against all other sources of variation in the accuracy of the individual assessments.[54] Moreover, although the regional factor was statistically significant, the differences were small, and the interpretation of the largest of the differences, the apparent underassessment of the North Midland counties, is perhaps less straightforward than might appear at first sight. Since all but three of the cases in that region came from the diocese of Lichfield, it is possible that it was not in fact the case that the subsidies were less adequately assessed there, but rather that probate valuations attained a more realistic level in that diocese.

Each of the remaining two factors in the table, the wealth of the taxpayer and the period in which the assessment was made, was unambiguously associated with the accuracy of the subsidy assessments. Both factors achieved relatively high beta scores (0.66 and 0.24, respectively), and both attained high levels of statistical significance. The figures in column 2 of the table show that the accuracy of the assessments declined systematically over time from 48.7% of the probate valuations in the period 1524–42 to 21.2% in the first thirteen years of Elizabeth's reign.[55] The figures in column 3 of the table bring out the point that the assessments made in Henry VIII's reign were more accurate than the average for the whole period studied, while those made latter were less accurate. In particular the assessments made before 1543 appear to have been considerably more accurate than was the case later, though it should be borne in mind that this result is based on only 20 cases. Thus, once the confounding effects of changes in other factors over time have been removed, it becomes apparent that the accuracy of the subsidy assessments of moveable goods experienced a similar decline between the reigns of Henry VIII and Elizabeth as was found in the case of assessments of annual incomes.

However, by far the most striking result to emerge from the analysis was the discovery that the factor with the strongest effect on the accuracy of the subsidy assessments was the wealth of the taxpayer. Indeed the beta scores in Table 9.4 suggest that it accounted for almost three times more variation in the accuracy of the assessments, than could be attributed to time period, the next strongest factor. The figures for the deviations for each wealth category in column 3 of the table show a clear and substantial downward progression, with the poorest being assessed at a much higher than average percentage of their probate valuations, and the richest at much lower than average percentage. Again, adding the deviations for each category to the overall mean, as in column 2 of the table, we find that once the effects of all other factors are held constant, those whose probated wealth was less than £10 were assessed in the subsidy at 59% of their probate valuation, while those whose probated wealth was above £100 were assessed at only 10% of their probate valuation. The allegations of Queen Elizabeth and her Privy Council that richer taxpayers were being more favourably treated than the poor in the later sixteenth century are amply confirmed. Throughout the entire period studied, from 1524 to 1572, an economic bias prevailed: the richer the taxpayer, the less his true wealth was captured by the subsidy assessments.[56]

Altogether, the six factors included in the analysis accounted for only about a half (48%) of the variation in the accuracy of the assessments amongst the 580 cases studied.[57] While we might be able to improve on this figure if we could identify and measure other relevant factors, a certain proportion of the variation in the historical record will always resist our attempts to comprehend it. Each subsidy assessment and probate valuation will have been subject to the vagaries of chance, error and the accidents of personality. And further error will have been introduced in the course of this study, for example through the misidentification of individuals in the two sets of sources.

The results reported above are also limited by systematic errors and biases lurking in the sources. As has already been emphasised, neither the feodaries' surveys nor the probate inventories can be assumed to have provided true valuations of the wealth of individuals, and so may give an over-generous impression of the extent to which the subsidy assessments captured taxpayers' wealth. Moreover, since the accuracy of the subsidy assessments has to be measured relative to valuations in other sources, in principle the differences in accuracy noted above may have been produced by systematic differences in the accuracy of alternative valuations rather than in the efficacy of the subsidy assessments. It has already been noted that this may have been so in the case of the apparent underassessment of the North Midlands, which may merely reflect the ability of the authorities in the diocese of Lichfield to secure more realistic probate valuations.

On the other hand, this is less likely to have been the case with the other factors. It is improbable that the accuracy of probate valuations varied systematically with the number of people being assessed for the subsidy. Nor is it likely that the goods of richer people, though more completely specified in the inventories, were so much more rigorously valued than those of poorer people as to produce the steep gradient by wealth in the apparent accuracy of the subsidy assessments. And it is improbable that the accuracy of the valuations in both the probate inventories and the feodaries' surveys actually increased over time, thereby generating a spurious apparent decline in the accuracy of the subsidy assessments.

In a comparative study of historical sources, as has been attempted here, there is plenty of room for error, and the results deserve to be regarded with a sceptical eye. Yet the main features of the story of the accuracy of the subsidy assessments which have emerged from this analysis, notably the decline over time and the favouring of the rich over the poor, are consistent with contemporary evidence. Above all, they confirm for the population at large the conclusion that Helen Miller reached in the case of the peerage, namely that the enforcement of the assessment clauses in the subsidy acts was a very different matter under Henry VIII from the farce to which it had degenerated by the second half of Elizabeth's reign.

In principle, the directly assessed subsidy should have given the Tudors a means of raising taxes that kept pace with the rapid inflation which afflicted the sixteenth century. In practice, standards of assessment deteriorated and the yields of the taxes declined, so much so that by the end of Elizabeth's reign parliament was driven to granting 'double subsidies'. There seems no doubt that responsibility for the long drawn-out erosion of the subsidy in the later sixteenth century rests squarely on the commissioners, who supervised the assessments. Their failure to implement the subsidy acts is a mark of their unwillingness to put public obligation before private profit, whether in the narrow sense of their economic interests, or in the wider sense of the local political capital they could make from favourable assessments.

With the subsidies, as with many other matters, the crown was dependent on the leading social classes to implement national legislation; but in this case there was an additional dimension to the problem. The dismal fact is that the very Privy Councillors who were making patriotic speeches in parliament and writing to the commissioners requiring them in the name of the queen to improve the accuracy of the assessments, took care that they themselves were assessed at sums which bore increasingly little relation to their true wealth. For example, Winchester, as Lord Treasurer, the senior financial officer of the realm, persistently reduced his assessment despite his evident affluence, and his successor, Burghley, continued to quote the figure at which he was assessed before he was ennobled.[58] It was not a problem of the centre being unable to command the shires; indeed, despite the rhetoric, in the matter of fraudulent self-interest, the centre was leading the way.

That a combination of personal self-interest and the exigencies of patronage politics conspired to undermine the directly assessed subsidy as a viable form of taxation under the later Tudors should, perhaps, not surprise us. After all, not only had direct assessment been tried in the past and abandoned as unworkable, but it was to be abandoned once more in the mid-seventeenth century and not to be revived again until the end of the eighteenth century. What is remarkable about the Tudor period is not the collapse of direct assessment in the later sixteenth century, but the ability of the crown in the earlier decades of the century to secure the co-operation of the leading social classes in obtaining valuations of incomes and wealth which were more realistic than could normally be achieved.

If the history of taxation in the later sixteenth century illustrated some of the limits of the Tudor state, its history in the reign of Henry VIII shows how political those limits were. In practice the crown could exercise no control over the subsidy commissioners, who were presiding over a system of taxation that was wide open to manipulation. Moreover, in the 1540s, along with others of their class, the commissioners were continually being asked to contribute by way of loans and non-parliamentary levies. Yet such was the political cohesion between the leading social classes and the crown that the former displayed an unparalleled willingness to operate a system of taxation, which, for its sophistication and attention to the principle of distributive justice, was several centuries ahead of its time. But it was a short-lived partnership; it would seem that, by the reign of Elizabeth, the relations between the crown and the political nation were no longer strong enough to hold the forces of individual and social advantage at bay.

Appendix I

Taxation Acts and Dates of Payment

Statute	Original[a]	Exchequer Copy	Year of enactment	Year of payment XV & X	Subsidy
Rot. Parl., VI, pp. 400–1	–	E175/File 5/14	1487	1488 1489	–
Rot. Parl., VI, pp. 401–2	–	E175/File 5/14	1487	–	1488
Rot. Parl., VI, pp. 420–4	–	–	1489[2]	–	1489[b]
Rot. Parl., VI, pp. 437–9	–	–	1490	1490–1[c]	–
7 H. VII c. 11	HL	–	1491	1492 (1)[d], 1492 (II)[d]	–
12 H. VII c. 12	HL	–	1497	1497 (I)[e], 1497 (II)[e]	–
12 H. VII c. 13	HL	–	1497	–	1497[f]
19 H. VII c. 32	HL	–	1504	–	1504
3 H. VIII c. 22	–	E175/File 6/5	1512 (3 H. VIII)	1512 1513 1514	–
4 H. VIII c. 19	–	–	1512 (4 H. VIII)		1513

Statute	Original[a]	Exchequer Copy	Year of enactment	Year of payment XV & X	Subsidy
5 H. VIII c. 17	HL	–	1514	–	1514
6 H. VIII c. 26	–	E175/Roll 70,71	1515 (6 H. VIII)	–	1515
7 H. VIII c. 9	HL	E175/Roll 70, 71	1515 (7 H. VIII)	1517	1516
14 & 15 H. VIII c. 16	–	–	1523	–	1524
					1525
					1526
					1527
26 H. VIII c. 19	HL	E175/Roll 78	1534	1537	1535
					1536
32 H. VIII c. 50	HL	E175/Roll 82	1540	1541	1541
				1542	1542
				1543	
				1544	
34 & 35 H. VIII c. 27	–	–	1543	–	1544
					1545
					1546 ('43)
37 H. VIII c. 25	–	–	1545	1546	1546 ('45)
				1547	1547

Notes:
a Preserved in the House of Lords Records Office.
b Almost identical grants made separately by Commons and Lords.
c First half payable 11 November 1490; second half payable 11 November 1491.
d One XV & X payable 1 April 1492; second XV & X payable 11 November 1492; third XV & X, granted conditionally, payable 11 November 1493, but never levied.
e One XV & X payable 31 May 1497; second XV & X payable 8 November 1497.
f Second subsidy payable 8 November 1497, but never levied.

Appendix II

Chancery Enrolments of Commissions

Date	C60 Fine Rolls	E371 Originalia	C66 Patent Rolls	Discrepancies, etc.
1. To collect fifteenths and tenths				
1488	–	/253 r. 50–6	–	
1489	/299 m. 1307	/254 r. 38–42	/598 m. 28d[a]	
1490–1	–	/255 r. 51–60	–	
1492 (I)	/302 m. 13–18	/257 r. 46–52	/598 m. 28d[a]	
1492 (II)	–	/258 r. 34–42	/598 m. 28d[a]	
1497 (I)	–	/262 r. 46–58	–	
1497 (II)	–	/263 r. 91–5	–	
1512	/323 m. 14–18	/278 r. 60–8	–	
1513	/323 m. 19–23	/278 r. 68–77	–	
1514	/324 m. 17–20	–	–	
1517	/328 m. 14–17	–	–	
1537	/348 m. 1–5	/303 r. 196	–	C60 lacks Hull and Worcester
1541	/352 m. 17–18[b]	/309 r. 57–8	–	
1542	/353B m. [19–20]	–	–	
1543	–	–	–	
1544	–	–	–	
1546	–	–	–	
1547	–	–	–	
2. To supervise the assessment and collection of subsidies				
1488	–	–	/568 m. 5d	
1489	–	–	–	
1497	–	–	–	
1504	–	/269 r. 74	–	
1513	/323 m. 24-33	–	–	
1514	/324 m. 21–6	/279 r. 127–42	–	
1515	/326 m. 20–5	/281 r. 75	–	
1516[c]	–	–	–	

221

Date	C60 Fine Rolls	E371 Originalia	C66 Patent Rolls	Discrepancies, etc.
1524	–	–	/642 m. 13d–20d	
1524a	–	–	/642 m. 20d–22d	
1525	–	–	/645 m. 1d–8d	
1526	–	–	–	
1527	–	–	–	
1535	–	–	–	
1536	–	/302 r. 94	–	
1541	/352 m. 1–16	/309 r. 58	–	C60 lacks King's and Queens's households
1542	/353B m. [1–18]	–	–	
1544	/355 m. 1–end	–	–	
1546 ('43)	–	–	–	
1546 ('45)	–	–	–	
1547	–	–	–	

Notes:
1524a   The Anticipation of part of the subsidy of 1524.
[a] In 1506 the order to the Chancellor of the County Palatine of Lancaster to appoint specified people as collectors was repeated.
[b] A commission was sent to the kinights of the shires and the burgesses of fourteen boroughs to appoint sufficient collectors, to give them full power to levy, and to return their names to chancery before 2 November. The names of those appointed as collectors are enrolled on E371.
[c] This subsidy was to be levied by the commissioners for the previous study.

The table shows that enrolment on the fine rolls was by no means a regular procedure, except in the years 1512–17. Enrolment on the Patent Rolls was very rare; and it is not clear why the four cases recorded were enrolled on these rolls. There were no enrolments of taxation commissions on the Close Rolls. Thus over half the commissions for the levying of taxes were not enrolled in Chancery.

Again over half the commissions are not to be found on the Original Rolls. However, with one exception, all the commissions were enrolled until 1516. It is clear from other sources, such as the Memoranda Rolls, that after 1516 the Exchequer was receiving such enrolments from Chancery on the Originalia, even when they do not appear on the Rolls.[1] The explanation for these omissions is probably that the officers of the Exchequer, by accident or design, omitted to include the Rotuli bearing the taxation commissions when they made up the rolls from the loose Originalia Rotuli sent to them from Chancery.

In the last three or four years of the reign of Henry VIII, enrolment appears to have ceased altogether.

Notes

Notes to Preface

1. It was printed as Schofield, 'Taxation and the political limits of the Tudor state' (1988), ed. Claire Cross, David Loades and J. Scarisbrick.
2. The search has been extended, as necessary, into the reign of Edward VI.
3. Briefly, all the guides, lists and indexes to manuscript collections that are to be found in the library of the Institute of Historical Research, Senate House, London WC1, together with the subject index of the National Register of Archives, have been consulted.

Notes to Chapter 1

1. It continued to be levied in the same standard form until 1623 (21 James I c. 33).
2. Each community made its own decision as to how the tax charge was to be apportioned amongst the inhabitants.
3. Until 1334. For a full study of the fifteenth and tenth and allied taxes from 1290 to 1334, see Willard, *Parl. Taxes, 1290–1334*.
4. Seven grants of subsidies were made as compared to twenty-eight grants of fifteenths and tenths, and of these seven grants only one (1472) was made after 1450. Subsidies: *Rot. Parl.*, III, pp. 546–7, 648–9; IV, pp. 318–19, 389–70, 486–7; V, pp. 172–4; VI, pp. 4–6. Fifteenths and tenths: Ibid., III, pp. 546, 568, 612, 635; IV, pp. 6, 35, 63–4, 95, 117, 336–7, 368, 425, 487, 502; V, pp. 4, 37, 68, 69, 142, 144, 228, 236, 498, 623; VI, pp. 39, 111, 149, 197.
5. For the dates of payment of multiple assessment taxes, see Appendix I.
6. That is, the latest date of payment of the tax by the collectors to the crown, as laid down in the subsidy acts. The assessment of the subsidies often took place some weeks or months before the statutory payment date. For the precise dates of payment and collection see Tables 3.7 and 5.18.
7. It should be obvious that each payment must be treated as a separate subsidy, if only to secure some measure of comparability between different subsidies. Hoskins cites the yield of the 'subsidy' of 1523 as being six times the yield of the subsidy of 1512, by way of proof that the former was 'the most all-embracing tax

since the poll tax of 1377'. But he fails to notice not only that the rates of the two subsidies were different, but also that the 1523 'subsidy' had four payments to the one payment of the 1512 subsidy. Hoskins, 'Early Tudor towns', p. 3.

8. The standard edition of Fortescue's text is *'De Dominio Regali et politico'*. For one summary of the constitutional position, see Chrimes, *Constitutional ideas*.
9. Fortescue, *Works*, pp. 455–8.
10. The actual sums involved in the different items of 'ordinary' and 'extra-ordinary' revenue and expenditure might be 'certain' or 'casual', that is, they might remain fixed or vary from year to year.
11. Fortescue, *Works*, p. 455.
12. Hody, CJ in the Rector of Eddington's case argued in exchequer chamber in 1441. *Year Books*, 19 Henry VI, Pas. pl. 1.
13. Fortescue, *Works*, pp. 458–9. See also *ibid.*, p. 453.
14. *Ibid.*, pp. 461–2.
15. Dietz estimates that the ordinary revenue of the crown in the early part of Henry VII's reign was approximately £52,000 per annum (Dietz, *English Government Finance*, p. 96). The total cost of Henry's diplomatic and military assistance to Anne, Duchess of Brittany, from December 1488 until April 1491, amounted to £108,088.17s.1d. WA 12240.
16. *Rot. Parl.* V, p. 572.
17. This short act was the second to be passed by the first parliament of Richard III's reign. *Stat. Realm* II, p. 478.
18. This is true both of benevolences and of loans which were later declared to be unrepayable. Benevolences: 1491: *Great Chronicle*, p. 245; 1544: *LP*, XX, pt. II, App. 4, §2; 1546: *LP*, XXI, pt. 1, 844. Loans: 1522: *LP*, IV, 214; 1542: *LP*, XVII, 194.
19. HLRO Original bill.

Notes to Chapter 2

1. 1497, 1523 and 1545.
2. No taxes were granted by the parliaments of 1485, 1495, 1510 and 1536. See Table 2.1.
3. The exception was the parliament of 1491. In 1523 the debate over the granting of subsidies extended well into the second session.
4. Hall, *Chronicle*, pp. 785–6.
5. For the extension of the activities and competence of parliament from 1529, see Elton, *Tudor Constitution*, pp. 228–30.
6. *Handbook Brit. Chron.*, pp. 497, 521–30.
7. No evidence is available for the grants of 1487, 1497, 1504, 1512 (4 Henry VIII), 1514, 1534.
8. The grant was made on 27 June (Hall, *Chronicle*, p. 657), and the session ended on 29 July (*Handbook Brit. Chron.*, p. 535).
9. The grant was concluded by the Commons on 15 March (*LJ* I, 218), and the session ended on 12 May (*Handbook Brit. Chron.*, p. 535).
10. 1490: dissolution same day as grant. *Rot. Parl.*, VI, p. 439; 1515; (7 H VIII) ?1 day after grant. *LJ*, I, p. 56; 1540: dissolution same day as grant. *LJ*, I, pp. 161–2.

11. 1489: prorogation same day as grant. *Rot. Parl.*,VI, p. 424; 1491: prorogation same day as grant. *Rot. Parl.*, VI, p. 444; 1512 (3 H VIII) 1 day after grant. *LJ*, I, p. 17; 1515 (6 H VIII) 3 days after grant. *LJ*, I, p. 41; 1545 prorogation 4 days after grant. *LJ*, I, p. 277.

12. The ceremony of presentation was held on many occasions in the fifteenth century, references as in p. [3] n. [4]. The first five grants of Henry VII's reign were presented in this manner, *Rot. Parl.*, VI, pp. 400, 401, 420, 438, 442.

13. No ceremonial presentation is recorded after 1492. Grants continued to be made in the last few days of the session, although not on the last day itself, until 1515.

14. 1540: *LJ*, I, pp. 161–2. In 1545 the grant was made just before Christmas, when parliament was prorogued until the beginning of Hilary term, 1547.

15. *Great Chronicle*, pp. 274–5; 12 Henry VII c. 12, 13.

16. *CSP Sp*, suppl (1513–42), 99.

17. Secret instructions to the commissioners, BM Cotton, Cleop. F. VI, ff. 316–20. For the timing of the commissions, Hall, *Chronicle*, p. 630.

18. CLRO Journals 12, f. 213.

19. *LP*, XIX pt. 2, 689.

20. Parliament assembled on 23 November 1545 (*Handbook Brit. Chron.*, p. 535). The Lord Chancellor referred to the costs of resisting the French in his opening speech; and taxation, together with other matters was discussed thereafter daily. *CSP Sp*, VIII, 174.

21. *LP*, II, 1364; VI, 299 (ix).

22. SP 2/Q/29–30.

23. *LP*, XV, 195, 321, 322, 438, 502.

24. 1532: SP 2/Q/29–30; 1534: *LP*, Add I, 899, SP 1/238, f. 203; 1540: *LP*, XV, 502, see also the earlier, and abortive draft, ascribed to 1539: *LP*, XIV pt. 1, 869.

25. Military expenditure was cited in the preamble to the act of 1529 which released the king from any obligation to repay the loans of 1522–3. Great emphasis was laid in the preamble on the fact that the loan money was only used for war purposes 'as doth evidently appere by the accomptes of the same [the king]', and thus might legitimately be termed taxation, and left unrepaid. 21 Henry VIII c. 24.

26. 26 Henry VIII c. 19.

27. *Ibid.*

28. 32 Henry VIII c. 50.

29. 34 & 35 Henry VIII c. 27. The use of the phrase 'politicque bodie' to mean parliament deserves noticing, since doubt about this had been expressed by Elton in *Tudor Constitution*, p. 320. Later in this same preamble the Commons and Lords are referred to as 'the king's Mates most loving and obedient subjectes assembled in this present parliament, being his civile and politicque bodie of this realm.' In addition to Henry's reference in his speech on Ferrer's case, again in 1543 (Holinshed, *Chronicles*, III, p. 826), there is Tunstall's statement in his sermon at the opening of the 1523 parliament that 'thys place ... ys the politike body of thys roialme'. SP 6/13/1.

30. The preamble to an act of the following year, releasing the king from any obligation to repay the loan of 1542, relied upon the conventional eulogy of the king's government together with a summary of military costs incurred by the crown. The statement that it was the Commons' duty 'to honour ayde maynteyne

and supporte his Majestie in all his just quarrelles' marks no advance upon Fortescue. Possibly the delicate nature of the matter in hand induced the crown to moderate its claims on the duties of its subjects. 35 Henry VIII c. 12.

31. 37 Henry VIII c. 25.

32. *Ibid.*

33. *Ibid.*

34. If Van Der Delft's observation that parliament in 1545 was ready to grant taxation 'owing to the hopes they have of peace', were correct, then one would have expected some reference in the preamble to the possibility of victory. *CSP Sp*, VIII, 174.

35. In fact parliament did oppose the grant of two feudal aids in 1504, not because they were illegal, for they admitted that they might be levied 'according to the auncient Lawes of this land'; but because of the 'gret vexacions trouble and inquietnes' that would arise in levying them. 19 Henry VII c. 32.

36. *Rot. Parl.*, V, pp. 172–4; VI, pp. 4–6, 149–53.

37. *Rot. Parl.*, VI, pp. 420–4.

38. Henry VII c. 11; 12 Henry VII c. 12, 13. In 1491 a third fifteenth and tenth was granted to be levied if the king stayed abroad longer than eight months. This was an additional grant proposed by the crown in its original grant, and not a parliamentary restriction of an agreed grant.

39. 'ye communys be not yt gred of that sum nother by their wylles that ye king sholde goo over'. *Trevelyan Papers*, pt. III, pp. 8–9. Parliament granted three fifteenths and tenths and a subsidy, the total gross yield of which was £126,745.

40. £160,000. 5 Henry VIII c. 17.

41. Except where otherwise indicated, this account is based on Hall, *Chronicle*, pp. 655–7. The most recent analysis of Wolsey's attempted negotiation with the Commons is in Guy, 'Wolsey and the Parliament of 1523'.

42. Letter written to Lord Surrey, Ellis, *Letters*, 1st ser., I, pp. 219–21.

43. According to Hall (*Chronicle*, pp. 656–7), these were 4s/£1 on lands and goods of £20 and above, 2s/£1 from £2 to £20, and a payment of 8d from those with lands and goods worth less than £2. These were to be paid over two years, at half the rates each year. The letter to Lord Surrey (Hall) differs in that lands and goods from £2 to £20 were to be taxed at 2s 8d/£1, and those with lands and goods less than £2 were to pay 1s 4d. Compare Wolsey's original demand of an overall rate of 4s/£1.

44. Hall, *Chronicle*, p. 657.

45. His appointment dates from 1521. *DNB*.

46. From 9 December 1503 until June 1513. Richardson, *Tudor Chamber Administration*, app. V, p. 9.

47. Since no gentlemen opposed the proposal, Hussey's suggestion may have been a well-timed manoeuvre. On the other hand, most of the gentlemen may have thought it inexpedient to come out into open opposition on a vote, and have left this, in vain, to the burgesses.

48. *Handbook Brit. Chron.*, p. 535.

49. This is scarcely enough evidence to warrant Brewer's remark that one half of the Commons was prepared to impeach the other half, *LP*, III, Introd., p. ccliii. Hall's classification of the opposing parties into knights of the shires and 'Commons'

raises difficulties. Hall himself (*Chronicle*, p. 657) says that the two sides were evenly matched in numbers; but there were far more members sitting for boroughs than there were for the shires, just as there were far more gentlemen than true burgesses. The division was probably between those who thought they would be liable to taxation on their lands, and those who thought they would be liable on their goods. Neale, *House of Commons*, pp. 146–8.

50. Hall, *Chronicle*, p. 657.
51. 3s/£1 on lands and goods worth £50 and above, at 1s/£1 for three years; 2s/£1 on lands worth up to £50, and on goods worth from £20 to £50, at 1s/£1 for two years; 1s/£1 on goods worth from £2 to £20; at 6d/£1 for two years; 4d payment in each of two years by those with lands worth £2 or wages at least £1.
52. In one speech, attributed by *LP* to Cromwell, it was argued that an invasion of France would be inadvisable. But an invasion of Scotland was proposed instead. *LP*, III, 2958, Introd., pp. cclviii–cclxii.
53. Lord Herbert, *Henry VIII*, pp. 134–6.
54. Commission: *LP*, III, 2484; Instructions: BM Cotton, Cleop. F. VI, ff. 316–20; Accounts: SP 1/234, f. 226, BM Cotton Cleop. F. VI, f. 340.
55. Letter to Lord Surrey; Ellis, *Letters*, 1st Ser., I, p. 219–21.
56. *Ibid.*
57. *Ibid.*
58. Hall, *Chronicle*, p. 656.
59. 'It was proved, that honest apparell of the commodities of this Realme, aboundance of plate, and honest viandes, were profitable to the realme, and not prodigall'. *Ibid.*
60. Preambles in general increase in length and explicitness with the Reformation parliament. This has been noted by Elton, *EHR*, lxiv (1949), pp. 178, n. 2. This growth is unlikely to have been spontaneous; the ministers of the crown were probably well aware of the propaganda value of the preambles.
61. *LJ*, I, p. 135. This lack of opposition was also noted by Holinshed, who reported the taxes as having been 'freelie granted without contradictions' (Holinshed, *Chronicles*, III, p. 815).
62. *LJ*, I, pp. 161–2.
63. *LJ*, I, p. 275.
64. *CSP Sp*, VIII, 174.
65. SP 1/230, f. 117.
66. SP 2/Q/29–30; SP 1/238, f. 203.
67. SP 1/159, ff. 33–46.
68. For references to the bills as enacted, see Appendix I.
69. Hall, *Chronicle*, p. 656; Lord Herbert, *Henry VIII*, pp. 134–5.
70. *LJ*, I, pp. 216–17.
71. *LJ*, I, pp. 214–15, 217–18.
72. *LJ*, I, pp. 274–80.
73. This is particularly clear with the clerical subsidy acts where the distinction between the original convocation grant and the clauses added by parliament is obvious.
74. Except that the act of 1504 was almost identical to that of 1497.
75. These subsidies are discussed more fully below, pp. 74–9.

76. This incorporation occurred mainly in the acts of 1514 and 1515 (6 Henry VIII).
77. Except in 1540 when three clauses favourable to the crown were added. They concerned the liability of orphans, the liability of aliens, and the cancellation of letters patent of exemption from taxation.
78. The five new clauses are discussed more fully on pages 90–2.
79. The Commons journals began in 1547. *CJ*, I, 1ff.
80. Before the parliament of 1536, Lords journals only survive for the parliament of 1510, the 1st session of the parliament of 1512, the parliament of 1515, and the 6th session of the parliament of 1529.
81. The bills for the following years are headed 'Soit baillé aux Seigneurs': 1497, 1504, 1512 (3 Henry VIII), 1514, 1515 (7 Henry VIII), 1534, and 1540. Appendix 1, HLRO originals. Otherwise from the journals: 1515 (6 Henry VIII); *LJ*, I, p. 41; 1523: Hall, *Chronicle*, p. 655–7; 1543: *LJ* I, p. 214; and 1545: *LJ*, I, p. 274.
82. Hall, *Chronicle*, p. 657.
83. In 1543 a proviso concerning the assessment of a suburb of Stamford was added in the Lords, *LJ*, I, p. 217. In 1545 the Lords returned the bill to the Commons after a first reading 'a quibusdam mendis reformanda', *LJ*, I, p. 275.
84. *Rot. Parl.*, as cited on p. 223, n. 4.
85. *Rot. Parl.*, III, pp. 546–7; VI, pp. 4–6, 420–4.
86. *Ibid.* The absence of any Commons Journal means that the critical question of whether the bills of the Lords' grants were read and passed in the Commons cannot be decided.
87. The Rector of Eddington's case, *Year Books*, 19 Henry VI, Pas. pl. 1.
88. *Year Books*, 21 Edward IV, Mich. pl. 6.
89. *Rot. Parl.*, VI, pp. 400–2, 420–4, 437–9, 444; *LJ*, I, pp. 161–2.
90. It is misleading to characterise late medieval taxation as being granted solely by the 'estate' that was to pay it, for Parliament was in a special position, because it could inflict taxes on aliens and on the clergy, who were underrepresented in that body.
91. 34 & 35 Henry VIII c. 27; 37 Henry VIII c. 25.
92. *Rot. Parl.*, as p. 223, n. 4 beginning at IV, p. 425, and omitting V, p. 68.
93. 1487, 1489, 1490, 1491, 1497 (c. 12), 1512 (3 Henry VIII), 1512 (4 Henry VIII), 1515 (6 Henry VIII), 1515 (7 Henry VIII) (part), 1523. See Appendix I.
94. Except for one revival in 1540, *LJ*, I, pp. 161–2.
95. 12 Henry VII, c. 13; 19 Henry VII c. 32.
96. 5 Henry VIII c. 17. This form of enactment by the king in the text of the act made a further royal assent superfluous. None has been found.
97. 7 Henry VIII c. 9, HLRO original.
98. 3 Henry VIII c. 22; 4 Henry VIII c. 19.
99. 12 Henry VII c. 12; 7 Henry VIII c. 9.
100. *Year Books*, 7 Henry VII, Trin. pl. 1; *Year Books*, 11 Henry VII, Trin. pl. 10. The judges probably based their opinions on the account of parliamentary procedure as it has been stated by officers of parliament in *Year Books*, 33 Henry VI, Pas. pl. 8.
101. A suggestion by counsel that all acts should bear the motto 'le Roy le veult' was dismissed by the observation that many undoubted acts lacked this. *Year Books*, 7 Henry VII, Trin. pl. 1.
102. 1514, 1543, 1545.

103. *Rot. Parl.*, VI, p. 402.
104. *Rot. Parl.*, VI, pp. 424, 438–9. Since the Lord Chancellor usually expressed the gratitude of the king on these occasions, probably here too he used the 'N're Sgn' le Roy remerciant' formula.
105. *Rot. Parl.*, VI, p. 444.
106. 12 Henry VII c. 13, HLRO original. This original is sewn to the foot of the original of 12 Henry VII c. 12, granting simultaneously two fifteenths and tenths. This latter act has no form of assent, unless the sign manual be held to extend to it also.
107. *Rot. Parl.*, VI, p. 534.
108. 3 Henry VII c. 22, HLRO original. Here again the traditional form lingered longer in connection with fifteenths and tenths.
109. Except 4 Henry VII c. 19, granting both a Fifteenth and Tenth and a subsidy, which had both forms, *LJ* (RP), I, p. xxxi. Otherwise 1515 (6, and 7 Henry VII): E175/Rolls 70, 71; 1523: *LJ* (RP), I, p. xc; 1534: *Ibid.*, p. ccxliv.
110. *LJ*, I, p. 162.

Notes to Chapter 3

1. *Rot. Parl.* III, 546–7, 648–9; IV, 318–19, 389–70, 486–7; V, 172–4, 497–8; VI, 4–6, 111–19. For a somewhat sketchy discussion of these taxes see Dietz, *English Government Finance*, 14–15. The text refers, of course, only to direct taxes on personal wealth, and not to indirect taxes on commodities. Alien poll taxes were granted six times before 1485: *Rot. Parl.* V, 6, 38, 144, 236; VI, 197–8, 401–2.
2. *Rot. Parl.* III, 546, 568, 612, 635; IV, 6, 35, 64, 95, 117, 336, 337, 368, 369, 425, 487, 502; V, 4, 37, 68, 69, 142, 144, 228, 236, 498, 623; VI, 39, 111, 149, 197.
3. *Rot. Parl.* IV, 409; V, 498; VI, 149–53.
4. *Rot. Parl.* VI, 151.
5. For the early history of the fifteenth and tenth, 1290–1334, see Willard, *Parl. Taxes 1290–1334*.
6. *Ibid.*, 11–12.
7. *Ibid.*, 134.
8. *Rot. Parl.* IV, 425.
9. *Ibid.*, as p. 61, n 2. IV, 425–V, 623, excepting V, 497–8.
10. *Ibid.*, V, 68
11. Where the act merely referred to customary allowances, the dependence on 1467–8 may be traced through the collectors' accounts in the Exchequer. E359/39, 43 *passim.*
12. 26 Henry VIII c. 19; E359/43, 26 H VIII, *passim*: 'sicut continetur in Rotulo Compotorum de Taxis de anno viij^{mo} Henrici vj^{ti}ac in diuersis aliis Rotulis de Taxis de diuersis aliis annis precedentibus'.
13. This appears to be a Tudor innovation; c.p. *Rot. Parl., loc. cit.* in p. 61, n. 2. The act of 1487 made no provision for the nomination of collectors, *Rot Parl.* VI, 400–1. The acts of 1497 and 1512 omit to specify where or when the collectors' names are to be certified, 12 Henry VII c. 12; 3 Henry VII c. 22.
14. 7 Henry VII c. 9.

15. E371/303 r. 196. Two such commissions were sent, one to the mayor and sheriffs of Kingston upon Hull, and one to the bailiffs of Worcester. In the latter case the two collectors originally appointed had died.

16. C60/353B m [19–20]. The collectors were notified of their appointment not by the usual commission and instructions; but by the sheriffs acting upon a writ of 'scire facias'.

17. The commissions were dated 4 August 1540, C60/352 m. 17–18. Parliament was dissolved on 24 July, *LJ* I, 163.

18. C60/352 m. 17–18; E371/309 r. 56. The usual instructions concerning the levy of the tax were omitted from these commissions.

19. After an extensive search, I have been unable to discover any certificates of appointments to collectorship of the fifteenth and tenth.

20. On the Originalia Rolls (E371). The individual commissions may also have been sent to the Exchequer. See pp. 33–5. For the somewhat haphazard enrolment of the commissions in Chancery, see Appendix II.

21. See p. 65.

22. C60 and E371 as in Appendix II; E359/39, 43 *passim*. Lincoln received a commission because its statutory exemption ceased in 1540. From 1542 separate commissions were sent to Kingston upon Hull and the 'comitatus' of Kingston upon Hull. In 1543 a commission was sent to Winchester, and in 1547 a commission was sent to Bedford.

23. And for wards, or groups of wards, within Lincoln.

24. It is doubtful whether a more detailed analysis of the many hundreds of collectors appointed between 1485 and 1547 would yield anything more precise than this. The names of the collectors are most conveniently found in the Chancery enrolments as in Appendix II. Where these are deficient, the names may be obtained from the collectors' accounts, E359/39, 43.

25. 32 Henry VIII c. 50; 37 Henry VII c. 25. Contrast the minimum qualifications required in 1439, when collectors were to be able to spend £5 a year in their county, *Rot. Parl.* V, 25.

26. Under the revenue law of the period the collectors were responsible for the tax due from their area to the full extent of their personal goods and estate.

27. The early Tudor form of the commissions was regularly used from 1401. CFR IV to XXII, *passim*. For early Tudor enrolled commissions, see Appendix II.

28. From this point the style 'vill' will be used to denote the smallest area upon which a fixed sum was assessed in 1334, and was levied at every fifteenth and tenth thereafter. The documents almost without exception refer to this unit as a 'villata', although a few local synonyms such as 'tything' or 'parish' are to be found. In towns receiving separate commissions the equivalent of the vill was usually the ward; but for convenience, in this study the style 'vill' will be used to include both the rural vill and the urban ward.

29. For enrolled commissions, see Appendix II. The commissions for the levying of directly assessed subsidies specified accompanying copies of the acts, which gave instructions to the commissioners for the levying of the tax.

30. Staffordshire possessed such a book, *c.* 1489: 'librum in custodia Willelmi Harper unius custodium pacis domini Regis remanentem pro utilitate inhabitancium totius comitatus predicti'. BM Stowe, 880, f. 45.

31. For books of reference see E164/7, containing the assessment for every vill for the fifteenth and tenth of 1415. Some entries are marginally annotated 'examinatur cum particulis de anno viij^{mo} Edwardi tercij'. Herefs., Bucks., Notts., and Nottingham are missing; Westmoreland is included. Interlineations in the calendar at the front of the volume noting royal events extend until the proclamation of Edward VI as king [1547]. In 1500 the Barons of the Exchequer ordered copies to be made of six worn out reference books, viz. two books of statutes, two books of manors, castles, and knights' fees, 'le Regester de taxacone' (Canterbury and York provinces, 1291) and the 'liber de taxacione de xvme et xme, as established for 1334. The volume E164/7 is clearly neither the worn out original nor the copy made in 1500. The collectors' enrolled accounts (E359) were kept in the Exchequer and referred to as 'Rotuli de Taxis'.

32. They are included in the artificial class E179. Other aspects of the form and the hands of these documents show them definitely to be products of the Exchequer; and preclude the possibility that they were compiled by the collectors. See especially E179/74/174; /71/143; /82/202.

33. For example E179/78/108–16; /97/200–13.

34. Some 'particule compoti' lack the third column of the net sum due. See E179/81/119.

35. E179/73/142; /104/129; /122/112; /133/127; /136/348–9; /141/123; /161/209; /165/115; /166/142; /189/166.

36. For example E179/81/120; /82/165, 202; /99/286.

37. The existence of separate commissions and 'particule compoti' shows that stuffing was not a general practice.

38. These were probably clerks in the king's remembrancer's department. All matters concerning casual accountants prior to their appearance for account were the concern of the king's remembrancer. The precedent book containing the 1334 charges is preserved amongst the records of the king's remembrancer. E164/7.

39. E359/39, 43, *passim*; E401/975–1167, *passim*.

40. 1491; 7 Henry VII c. 11. The acts of 1497 and 1512 increased the number of justices of the peace to two; 12 Henry VII c. 12, 3 Henry VIII c. 22. Another act of 1512 required that one of these justices should be of the quorum; 4 Henry VII c. 19. The act of 1515 allowed the individual to complain directly to the justices instead of through a local officer; 7 Henry VII c. 9.

41. It is unlikely that informal proceedings of this nature found their way into the records of local government.

42. For enrolled commissions, see Appendix II.

43. For example, class A may be more successful than class B at resisting tax collectors; hence more actions against class A are brought in the courts than are against class B. From the legal records alone it would obviously be unwise to conclude that class A were in fact more liable to taxation than class B.

44. CFR XXII, 225; *Medieval Latin Word List*, 'prepositus'.

45. 1537: Ilford, Essex, REQ2/2/50; Malden, Surrey, E111/16; Lakenham, Norfolk, C1/1037/18–20. 1542: Wendover, Bucks., E159/321 Recorda P.r.56., Cornilo Hundred, Kent, E159/321 Recorda P.r.35., Maidstone Hundred, Kent, E1. 59/322 Records T.r.40. In the last two instances the constables of the hundred were responsible for the assessment for every vill within the hundred.

46. 1537: Lydney, Glos., SP1/142 f.46. Here the collectors collected the individual contributions themselves.
47. 1542: Burford, Oxon, St.Ch.2/7/51.
48. 1537: Plymouth, Devon, SP1/125 f.45. 'yn his Guyldhall with hys bretherne assessying ther quyndecym'.
49. Wendover, Cornilo Hundred, Maidstone Hundred, as cited above.
50. Those entrusted with the local levy of the fifteenth and tenth were to 'leuare' the money due from the vill. The commission avoids any precise word such as 'assidere'. 'Leuare' is as imprecise as the English verb 'to raise'. *Shorter Oxford Dictionary*, 'raise' III, 8. For enrolments of commissions, see Appendix II.
51. See Table 3.2. Similarly outlying hamlets sometimes bore a fixed proportion of the total vill charge: Stepney, E159/322 Cssns T.r–; Wendover (disputed), E159/322 Cssns H.r–; E111/42E.
52. For enrolment of commissions, see Appendix II.
53. 1492(II) – Langton, Oxon., E159/269 Recorda H.r.33d; 1512 – Islington, Middx. E; 159/294 Recorda M.r.25–6; 1541 – Barnstaple, Devon, St.Ch.2/3/289–302.
54. 1488 Sunbury, Middx. E159/264 Recorda T.r.11d; 1512 Crowchestoke, Norfolk C1/364/32; c. 1541–4 Luton, Beds. C1/776/36–7; 1542 Burford, Oxon. St.Ch.2/7/51–71; 1542 Willoughby, Kesteven. St.Ch.2/32/99; 1547 Wendover, Bucks. E111/2E.
55. St.Ch.2/7/51–71.
56. Johnson, *Surrey Rec. Soc.*, XI, lxxv.
57. Dietz, *English Government Finance*, 14.
58. That a subdivision on to parcels of land may have 'illegally' occurred fairly early is suggested by Tait, *Chetham Soc. N.S. 83* (1924) xxxi, n. 1: 'Professor Willard has noticed a tendency in this direction soon after the standardising of the tax in 1334'. Willard indeed makes such an observation, *Engl. Hist Rev.* xxx (1915), p. 71, but only provides one satisfactory example. But the point remains that the assertions of Johnson and Dietz, not being based on any evidence, are false inferences from the standardisation of 1334.
59. C193/1 f.118.b.
60. Jacob, *Law Dictionary*, 'chattels'.
61. For enrolled commissions, see Appendix II.
62. 7 Henry VII c. 11. Only slight variations in the wording occur in the other acts.
63. 1542: Nursling, Hants., E111/15; 1546–7: Betteshanger, Kent, E159/326 Cssns P.r–.
64. E111/23, 42D.
65. E111/42D.
66. E159/326 Cssns M.r–.
67. There is one case of a recognisance being given in the Exchequer, voidable if the recognizor paid the contribution assessed on him by the Barons, E159/324 Recogn M.5– (1537). In another instance, in 1546, the Barons ordered a reassessment in Dowsthorp, Northants, following upon a complaint of extortionate assessment, E159/325 Recorda H.r.29. In neither case was there any question of altering the basis of the assessment.
68. See Table 3.9. The exception is for land in Erith and Plumstead, Kent, for which the collectors secured exoneration on account of flooding. The local inquisition

returned that the land was traditionally assessed at 1 ½d per acre, E368/315 SVC P.r.4.

69. E368/265 SVC M.r.11. The collectors were only exonerated from the £1 0s 0d that they originally claimed.

70. E368/331 Recorda T.r.31, inquisition of 1553, Bedington Park, Surrey. The inquisition of 1547, concerning lands in Ampthill, Beds., used a similar phraseology, E368/323 SVC M.r.5. The exonerations of collectors for religious houses exempted by prerogative grant were made 'pro porcions bonorum et catallorum suorum [the religious community] in diuersis Villis et hundredis comitatus predicti'. E359/39, 48 *passim*.

71. But one form of a writ of supersedeas from Chancery calling in a commission, and referring to the assessment of goods and lands has been found. This does not affect the point that in theory assessments were to be made on bona et catalla, but that in practice lands also were assessed. C193/1 f.118d.

72. As at Godalming, 1488: E368/265 SVC M.r.11.

73. C193/1 f.118. In 1543 the Privy Council wrote to the president and Council of the Marches in favour of one Horton 'being inhabitant wythin the Cite of London and neverthelesse ceassed for the xv in the sayde Marches' *APC*, I, 124.

74. E159/294 Recorda M.r.25–6.

75. 1541 Barnstable suburbs, Devon: St.Ch.2/3/289–302; 1542 Chessington, Surrey: E111/16; 1543 Stepney, Middx: E159/322 Cssns T.r–; 1544 Downesell, Essex: E159/323 Cssns M.r–; 1544 Boscombe, Wilts: E159/323 Cssns H.r–; 15467 Betteshanger, Kent E159/326 Cssns P.r–.

76. This is especially clear in the case of farmers of lands held by religious houses, C1/773/70–1. Sometimes the owners of the lands refunded their tenants for the money paid by them towards the fifteenth and tenth; Chessington and Betteshanger, as above.

77. *c.* 1541–4 Luton, Beds, C1/776/36–7.

78. 1542, St.Ch.2/32/99.

79. 1537 Lakenham, Norfolk C1/1037/18–20. In the latter part of the fourteenth century the inhabitants of Colchester twice assessed 'forinceci' and those non-residents who used the markets, *Colchester Red Paper Book*, 7.12.

80. Non-residence was cited in a Star Chamber suit as grounds for exemption. It is not known if this claim was successful. St.Ch.2/32/99.

81. Somewhat similar was the customary payment of the tax charged on the hamlet of Alcyter, Dorset, out of the common box of Shaftesbury, C1/943/15.

82. Jordan, *Philanthropy in England*, 276; *Charities of London*, 197. *Rural Charities*, 50, 295.

83. Jordan, *Rural Charities*, 143–4.

84. E111/16, 42E; E159/317 Recorda T.r.2,23; /320 Recorda P.r.1d; /321 Recorda P.r.35; /322 Recorda P.r.55, 56, T.r.40; C1/960/3; /1037/18–20; REQ2/2/50; St.Ch.2/7/51–71; SP1/142 f.46.

85. E111/42E; St.Ch.2/7/51–71. In one case the collectors collected the individual contributions themselves, Sp1/142 f.46.

86. By 43 Henry III c. 15 and 52 Henry III c. 23 it was illegal for anyone to distrain 'extra feodum suum neque in regia aut comuni strata, nisi Domino Regi et ministris suis'. For a convenient summary of the law of distress between private

parties, see Jacob, *Law Dictionary*, 'Distress'; Cowell, *Law Dictionary*, 'Distress', and Coke, *1st Institute*. The law relating to distress for the king's debts is not discussed by Jacob and Cowell. Coke notices some of the statutes mentioned below; but adds nothing material in his commentary on them, *2nd Institute*, 106–7, 130–3.

87. Magna Carta c. 9.

88. 51 Henry III stat. 4. The clauses concerning distress are headed 'Districciones de Scaccario' and apear to have been inserted between articles 13 and 14 of the 'Estatuz', *Stat. Realm*, I, 197. This clause, but excepting sheep, also appears in the *Articuli super Cartas*, 28 Edward I c. 12, *Stat. Realm*, I, 139; and both confirm Exchequer practice as described in the *Dialogus de Scaccario*, 111–12.

89. *Dialogus de Scaccario*, 110-11.

90. Articuli super Cartas, *loc. cit.*

91. 51 Henry III stat. 4: 'Districciones de Scaccario'.

92. *Ibid.*, and *Articuli super Cartas*, *loc. cit.*

93. 51 Henry III stat. 4: 'Districciones de Scaccario'.

94. *Articuli super Cartas*, *loc. cit.*, but only 'jesques a un jour deinz le jour le visconte'.

95. In private distress, where sale was illegal, this was the only purpose.

96. For successful distresses see *LP* XIII, pt. I, 966; REQ2/10/244; C1/1037/18–20.

97. A wrongful recovery of a distress was known as a 'rescue'. See Jacob, *Law Dictionary*, 'Replevin', 'Rescue'.

98. Although collectors were exempt by statue from all fees in the Exchequer, 'concernyng [their] accompte and euery parte therof', it is doubtful whether these proceedings would have been considered as falling within the terms of this exemption.

99. See Table 3.4.

100. For example, E159/266 Recorda P.r.15.

101. Different weapons, combinations of weapons, extents and forms of violence, injuries, abuse and threats were alleged.

102. See Glossary.

103. Return days in the Exchequer, see E202/275-296, *passim*.

104. 1517 Kent: E159/297 Recorda M.r.10d; 1537 Dover: E159/320 Recorda P.r.63; 1537 Middx: E159/317 Recorda H.r.9; 1537 Staffs: E159/317 Recorda P.r.18d; 1542 Bucks: E159/322 Recorda P.r.56; 1542 Kent: E159/321 Recorda P.r.35; 1544 Bucks: E159/322 Recorda H.r.43 – the writ of subpoena was served on the defendant by the plaintiff himself.

105. Staffordshire, as above. On another occasion the defendants appeared, but did not reappear after an adjournment. A writ of attachment was issued, Buckinghamshire (1542), as above.

106. 1537 Staffordshire: E159/317 Recorda P.r.18d, T.r.23. Both these cases arose out of the same dispute.

107. The sheriffs' answers are generally noted on the Memoranda Rolls (E159). The original write with the sheriffs' endorsements survive in E202/175–296. In one case the sheriff returned that his attachment had been rescued, E159/274 Recorda T.r.4d.

108. The Memoranda Rolls describe their appearance: 'Tamen ad eundem diem inuenti sunt in Curie'.

109. 1492(II) Norfolk: E159/270 Recorda P.r.12d; 1537 Somerset: E159/318 Recorda M.r.32; 1541 Bucks E159/320 Recorda P.r.1d.
110. Norfolk and Buckinghamshire, as above.
111. In such cases the enrolment on the Memoranda Roll ends 'vlterior execucio vt in ligula breuium'. The original writs, preserved on their original Exchequer files, are extremely numerous, dirty, and awkward to handle. A few cases have been followed through several years, but without any result. A full search for all the 62 unaccounted for cases would be a very lengthy undertaking, and unlikely to yield much information. E202/175–296.
112. The fees payable in 1562 are given in Jessop, *The Oeconomy of the Fleete*, 152 (table facing). The somewhat lax regulations of the prison are printed *Ibid.*, 155–9.
113. 1488 Kent: 5 days (E159/266 Recorda M.r.23d); 1488 Worcs: 5 days (E159/264 Recorda T.r.16); 1492(I) Warwickshire: 10 days (E159/268 Recorda P.r.7d); 1514 Shropshire: 4 months (E159/293 Recorda H.r.1d) – awaiting empanellment of jury; 1542 Bucks: 2 days (E159/322 Recorda P.r.56).
114. For forms of defence, see Jacob, *Law Dictionary*, 'Defence'.
115. 1512 Wilts E159/292 Recorda H.r.19: 'petunt pro transgressis predictis ex Gracia Curie ad racionabiles fines cum Domino Rege in premissis faciendas admitti. Et admissi sunt'.
116. 'se ponunt super patriam': 1488: Worcs. E159/264 Recorda T.r.16: 1492(I): Warw. E159/268 Recorda P.r.7d 1537: Staffs. E159/317 Recorda P.r.18d, T.r.2,23: 1541: Bucks. E159/320 Recorda P.r.1d; 1541: Kent E159/320 Recorda P.r.34. 1542: Kent E159/321 P.r.35; 1544: Bucks. E159/322 Recorda H.r.93.
117. Worcs., War., Kent and Bucks. (1544) as above.
118. 'sed ut parcantur misis et expensis super capcionem Inquisitionis inter Dominum Regem et ipsos [AB and Cd] in premissis capiendam ijdem [AB and CD] petunt ex gratia Curie se ad rationabilem finem cum Domino Rege admitti'.
119. The fines levied are sometimes given in the main enrolment of the cases on the Recorda of the Memoranda Rolls; but more often they appear in the section 'Fines, manucapciones, Dies dati, respectus visus etc' for the term in which they were levied. This may be in a different roll from main enrolment which is filed under the term in which the original information was laid. But the main enrolment always carries a refrence to where the fine may be found: 1488: E159/266 Fines H.r–; 1489: E159/266 Fines P.r–, T.r–; /269 Fines M.r–, H.r–; /274 Fines H.r–; 1490–1: E159/ 267 Fines M.r–; /268 Fines T.r–; /269 Fines P.r–; /271 Fines P.r–; 1492(I): E159/269 Fines P.r–, T.r–; /271 Fines P.r–; /272 Fines T.r–, M.r–; 1492(II): E159/270 Recorda H.r.11, 11d; Fines P.r–; /271 Recorda M.r.13; /271 Fines P.r–, M.r–; /273 Fines M.r–; /274 Fines T.r–, M.r–; 1497(II): E159/275 Fines T.r–, M.r–; /276 Fines M.r–; /280 Fines M.r–, H.r–; /281 M.r–; 1512: E159–293 Fines P.r–; 1537: E159/ 320 Recorda P.r.63; 1541: E159/320 Recorda P.r.34; 1542: E159/322 Recorda P.r.56. In five cases the amount of the fine is not known: E159/264 Recorda T.r.11d, 16; /265 Recorda T.r.24d; /268 Recorda M.r.13; /269 Recorda H.r.13.
120. 'Idcirco versus ipsos pro premissis non fiat hic vlterior execucio'.
121. 1514 Shropshire: E159/293 Recorda H.r.1d; /297 Recorda H.r.3; 1517 Kent: E159/ 297 Recorda M.r.10d; 1547 Shropshire: E159/326 Recorda T.r.25, 25d. The effect of acts of general pardon is discussed on p. 156, n. 78.
122. The records of the Courts of King's Bench and Common Pleas could not be

searched on account of their vast bulk. Unfortunately contemporary docket rolls give only the form and not the substance of each action. IND 1–9; 1325–1337.

123. The number of cases brought before Courts other than the Exchequer may have been higher than this, for whereas the cases in the Exchequer are recorded on a continuous series of Memoranda Rolls (E159; E368), record of cases in Chancery, Star Chamber and Requests is dependent upon the survival of the original bills, answers, depositions and interrogatories (C1; St.Ch.1, 2; REQ2), of which some may have been lost. No decisions in cases concerning fifteenths and tenths are recorded on the Chancery Decree Rolls (C78/1–3), or in the Decree and Order Books of Chancery (C33/1–2), and requests (REQ1/1–8). The Decree and Order Books of Star Chamber for the early Tudor period have not survived.

124. 1488 Melcombe Regis, Dorset: E159/266 Recorda M.r.7; 1490–1 Otterton, Devon: E159/268 Recorda M.r.13; 1490–1 Southwark Surrey: E159/267 Recorda M.r.16; 1498(II) Exeter, Devon: E159/275 Recorda H.r.6; 1497(II) Northmundham, Sussex: E159/274 Recorda T.r.4d; 1537 Dover, Kent: E159/320 Recorda P.r.63; 1537 Ilford, Essex: REQ2/2/50; 1541 Burford, Oxfordshire: St.Ch.2/7/51–71; c.1546–7 Linby, Nottinghamshire: REQ2/12/118.

125. For example, in 1512 two men were presented before the Court of Aldermen in the City of London for making an affray against the collectors whilst levying a distress. CLRO Repertory 2. f. 147.

126. 1492(II) – Kent: E159/271 Recorda M.r.13d; Surrey: E159/270 Recorda P.r.10. 1497(II) – Essex: E159/275 Recorda P.r.5d; Kent: E159/275 Recorda H.r.14; Wilts: E159/275 Recorda M.r.10, 10d. 1517 – Staffs: E159/297 Recorda T.r.12d. 1541 – Kent: E159/320 Recorda P.r.34. 1544 – Bucks: E159/322 Recorda H.r.43.

127. 1488 – Notts: E159/265 Recorda M.r.11d; Worcs: E159/264 Recorda T.r.16. 1489 – Hants: E159/266 Recorda H.r.12d. 1490–1 – Shropshire: E159/269 Recorda M.r.21d, 29d, and 20d, 21, 24, 24d, 28, 29. 1492(I) – Kent: E159/269 Recorda T.r.6; Lindsey: E159/268 Recorda T.r.6; Shropshire: E159/269 Recorda M.r.22, 22d, 26d, and 13, 13d, 14, 27, 27d; Staffs: E159/269 Recorda M.r.30d, 9d, 15d, 16, 16d, 20, 23, 23d, 26; Warw: E159/268 Recorda P.r.7d. 1492(II) – Rutland: E159/269 Recorda P.r.4; Surrey: E159/270 Recorda P.r.10d; Wilts: E159/271 Recorda M.r.13. 1497(II) – Herefs: E159/274 Recorda P.r.17; Wilts: E159/295 Recorda M.r.17. 1512 – Shropshire: E159/292 Recorda P.r.4d; Wilts: E159/292 Recorda H.r.19; Yorks (ER): E159/291 Recorda M.r.9. 1513 – Shropshire: E159/293 Recorda H.r.1d. 1514 – Shropshire: E159/297 Recorda H.r.3. 1517 – Kent: E159/297 Recorda M.r.10d. 1537 – Somerset: E159/318 Recorda M.r.32. 1546 – Essex: E159/325 Recorda M.r.43d.

128. 1489 – Staffs: E159/267 Recorda T.r.12. 1492(II) – Norfolk: E159/270 Recorda H.r.1, 11d, 12d; and 17d. 1497(II) – Essex: E159/274 Recorda P.r.13d, /275 Recorda M.r.11. 1547 – Shropshire: E159/326 Recorda T.r.25, 25d.

129. 1488 – Worcs: E159/265 Recorda H.r.11d.

130. 1488 – Kent: E159/266 Recorda M.r.23d. 1489 – Oxon: E159/266 Recorda P.r.15; Shropshire: E159/266 Recorda T.r.17; Sussex: E159/267 Recorda T.r.17d. 1490–1 – Middx: E159/274 Recorda H.r.9; Notts: E159/268 Recorda M.r.11d. 1492(II) – Cornwall: E159/269 Recorda M.r.17; Wilts: E159/268 Recorda P.r.14. 1492(II) – Derbs: E159/270 Recorda P.r.9d; Dorset: E159/269 Recorda H.r.20d; Herts: E159/269 Recorda P.r.7; Kent: E159/270 Recorda T.r.14d; and H.r.8d; Surrey: E159/

270 Recorda P.r.9. 1497(II) – Hants: E159/274 Recorda T.r.3; and 3d; Herts: E159/274 Recorda T.r.6. 1537 – Middx: E159/317 Recorda H.r.9; Staffs: E159/317 Recorda T.r.23.

131. On the inhabitants generally: 1492(I) Staffs: E159/269 Recorda M.r.19d; 1514 Shropshire: E159/293 Recorda H.r.1d. On named individuals: 1537 Staffs: E159/317 Recorda P.r.18d, T.r.2; 1543 Kent: E159/321 Recorda H.r.45.

132. 1488 – Middx: E159/264 Recorda T.r.11d. 1489 – Herefs: E159/266 Recorda M.r.26; Holland: E159/265 Recorda T.r.24d. 1492(I) – Oxon: E159/270 Recorda M.r.7. 1492(II) Wilts: E159/269 Recorda H.r.13. 1497(II) – Norfolk: E159/274 Recorda P.r.8d; Sussex: E159/274 Recorda T.r.4. 1512 – Yorks (WR): E159/293 Recorda M.r.16d. 1517 – Beds: E159/297 Recorda T.r.8; Bucks: E159/297 Recorda T.r.10d. 1541 – Bucks: E159/320 Recorda P.r.1d; Devon: St.Ch.2/3/289302. 1542 – Bucks: E159/322 Recorda P.r.56; Kent: E159/321 Recorda P.r.35; and /322 Recorda T.r.40; Kesteven: St.Ch./2/32/99. 1543 – Herefs: E159/322 Recorda P.r.55.

133. The correct way to recover a wrongful distress was to petition the sheriff to 'replevy' the goods seized, see Jacob, *Law Dictionary*, 'Replevin'. It is not clear whether this form of recovery could be used where the crown's interests were involved. It was barred in such cases in the later seventeenth century, Jacob, *Ibid*. No record has been found of replevies for taxation distresses for the early Tudor period.

134. Because the point at issue was held to prevent the collector from discharging his duties as a debtor to the crown: 'quominus predictus [AB] dicto Domino Regi nunc satisfacere valeat de debito et compotis in quibus eidem Domino Regi nunc tenetur ad dictum Scaccarium Dicti Domini Regis nunc'. Since most of the cases in the Exchequer of pleas were actions of debt against the collectors, the 'quominus' reason does not seem very compelling. Twenty-six cases have been noted which can be shown to have concerned collectors of fifteenths and tenths in a purely private capacity; most of which were for the recovery of debts contracted before appointment to collectorship. E13/173 M.r.11; /174 M.r.12d, H.r.3d; /175 P.r.2d, T.r.[16]d, M.r.13d; /178 M.r.7d, H.r.12d; /184 P.r.4d; 189 M.r.5d; /192 H.r.1d; /193 P.r.2d, 6; /194 T.r.1d; /196 M.r.10, 12d; /197 H.r.–d; /210 M.r.4, H.r.5; /216 T.r–d; /223 P.r.[7].

135. This rendered a private distress wrongful. It is not known whether a distress taken by royal officials for debts to the crown was subject to this restriction or not. Jacob, *Law Dictionary*, 'Distress'.

136. Few enrolments of all types of action in the Exchequer of pleas extend as far as a decision. E13/171–225.

137. E159/291 Recorda M.r.28d.

138. C1/360/32, /567/94.

139. 1488 – Glos: E159/266 Recorda H.r.13d account only. 1490–1 – Yorks (NR): St.Ch.1/2/83 account and expenses; Derbs: C1/237/56, /258/35 account and expenses. 1514 – Lancs: E159/325 Recorda P.r.11 account only. 1517 – Glos: E159/304 Recorda T.r.4d account only. 1537 – Bucks: E159/319 Recorda H.r.9d expenses only.

140. E459/39, 43, *passim*.

141. The same sums as were allowed in 1415; E164/7; but less than the allowances of 1334; Willard, *Parl. Taxes 1290–1334*, p. 205.

142. The collectors for Bristol were allowed £3 0s 0d in 1537, and £2 0 s 0d from 1541 to 1547. E359/43, 26 H VIII, r.4; 32 H VIII, 1st payment, r.8d, 2nd pmnt, r. 13, 3rd pmnt, r.4, 4th pmnt, r.7d; 37 H VIII 1st pmnt, r.1, 2nd pmnt, r.1. The collectors for Gloucester were allowed 10s 0d in 1541 (E359/43 32 H VIII, 1st pmnt, r.11d), 17s 6d form 154244 (*ibid.*, 2nd pmnt, r.13, 3rd pmnt, r.11, 4th pmnt, r.7), and 13s 6d in 1546 (*ibid.*, 37 H VIII 1st pmnt, r.1). The collectors for Exeter and Derby, who accounted separately from 1541, were somewhat irregularly allowed a portion of the traditional county allowance: E359/43 32 H VIII 1st pmnt, r.8d, 11d; 2nd pmnt, r.5, 13; 3rd pmnt, r.13, 18; 4th pmnt, r.4, 2d; 37 H VIII 1st pmnt, r.1, 1d; 2nd pmnt, r.1, 1d.

143. More precisely 0.97%. The proportion is not exact because while the allowances were traditional rounded figures, the gross yields of the counties, although also traditional, were not rounded.

144. A statutory allowance of 2d/£ to each of the three groups of officials, the commissioners, the high collectors, and the petty collectors. It is impossible to compare the remuneration of the collectors of the fifteenths and tenths with any one of these groups, because their work was so different.

145. Beds, Cornwall, Derbs, Essex, Herts, Holland, Hunts, Isle of Wight, Kent, Lancs, Lindsey, Middlesex, Rutland, Shropshire, Surrey, Sussex, Yorks (ER), Yorks (WR). E359/43 26 H VIII, *passim*.

146. E359/43 26 H VIII, *passim*.

147. E359/43 26 H VIII, *passim*; E368/312 SVC M, *passim*.

148. E368/313 SVC P.r.1.

149. E359/43 26 H VIII, r. 3.

150. E359/43 32 H VIII, *passim*.

151. The local assessors of directly assessed subsidies received no remuneration. The commissioners who supervised the assessments got 2d/£, and the local, or petty, collectors also received 2d/£. See below, p. 121.

152. St.Ch.2/7/51; C1/809/56; /960/3. In another case the attorney general prosecuted, E159/294 Recorda M.r.25–6. These cases are, of course, no argument against the possibility of overcharging by the local collectors, for the essence of such overcharging was that it was secret.

153. Under the act, 18 Henry VI c. 1, letters patent were to bear a date not earlier than the date of the receipt in Chancery of the warrant authorising their issue.

154. These are discussed below in Chapter 6.

155. 7 Henry VII c. 11, which also exempted those who had been collectors of a fifteenth and tenth granted the year before; 12 Henry VII c. 12; 3 Henry VIII c. 22; 32 Henry VII c. 50; 37 Henry VIII c. 25.

156. If it could be proved before the Lord Chancellor that a member of the commons had accepted such bribes, the member was to be committed to ward 'unto the tyme he have satisfyed the partie the double ([1491] x times so much) of his or their Receits or Rewards', and further at the discretion of the Lord Chancellor until fine had been made to the king for the contempt. *Rot. Parl.* VI, 437–9; 7 Henry VII c.11. No such cases have been found amongst the records of Chancery.

157. By no means all letters patent were enrolled. See Appendix II, also Maxwell-Lyte, *The Great Seal*, pp. 363–6.

158. Dietz, *English Government Finance*, p. 14.

159. Johnson, *Surrey Rec. Soc.*, XI, lxxv.
160. C193/1 f.119.
161. Willard, *Parl. Taxes* 1290–1334, 94–6.
162. For enrolments of commissions, see Appendix II.
163. E159/274 Recorda T.r.4d.
164. 1492(I) Berwyk Oxon: subcollector cited after a successful distraint, E159/270 Recorda M.r.7; 1492 (I) Langton Oxon: assessors cited for assessing two fo the rector's farmers, E159/269 Recorda H.r.33d.
165. 1542 Willoughby, Kesteven. A lessee of lands formerly belonging to the Abbey of Crowland was assessed by his fellow inhabitants for these lands for the fifteenth and tenth. The lessee brought a bill of complaint in the Court of Augmentations, alleging that the lands had always been included in the Abbot of Crowland's disme payment, and had thus traditionally been exempt from fifteenths and tenths. The inhabitants denied this, and brought a counter suit in Star Chamber, alleging malicious maintenance of the lessee by a local knight. E321/10/13; St.Ch.2/32/99.
166. Dietz, *English Government Finance*, p. 14.
167. Ramsay, *Lancaster and York*, II, p. 259.
168. Vickers, *England in the Later Middle Ages*, p. 335.
169. *Nottingham Records*, II, p. 286.
170. *Rot. Parl.* VI, pp. 4–8.
171. Willard, *Parl. Taxes 1290–1334*, p. 163.
172. This clause first appeared in the commission of 1377. Thereafter it occurs somewhat irregularly until 1401. *CFR* IV–XXII. For enrolment of commissions 1485–1547, see Appendix II.
173. *CFR* IV, 480–1.
174. 4 Henry VII c. 19.
175. 1517, Richard, Earl of Kent's lands in Clophill, Bedfs., E159/297 Recorda T.r.8.
176. The northern counties seem to have been required to pay most fifteenths and tenths before 1392. From 1392 to 1415 they were called upon irregularly; and after 1415 scarcely ever at all. *CFR* IV–XXII.
177. BM Cottonian Cleop. F.VI, 244. A summary of the yield of a fifteenth and tenth temp. James I.
178. Henry VII to the commissioners at York (1512) *LP* XVII, 799; Sir Thomas Wharton's remembrance (1543) *LP* XVIII, pt. I, 799. *Hamilton Papers*, I, No. 163. Certain parts of Yorks. (NR) were also liable to border service; but enjoyed no exemption from fifteenths and tenths.
179. See Appendix I.
180. Since 1463 the assessment had been reduced from £46 12s 2½d to £20 0s 0d. E368/262 SVC H.r.7.
181. 3 Henry VIII c. 22.
182. 7 Henry VIII c. 9.
183. E368/262 SVC M.r.16d; /263 SVC T.r.8; /266 SVC T.r.6, M.r.11, 12d; /270 SVC T.r.7d.
184. E359/39, 43 *passim*, Hants. Possibly because the exemption was first grnated by statute as long before as 1407. *Rot. Parl.* III, p. 620.
185. E368/263 SVC M.r.11.

186. E368/264 SVC P.r.15.
187. E368/265 SVC T.r.8.
188. E368/266 SVC M.r.11.
189. E368/317 SVC P.r.7.
190. E368/317 SVC P.r.4.
191. E159/264 Bre.Dir. T.r.17d; /265 Bre.Dir. T.r.9d; /267 Bre.Dir. P.r.4, cite letters patent of Edward I, confirmed 13 Dec 1487. The procedure was for the property of members of the Cinque Ports and their outliers, wherever it was situated, to be assessed; and on the basis of these detailed assessments the collectors of Kent and Sussex claimed their allowance. E179/124/168–76; /237/55–6, etc. On 7 May 1491, at the request of the King and council, the Barons of the Cinque Ports entered into a recognisance for 2,000 marks that the total assessment of the goods of the inhabitants of the Cinque Ports should not exceed £500. E159/267 Recorda P.r.12d. In the two previous fifteenths and tenths the total assessments of the Cinque Ports had been £576 4s 0d and £608 13s 10d. E368/262 SVC P.r.12; T.r.9; /263 SVC H.r.9; /264 SVC M.r.6. The entire hundred of Tenterden in Kent was annexed to the Cinque Ports by letters patent of 1 Aug. 1449. E159/272 Bre.Dir. P.r.4d. In 1540 and 1546 letters to the collectors inhibiting levying on the Cinque Ports were sent by the Privy Council. Nicholas, *Ordinances* VII, p. 165; *APC* I, 422.
192. By charter of Edward IV, E159/265 Recorda M.r.5d; /267 Bre.Dir. P.r.3d.
193. *LP*. Ed I, confirmed 1 Mar 1309 and 20 Feb 1462.
194. By letters patent of 12 Dec 1485, *CPR* (1485–1494), 118; E159/264 Recorda T.r.10.
195. By charter of 7 Dec 1461, confirmed by letters patent of 21 April 1507, E159/285 Bre.Dir. P.r.1.
196. By charter of Edward III, E159/268 Bre.Dir. M.r.1; /271 Bre.Dir. M.r.3; /287 Recorda M.r.2.
197. E368/317 SVC M.r.3.
198. By letters patent of 20 Feb. 1483, confirmed by letters patent of 4 June 1488, for 65 years. The reduction was granted because of inundation by the sea and consequent de-population. E159/265 Recorda H.r.16, T.r.23, Bre.Dir. M.r.6. Upon suit to the crown the reduction was prolonged for a further 50 years, by letters patent of 25 June 1543, E159/325 Recorda H.r.14.
199. Reductions consistently granted by commissioners temp. Henry VI were annulled by the act of resumption, 28 Henry VI; but were restored by letters patent of 27 Nov 1489. E371/255 r.14; E159/267 Bre.Dir. M.r.2, Recorda M.r.13.
200. E359/39, 43 *passim*. The allowance for the Cinque Ports averaged approximately £450 out of an average total of approximately £550.
201. *Rot. Parl.* VI, 418–20.
202. 7 Henry VII c. 5.
203. E359/39 3 HVII, 2nd payment, *passim*; 5 HVII, *passim*.
204. 32 Henry VIII c. 50.
205. E359/43 32 Henry VIII, *passim*.
206. LAC L1/1/1/1 f.289.b.
207. *LP* XVII, 326 (68).
208. E159/321 Recorda T.r.23.
209. E159/320 Recogn. H.r.

210. *YB* 20 Henry VI M. pl. 25; *YB* 21 Edward IV M.pl.6. The Rector of Eddington's case, although concerning a fifteenth and tenth, is irrelevant because there was no clause in the grant annulling prerogative grants of exemption. *YB* 19 Henry VI P.pl.1. Sgjt. Markham's argument.
211. Plucknett, *Lancastrian Constitution*; Chrimes, *English Constitutional Ideas in the Fifteenth Century.*
212. The terms of clerical grants were merely certified by the archbishop into Chancery.
213. The standard form of acceptance ran: 'Le Roy, en merciant a cez Comoenz de lour boens coeurs en faisantz les Grauntez suisditz, mesmes les Grauntez, ovecque toutz les Articeles en ycelle contenuz, ad excepte, & graunte.' Individual words may vary. *Rot. Parl.* VI, 444.
214. In 1482 the case was brought by the abbot into the Exchequer chamber because, although the Barons of the Exchequer had already ruled in his favour, the sheriff was still distraining upon him. *YB* 21 Edward IV M. pl.6.
215. See Table 7.1.
216. See the first few pages of Chapter 8.
217. It is significant that until 1516, with the exception of the subsidy of 1513, the acts granting directly assessed subsidies all specified the sum that the taxes were designed to yield.
218. The act granting a directly assessed subsidy in 1489 expressly prohibited the return of any ssessments to a court of record. *Rot. Parl.* VI, pp. 420–3.
219. 4 Henry VIII c. 19.
220. Although non-parliamentary taxes are traditionally associated with Henry VII, they were in fact most often resorted to between 1542 and 1546.
221. 21 James I c. 33. Three fifteenths and tenths were granted in customary form. No fifteenths and tenths were ever granted to the crown again.

Notes to Chapter 4

1. 1404: *Rot. Parl.*, III, pp. 546–7; 1411: *ibid.*, pp. 648–9; 1427–8: *ibid.*, IV, pp. 318–19; 1431: *ibid.*, pp. 369–70; 1435: *ibid.*, pp. 486–7; 1450: *ibid.*, V, pp. 172–4; 1472: *ibid.*, VI, pp. 4–6.
2. 1431: *ibid.*, IV, p. 409; 1472: *ibid.*, VI, p. 151. An attempt in 1463 to levy the £6,000 usually deducted from fifteenths and tenths by way of direct assessment also failed, and was withdrawn. *ibid.*, V, pp. 497–8.
3. No directly assessed subsidy in the fifteenth century was ever repeated.
4. *Rot. Parl.*, IV, p. 409.
5. *Ibid.*, V. pp. 172–4.
6. *Rot. Parl.*, VI, pp. 4–6.
7. 1439: *ibid.*, V, p. 6; 1442: *ibid.*, p. 38; 1449: *ibid.*, p. 144; 1453: *ibid.*, p. 230; 1482: *ibid.*, VI, pp. 197–8.
8. *Ibid.*, pp. 401–2.
9. i.e. 6 April 1488.
10. Before 6 April 1488. C66/568 m.5[17]d; *CPR* (1485–94), pp. 239–43. Including the northern border shires, but excluding Lancashire. Although the town of Oxford

did not receive a separate commission, it none the less accounted separately at the Exchequer. E159/266 Fines T.r–.

11. Apart from the records cited below, only one return of an inquisition (E179/124/154), and five auditors' accounts concerning this tax are to be found amongst the Exchequer records: E179/161/14; E179/180/116; E179/284/32; E179/285/27; E179/287/30.

12. These claims were made by the collectors when they accounted at the Exchequer. Collectors for fifteen shires and boroughs claimed exoneration for £90 9s 0d. Beds: E368/262 SVC T.r.8; Cambs: E368/263 SVC H.r.8; Cornw: E368/262 SVC M.r.19; Devon: *ibid.*, M.r.17; Essex: *ibid.*, M.r.8; Herefs: E368/261 SVC T.r.8; Herts: E368/264 SVC H.r.5; Hunts: E368/261 SVC T.r.8; Lindsey: *ibid.*, Norfolk: *ibid.*; Suffolk: E368/262 SVC M.r.18; Sussex: *ibid.*, M.r.10; Warwicks: *ibid.*, T.r.8; Canterbury: E368/261 SVC P.r.24; Oxford: E368/264 SVC T.r.9. The petition of the Norfolk collectors included a claim for exemption of three Hanse merchants assessed in Bishop's Lynn. They cited letters patent dated 12 June 1488, reminding them that the Hanse merchants residing in the Steelyard were exempted by the act of parliament. But there is no such clause in the act. Nevertheless the Barons exonerated both the collectors and the merchants. E368/261 SVC T.r.8. Letters patent enrolled in E159/264 Recorda T.r.5.

13. These sums were generally levied by the sheriff by way of the Summons of the Pipe. For the difficulties of tracing such levies see pp. 165–7.

14. Eight such claims were made, totalling £4 15s 4d. Namely, Beds: E159/265 Recorda T.r.8; Cornwall: E159/264 Recorda T.r.14; Essex: *ibid.*, T.r.7, 14, E159/265 Recorda M.r.1, 9d; Norfolk: E159/264 Recorda T.r.6. The Cornwall claim was made by the collectors, on the basis of a testimonial signed by many people.

15. Norfolk: E159/264 Recorda T.r.11.

16. Both London. In one the defendant appeared in the Exchequer before the day assigned for the return of the writ: E159/264 Recorda T.r.17d. In the other the defendant was attached and produced in the Exchequer by the sheriff eighteen months after the original writ was issued: *ibid.*, T.r.20.

17. Notes giving the outlines of some of the accounts have been preserved on the Memoranda Rolls; but no information has survived for Berks., Bucks., Cumbs., Derbs., Glos., Kent, Kesteven, Middlesex, Northants., Salop, Staffs., Surrey, Westmorland, Yorks., and the Cinque Ports, Lincoln, and York.

18. This figure has been calculated by collating the accounts, cited in the Memoranda Rolls, with the records of the actual receipt of money in the Exchequer of Receipt, from those counties for which no accounts survive. No traces of receipts from this tax have been found in any other treasury. E368/261 SVC P.r.24, T.r.8; E368/262 SVC M.r.10, 17, 18, 19, T.r.8; E368/263 SVC M.r.10, H.r.8; E368/264 SVC H.r.4, T.r.9; E159/265 Recorda H.r.2d, T.r.23d; E364/119/[45]d. E401/961, 964, 965, 966, 967, all *passim*; E405/75, 78, all *passim*.

19. No separate taxes, that is. Alien polls were often included in directly assessed subsidies of general incidence. See pp. 106–7.

20. *Rot. Parl.*, VI, pp. 420–4.

21. *Ibid.*, pp. 4–6.

22. There was some dispute over the proportions of the two grants, *CSP Ven.*, (1202–

1509), 550. For the Canterbury grant see Wilkins, *Concilia*, III, pp. 625–6; *CFR*, XXII, 267.

23. This clause appears at the end of the act after the main provisions for levying the tax. *Rot. Parl.*, VI, p. 423.
24. Or, if dissolved, to the next parliament. *Rot. Parl.*, VI, p. 422.
25. *Ibid.*, p. 423.
26. That is, lands in England, Wales, and the Marches. The form of tenure was immaterial.
27. *Rot. Parl.*, VI, pp. 420–3.
28. *Ibid.*, pp. 423–4. The Lords' grant also specified that those enjoying the use of lands, though not seised of them, were nevertheless to be liable to the subsidy.
29. *Rot. Parl.*, VI, p. 421. No copies, or Chancery enrolment, of this commission have been discovered.
30. *Ibid.* A few transcripts of these inquisitions have survived. BM Stowe 880, ff.44–5; BLO Dodsworth 4192, ff. 39–79; E179/149/186, 187; E179/151/353.
31. *Rot. Parl.*, VI, p. 421.
32. But not anyone who either had been, or still was, a collector of the two fifteenths and tenths granted in 1487.
33. *Rot. Parl.*, VI, p. 422. Four such cases of default by the collectors are recorded and in none of these is certification by the commissioners mentioned. The information against the Staffs. collectors was led by the attorney general. Kent: 'distringas', E368/269 Recorda M.r.11; Lincs: 'distringas', E159/267 Recorda P.r.17; Glos: 'capias', E159/271 Bre.Ret.P.r-d; Staffs: 'subpeona/attachias', E159/271 Bre.Ret.M.r.16d. For an explanation of the forms of process see the Glossary, below.
34. *Rot. Parl.*, VI, p. 421.
35. It is interesting that no collectors brought actions in the Exchequer against 'rescues' of distresses.
36. Apparently only one collector took advantage of this provision, and the information was given to the Barons on oath rather than by certificate. The Barons issued a writ of 'venire facias' to the sheriff; but the enrolment of the case breaks off before the return of the writ is recorded. E159/268 Recorda H.r.14.
37. *Rot. Parl.*, VI, pp. 422–3.
38. But three transcripts of inquisitions held in Norfolk and giving individual assessments have survived amongst the Exchequer records: E179/149/186, 187; E179/151/353. Although the class E179 is artificial, it is clear that these inquisitions somehow came into official hands. Probably they were brought in by the Cellarer of the abbey of St Edmund at Bury when he delivered the money from Norfolk and Suffolk: E36/125, f.143. An eighteen-folio paper book in an Exchequer hand contains accounts for all collectors who paid money to the Cellarer. E179/280/11. The attorney general delivered a list of collectors and commissioners who had not yet sent in certificates for Salop. E179/166/111.
39. Parliament estimated the yield of the tax at less than £27,000, *Rot. Parl.*, VI, p. 437. £18,300 7s 11½d was paid into the Exchequer by the collectors: E401/965, 966, 967, 970, 971, 972, 974, 978, *passim*. Instructions to pay the proceeds of the subsidy to the Exchequer may have been included in the 'lost' commissions.
40. E36/125, f. 143. The Cellarer was allowed £10 for storing and conveying £1468 7s 2d.

41. £323 6s 8d was paid to military paymasters in the north, and £1022 6s 7½d to the Treasurer of the Chamber, all through the hands of William Beverley, Dean of Middleham, and general paymaster in the north. E101/413/2/2, ff. 1b, 2b; E404/ 80/4 HVII/118; E404/80/5 HVII/109, 194.

42. 'at our straicte commaundment', E404/80/4 HVII/91.

43. No warrant mentioned, E404/80/5 HVII/239.

44. No warrant mentioned, E179/242/99.

45. £241 10s 1½d was assigned to four persons in repayment for loans to the crown. E401/967, on 10 Feb. and 14 Feb., E401/972 on 7 Feb., and E401/974 on 16 Feb. £7 6s 8d was assigned for the payment of fees and annuities. E401/974, on 5 Dec. and E401/977 on 19 July.

46. Except that three collectors for Lincolnshire accounted before an Exchequer auditor. Possibly they had been cited as defaulters by the commissioners E159/ 267 Recorda P.r.17. The complete absence of documents relating to the accounting process makes it very unlikely that other collectors accounted at the Exchequer.

47. See pp. 141–5. The collectors paying their money directly to the tellers in the Exchequer received tallies according to the ordinary course of the Exchequer, see p. 141.

48. The tallies were struck on the authority of writs issued under the Privy Seal and addressed to the Treasurer and Chamberlains of the Exchequer. The writ recited the payments to other royal officials and demanded that tallies be struck for the acquittance and discharge of the collectors. E404/80/4 HVII/91, 118; E404/80/5 HVII/109, 194, 239.

49. *Rot. Parl.*, VI, p. 437.

50. E401/965, 966, 967, 970, 971, 972, 974, 977, 978, *passim*: E405/78, *passim*; E36/ 125, f.143; E404/80/4 HVII/91, 118; E404/80//5 HVII/109, 194, 239; E179/242/99: adjusted to eliminate, as far as possible, double counting.

51. No provision for the remuneration of collectors was made in the act of parliament; but a letter under the royal signet to the commissioners for Essex states that the 'conveyours' of the tax money will be rewarded '[accord]yng to reason'. *Colchester Red Paper Book*, pp. 145–6.

52. Also the only receipt roll for the important term of Michaelmas 1489 is cut off short at 18 Feb. 1490. E401/967, pts I and II.

53. Another contemporary estimate of the yield was 'lytill ovyr a ffyfftene' *Great Chronicle*, p. 243. Since the *net* yield of a fifteenth and tenth at this period was about £29,500, the estimate is improbable.

54. *Two London Chronicles*, 194; *Great Chronicle*, 243.

55. BM Stowe 880, ff. 44–5; BLO Dodsworth 4193 ff. 39–79; E179/149/186, 187; /151/ 353.

56. Handbook of Brit. Chon. 534. *Rot. Parl.*, VI, 437. The subsidies of 1431 and 1472, which also failed, were replaced by grants of fifteenths and tenths, *Ibid.*, IV, 409; VI, 149–53.

57. *Ibid.*, VI, 438.

58. The next comparable subsidy was granted in 1514, 5 Henry VIII c. 17. A directly assessed poll tax, not a full rate per pound subsidy was granted two years earlier, 4 Henry VIII c. 19.

59. *Rot. Parl.*, VI, 437–9; 7 Henry VII c. 11.

60. The council consisted of the king, the lords spritual and temporal, and 'ffrom every Cyte bourgth & good toun of Engeland certayn Cytyzins & bourgeysis'. Parliament was called because the 'generall counsayll ... was not Suficient auctoryte for the levyying thereof' that is of the grant of £120,000. *Great Chronicle*, 274–5.

61. 12 Henry VII c. 12.

62. 12 Henry VII c. 13.

63. That is, the sixteen cities and towns which traditionally received separate commissions to levy fifteenths and tenths. See p. 73.

64. Those who enjoyed the use of profits from lands of which they were not seized were nevertheless liable to assessment.

65. Nevertheless seven cases are known in which such incomes and annuities were assessed. E159/274 Recorda P.r.18d, H.r.18d, 25d; /175 Recorda P.r.9, M.r.22d.

66. Nevertheless four cases are recorded where dismable lands were assessed. Those so assessed brought actions against the commissioners in Chancery. Oxon: C1/196/85; Herefs: *ibid.*/86; Salop: C1/205/50; Lindsey: C1/223/67.

67. 12 Henry VII c. 13.

68. CLRO Repertory 1, f. 18b.

69. The names of the commissioners are conveniently printed in *Stat. Realm*, II, 646–7.

70. Except that eight commissioners were appointed for both London and Southwark.

71. The names of the sheriffs are given in *Lists and Indexes*, XI; for justices of the peace, see *CPR* (1494–1509), 629–69. The act required for the purposes of assessment a quorum of six commissioners in the shires and four in the towns.

72. Members of the Commons, justices of the peace, clerks of parliament, and commissioners of the subsidy were not to be appointed collectors. Corporate towns were to arrange for the collection within their own limits and hand over the money to the county collectors.

73. In 1489 the collectors might commence collecting immediately after the assessments had been made. The subsidy of 1497 was payable in two parts, each part being equivalent to one fifteenth and tenth. The two latest payment dates at the Exchequer were 31 May and 8 November 1497. The commissioners were to have certified the names of the collectors to the Exchequer by 5 May and 1 October, and were to give the collectors the lists of assessments before 13 May and 15 October. The assessment for the second part was not to begin before 15 August.

74. But like the collectors of fifteenths and tenths they were subject to the dangers of collective responsibility. See pp. 12–14. Only one action at law brought by collectors against recalcitrant colleagues has been found: Yorks. (NR) C1/89/9. The outcome is unknown.

75. As under the act of 1489 the tenant was authorised to recoup his losses by deduction from subsequent rent payments.

76. No record of such a committal to ward has been discovered. But the *ad hoc* nature of the procedure makes it unlikely that it would have been formally recorded.

77. For a description of this process see p. 53. Yet three collectors brought actions against rescuers of distresses in the Exchequer. In one case the enrolment ends before the sheriff returned the writ of attachment, Wilts: E159/277 Recorda P.r.8. In the two other cases, both occurring in Glos., the writs of attachment were

unsuccessful, but the defendants appeared in the Exchequer some years later. All pleaded not guilty, but requested to be admitted to fines rather than be tried by jury. Two were fined 5s 0d each for one of the rescues: E159/279 Recorda M.r.20d; and two others were fined 3s 4d each for the other rescue: E159/275 Recorda M.r.11d.

78. The certifications for defaults came from the following counties: Berks., Cambs., Essex, Herts., Holland, Lindsey, Notts., Oxon., Surrey, Sussex; the cities of Canterbury and Lincoln; and the town of Colchester. 120 of the defaulters were assessed at £37 12s 2½d on goods, and 75 at £14 19s 1¼d on lands, tenements and fees. Most defaults were from Lindsey (65) and Herts (30), all assessed on goods. E159/274 Recorda M.r.12d, H.r.18d, 25, 25d, P.r.18d, 22; /275 Recorda M.r.22d, H.r.14d, P.r.9, T.r.5; /276 Recorda M.r.5d, 19d; /277 Recorda M.r.11d, 18; /280 Recorda T.r.15.

79. The Earl of Surrey, after eight days, paid £1 5s 0d assessed on him in Surrey for an annuity. E159/274 Recorda H.r.18d.

80. The Memoranda Rolls give a reference to the place on the pipe rolls where the sheriffs were charged. Levy of these sums was by the summons of the pipe. Reference to £60 17s 11d of these debts has been found on the pipe rolls: E372/353 Cambs., Hunts., Lincs., Essex-Herts.; /354 Essex-Herts. But it cannot be determined whether the sheriff actually levied these sums or not, see pp. 165–7. A further £2 13s 4d due from five persons was levied by assigned tally issued to the Treasurer of the Wars: E401/990, 10 May, 27 June.

81. The Queen was also exempted in one of these clauses. Exemption for the academic colleges of Oxford, Cambridge, Eton and Winchester was granted by the king after engrossment, and a proviso to this effect with the royal sign manual was stitched to the original act. 12 Henry VII c. 13 HLRO.

82. *Great Chronicle*, 275–81.

83. 19 Henry VII c. 32. This is all rehearsed in the preamble. Arthur was made knight of the Bath in 1489, and knight of the Garter in 1491. He died on 2 April 1502. Margaret was married to James, King of Scotland, in January 1503. *DNB*.

84. There is no convenient summary of the financial position of the Exchequer; in October 1502 the accumulated cash and bullion, noted in a memorial in the king's hand, was £46,381 1s 7d, E101/413/2/3, ff. 1–5. The clear balance of receipts over expenditure in the treasury of the Chamber for the period October 1502 to October 1505 was £22,729 1s 0d, *ibid.*, f. 240. The gain to the crown was probably more than this because some of the expenditure was on investments such as jewels and plate, Dietz, *English Government Finance*, 85–7.

85. *Ibid.*, 28, and n. 20.

86. Richardson, *Tudor Chamber Administration*, *passim*, but especially 192–214. Increased activity in enforcing feudal incidents is reflected in the Memoranda Rolls from 1502 E368/276 Bre. Ret. *passim*; /277 *ibid.*, /278 *ibid.* See also Elton, *HJ* I (1958) 21–39.

87. 19 Henry VII c. 32, preamble. This also suggests that the well-known opposition of Sir Thomas More was not so much that of a subject to a grant of money to the crown, as that of a common lawyer to a general inquisition of tenures. Roper, *Life of More*, 7–8.

88. In a schedule attached to the act. 19 Henry VII c. 32 HLRO.

89. Cumberland was to pay £133 6s 8d, Westmorland and Northumberland £200 0s 0d each.
90. Probably because Yarmouth, usually exempt from fifteenths and tenths, was not exempt from this subsidy.
91. The order of the clauses is exactly the same as in the act of 1497, and only some details are changed. It appears, therefore, that the entire act was laid before the Commons in the crown draft.
92. 19 Henry VII c. 32. HLRO. The names of the commissioners are conveniently printed in *Stat. Realm*, II, 677–82.
93. *Ibid.* A quorum of four commissioners was required both in counties and in the boroughs.
94. Both the collectors and the commissioners received the sums traditionally allowed to collectors of fifteenths and tenths, see Table 3.6 (p. 55). The collectors were allowed both sums when they accounted, and were required by the act to pay the commissioners their part when they returned. One of the commissioners for Nottinghamshire sued the collectors in the Exchequer of Pleas for detaining such money due to him. The Barons ordered the sheriff to levy this, and to pay it to the commissioner within six months. E13/186/T.r.7. For some unknown reason the commissioners for Northants were not allowed any remuneration in the collectors' accounts. E359/38, 19 HVII, r.2d.
95. Assessments were to be completed before 29 September. Only the academic colleges of Oxford, Cambridge, Eton and Winchester, together with the Charter-houses and the house of Syon were exempt. The town of Shrewsbury was assessed in the act at £79 0s 8d; but the collectors claimed exemption in the Exchequer by virtue of their letters patent of 12 December 1485; *CPR* (1485–1494), 118. The attorney general contested the sufficiency of their patent, and the Barons decided against the collectors. But nothing was paid until 14 May 1509 when the collectors successfully sued a pardon of 10 May 1509 releasing them from all tax debts contracted during the reign of Henry VII. E159/284 Recorda P.r.7. But in a similar case concerning the town of Ludlow, the Barons were still considering their decision when Henry VII died, and at this point the enrolment breaks off. E159/285 Recorda P.r.22. But in the summer of 1510 two inhabitants of Ludlow claimed that a collector had extorted the £12 due from them by threatening to seize the goods of outlaws. The collector denied the charge, and the Barons' decision is unknown. E13/187 T.r[7]d.
96. Within eight days of completing the assessments. As in 1497 the collectors were not to start levying the tax before this period had elapsed.
97. Before 1 November 1504.
98. For a definition of these terms see the Glossary.
99. Cumbs: E159/284 Recorda M.r.38d; Notts: *ibid.*, r.34; Salop: *ibid.*, H.r.17, /285 Recorda H.r.9; Southwark: /283 Recorda M.r.22d.
100. Cumbs. (two cases): E159/284 Recorda M.r.38d; Lindsey /285 Recorda M.r.23, 23d, H.r.9d.
101. At 6s 8d each.
102. After attempts lasting fifteen months to get a local jury to come to the Exchequer, the case was committed to the assizes. Warwicks: E159/283 Recorda M.r.22.
103. 22 & 23 Chas II c. 3.

104. 4 Henry VIII c. 19.
105. 1s 0d was levied on every man and woman over the age of fifteen years. *Rot. Parl.*, III, 90. Both Hoskins and Cornwall in their claims for the subsidies of 1524–7 seem unaware of the terms of the subsidies of 1513–16. Hoskins, *TRHS* 5th Ser. 6, 2–3; Cornwall, *Sussex Subsidy Rolls*, xxi. In fact the act for the subsidies of 1524–7 specifies a *smaller* taxable population than do the acts for the subsidies of 1513 and 1514, see Table 5.7 (p. 107).
106. Written local assessments revised by nationally appointed commissioners were characteristic of directly assessed taxes between 1290 and 1334; but the commissioners were also collectors. Willard, *Parl. Taxes 1290–1334*, 39–68, 183–92. In contrast in the later fifteenth-century subsidies, while the commissioners and the collectors were two separate groups, there was no 'two-tier' system of supervised written local assessments. *Rot. Parl.*, VI, 4–6, 420–4; 12 Henry VII c. 13; 19 Henry VII c. 32.
107. Fines were to be certified to the Exchequer to be levied by writ of *fieri facias*.
108. The draft was made by John Hales, of Gray's Inn.
109. These clauses were very much the same as in 1497 and 1504. The exempt colleges were those of Oxford, Cambridge, Eton and Winchester. The general exemption of spriutal persons was new.
110. The collectors were to be allowed for both at their account, and were to pay the commissioners on their return. In default of payment the latter were to have an action at law for debt, in which 'the defendaunte shall not wage hys lawe'. See Glossary.
111. 5 Henry VIII c. 17.
112. Hence the provisions in the act, described below, for the levy of a further subsidy if necessary.
113. More precisely, £50,804 16s 7d, E359/38 5 HVIII.
114. The subsidy of 1489 was equally demanding for the assessment of lands, but not so demanding for the assessment of goods, and required no assessment of wages. *Rot. Parl.*, VI, 420–4.
115. The commissioners were empowered to punish by fine and imprisonment those who changed their place of residence in order to escape assessment altogether.
116. They were to retain this sum from the money that they handed over to the high collectors.
117. Willard, *Parl. Taxes, 1290–1334*, 198–214. *Rot. Parl.*, III, 546–7, 648–9; IV, 318–19, 369–70, 486–7; V, 172–4; VI, 4–6, 420–4; 12 Henry VII c. 13; 19 Henry VII c. 32; 4 Henry VIII c. 19. For fifteenths and tenths, see above.
118. Clauses concerning double assessment, the powers of commissioners over recalcitrant local officials, the exemption of members of the Commons from appointment as collectors, the exemption of collectors from fees in the Exchequer.
119. Clauses concerning legal tender, total exemptions from the subsidy and collectors' remuneration remained at the end of the act.
120. The committee consisted of the Lord Treasurer, the 'Justices of either Benche', the speaker of the Commons, one knight from every shire, two of the London burgesses, one burgess from Bath, Bristol, Canterbury, Coventry, Gloucester, Kingston upon Hull, Leicester, Lincoln, Norwich, Nottingham, Oxford,

Rochester, Salisbury, Shrewsbury, Southampton, Southwark, Worcester and York, as many burgesses from other corporate towns as wished to attend. No quorum was specified.

121. By 1 July 1514. Certificates were also to be sent to the Exchequer before 18 June.

122. Fines were to be certified to the Exchequer and levied by the collectors together with the assessments.

123. 'as yf the same ambyquytes doubtes and questions or any of them were in this present act especyally reherced and the Remedyes declaracion or reformacion of them put in certentie or otherwyse by auctoryte of this present perlement remedyed.' 5 Henry VII c. 17.

124. The size of the deficit and the new rates were to be publicly proclaimed and certified to Chancery, who were to issue fresh commissions to the original commissioners.

125. The sums certified by the commissioners amounted to 'ryght letill above fyfty thousand poundes'. 6 Henry VIII c. 26, preamble.

126. *Ibid.* The reasons advanced were (1) that commissioners were not appointed for 'diverse parties of this realme', and (2) that not all the commissioners had returned full certificates. Since the committee was empowered to deal with both these cases, it is probable that the real reason for the fresh act of parliament was that the committee was unable to enforce the powers entrusted to it. Certificates were made to the Exchequer from all counties except Beds, Bucks, Cambs, Cornwall, Devon, Hunts, Lancs, Kesteven, Yorks, Bristol, Hull, York, Royal Households before 22 July. Certificates from Kesteven, Lancs, and King's Household, came in a few months later. E179/279/2.

127. Clauses concerning the remuneration of commissioners and collectors were incorporated into the main text.

128. Clauses concerning exemptions from liability to the subsidy, legal tender, the liability of the clergy except for their dismable possessions, and an extended clause empowering commissioners to order royal officials outside their area to levy distress on, or arrest, defaulters. This last clause was probably a crown proposal.

129. It consisted of the Lord Chancellor, the Lord Treasurer, the Chief Justices of either Bench, the Chancellor of the Duchy of Lancaster, the Speaker of the Commons, the Justices of Assize for every shire, the Recorder of London, the Master of the Wardrobe, the Under-Treasurer of England, the Queen's Attorney, theAttorney of the Duchy of Lancaster, and the knights and burgesses of the Commons. No quorum was specified.

130. But in case of default of certification by the commissioners, the committee might assess the whole area concerned themselves, and certify the sums to the Exchequer. The Exchequer was to arrange for these to be levied by *fieri facias*, or otherwise.

131. Within eight days of casting up the yield the committee was to certify Chancery to renew the commissions to the former commissioners. The payment, assessment and certification dates were to be the same as before, but one year later.

132. Within the counties the commissioners were to apportion these sums according to the assessed value of goods and of income from lands, fees, offices and wages, always so that the value of each category carried an equal burden.

133. The estimated yield of the first subsidy, according to the preamble to the act granting the second subsidy, was £45,637 13s 8d. 7 Henry VIII c. 9, preamble.

134. *Ibid.* The act also provided relief for collectors of the previous subsidy overcharged in the Exchequer through faulty adding up of the assessments, and relief for those doubly assessed who had been unable to secure such relief under the provisions of the earlier act. In both cases claims were to be made to the Barons of the Exchequer supported by certificates from the commissioners. Only one such claim has been noted, and this was supported by a writ under the privy seal requesting relief to be given to the collectors by way of tallies of assignment. E404/91/9 HVIII/-.

135. The subsidy of 1514 had yielded just over £50,000, the subsidy of 1515 about £44,600. The fifteenth and tenth would yield another £29,000, leaving but £35,000 to be raised by the new subsidy. For the actual yields see Table 7.1 (p. 170).

136. But the act specified that distresses 'ad verificationes liberandas' were to be made according to the following scale. First distress: £1, second distress: £2, further distresses: £5. The Barons were also empowered to attach the commissioners and to seize their lands 'nomine districcionis' until certificates were forthcoming. For forms of process, see Chapter 6, pp. 151–67.

137. For the 'drawinge writinge & ingrocying' of these two acts Hales was paid £10. SP1/230, f. 117. Hales was appointed reader of Gray's Inn in October 1514, third Baron of the Exchequer from 1522 to 1528, second Baron of the Exchequer from 1528 until his death in 1539. Foss, *Judges of England*, 5, 185.

138. 14 & 15 Henry VIII c. 16.

139. Cornwall, *Sussex Subsidy Rolls*, xxiv has badly misunderstood this: 'Peers were to tax themselves separately as were the Clergy in Convocation'. There was no question of a separate grant by the peerage, nor were the peers assessed by other peers.

140. Miller, *BIHR* XXVIII (1955), 15–34 provides an excellent discussion of the assessment of the peerage. See also *LP* IV, 1117, 2972; BM Add. 25, 460, f. 7.

141. But only after a valuation by between two and four local inhabitants. This should be compared with the fifteen days' grace generally allowed by statute. 51 Henry III stat. 4.

142. Details were to be certified to the Exchequer by at least two commissioners. The assessments were then to be levied by process out of the Exchequer.

143. The crown draft of the bill, as it was engrossed, naturally contained the reduced rates and extended payment period forced by the opposition in parliament. Further efforts seem to have been necessary to incorporate provisions for the acceptance of plate and the other clauses in the subsidy bill.

144. 26 Henry VII c. 19. The deficiencies of this act are particularly surprising since it is known that Cromwell had studied earlier subsidies. March 1533: *LP* VI, 299 (ix), see *LP* II, 1371; July 1534: *LP* VII, 923 (xviii). The deficiencies of the act seem to have borne fruit for Cromwell's remembrances contain several references to 'the deceit of the king in his subsidy'. Jan. 1535: *LP* VIII, 147; Feb. 1536: *LP* X, 254; Apr. 1537: *LP* XII, pt, I, 1091; Dec. 1537: *LP* XII, pt. II, 1151, §2, 3; Jan. 1538: *LP* XIII, pt. I, 187; Apr. 1538: *LP* XIII, pt. I, 879.

145. The act of 1534 also required payment to be made to the Treasurer of the Chamber rather than to the Exchequer.

146. Such as increases in fines for various offences under the subsidy acts, and an

increase in the number required for a quorum of commissioners. 32 Henry VIII c. 50; 34 & 35 Henry VIII c. 27.

147. 37 Henry VIII c. 25.

148. An income of £10 per annum in lands, or the possession of goods to the value of £66 13s 4d Similar qualifications had been required for the collectors of the fifteenths and tenths granted in 1540. 32 Henry VIII c. 50.

149. The recognisances were to be taken by the commissioners and certified to the Exchequer. Collectors refusing to subscribe to recognisances and commissioners failing to certify them were to be fined £10.

150. This clause applied both to the fifteenths and tenths and to the subsidies. While exemptions from subsidies were disadvantageous to the crown in that they reduced the yield of the tax, exemptions from fifteenths and tenths were disadvantageous to other taxpayers, because, since the yield remained fixed, a greater burden was placed on them. Prerogative grants of exemption from subsidies were very rare. This, together with the fact that the crown ignored this clause as far as the fifteenths and tenths were concerned (see Chapter 3, pp. 27–71), suggests that this clause was promoted by the Commons rather than by the crown.

Notes to Chapter 5

1. Unless otherwise stated all references in this chapter are to the subsidy acts. It would be tedious to cite the reference for each act on every occasion; these references are gathered together in Appendix I.

2. As Appendix I. No schedules were attached to the act of 1523. The names of the commissioners are conveniently printed in *Stat. Realm*, III (1513) pp. 79–89; (1514) pp. 112–19; (1515–16) pp. 168–75; (1524) *LP*, III, 3283; (1525) *LP*, IV, pt. I, 547.

3. See Appendix II.

4. See Appendix II.

5. See Appendix I, 'Exchequer copy'.

6. See Appendix II.

7. 'THE ACTE OF SVBSIDIE', printed in black letter on 20pp foolscap by Berthelet, the king's printer. SP1/86 ff. 170–81. See also *LP*, XIII, pt. II, 98; and for the 1545 act. *LP*, *Add.*, 1714; SP1/245 ff. 49–53.

8. For the actual dates specified by the subsidy acts, see Table 5.18.

9. The East, North and West Ridings of Yorkshire, and the parts of Holland, Kesteven and Lindsey in Lincolnshire.

10. Commissions to certain shires are sometimes lacking in the Chancery enrolments; but this is due to clerical error, since collectors from the areas concerned accounted in the Exchequer.

11. The maximum number of 'auxiliary' commissioners that might be appointed for the subsidy of 1514 was ten.

12. Care must be taken not to include those gentlemen to whose names were appended the name of their seat, but who nevertheless were full commissioners.

13. Possibly also to other factors such as the number of gentry available. But there is no evidence of any desire to serve on the subsidy commissions similar to the desire for inclusion in the Commissions of the Peace, unless the amendments made by

the Privy Council to some of the commissions in 1541 were prompted by such considerations.

14. The names of both sets of commissioners can most readily be compared for the subsidies of 1513 and 1514. Subsidy commissioners: *Stat. Realm*, III, pp. 79–89, 112–19; Commissioners of the Peace: *LP*, I, pt. II, app. 1.

15. But some peers were appointed as commissioners for the anticipation of the subsidy of 1524. *LP*, III, 3504.

16. This is especially clear for the subsidies of 1524 and 1525, and for the subsidies of 1541 and 1542. See Appendix II. The commission for the subsidy of 1547 in Lincoln was sent to those who had been commissioners for the subsidy of 1546 ('45). LAC L1/1/12 f.43b.

17. See Table 5.9.

18. The names of the commissioners for the peerage were certified by Wolsey to the Exchequer. E179/69/11; E159/308 Recorda H.r.15.

19. E359/44 26HVIII, 1st payment, r.13; 2nd payment, r.11; 32HVIII, 1st payment, r.17; 2nd payment, r.7; E359/42 34 & 35HVIII, 1st payment, r.19; 2nd payment, r.18d; 3rd payment, r.14d; 37HVIII, 1st payment, r.15; 2nd payment r.13d.

20. For the subsidies of 1541 and 1542 the commissioners wrote to Lord Cobham asking for his own valuation of his assessment. *LP*, XVI, 584; XVII, 141.

21. See Collectors' Accounts, and *LP*, XIII, pt. 2, 672.

22. Derbs: E159/303 Recorda M.r.22d; Yorks. (WR): E159/306 Recorda H.r.36.

23. Norfolk: E159/313 Recorda P.r.31.

24. 7 Henry IV c. 11.

25. Cornwall, *Sussex Subsidy Rolls*, xxv, states that the subsidy acts exempted members of parliament from appointment as commissioners. He is mistaken. As this introduction contains a number of errors, it is best disregarded.

26. According to the commissioners' certificates, almost all commissioners returned a single certificate for the subsidy of 1513, while most did so for the subsidy of 1514. For the subsidy of 1515 most commissioners returned several separate certificates for portions of the commission area, and by 1523 only the towns were each returning one consolidated certificate for the whole commission area. E179, *passim*; E359/38, 41, 42, 44, *passim*.

27. *LP*, XVI, 112.

28. *LP*, XV, 1004 (county unknown: 1 addition); 1008 (Bucks: 6 additions); XVI, 8 (Oxon: 1 addition)

29. *LP*, XVI, 157, 168, 214, 223, 361, 533, 1104, 1141.

30. *LP*, XVI, 435.

31. *LP*, XX, pt. 2, 1049 (Sussex: Bishop of Chichester in place of Sir John Gage).

32. A formal warrant was to follow. The collectors were to bring the Treasurer's Bills of Receipt to their account at the Exchequer. APC I, 332, 336.

33. A 'good lesson and exhortation' for 'misdemeanour' towards two commissioners: (1542), *LP*, XVI, 1299. The examination of the collectors for the peerage and the committal of one of them to the Fleet for embezzlement: (1543) *LP*, XVIII, pt. I, 24. The committal of a collector who had forged an Exchequer tally to three hours on the pillory: (1543) E159/321 Recorda T.r.45. There were possibly more cases than these; but no cases concerning subsidies were brought either before Star Chamber or Requests.

34. Except for the subsidies of 1514 and 1515 where control of the commissioners was entrusted by the subsidy acts to committees in the 'Cheker Chamber'.
35. This clause was omitted by the act for the subsidies of 1535–6.
36. 5 Henry VIII c. 17. All subsequent subsidy acts had similar definitions. The earlier act, for the subsidy of 1513, enumerated lands, tenements, and rents, both free and copyhold, offices, annuities and corrodies.
37. But not for subsidies up to, and including, 1525 when wages were assessed under a separate category: see below. A large number of servants were assessed in Southwark for the subsidy of 1546 ('45); but they were exonerated because their wages were paid by the week and not by the year. E368/322 SVC M.r.4.
38. This excusable shorthand is frequently employed by editors of record society publications of subsidy rolls. See, for example, Cornwall, *Sussex Subsidy Rolls*; Chibnall and Woodman, *Bucks. Record Soc.*, viii (1950).
39. For example by the sale of surplus produce.
40. Especially for the purpose of calculating the selling price of the land.
41. The wording is that of 4 Henry VIII c. 19.
42. The act for the subsidies of 1546 ('45) and 1547 specified a minimum assessment of £2 for annual wages received by servants, as compared to the general minimum assessment of £1 for other annual incomes.
43. The wording is that of 4 Henry VIII c. 19.
44. 5 Henry VIII c. 17.
45. 6 Henry VIJII c. 16.
46. Exceptions from the exemption for clothing were: for the subsidies of 1524–7, 'Juels of golde'; for the subsidies of 1535–6, 'jewells'; for the subsidies of 1541–6 ('43), 'Juels sylver stoune and othir'; and for the subsidies of 1546 ('45)–7, 'Juels sylver stoune and pearls'.
47. For example, Lord Lawarr estimated the value of his jewels, plate and household stuff at 1,400 marks; but he was also owed 1,100 marks which he had lent to two other peers. Thus his subsidy assessment would have been considerably higher than what would have been shown by an inventory of his tangible wealth. BM Add.MSS 25,460, f.7. And the subsidy assessment of a merchant, who owed large debts, would be much smaller than a valuation of his apparent wealth.
48. There was also a poll tax on aliens not otherwise liable to the subsidy.
49. Except that a minimum age qualification was also imposed on assessments on wages for the subsidy of 1513.
50. Leicester: about 33 per cent; Exeter: 36.5 per cent; and Coventry: 48.5 per cent. Hoskins, *TRHS*, 5th Ser., vol. 6, 17. For Leicester, Hoskins cites *Trans. Leics. Arch. Soc.* XXV (1949), 74, 84.
51. Smith, *Land and Politics*, pp. 109–10.
52. Holdsworth, *History of English Law*, III, pp. 520–33.
53. E179/*passim*. In 1545 a woman married during the assessment of the subsidy. Her goods were assessed twice, once under her maiden name and once under her husband's name. The assessment under her maiden name was quashed. E359/42 34 & 35 HVIII, 2nd payment, 7d.
54. Holdsworth, *History of English Law*, III, p. 516.
55. Except for assessment on wages for the subsidy of 1513. See Table 5.7.
56. A claim was made by the executors of a man who died after having been assessed

for the subsidy of 1547, and whose lands escheated in wardship to the crown on account of the minority of his son. The executors paid the subsidy on the deceased's goods instead. E159/326 Records T.r.53. A similar claim was made for the subsidy of 1524: E368/298 SVC H.r.19. Three exemptions were claimed for exoneration from assessments on goods subsequently forfeit to the king. 1542: Yorks. (WR), felon, E159/321 Recorda H.r.86; 1536: London, felon, E359/44 26HVIII 2nd payment, r.2d; 1544: London, E359/42 34 & 35 HVIII, 1st payment, r.17.

57. Nevertheless, a commission to assess the inhabitants was sent out for the subsidy of 1514. LP, I, 862 § 7. For the subsidy of 1516, the inhabitants of Walmer, Deal, Folkestone, Romney, and various towns on the isle of Thanet were required by the Barons in the Exchequer to prove their incorporation with the Cinque Ports. The case was undecided. E159/302 Recorda M.r.16. The inhabitants of Lydd produced their charter in the Exchequer and secured exemption from the subsidy of 1524. E159/306 Recorda H.r.8. For the later subsidies a few of the inhabitants were assessed elsewhere and claimed exoneration from these assessments: 1544: 150 persons in Kent at £65 7s 4d, E359/42 34 & 35, HVIII, 1st payment, r.18d and 7 persons in Sussex at £8 12s 8d, ibid., r. 15d; 1545: 1 person in Kent at £3.0s.0d, ibid., 2nd payment., r.11d; 1546 ('43): 1 person in Kent at £0 3s 4d, ibid., 3rd payment. r.2; 1547: 1 person in Westminster at £6 13s 4d, E359/42 37 HVIII 2nd payment, r.14d.

58. Who was styled 'Ladye Katheryn Princes Dowager late Wyff of Prynce Arthure'.

59. The Minories, London; Denney, Cambs., and Bruisyard Suffolk. These were the three abbeys of Franciscan nuns in England. Knowles & Hadcock, Medieval Religious Houses, p. 232.

60. In addition, a schedule under the royal Sign Manual, granting exemption to the Colleges, but with the names of the other Houses struck through, was attached to the act. 7 HVIII c.9. HLRO original.

61. But there was no specific statutory exemption for the subsidies of 1513, 1514 and 1535–6.

62. But there was no specific statutory exemption for the subsidies of 1535–6 and 1544–6 ('43). For other forms of exemption for these subsidies, see below.

63. That is, lands acquitted after the Taxation of Pope Nicholas.

64. 'Temporal' lands of the clergy were, generally, those acquired after the Taxation of Pope Nicholas of 1291, and were therefore not dismable.

65. 'he or they shalbe oonlie chardged by the vertue of this acte for his or theyre saide Manoures landes, tenementes, hereditaments or spirituall possessions or oonlie for his saide Goodes and Catalls, The beste of all to be taken for the King, and not to be chardged for bothe or double chardged for any of them'. On the other hand, the two acts for the clerical subsidies both contain clauses, added by parliament at the same time as the lay subsidy acts were being debated, which required lay persons holding any 'spirituall promocion' together with temporal lands and goods to pay the clerical subsidy on the spiritual promotion and the lay subsidy on his temporal lands or possessions. 34 & 35 Henry VIII c. 28, 37 Henry VIII c. 24. The clauses in the clerical acts are more consonant with fifteenth and sixteenth century taxation practice; but it does not seem possible to construe the clauses in the lay acts to this effect.

66. Many of these claims concerned monastic pensions, which, being liable to the clerical subsidies, were classed as spiritual incomes. On the other hand, a clerk of Peterborough cathedral claimed before the Barons of the Exchequer that he had not been assessed for temporal lands which he held in Kent, either for the subsidy of 1544 or for the subsidy of 1545, and asked to be assessed accordingly. E159/324 Recorda P.r.11.

67. The act for the subsidies of 1535 and 1536 lacked this clause. The towns of Shrewsbury and Ludlow successfully sued their letters patent of exemption for both these subsidies. Ludlow: E359/44 26HVIII, 1st payment, r.11, E159/316 Bre.Dir. T.r–; E359/44 26HVIII, 2nd payment, r.9d, E159/319 Bre.Dir. T.r–. Shrewsbury: E159/321 Recorda H.r.85, /317 Recorda H.r.40. As from 1523 the subsidy acts had a further clause saving the future rights of the franchises and other prerogative grants.

68. For the significance of the position of clauses in the subsidy acts, see pp. 19–21. The acts for the subsidies of 1541–2, in addition to the usual clause has a proviso attached to the act, which was therefore probably introduced into parliament after engrossment of the act, suspending prerogative grants both for the subsidies and for the fifteenth and tenths. For the effect of this proviso on the numerous exemptions from fifteenths and tenths, see p. 69.

69. The wording is that of 6 Henry VIII c. 26.

70. The wording is that of 14 & 15 Henry VIII c. 16.

71. The wording is that of 4 Henry VIII c. 19.

72. No such provision was made by the act for the subsidy of 1514. Sir Thomas Wyatt was abroad, and was assessed on the evidence of his neighbours to the subsidy of 1546 ('45) E159/325 Recorda P.r.66. On the other hand, Lord Sandys, Treasurer of Calais escaped assessment towards the subsidy of 1525, but not in 1524, because he was 'in the kinges service at Caleis', and Lord Berners, the deputy, escaped assessment for both subsidies. E179/69/19 cited by Miller *BIHR* XXVIII, (1955), 17, n. 2. Lord Lisle, a later Deputy of Calais, tried to avoid paying the subsidies of 1535 and 1536, and succeeded at least until 1548. *LP*, XII, pt. 2, 337, 423; XIII, pt. 1, 579; pt. 2, 590, 644, 672; XIV, pt. 1, 53, 81. E359/44 26HVIII, 1st payment, r.13; 2nd payment, r.11; E372/387, 391, 394, all Ad. It. London.

73. For the procedure of certification, see pp. 128–31. For the statutory payment date, see Table 5.18.

74. This calculation is highly hypothetical. However, it yields the reasonable conclusion that the incidence of double assessments because of double residence was higher amongst the richer classes.

75. The subsidies of 1544 and 1546 ('45) are compared because they are the first of a series. See below. If it is assumed that the known decline of 70% in the number of persons assessed in the West Riding of Yorkshire between the subsidies of 1545 and 1546 ('45) is typical of the fall in the number of persons assessed over the country as a whole, then the considerably smaller decline of 18½% in the number of double assessments confirms once again the impression that double assessments for double residence were mainly confined to the richer classes. Smith, *Land and Politics*, pp. 109–10. It is also assumed that the numbers assessed in 1544 and 1545 were the same.

76. E159/326 Recorda M.r.26.
77. The act for the subsidies of 1535–6 did not punish removal into exempt areas.
78. The Attorney General claimed in the Exchequer that during the assessments for the subsidy of 1546 ('45) John Jones, clothier of Abingdon and of Burford, Oxon., claimed in each place that he had been assessed in the other. The enrolment of the case ends after the attorney general had requested a trial by jury. E159/325 Recorda P.r.11.
79. Proceedings taken by the Justices of the Peace were probably informal, and are unlikely to have left any documentary record. No fines certified by the Justices to the Exchequer have been noted.
80. See Table 5.18, p. 132, below.
81. For the subsidies of 1513, 1514 and 1535–6 no minimum number was specified by the subsidy acts. For the subsidies of 1544–7 the minimum number was raised to three. As from 1515 the subsidy acts exempted commissioners and members of the commons from appointment as assessors. The act for the subsidies of 1544–6 ('43) also required the attendance of all the commissioners at the preliminary meeting 'having no sufficient excuse for his absence'.
82. But not for the subsidies of 1513 and 1514. From 1535 the fine was raised to £2. The act for the subsidies of 1535–6 made no provision for excuses.
83. No oath was required from the assessors for the subsidies of 1513 and 1535–6.
84. The act for the subsidies of 1544–6 ('43) required the oath to be taken first by 'oone of the moste substaunciall inhabitauntes or officer', and then by the other assessors.
85. The text is as for the subsidies of 1515 and 1516. This form of oath was repeated by the act for the subsidies of 1525–7 with two very minor additions. The act for the subsidies of 1541–2 omitted the references to wages, and altered the invocation of the saints to an appeal to the 'contentes of this Booke'. The act for the subsidies of 1544–6 ('43) mentioned 'debtes and other things' for the first time, and the act for the subsidies of 1546 ('45)–7 repeated this form verbatim. Otherwise the original form of the oath was retained substantially unaltered until the end of the period.
86. As from 1515; but there was no fine for the subsidies of 1535–6 because no oath was specified by the subsidy act. As from 1541 the fine was raised to £2.
87. 1545: LAC, L1/1/12, f.25b; 1547; Ibid., f. 43b.
88. For the subsidies of 1514 and 1515 the commissioners for the city of London printed a summary of the assessment rates and rules, together with an order for certification to be made by a certain day, for distribution to the assessors. Steele, *Proclamations*, vol. I, 71, 72. A torn copy of No. 72, with additions in a contemporary hand, may be found in WA 12409.
89. From 1515. From 1535 this fine was raised to £2. A curious discrepancy occurred in the last three acts for the subsidies of 1541–7. The assessors were to be warned by the commissioners at the preliminary meeting that failure to appear at the next meeting with their certificates would incur a fine of £1. But in the clause dealing with this second meeting the acts specified the fine for non-attendance as £2. This discrepancy was not resolved until 1553, 7 Edward VI c. 9, which settled on £2.
90. The wording is that of 6 Henry VIII c. 26.
91. No such provision was made by the act for the subsidies of 1535–6.

92. Thus for the subsidies of 1515–16 and 1524–7. For the subsidies of 1513 and 1514, only 'sufficient warning' was required. The acts for the subsidies of 1541–6 ('43) omitted 'at their parisshe churches', and the act for the subsidies of 1546 ('45)–7 omitted 'opyn proclamacions'.
93. For the subsidies of 1513 and 1514 they were only to be charged at the highest available assessments.
94. Text as from 1515. This form of oath suffered the same minor changes in subsequent subsidy acts as have been described for the assessors' oath.
95. This was not available under the act for the subsidy of 1513.
96. Naturally this testimony had to be given before the commissioners certified the assessments to the Exchequer. This procedure was not recorded in the commissioners' certificates, and so no estimate can be made as to how frequently it was resorted to. It was used at least once in London for the subsidy of 1525. CLRO Repertory 4, f. 216b. During the assessment of the subsidy of 1515, a taxpayer alleged that one of the London commissioners had refused to allow him to volunteer his own assessment on oath. CLRO Repertory 3, f. 1b.
97. Proof was to be 'by witnes his own confession or other lawful waies or meanes'. No court was specified as being competent to try such cases, and no procedure for the levying of the fine was indicated. The Exchequer would have been the most likely court for such actions; but none have been noticed there.
98. No date was specified by the act for the subsidies of 1535–6. See Table 5.18.
99. No dates for assessment were specified by the act for the subsidies of 1535–6; but for the subsidy of 1535 there is evidence that assessments were being made on 1 July, and on 9 September. *LP*, VIII, 968; IX, 308. The commissions for the subsidy of 1536 were received in Norfolk on 5 September, *LP*, XI, 404, but on 3 October the assessments were suspended, first in Lincolnshire and Yorkshire, and then in many other parts of the country, because of the disturbances. *LP*, XI, 533–4, 679, XII pt. 1, 32, 344.
100. See Table 5.18.
101. For payments by collectors other than to the Exchequer see Table 6.2 (p. 151), notes 1, 3, 4.
102. See Table 5.18. The subsidy acts required at least two commissioners to be present for the appointment of the petty collectors and for the preparation of their lists. The acts for the subsidies of 1544–7 raised this number to three.
103. This depended on the size of the hundred, which varied considerably from county to county. In Sussex, where the hundreds were very small, collectors were usually appointed for each rape. It was very rare for two collectors to be appointed for the same area. E359/38, 41, 42, 44, *passim*.
104. The names of the collectors can be obtained from the Collectors' Accounts. E359/ 38, 41, 42, 44, *passim*.
105. Only one claim against such a consecutive double appointment has been found. The collector's name was certified in error for his son's. E159/320 Recorda T.r.30.
106. The act for the subsidies of 1535–6 extended this to exempt anyone from appointment as high collector outside his own county.
107. These qualifications were required of collectors of fifteenths and tenths since 1541. 32 Henry VIII c. 50.

108. For the use of recognisances in the procedure of the Exchequer of Account, see pp. 161–4.

109. The collectors were to pay all the cash that they had in hand by 1 April in 1546 and 1547; and the balance due from their area within one month.

110. No such fines have been found. Nevertheless, some of the commissioners' certificates were endorsed by the officers of the Exchequer as 'sine obligacione'. E179/151/346. Some of the commissioners' certificates incorporated the form of the recognisances in the text of the indentures, while others stated that separate recognisances were enclosed. No separate obligations have been found. These have probably been preserved in the class E114, Exchequer, King's Remembrancer, Bonds, which is at present described as '98 bundles, temp. Henry VIII to Victoria'. PRO 'King's Remembrancer, class list', vol. I, 146a. Only one additional recognisance, taken by the Exchequer, has been found. 1547: Somerset (Brent hundred) E159/327 Recogns. H.r.–.

111. The wording is that of 4 Henry VIII c. 19. As from 1524 the presence of a majority of the commissioners was necessary for the appointment of high collectors and for the preparation of their indentures.

112. See Table 5.18. The act for the subsidies of 1546 ('45) and 1547 required the indentures to be given to the high collectors some four and a half weeks before the indentures were to be given to the petty collectors. Since this last date, as specified by the act, was only one day before the high collectors were meant to have paid the bulk of their money to the Exchequer, it is probable that at least the date specified for the petty collectors is erroneous.

113. But not for the subsidy of 1513 when the petty collectors were allowed any remuneration by the subsidy act.

114. For the subsidies of 1535–6 the money was to be paid to the Treasurer of the Chamber.

115. The official Exchequer fees were laid down by an ordinance of the Council dated 28 July 1456, and enrolled on E159/234 Recorda M.r.56. These fees were printed regularly until 1552. *Bibliography of Early English Law Books*, pp. 136–8. They were also hung up in tabular form in the Exchequer. UL, 1921 Catalogue, No. 9, f. 41–3. The act for the subsidies of 1546 ('45)–7 imposed a fine of twenty times the sum in question on any officer of the Exchequer who charged the collectors any fee, together with imprisonment at the king's discretion.

116. These indentures were not normally certified to the Exchequer. Only one indenture handed to a petty collector has been found. 1515: Oxon. (Binfield hundred) E179/274/53.

117. Compare the position of the collectors for fifteenths and tenths, discussed on pp. 45–6.

118. 'Spurred pennies' are not mentioned in the subsidy acts after 1523. They were first downvalued to ½d by the act of 1504 'Pro Reformacione Pecuniarum', 19 Henry VII c. 5. The description seems to apply to all pennies minted in the reigns of Richard III and Edward IV, and to those minted in Durham between 1485 and 1489. Brooke, *English Coins*, 162–73, plates XXV, XXXVII.

119. There was no provision in the subsidy act of 1534. Although the act for the subsidies of 1524–7 gave some exchange rates in full, it also cited the proclamation on exchange rates issued before the first day of the parliament. No such

proclamation is noted in Steele, *Proclamations*. The acts for the subsidies of 1541–6 ('43) cited a proclamation of 27 March 1539, and the act for the subsidies of 1546 ('45)–7 cited the last relevant proclamation. No proclamations concerning exchange rates have been noted by Steele for these dates. See Steele, no. 88, and I, 179a.

120. For 'wastage' see Craig, *The Mint*, p. 86; and for the costs of coinage see *ibid.*, appendix 2.

121. In 1542 a collector brought in silver to the value of £12 10s 0d which he had seized in default of payment, and this was accepted by one of the tellers. E359/44 32 HVIII, 2nd payment, r.12d.

122. E405/483, no foliation.

123. These coins were not minted in Henry VIII's reign. Brooke, *English Coins*, pp. 174–5.

124. The document refers to 'Argentum'. Since all other silver coins are specified by name, it has been inferred that this style refers to halfpennies and farthings.

125. Described as 'Solles'.

126. This liability ceased with the abandonment, after 1525, of wages as a separate assessment category.

127. It seems to have been a general principle that assessments on goods were made on whoever held them, regardless of where the legal title lay.

128. Except that for the subsidies of 1544–6 ('43) landlords were only to be held liable after a default in payment by aliens.

129. For the subsidies of 1524–7, tenants and lessees of spiritual persons, bound by oath or covenant to pay taxes, were required by the subsidy act to pay to the landlord at each assessment the value of one disme only, even if the land were not ordinarily liable to the clerical tenth.

130. Only one such action has been found. It was brought in Chancery, but the outcome is unknown. 1526: Lincs., C1/977/25.

131. No provision for distress outside the collector's area was made by the act for the subsidies of 1535–6.

132. It had long been established that a debt to the crown did not expire upon the death of the debtor, but was inherited by the heirs, executors, administrators, or anyone holding the property of the deceased. Normally the recovery of such a debt was undertaken by the Exchequer by means of a combined writ of 'diem clausit extremum', 'capias', 'distringas' and 'fieri facias', addressed to the sheriff. For this process, see pp. 157–8. The subsidy acts thus considerably streamlined the traditional procedure, eliminating the Exchequer, the sheriff and the inquisition post mortem.

133. The wording of this clause in the act for the subsidies of 1535–6 implies, incorrectly, that lands and tenements were generally liable to distress for subsidy debts.

134. The same fee as was allowed to the sheriff for making arrests by an act of 1444. *Rot. Parl.*, V, p. 110.

135. Either by the king's remembrancer, or by means of the summons of the pipe. See pp. 164–5.

136. The claims are best taken from the Collectors' Accounts as enrolled on E359, since the original certificates have generally not survived. For an original certificate, see E179/71/121.

137. See pp. 164–5.
138. Some went to the wars in France. E359/42 34 & 35 HVIII, 2nd payment, r. 6, 16d; 3rd payment, r.2d.
139. A fine of £1 was suggested by the subsidy acts, but the commissioners were quite free to augment this. For most of the subsidies the presence of two commissioners was required for the imposition of fines. For the subsidies levied between 1514 and 1527 the number of commissioners required was three.
140. 1515: Essex. £1 for disobedience to the commissioners. E179/279/3/22. 1544: Beds. Offence unspecified. E179/71/136.
141. For the actual dates, see Table 5.18.
142. But for some of the later subsidies the certification date was still close to the payment date. For the subsidies of 1535–6, however, very few people were assessed because of the high minimum assessments. E179/ various counties 14 Henry VIII–1 Edward VI, *passim*.
143. See pp. 133–4.
144. Unless the device of the Anticipation had been decided upon, but kept secret, during the passage of the subsidy act through parliament. Several of these certificates have survived amongst the state papers. *LP*, IV, 969, 1117, 1299, 1779, 2811. It was probably on the basis of these certificates that the decision was taken to order a re-assessment in February 1524.
145. Needless to say, the commissioners did return the names of the collectors. E359/ 38 6 HVIII, 7 HVIII, *passim*.
146. Increased to eight days for the subsidies of 1546 ('45) and 1547.
147. E179/ various counties, 14 Henry VIII–1 Edward VI, *passim*.
148. For the forms of Exchequer process, see pp. 152–4.
149. For the subsidies of 1513–16 no dates for the beginning of assessment were specified in the acts. If, as for later subsidies, the assessment took approximately six weeks, then the total time for assessment and collection for these subsidies was as follows: 1513 and 1514: about 18 weeks. 1515 and 1516: about 13 weeks.
150. The subsidy was granted because the previous subsidy appeared extremely unlikely to yield the sum granted to the crown.
151. This was recognised by Paget in his memorandum of November 1544, in which he discusses the different ways, including a 'benevolence', of raising revenue. *LP*, XIX, pt. 2, 689.
152. The average number of commissioners appointed was seven.
153. That is, mayors, sheriffs, Justices of the Peace, bailiffs or similar officers.
154. That is, to the same towns that received separate commissions for the subsidy of 1524, with the exception of Hereford, Kingston upon Hull, London, New Windsor, Southwark, Yarmouth and York, and with the addition of Cambridge, Wells and Winchester. A separate commission, not included in the Chancery enrolment, was sent to various judges to practise with the legal profession for the Anticipation. E359/41 1st payment, Anticipation, r.5.
155. The names of the commissioners are conveniently printed in *LP*, III, 3504. The full instructions to the commissioners were delivered into the Exchequer by a Chancery clerk on 18 February 1524, and were enrolled by the king's remembrancer. E159/305 Recorda P.r.18, M.r.29.
156. These were the only assessments available on 2 November 1523.

157. Nevertheless the collectors accounted at the Exchequer. E359/41 1st payment, Anticipation, *passim*. For the failure of some of the collectors to levy before the collectors of the subsidy, see Table 7.1 (pp. 170–2). Certificates of the sums to be collected in anticipation were to be sent by the commissioners to the Council at Westminster. E159/305 Recorda P.r.18, M.r.29.

158. The commission arrived in Kent before 16 June. *LP*, XX, pt. I, 957. But it arrived in Norfolk between 21 and 27 June, *ibid.*, 999, 1031.

159. *LP*, XX, pt. I, 675. LAC, L1/1/2 f.32–32b.

160. *LP*, XIX, pt. II, 689; XX, pt. I, 674; pt. II, 366, 769, 853.

161. By a general proclamation. *LP*, XX, pt. I, 703.

162. LAC L1/1/1/2 f.32–32b.

163. *Ibid.*, f. 26. For the success of these devices to speed the collection of the subsidies see Table 8.1 (pp. 179–81).

164. E179/279/1. But certificates from about 70% of the commission areas are missing from the file.

165. E179/279/2. But certificates from about 20% of the commission areas are missing from the file.

166. The two missing indentures were for the two Royal Housholds. E179/279/3. But certificates from about 20% of the commission areas are missing from the file.

167. See Table 5.18.

168. These are scattered all over the class E179, and are at present classified according to counties and somewhat arbitrarily, into miscellaneous oddments.

169. Gross lateness in certifying the assessments would have seriously hindered the collectors in accounting at the Exchequer, and would have occasioned severe process out of the Exchequer. For the speed at which the collectors accounted, see pp. 184–7. For process against the collectors, see pp. 151–6.

170. 1536: Cornwall. John Arundel, the commissioner, was found in the Exchequer and committed to the Fleet. He was released upon payment of a fine of 10s 0d. E159/320 Recorda M.r.53. The other case was 1535; Lancs., and the outcome is unknown. E159/317 Recorda H.r.18d.

171. The commissioners were John Malory and John Norton.

172. John Malory had died, so John Norton accounted alone. The fraud was discovered because the sheriffs returned the writs of attachment issued against the collectors when they did not appear to account at the Exchequer, with the endorsement 'non est talis persona'. E159/303 Recorda H.r.23d; E159/306 Recorda M.r.42.

173. Cope admitted his offence. E159/324 Recorda P.r.39.

174. C1/1004/74.

175. The name of the commissioner delivering the certificates was endorsed on the certificates by the officers of the Exchequer. E179/279/2.

176. E179/279/3.

177. The certificates must have arrived in the Exchequer because the collectors accounted. E359/38 5 HVIII, 6HVIII, *passim*.

178. About 70% of the certificates due are missing from the file. E179/279/1.

179. They are scattered throughout the class E179. Very many more commissioners sent in separate certificates for parts of each commission area than had been the case before. It would have been inconvenient to keep such large numbers of

certificates on a single file. For the increase in the number of collectors accounting, see Table 8.2 (p. 185).

180. See Table 8.2. The additional certification of individual names and tax charges also made the certificates very bulky.

181. Similar writs of 'distringas ad extractas liberandas' were issued regularly against commissioners of sewers, oyer and terminer, gaol delivery, and of the peace. See the section Bre.Ret. in E159/262–327.

182. The writs were returnable on the quindene of Trinity. It was normal Exchequer practice to send out writs in the middle of the previous term, E202/175–296, *passim*. These writs were therefore probably sent out in mid-April. E159/303 Bre.Ret. P.r–. See Table 5.18.

183. For the revision of the assessments, ordered by a signet letter of 26 February 1524, see p. 183.

184. Staffs, Sussex, Yorks (ER) and (WR). E159/304 Recorda T.r.9d, 10, 12. These instances have been noted because the sheriffs were fined for making an insufficient return to the writs. There may well have been other cases, but in which the writ was properly returned. Writs against some of the commissioners for the peerage were issued as late as November 1529. E159/308 Recorda H.r.15, Dies Dat. M.r–, Bre.Ret. T.r–. For the statutory certification dates see Table 5.18.

185. Returnable on the octave of Hilary. E159/319 Bre.Ret. M.r–.

186. E159/320 Bre.Ret. M.r–.

187. But at least all these commissioners certified before the return day. E159/322 Bre.Ret. H.r–.

188. E368/303 Recorda T.r.4, 10, 14; E372/366 It.Ebor. It is very difficult in most cases to distinguish subsidy commissioners from other commissioners, for most entries refer to them merely as 'unus Assignatus Regis'.

189. E159/308 Bre.Ret. T.r–, M.r–, Recorda H.r.15, Dies Dat. M.r–; /309 Dies Dat. M.r–d.

190. For the fifteenth century, see Pugh and Ross, *BIHR*, XXVI (1953).

Notes to Chapter 6

1. For the concept of a 'Court of Record', see Elton, *Tudor Revolution in Government*, pp. 47, 51, 120, 168, 195, 204–5, 222, 281.

2. E159, E368, *passim*.

3. From Easter 1505 until Easter 1551, an annual 'Declaration of the State of the Treasury' was drawn up by the under-Treasurer, the head officer of the Exchequer of Receipt. The 'Declarations' classified receipts into cash payments and assignments, and then by class of revenue, and type of assignment. Details of the movement of cash and tallies between the Exchequer and the Treasury of the Chamber were also given. From 1514 the 'Declarations' contain no record of revenue derived from taxation. BM Lansdowne, 156, f. 124 ff.; E405/183–212. The 'Declarations' for nine years are missing.

4. The subsidy of 1489 was to be paid to designated receivers in the counties. The subsidies of 1535–6 were to be paid to the Treasurer of the Chamber, as was the anticipation of the subsidy of 1524.

5. This account is based mainly on various documents (numbered but disorganised) in E407/71, relating to disputes between officers of the Exchequer during the reign of Elizabeth. Several of the documents attempt to describe the practice of the Exchequer as it was in the time of Henry VII. For this dispute, see Elton, 'The Exchequer: War in the Receipt'. For tallies, see Jenkinson, *Archaeologica, LXII* (1911), pp. 367–80.

6. For the early Tudor period, E405/477, 480–3, 385–6, 560; E407/60.

7. For the early Tudor period: E405/75–124.

8. For the early Tudor period: E402/57–99.

9. For the early Tudor period: E401/975–1181.

10. For the early Tudor period: E402/1–3g.

11. For the period 1485–94 the Tellers' Rolls contain approximately twelve rotuli sides per annum. For the rest of the reign of Henry VII, with the exception of 1497–9 and 1503, the Rolls contain about half this number. The change is too sudden and drastic to be accounted for solely by the rise of the Chamber system; something else must have been responsible for this change.

12. Following Steel, *The Receipt of the Exchequer, 1377–1485*, pp. 7–13, the Treasurer's Roll has been used wherever possible. The Treasurer's Roll by no means always bears its characteristic dots in the left-hand margin. The practice, noted by Steel, *ibid.*, p. 9, of writing the name of the Roll in the overlap where two membranes had been stitched together was not current in the early Tudor period. Instead the same place was used to inscribe the date. Serious discrepancies between the Rolls have been found. See, for example E401/971 and 972, 22 Nov.

13. For some of the years only one of the Chamberlain's Rolls has survived. Elton's statement in 'The Exchequer: War in the Receipt', p. 216, that by 1550 no counterpells had been enrolled for decades, is incorrect, as can be seen from the list of Receipt Rolls kept in the National Archive.

14. E404. The warrants for the early Tudor period are at present in some confusion. Where several numerical series appear on the warrants, the series appearing on the face of the warrants has been taken. Where no numeration of the warrants exists at all, I have arranged the warrants for the reign of Henry VII in date order. Unfortunately I did not have the time to continue this procedure for the warrants of the reign of Henry VIII.

15. E404/80/5HVII/139. The Issue Roll, said by Giuseppi, *Guide to the PRO*, p. 184, and believed by all, to have lapsed between 19 Edward IV and 9 Elizabeth, is frequently quoted by Exchequer documents until at least the second decade of the sixteenth century. E159/264 Recorda T.r.4; E159/298 Recorda T.r.11d; E159/299 Recorda M.r.21d; E159/304 Recorda H.r.9d, 22; E159/305 Recorda T.r.1d; E159/306 Recorda H.r.19d; E159/308 Recorda T.r.31. Three further references, later in the reign of Henry VIII, may possibly be referring to the right-hand column of the Receipt Rolls where assignments were enrolled. On the other hand, the form of the quotation is undoubtedly that of an Issue Roll. E159/321 Recorda P.r.42, 42d; E159/324 Recorda M.r.15.

16. £260 to the Earl of Surrey, warden of the Eastmarches, £13 6s 8d to Sir Richard Chomley, Treasurer of Berwick, £26 13s 4d to Rogier Hopton, £10 0s 0d to Sir Richard Tunstall, for the repair of the city of York; and the balance of £241 4s 2½d to the Treasurer of the Chamber.

17. E404/80/4HVII/118.
18. E401/967 28 Oct.; E405/78, Pierson, r.1d.
19. The whole subject of assignment before 1485 has been exhaustively discussed by Steel, *The Receipt of the Exchequer, 1377–1485.* For the procedure of assignment see especially *ibid.*, pp. xxix–xxxiv.
20. No evidence has been discovered of the practice noted by Willard, *Parl. Taxes 1290–1334*, p. 233, n. 20 of sending out accompanying writs ordering payment together with the assigned tallies. Willard's contention that this rendered assigned tallies non-negotiable except by the 'legal' holder requires that the writs specified the name of the 'legal' holder. But Willard does not say if this was the practice of the Exchequer or not.
21. Steel, *The Receipt of the Exchequer 1377–1485*, pp. xxxii–xxxiii.
22. Compared with figures for previous reigns, 'mutua per talliam' were very rare in the early Tudor period. See Steel, *ibid.*, app. D, tables D1–10.
23. E13/176 T.r[14]d.
24. E13/177 P.r.7d.
25. This procedure was commonly used in the reign of Henry VII to regulate the payment of taxes levied in Yorkshire to Treasurers of military operations on the Scottish border. In the earlier part of the reign William Beverley, Dean of Middleham, was the chief Treasurer in the north. E404/80/4HVII/118; E404/5HVII/59, 109, 194, 219, 252. In the later 1490s his place was taken by William Severs, bishop of Carlisle. E404/82/12HVII, 6 November, 25 January; E404/83/14HVII/13 February, 12 April; E404/84/17HVII, 14 March. Severs' accounts: Salisbury MSS, 212/2,9 (BM microfilm No. M 485/56).
26. See, for example, E368/266 SVC T.r.6; E368/267 SVC M.r.11.
27. See, for example, E404/80/5HVII 89, 113. The practice noted by Willard, *Parl. Taxes 1290–1334*, p. 233, of requiring the production by the collectors either of the original writ ordering the payment or the indenture of receipt from the payee was not current in the early Tudor period. Only one example has been noted where the original warrant and indenture of Receipt were produced in the Exchequer E404/81/8HVII, 12 June. Otherwise the Privy Seal warrant to the Treasurer and Chamberlains seems to have been considered sufficient authority in itself for the levy of the tally.
28. Payments were usually recorded in the collectors' accounts as having been made in so many tallies 'de sol.' (Solucione), or 'de sol. et pro', or 'pro AB'. See especially E359/38, 39, *passim*.
29. Such as losses through robbery, E404/81/9HVII 23 May. Or remission of money assessed on the Cinque Ports, E401/1053, 3 Feb.
30. The striking of assigned tallies involved far more work in the Exchequer of Receipt; but the collectors were exempted by statute from liability to fees there. See Appendix I.
31. Assignments, especially for short-term loans, were very common in the early years of Henry VII's reign, but after 1495 became increasingly rare.
32. A tenth granted by the convocation of Canterbury, held in 6–7 Henry VII, (Wilkins, *Concilia*, III, p. 634) and payable 23 April 1492 *(CFR XXII, 434).*
33. E404/81/7HVII/5 Apr.
34. E401/976–982.

35. The Under-Treasurer was the head officer of the Exchequer of Receipt.
36. E404/82/12HVII/17 Mar.
37. E401/986–94.
38. But at least two of the Tellers were peripatetic, possibly collecting the loan money. E36/126, f.78. On both occasions part of the taxes was assigned elsewhere, and a very small proportion was paid directly to the Exchequer of Receipt in the normal way.
39. E404/85/20HVII/71.
40. E401/996, 998, 1000, 1002–3.
41. E405/183 f.31, 124b, Declaration of the State of the Treasury. John Daunce, Teller delivered £30,745 6s 9d to the Treasurer of the Chamber.
42. E159/305 Recorda P.r.18.
43. E159/303 Recorda M.r.1. The Barons were to allow these sums collected by way of anticipation to the collectors of the subsidy of 1524 when they came to account. Some unexplained difficulty seems to have arisen in the case of London. This was solved by issuing a tally to the collectors of the subsidy showing the money collected by way of anticipation as assigned to the Chamber. E404/96/ 19HVIII/62; E401/1100, 6 July.
44. E359/44 26HVIII, 1st payment, *passim*.
45. E404/100/27HVIII/11.
46. E401/1130, 28 May. Further batches were also struck on 22 June, 3 November, 15 January, 18 April, and so on. Tallies for the subsidy of 1536 appear to have been struck on certain dates in the same manner. E401/1130, 1133, 1135, 1137, 1140, *passim*.
47. The officers of the Exchequer of Receipt were prohibited by statute from claiming fees from collectors of parliamentary taxes. See Appendix I. For the collectors there was the expense of further delay and of a prolonged residence in London, or the costs of the retention of an attorney.
48. The courts of law kept the following terms: Michaelmas: 6 October to *c.* 25 November; Hillary: 20 January to 2–17 February; Easter: Quindene to *c.* Ascension; Trinity: Octave to 8 July. *Handbook of Dates*, pp. 67–8. Terms in the Upper Exchequer began one week earlier. E159/262–325; E368/259–322; E202/175–296.
49. E401/975–1181. Terms could straggle on until late in April and until early September; but this was rare. See, for example, E401/968, 986. All this confirms the account given by Steel, *The Receipt of the Exchequer, 1377–1485*, p. 2.
50. This again confirms Steel, *ibid.*, who notes that the Exchequer of Receipt was never open more than 164 days in any one year.
51. E401/975–1181.
52. E159/262–325; E368/259–322.
53. A similar policy has been noted by Willard, *Parl. Taxes 1290–1334*, p. 276.
54. From Chancery by way of the Originalia Rolls (E371).
55. For copies of acts granting taxes in the Exchequer, see Appendix I. Occasionally these acts might be enrolled on the King's Remembrancer's Memoranda Rolls. See, for example, E159/319 Recorda H.r.38.
56. The original writs are preserved, in most cases on their original files, in the class E202.
57. Such as 1s 0d: E159/269 Recorda T.r.11d; 3s 4d: E159/273 Recorda T.r.12d; 5s 0d:

E159/274 Dies dati T.r–; 6s 8d: E159/269 Dies dati H.r–. See also E202/175–296, *passim*.

58. Return days in the Exchequer were usually the morrow, the octave and the quindene of Michaelmas, Hillary and Trinity, and the octave (known as 'Crastino Clausi Pasche'), the quindene and month of Easter. Mid-term return days, such as the morrow, octave, and sometimes the quindene of the feasts of St John the Baptist, St Martin, the Purification and the Ascension were less frequently used. E202/175–296, *passim*.

59. Most writs bear a 'Teste' date falling in the middle of the term immediately before the return date. For the possibility of general 'liberate' or 'sealing' days in the Exchequer, see Vernon, *Considerations for Regulating the Exchequer*, p. 18.

60. Writs for distress were only enrolled on the Memoranda Rolls if there were a subsequent process for attachment (see below), and in these cases often only the immediately previous writ of distress is cited. The class E202 is too vast to search to discover the first date of the issue of these writs.

61. Fifteenth and tenth of 1497(II): commission sent out late, see Appendix I and Table 6.2. Anticipation to subsidy of 1524: letter to the Barons to distrain the collectors, 15 November 1524, but no list of commissioners sent from chancery until April 1526. E159/303 Recorda M.r.1; E159/305 Recorda P.r.18; the subsidies of 1535 and 1536 were affected by the difficulties in substituting tallies for the Treasurer of the Chamber's bills of Receipt, see pp. 149–50. The fifteenth and tenth of 1537 may well have been affected by the Pilgrimage of Grace, in that a great backlog of work on the delayed accounts of the previous subsidy had built up in the Exchequer, see Table 8.2. No explanation can be suggested for the apparent delay for the subsidies of 1525, 1526 and 1547.

62. See Table 6.2.

63. These forfeits are not systematically enrolled on the Memoranda Rolls, because not all writs for distress are enrolled there. Possibly they could be partially reconstructed from E101, amerciaments before the Barons; but the incompleteness of this source and the complexities of the sheriffs' accounts would make such a reconstruction of little value.

64. The process was not used for summoning the commissioners to send in their certificates.

65. The procedure of attachment is described in the Glossary.

66. In practice, the sheriffs endorsed the writs, first with their answer concerning the attachment, and secondly with full details of the location, the extent and the annual value, together with the date of seizure, of seized lands. From these returns it would be possible to compile a table of the distribution of the value of land per acre over most of England over a considerable period of time.

67. The Memoranda Rolls rarely specifically say 'quod manus regis amoveantur'; but the sheriffs' accounts for the seized lands show clearly that the seizure lapsed upon the collectors' completion of their accounts. See, for example, E379/116/10–11HVII, 11–12HVII, Salop.

68. Compare the process described immediately below issued by the Lord Treasurer's Remembrancer where seizures were allowed towards the reduction of the collectors' debts.

69. Seized goods were charged immediately to the sheriffs on the Pipe Rolls. For

seized lands the sheriffs underwent a special account before auditors and the Barons. After a seizure, writs were sent to the coroners to distrain the sheriff to account for the lands on the next return day. No writ addressed to the coroners in the early Tudor period was ever returned by them to the Exchequer.

70. 'recesserunt sine licencia Curie'. The Barons were quite prepared to license adjournments. See below.

71. While the King's Remembrancer's writ instructed the sheriff to seize all the collectors' lands and possessions ('in manus Regis capias') without limit, the Lord Treasurer's Remembrancer's writ ordered him to seize lands and possessions to the value of a specified sum, via the writ of *fieri facias*.

72. See, for example, E368/272 SVC T.r.2; E368/283 Recorda H.r.22, 26d; E368/284 Recorda M.r.38.

73. For the writs issued by the Lord Treasurer's Remembrancer, and for the consequent seizures, see references to Table 8.3.

74. See references to Table 8.3.

75. But they were probably, nevertheless, liable to fees in the Fleet. For the fees in 1562 see Jessop, '*The Oeconomy of the Fleete*', table facing p. 152.

76. See, for example, E159/268 Dies dati, M.r–.

77. The longest period of imprisonment suffered by the collectors that has been noted is eight months, E159/268 Recorda P.r.15. But the conditions of imprisonment in the Fleet were very lax, see Jessop, '*The Oeconomy of the Fleete*', pp. 157–9.

78. E159/294 Recorda P.r.18, T.r.12d; E159/297 Recorda H.r.11d, 13; E159/304 Dies dati T.r–; E159/305 Dies dati T.r–, H.r–, Fines P.r–, E159/306 Recorda P.r.21d, 28d, Fines H.r–; E159/307 Recorda M.r.45; E159/317 Recorda P.r.36d, 58; E368/290 Bre.Ret.H.r.2; E368/323 Bre.Ret.M.r–.

79. This process was rarely successful and was usually abandoned. See, for example, E368/305 Recorda H.r.2d.

80. The fines were paid to the Remembrancers, who accounted for them on the Pipe Rolls, E159, E368, Fines, *passim*.

81. E159/265 Recorda M.r.24; E159/267 Recorda M.r.23, 44.

82. E159/270 Recorda M.r.15d; E159/272 Recorda M.r.14; E159295 Recorda M.r.16d; E159+/299 Recorda H.r.23, Dies dati T.r–; E159/303 Recorda M.r.21, H.r.17d, 19; E159/304 Recorda T.r.9, H.r.18d, Dies dati H.r–; E159/305 Fines P.r, P.r-d; E159/312 Bre.Ret.P.r-d; E159/314 Dies dati M.r–; E159316 Dies dati P.r–; E159/317 Dies dati M.r–; E159/321 Dies dati P.r.3. E368/269 Recorda P.r.19; E368/274 Bre.Ret. M.r.4d; E368/279 Recorda H.r.26d, 27; E368/282 Recorda H.r.16; E368/297 Bre.Ret. H.r–; E368298 Recorda M.r.17d, 53, H.r.45, T.r.15; E368/303 Bre.Ret.T.rd; E368/305 Bre.Ret. H.r.2; E368/308 Recorda T.r.1, 29; E368/309 Bre.Ret.T.r.3; E368/310 Recorda P.r.4, Bre.Ret. T.r.11d; E368/311 Bre. Ret. M.r.1d; E368/317 Recorda M.r.9d; Bre.Ret. M.r.1d; E368/319 Recorda M.r.35; E368/323 Bre.Ret. M.r–, M.r.–d.

83. E159/315 Recorda P.r.11; E368/286 Recorda H.r.8, T.r.24; E368/298 Recorda M.r.53, H.r.45; E368/314 Recorda M.r.81; E368/324 Recorda P.r.7.

84. c. 9. *Stat. Realm*, II, p. 21.

85. For example, out of fifty-four groups of collectors for the fifteenth and tenth of 1488, eight employed professional attornies, forty-one appointed one or more of their number as their attornies, and in only five cases did all the collectors appear

in the Exchequer. E159/264 Attornati T.r-; E159/265 Attornati M.r-, H.r-, P.r-. In six cases, 'special' attornies were admitted on account of the infirmity of a collector, E159/305 Dies dati P.r-; E159/307 Recorda M.r.45, H.r.18, 18d; E159/316 Recorda P.r.30d. In one earlier case the officers of the Exchequer refused to accept such an attorney and required the collector to take the oath of faithful accounting before the justices of assize and to give bond for the due payment of his debt. E159/301 Recorda T.r.14.

86. E159/303 Recorda H.r.18; E159/317 Recorda M.r.58, H.r.39, P.r.36d, Dies dati M.r-, Fines P.r-, M.r.
87. No form of this oath has been discovered.
88. UL, 1921 Catalogue No. 9, p. 39. Each of the six auditors appears to have borne an equal share of the business.
89. The auditors 'take no peny for the Same but bereth the charges of perchement at their owne costes', *ibid.*, p. 36.
90. Such as E164/7.
91. E179, *passim.*
92. The accounts are scattered throughout the class E179. For example, for the fifteenth and tenth: E179/122/81; and for the subsidy: E179/114/270.
93. The Exchequer ordinance of June 1326: 'Et les allowances a faire par brefs et tailles a la fyn de tieux acomptes se facent en plein Eschequier'. *Red Book of the Exchequer*, III, p. 933.
94. This division is also reflected in the division between the functions of the two Remembrancers. The King's Remembrancer was responsible for the presence of the collector until the charge had been prepared and the account heard by the Barons, while the Lord Treasurer's Remembrancer was responsible from the audit by the Barons until the collectors were acquitted of their account. E159, E368, *passim.*
95. For the early Tudor period: E368/259–325, SVC, *passim.*
96. The enrolled accounts of the collectors, E359/38, 39, 41–44. These accounts, in turn, refer to the Memoranda Rolls for the Barons' decisions on new allowances.
97. The fact that reference is made to a fuller version on the enrolled accounts suggests that it is very likely that this abbreviation was no more than a clerical convenience.
98. Willard, however, claims that in the early fourteenth century some allowances did appear on the auditor's account sheet. Willard, *Parl. Taxes 1290–1334*, p. 328.
99. Baronial supervision of the auditors was enjoined by the Exchequer ordinance of 1326: 'Et certeins Barons soient assignez a surveer et examiner les faitz et l'exploit des auditours de tieux acontes'. *Red Book of the Exchequer*, III, p. 933. The heading on the auditors' charges was in the form 'Auditores N. Lathell Baro. J. Clerk Clericus' and this form was repeated at the head of the collectors' enrolled accounts. As far as can be seen the business was equally divided between the second, third and fourth Barons.
100. For claims for exoneration drawn up in the auditors' style, and in an auditor's hand, see E179/124/177; E179/159/113A; E179/180/116; E179/274/43.
101. Willard infers for the early fourteenth century that routine allowances were made by the 'auditors', one Baron and one auditor, before the accounts were heard in full Exchequer. But he does not apply the crucial test of whether the 'audito

compoto' sum on the Lord Treasurer's Memoranda Roll was the same, or less than, the 'summa onerabilis' as given by the auditors' charge-sheets. Willard, *Parl. Taxes 1290–1334*, pp. 317–29.

102. This account is based on an Elizabethan document which purports to describe the practice of the Exchequer as it was in the reign of Henry VII. However, the document implies that for the allowance of tallies, the accountant had merely to ask the Secondary of the Pipe to enter them on the enrolled account without any reference to a formal account before an auditor or the Barons. E407/71.

103. Only one case of forgery has been noted. On suspecting a tally, the Barons ordered a check, which revealed that there was no foil with the Chamberlains' Deputies and no entries in the Receipt and Tellers' Rolls. The collector was held in the Fleet for eight months while his alibis were checked and found wanting. Norfolk, as Treasurer, committed the collector to the council in Star Chamber, who in turn committed him to three hours on the pillory. E159/321 Recorda T.r.45.

104. E164/7.

105. Except for the subsidy of 1513, when the remuneration was 4d/£, 4 Henry VIII c. 19.

106. Such citations are common on the enrolled accounts of collectors for fifteenths and tenths, E359/39, 43, *passim*.

107. The 'breuia directa' were enrolled on the King's Remembrancer's Memoranda Roll (E159); and citations of this enrolment were noted on the Lord Treasurer's Memoranda Roll (E368). 'Breuia directa' were probably required in order to have some form of record of the authority in the Exchequer. Thus claims based on statutes, which were already of record in the Exchequer, did not require 'breuia directa' in support of them.

108. 'quos remittunt Regi', E359/38, 39, 41–4, *passim*.

109. Sometimes to other collectors, for example, E368/319 Recorda H.r.8; and sometimes to other officers of the crown, usually sheriffs, for example, E368/322 Recorda T.r.65.

110. 'visus compoti'.

111. See, for example, E179/122/92. For a 'visus' bearing a Baron's name, see E179/117/80.

112. If the collectors appeared before a writ of attachment was issued against them, and accounted without ever withdrawing from the Exchequer without licence, no record was made on the Memoranda Rolls of any adjournments that may have been granted.

113. The longest period of consecutive adjournments that has been noted is two-and-a-half years. E159/274 Datus dies T.r–.

114. Recognisances were usually enrolled in the King's Remembrancer's Memoranda Roll. A few were also enrolled on the Lord Treasurer's Remembrancer's Roll.

115. 'percomputare'.

116. Two, three or four six-monthly, or yearly, instalments were the most common.

117. For the total number of groups of collectors appointed for each tax, see Table 8.2.

118. 37 Henry VIII c. 25. Recognisances from the collectors of the subsidies were to be taken by the commissioners and recognisances from the collectors of the fifteenths and tenths by the members of the commons who appointed them. The

statutory penalty for either omitting to take, or refusing to subscribe to, a recognisance was £10.

119. But one recognizance was taken by the officers of the Exchequer from a collector of the fifteenth and tenth of 1547, and another from a collector of the subsidy of 1547, see Table 6.6. These recognisances were required by the statute; but no process to levy the statutory fine has been noted.

120. Subsidy of 1514: Glos., E159/310 Recorda P.r.37; subsidy of 1524: Derbs., Morleston and Lutchurch hundred, *ibid.*, P.r.38.

121. Only six cases have been noted, all from the taxes payable in 1497. E368/271 SVC T.r.6, 6d; E368/274 SVC P.r.12: E368/277 SVC M.r.24d; E368/278 SVC M.r.24d, T.r.21.

122. Under the Statutum de Finibus of 27 Edward I c. 2, the sheriffs were held personally responsible for all debts to the crown contracted by those resident within their sheriffwick and during their term of office, even when they could not levy the sum from the parties concerned. *Stat. Realm*, I, p. 129.

123. In the collectors' enrolled accounts, references were given as to where on the Pipe Rolls the sums were to be answered.

124. According to the Exchequer ordinance of June 1326, debts on the Exannual Rolls were to be read to the sheriffs after they had been apposed on their accounts to see if they might possibly be levied. *Red Book of the Exchequer*, III, pp. 855–7. No case of a debt on the Exannual Rolls ever having been levied has been found for the early Tudor period. E363/6–8.

125. See Table 3.10. Some of these debts were even marked as being subject to writs of exemption in the particulars of account sent out to the collectors. See, for example, E179/73/142.

126. The immediate transference of some of these sums to the Exannual Rolls was a virtual recognition of the validity of the claim to exemption. But the officers of the Exchequer do not appear to have been consistent in their discrimination between debts transferred to the Pipe and those transferred to the Exannual Rolls.

127. 'In Tho', that is, 'in thesauro'. Sometimes these entries are accompanied by the marginal annotation 'tallia inde'.

128. 'Sed non debent'. Religious houses would often allow considerable periods of time to elapse and then, appearing by attorney, claim exemption from debts incurred for several taxes by citing a previous enrolment of their charter or letters patent of exemption in the Exchequer. See, for example, E372/345 It. Wilts.

129. But some sheriffs petitioned for these allowances. See, for example, E368/264 Precepta H.r.2.

130. It is not clear whether this sign signifies 'respondit', or any of the inflexions of this verb, or rather 'recordatus'. At any rate the mark does not in any way correspond with the answer to the debt in the new place of enrolment; rather it seems to be a check mark denoting the completion of the transference to the entry to the other Roll, or membrane.

131. The writ of 'diem clausit extremum' commanded the sheriff to hold an inquisition post mortem and to seize the lands and goods of the deceased, as described above. The writ of '*fieri facias*' was an order to levy a specified sum from the lands and possessions of the debtor.

132. 12 Edward I. *Stat. Realm*, I, p. 70.

133. See, for example, E372/391 Res. Kanc, Johannes Bull; E372/392 *ibid*.
134. Sometimes between one and three dots were arranged in certain patterns around the 'T'. These patterns denoted that the owners, or bailiffs, of certain liberties had levied the sums and were to account for them in their own separate accounts. E372/331–392, *passim*. See Fanshawe's comments in BM Lansdowne 171, f. 423b. The printed edition, Fanshawe, *The Practice of the Exchequer Court*, is of limited use in this context because the printer was unable to reproduce the diagrams showing the patterns of the dots.
135. See, for example, E372/378 It. Herefs. Debts marked 'O' are to be found in the sheriffs' accounts on the subsequent Roll. See, for example, E372/392 and 393, Salop.
136. Orders on the sheriffs' accounts are scattered through both Memoranda Rolls, but are mostly concentrated in the section 'Precepta' on the Lord Treasurer's Memoranda Rolls (E368). The sheriffs' accounts extend over several years on the Pipe Rolls, with sheriffs attempting to levy their predecessors' debts by distraining on them. The confusion mounts rapidly.
137. Coke, *Fourth Institute*, p. 116.
138. Gilbert, *Treatise on the Court of Exchequer*, pp. 116, 150.
139. Thomas, *The Ancient Exchequer of England*, p. 56, describes 'T' and 'On^i' as alternative charge marks, without explaining the difference between them. He is unaware of the combined form of 'On^i T'.
140. Vernon, *Considerations for Regulating the Exchequer*, pp. 12–13.
141. The consolidated sheriffs' accounts consisted of a gross total of debts together with additional items separately specified. E372/331–392, *passim*.
142. Sometimes the year is specified. 'R' in Exchequer documents always denotes the Great Roll, of the Pipe Roll.
143. See, for example, E372/391 It. Berks. collector for Faircross and other hundreds for the fifteenth and tenth of 1541; E372/394 *ibid*.
144. See, for example, E372/391 Devon, Collector for Axminster and other hundreds for the fifteenth and tenth of 1541; E372/392 *ibid*.
145. This would be shown by the phrase 'Sed non debent'.
146. See, for example, E368/270 Recorda M.r.9.

Notes to Chapter 7

1. Dowell, *History of Taxation and Taxes*, I, p. 125.
2. Dietz, *English Government Finance*, appendix, table VII.
3. For example Dietz's figure for the yield of the fifteenth and tenth of 1490–1 is only £20,830 (*ibid*.)
4. Only one contemporary summary of the yields of the taxes has been discovered. This was drawn up late in Elizabeth's reign and covers the subsidies from 14 Henry VIII to 23 Elizabeth, but omits the subsidies of 1535–6. The figures appear to be of the net yields of the subsidies and are accurate to within a few hundred, or in some cases thousand, pounds. E179/241/332.
5. For the number of accounts for each tax, see Table 8.2.
6. E179/ *passim*.

7. E368/259–325 SVC *passim.*
8. At the statutory rate of 6d/£ or 2½% of the gross charge.
9. E179/ *passim.*
10. E401/975–1181 *passim.*
11. For reasons of clarity the totals have been shown as correct to the nearest pound. Transcripts were taken to the nearest fraction of a penny.
12. E164/7.
13. E179/ *passim.*
14. 12 Henry VII c. 13; 19 Henry VII c. 32.
15. See Appendix I.
16. E159/303 Recorda M.r.1.
17. For example, Yorkshire for the fifteenth and tenth of 1492 (II).
18. As possibly with aliens in the northern border counties for the subsidies in the 1540s. The commissioners may well have returned that no one was eligible for assessment. See, for example, E179/158/70. But many of these returns may not have survived.
19. Dietz's estimate of the yield is 30 per cent too low.
20. 1492 (II) low because of the omission of the commission to levy in Yorkshire. 1537 high because the £6,000 traditionally allowed for decay was levied. 1541–47 are slightly low because of the absence of accounts for several reasons.
21. If all the original commissioners' certificates were extant this would be possible, since the relative proportions of the whole comprised by each of the tax charges and assessments could, somewhat laboriously, be calculated. But hundreds of the certificates are missing. Sampling would be very dangerous because one area may well have differed quite considerably from the next.
22. Such as the inclusion of Wales in 1544.
23. Compare the subsidies of 1526 and 1527 with the subsidies of 1524 and 1525. The rates were the same for these subsidies; but in the later two higher minimum assessments prevailed.
24. For some measure of the progress of inflation see Brown and Hopkins, *Economica*, 22 (1956), fig. 1 on p. 299 and appendix B, p. 312.
25. Unless it can be shown the wages paid to soldiers and the prices of military supplies increased at a slower rate than the overall rise in prices. The delay between the assessment of the subsidies and their payment to the crown would have reduced their real value.
26. Except the subsidies of 1514, 1515 and 1516 for which there were separate statutes. See Appendix I.
27. The reduction between 1489 and 1490 was because of an obligation for £1333 6s 8d entered into by the Barons of the Cinque Ports that they would not ask for deductions greater than £500. E159/267 Recorda P.r.12. No explanation is offered for the reduction after 1517.

Notes to Chapter 8

1. The question of whether the yields of the taxes were large enough to cover the military expenses incurred by the crown is too large a question to be fully

examined within the scope of this study. However, it may be noted that while the cost of Henry VII's campaign in France and Brittany between 1489 and 1492 was but £108,000 and therefore covered by the yields of parliamentary taxes, the cost of the wars in France and Scotland between September 1544 and September 1545 was £560,000 and required in addition to parliamentary taxation the levy of loans and benevolences, the debasement of the coinage, and the sale of considerable quantities of the crown lands. Henry VII; WA 12240; Henry VIII: *LP* XX pt. 2, 324; XIX, pt. 1, 272.

2. In the case of anticipatory assignments the effective use to the crown of the taxation money really dates from the moment that the collector received the money. In the case of retrospective assignments for bookkeeping purposes, the crown had effective use of the money much earlier.

3. These recognisances were required by statute, and were to be taken from the collectors of the fifteenths and tenths by the members of the commons, and from the subsidy collectors by the commissioners. In both cases the recognisances were to be for twice the value of the money which the collectors were to collect. 37 Henry VIII c. 25.

4. According to the statute the commissioners were to have received their commission before 4 January 1547; but the commissions were not sent out until 21 February. L1/1/1/2, f. 43b.

5. Steele, *Proclamations*, I, 304, 308; citing BM Titus B.II.3.

6. E401/1176 *passim.*

7. For details of this Anticipation, see p. 133.

8. For details of this Anticipation, see p. 134. Also the collectors for ten areas were so slack that in the event the money was collected by the subsidy collectors. See note f in Table 7.1.

9. Fifteenths and tenths: 1488: Salop, whole sum E159/265 Dies dati M.r-; 1489: Hants, 10 per cent E368/308 Recorda T.r.1; 1490–1: Salop, 96% E368/297 Recorda P.r.15; Staffs., 64% E368/295 Recorda M.r.7; 1492 (II) Salop, 74% E368/ 289 Recorda M.r.33; Staffs, 8% E368/293 Recorda T.r.13; 1497 (I) Salop, 74. E368/289 Recorda M.r.35; Yorks (WR) 9% E368/298 Recorda T.r.15. Subsidy: 1497: Salop, 89% E368/283 Recorda T.r.16; Yorks (WR), 23% E159/277 Recorda M.r.7. These sums pardoned amounted to £2,578.

10. Except that for the subsidy of 1515 a very slightly larger proportion was paid in before one month.

11. This was required by statute. 32 Henry VIII c. 50.

12. See Table 5.7.

13. The dates given for 'account' are perforce those for the audit of the accounts by the Barons in full Exchequer. The dates of the closure of the accounts are not known; but in the majority the notes of the accounts on the Lord Treasurer's Remembrancer's Memoranda Rolls show that the allowances claimed by the collectors presented no unusual difficulties and it may therefore be assumed that the accounts were closed in the same term. E368/259–325 SVC, *passim.*

14. The subsequent term never began within one month after the payment date. See Table 6.2.

15. These returns were not enrolled in the Memoranda Rolls unless a writ of attachment happened to be issued in the term immediately following. The

original writs as filed on their return to the Exchequer are preserved in the class E202; but they are almost impossible to use on account of their vast bulk and the somewhat bizarre way in which they were filed by the officers of the Exchequer.

16. The sheriff for Salop returned in answer to a writ to attach the collectors of the subsidy of 1497: 'Certifico quod non est aliquod subsidium siue Auxilium assessatum siue taxatum infra balliuam meam', and further claimed for good measure that the writ had been delivered too late for him to execute it. The Barons treated this as a 'contempt', and fined the sheriff £2. E159/275 Recorda H.r.25.

17. If the collectors' account had been heard by the Barons, the seizure was to extend only to the value of the debt outstanding upon their account.

18. BM Additional MSS 30, 198, f. 41.

19. UL 1921 Catalogue No. 9, p. 43.

20. Usually upon the evidence of a witness in the Exchequer.

21. Sometimes the sheriffs were fined for failing to return whole files containing several dozens of writs. It is impossible to be certain whether writs against tax collectors were included within those files or not, and such cases have been excluded from the table.

22. Writs returned to the Exchequer with no endorsement were known as 'breuia alba'.

23. 6s 8d: E159/305 Dies dati T.r–; £10: E159/284 Recorda M.r.49.

24. An anonymous writer on the Exchequer. UL 1921 Catalogue No. 9, p. 43.

25. Polydore Vergil, *Anglica Historia*, 38–9. *Great Chronicle of London*, 242. The Chronicle places the revolt before the grant of the subsidy.

26. *Paston Letters*, VI, No. 1037, p. 127; *CSP Venet*, 1202–1509, 553.

27. Plumpton Correspondence, No. 25, p. 61. Unless the Earl of Northumberland changed his tactics at the last minute, the Earl of Oxford's claim that the Earl of Northumberland 'addressed hym self towardes theym wihtoute any harneys in pesible maner' appears somewhat unlikely. *Paston Letters*, VI, No. 1037, p. 127.

28. William Paston sent a copy of the rebels' proclamation to John Paston. *Ibid.*, VI, No. 1039, p. 129.

29. Holinshed, *Chronicles*, III, 492–3.

30. *Great Chronicle of London*, p. 278; Polydore Vergil, Anglica Historia, pp. 91–3; *Two London Chronicles*, p. 213. Pollard, *Reign of Henry VII from Contemporary Sources*, I, p. 159.

31. *Great Chronicle of London*, p. 278; Polydore Vergil, *Anglica Historia*, pp. 91–3.

32. For the rebellion in Yorkshire see Dods, *Pilgrimage of Grace* and Bush, 'Up for the Commonweal'.

33. Hallom alleged that 'It was concluded at Doncaster that there should be no more payments gathered till the Parliament time'. *LP* XII, pt. 1, 201 (p. 86). And rumours that this agreement was about to be broken were cited as a cause of the second conspiracy. *Ibid.*, 202 (p. 103).

34. The Papal Envoy ascribed the refusal of the Yorkshire rebels to pay the subsidy of 1489 to the extraordinary nature of the tax. *CSP Venet*, 1202–1509, 553.

35. *LP* IV, 377.

36. Polydore Vergil, *Anglica Historia*, pp. 202–3, reports that there was a general recourse to arms; but in the absence of any contemporary evidence to support his contention, it is probably best disregarded.

37. E179/279/1, Yorks (WR), Staincliffe and Ewcross.
38. E404/96/20HVIII/114.
39. E179/279/1, Yorks WR, Staincliffe and Ewcross. Sedbergh and Dent persisted in their refusal to pay. For the collectors' account see E359/38 4HVIII, 4a, Skipton and Staincliffe. Surprisingly, no evidence has been discovered of any trouble over the subsidy of 1514, which was being assessed in the meantime.
40. Except no rescues have been recorded for Berkshire, Gloucestershire, the Isle of Wight and the North Riding of Yorkshire.

Notes to Chapter 9

1. For a path-breaking attempt to relate changes in taxation to social, political and economic developments in early modern Europe see R. Goldscheid, 'A sociological approach to problems in public finance', pp. 203–13.
2. Directly assessed taxes in the Middle Ages are discussed in Willard, *Parliamentary Taxes*.
3. There were two further short-lived attempts at direct assessment of incomes: in 1670–1 and 1689–98. Taxation practice in the late seventeenth and eighteenth centuries is summarised in Kennedy, *English Taxation*, pp. 38–50.
4. The classic exposition of late medieval doctrine is by Fortescue, in the *De dominio regali et politico*. The most recent discussion of these issues is in Alsop, 'Theory and practice of Tudor taxation', pp. 19–30.
5. The question of how far the case for taxation contained in the preambles, especially those of 1534 and 1543, was widened to include ordinary expenditure has been keenly debated since it was first raised. The latest contribution to the debate is by Alsop, 'Tudor taxation'. Further readings on its relevance have been attributed by Harris in two articles in *English Historical Review* (1978). Hoyle, 'Crown, Parliament and Taxation', gives a measured, 'constitutional', reading of the debate.
6. Later in the sixteenth century, the Commons deliberately delayed readings of the subsidy acts in 1566, 1589 and 1601 during debates on the succession, on the reform of abuses in purveyance and the Exchequer, and on monopolies, respectively. Neale, *Elizabeth and her Parliaments, 1559–1581*, pp. 136–9, 143, 166, 168–9 (1566); Neale, *Elizabeth and her Parliaments, 1585–1601*, pp. 206–15 (1589), 252–679 (1601). The lack of any surviving Commons Journals and diaries makes it impossible to detect whether similar tactics were used at an earlier date.
7. For the late medieval period, see Harris, '*Aids, loans and benevolences*', pp. 1–19.
8. See, for example, the *pro forma* letter inviting contributions to the 1497 loan and specifying the date of payment SC1/51/116. Repayments are recorded in the Exchequer Tellers' book E405/79. For a later sixteenth-century example, see the terms of the Privy Seal loan of 1570 in E407/16, fols 16–18. Repayment from the Exchequer was ordered within a year, as promised in the Privy Seal letter. Dietz, *English Public Finance Rev*, pp. 25–6.
9. Examples of instructions to commissioners levying loans and benevolences as to how to justify them and secure individual consent can be found in Nicholas,

Proceedings of the Privy Council, v, pp. 418–21 (1491 benevolence); *LP* xii, 194 (1542 loan); *LP* xx (2) 6, App. 4, s.2 (1545 benevolence).

10. The benevolence of 1491 was written off by 11 Henry VII c. 10, the loan of 1522 by 21 Henry VIII c. 25, the loan of 1542 by 35 Henry VIII c. 12, and the benevolence if 1545 by 37 Henry VIII c. 25. In addition, Mary's loan of 1556 was not repaid by Elizabeth, nor did she repay the loan of 1597. Dietz, *English Public Finance*, p. 81.

11. Accounts of the attempt to raise the Amicable Grant and the hostility it aroused can be found in Hollinshed, *Chronicles*, pp. 684–6, and in Hall, *Chronicle*, pp. 694–9. The quotations are from *ibid.*, p. 696. Correspondence between hard-pressed commissioners and Wolsey, fomenting on the nature of the apposition, are calendared in *LP*, iv 1235, 1243, 1260, 1263, 1266–7, 1345, App. 39.

12. S. d'Ewes, *The Journals of all the Parliaments During the Reign of Queen Elizabeth* (London, 1682), p. 633; facsimile reprint (Shannon, 1973).

13. D'Ewes also reports that Mildmay admitted in the 1576 parliament that under-assessment was common (*ibid*, p. 246). By 1587 Mildmay was claiming in parliament that the assessment practice was so lax that 'not the sixth part of which is given doth come to her Majesty's coffers'; Parliamentary diary cited in Neale, *Elizabeth and her Parliaments*, ii, p. 168. Undervaluation was frequently mentioned in the debates on the subsidy in the 1593 and 1601 parliaments. D'Ewes, *Journals*, pp. 477–94, 629–33.

14. Marillac reported that the subsidy commissioners for London were accused of disobeying royal commands by making assessments that were too low, and were threatened by punishment as traitors. Whereupon the mayor and magistrates allegedly begged for mercy and promised to pay at double rates. *LP*, xvi 223.

15. 'Concernyng the Subsidy with the remedy for the deceit used therein'. *LP*, xiii (1) 187.

16. Corporation of London RO, Repertory, iii, fol. 116.

17. From a signet letter to the commissioners for Wiltshire, dated 26 February 1524. SP/1/30. fol. 141. For an example of a certificate containing revised assessments, dated 26 May 1524, see E1789/133/117.

18. R.G. Lang, *Two Tudor Subsidy Rolls*, pp.xvi–xxvi.

19. For examples of earlier letters from the crown to commissioners with no mention of undervaluation see GMR, Loseley MSS, 1484 (1541): Bodleian, North (Wroxton) MSS, a 1, fols 27ᵛ–28ʳ (1549).

20. GMR, Loseley MSS, 1488/1. Copies of the text can be found in SP 12/4, fols 96–97ᵛ, and in BL, Add. MSS 48018, fol. 151 (Beale's precedent book).

21. GMR, Loseley MSS 1488/2; SP 12/4, fols 98–9ᵛ; BL, Add. MSS 48018, fol. 151.

22. SP 12/107, fol. 97–8ᵛ.

23. D'Ewes, *Journals*, p. 458.

24. *Acts of the Privy Council*, xvii, pp. 423–5.

25. From a letter from the Privy Council to the Northants. subsidy commissioners in December 1601, in J. Wake, ed., *Musters, Beacons, Subsidies, etc.* iii, pp. 81–3.

26. Letter from the Privy Council to the subsidy commissioners, 9 July 1593. *APC*, xxiv, p. 378. On 2 December 1593 the Privy Council wrote to the Lord Keeper instructing him to put out of the commission of the peace all who refused to be assessed at £20 in annual incomes. *APC*, xxiv, p. 514.

27. *APC*, xxviii, pp. 625–7.
28. *Rural economy in Yorkshire in 1641, being the farming and account of Henry Best of Elmswold in the East Riding in the county of York* (Surtees Society, 33, 1887), pp. 186–9.
29. Miller, 'Subsidy assessments of the peerage in the sixteenth century', *BIHR*, xxviii (1955), 15–34.
30. *Ibid.*, 18.
31. *Ibid.*
32. *Ibid*, p. 24, n. 1.
33. *Ibid.*, pp. 24–31. Despite finding two cases of underassessment 'on a considerable scale'. *Ibid.*, pp. 30–1.
34. Although after 1540 the subsidy acts no longer specified 'clear' annual values, it seems likely that it was standard sixteenth-century practice in assessing annual incomes to take net, rather than gross, values.
35. For a discussion of the jurisdiction of the Courts of Wards and Liveries and of the activities of the feodaries, see H.E. Bell, *An Introduction to the History and Records of the Courts of Wards and Liveries*, especially pp. 1–4, 40–2, 54–6, 76–9. The engrossed accounts are in Wards 9.
36. In a few cases where it is possible to compare the valuations returned by the feodaries and escheators for the same estate, Bell finds that at the end of Elizabeth's reign the feodaries' valuations were 5–25 per cent higher than those of the escheators. *Courts of Wards and Liveries*, p. 56. However, Smith finds little to choose between the valuations of the two officials in the West Riding in the period 1520–79. *Land and Politics*, pp. 274–5.
37. The feodaries' valuations were taken from PRO, Wards 9/129, 131, 135, 137–8, 579; and matching subsidy assessments from PRO, E179.
38. Except for two cases in the mid-1540s in which the subsidy assessments were 29 and 30 per cent of the feodaries' valuations, respectively.
39. The subsidies levied between 1549 and 1552 were assessed only on goods. See Appendix II.
40. The probability that the difference between the distributions of the individual results obtained in the two periods could have arisen merely by chance is less than 1 in 50 (2 per cent). A Kolmogorov–Smirnov, two-sample, 1-tailed test with chi-square approximation yielded a value of p between 0.01 and 0.02. This test is clearly explained in Siegel, *Nonparametric Statistics*, pp. 127–36.
41. Sixteenth-century canon and statute law on the subject is conveniently summarised in Swinburne, *Brief Treatise of Testamentes and Last Willes*, fols 217[v]–221[r].
42. *Ibid.*, fols 220[v]–221[r].
43. *Ibid.*, fol. 220[r].
44. *Ibid.*, fol. 218[v].
45. Overton, 'Estimating crop yields from probate inventories', *Journal of Economic History*, 39 (1979), p. 373.
46. The data were collected in 1963–6.
47. In a further 683 cases there was no entry in the subsidy assessment list for the vill of residence of an individual whose probate inventory had been recovered. Because it is uncertain whether the individuals concerned were absent from the

vill, or were present and assessed at a figure below the exemption limit, these cases were omitted from the main investigation. The analysis was repeated including them with the subsidy assessments arbitrarily set to 10 shillings below the appropriate exemption limits. The results were close to those of the main investigation, and the few differences of any consequence will be reported below.

48. In a few cases in which the date of the subsidy assessment was missing, the interval was arbitrarily set to the average figure.

49. If two individuals were found with the same name in the subsidy assessment, even if in adjacent vills, the case was discarded.

50. Debts were sometimes noted on the will rather than on the inventory. Unfortunately many inventories lacked an accompanying will. Two further problems are the variable degree with which apparel was specified in the inventories, and the seasonal cycle of crops. Where the subsidy assessment was before the harvest and the probate valuation after it, crops in the barn were deducted. However, when both valuations were after the harvest no correction was made for the consumption of crops in the intervening interval.

51. Expressed formally, the problem is one of multivariate analysis of variance with unbalanced data. The analysis was performed using the ANOVA procedure in the SPSSX statistical package with option 3 (main effects only): *SPSSX Users' Guide* (Chicago, 1983), pp. 439–50. The analysis was replicated using the procedure GLM with statements MEANS and LSMEANS, in the SAS statistical package, and similar results were obtained. *SAS Users' Guide: Statistics* (Cary, NC, 1982), pp. 139–204.

52. This can only be achieved if each of the factors has the same proportional effect across the full range of values of the other factors. Where this is not so, as, for example, would be the case if the effect of region was not constant over time, the factors are said to 'interact' to produce a 'crossed effect' over and above the simple combination of their independent effects. If this occurs, it is impossible to estimate the independent effect of each factor net of the effects of the others. Tests were made for interactions between the factors using the more efficient GLM procedure in SAS (see previous note). No statistically significant crossed effects were found.

53. More formally, beta is a standardised regression coefficient in the sense used in multiple regression. It should be noted that the unequal numbers of cases in the different categories in the table means that the squares of the betas do not measure directly the proportion of the variance accounted for by each factor, and so do not sum up to the R^2 figure given at the foot of the table. However, the beta figures do properly represent the *proportional* differences in the degree to which the various factors account for the variance in the data.

54. If cases with missing subsidy assessments are included, with valuations arbitrarily set at 10s below the exemption limit, not surprisingly the exemption limit emerges as the factor with the highest beta value, and is statistically significant at the 1 per cent level.

55. If the cases with missing subsidy assessments are included, the figure for the 1543–5 period rises to a level much closer to that achieved in the earlier part of Henry VIII's reign. The accuracy of the assessments in the immediate post-Henrician period is also reduced. The deviations for the six periods become 20.1, 15.3, 2.1, −8.6, −5.0, −3.3. The beta figure, indicating the relative importance of the time period, is substantially higher at 0.42.

56. The strength of the relationship is further attested by the fact that it is present to the same degree in the data even before the effects of other factors are taken into account; and it is unchanged when cases with missing subsidy assessments are included in the analysis.
57. Table 9.4: multiple R^2 = 0.484.
58. Miller, 'Subsidy assessment of the peerage', p. 22.

Notes to Appendix II

1. E159/322 Bre. H.r– where names of the commissioners fot eh subsidy of 1544 are 'Teste per Originalia anno xxv^{mo}'.

Glossary

In a study of this nature a large number of technical terms have, of necessity, to be used. The significance of most of these either has been apparent, or has been explained, in the context in which they occurred. The following list is short and is confined only to those terms, which it has not been possible to define fully so far. The list therefore amounts in no sense to a complete catalogue of all the technical terms employed in this book. Unless otherwise stated, all quotations are from Jacob, *Law Dictionary*.

Attach
'signifies to take or apprehend by commandment of a writ or precept. It differs from arrest, in that he who arresteth a man carrieth him to a person of higher power to be forthwith disposed of; but he that *attacheth* keepeth the party *attached*, and presents him in Court at the day assigned'.

Attachment
'is a process that issues at the discretion of the judges of a court of record, against a person for some contempt'.

Chattels
'Chattels, or Catals, comprehend all goods moveable or immoveable, except such as are in the nature of freehold, or parcel of it ... chattels real concern the realty, lands and tenements, leases for years, interests in advowsons, in statutes merchants &c. ... An owner of chattels is said to be possessed of them; as of freehold the term is, that a person is seised of the same'.

Dismable
Liable to taxation with the clerical tenth. Usually denotes the spiritualities, and temporalities annexed to spiritualities, listed and assessed in the Taxation of Pope Nicholas of 1291.

Essoin
'signifies an excuse for him that is summoned to appear and answer to an action ... by reason of sickness and infirmity, or other just cause of absence.'

Protection
'Protection is an immunity granted by the King to a certain person, to be free from suits at law for a certain time, and for some reasonable cause; and 'tis a branch of the King's prerogative so to do.' Protections were given to those going overseas, to debtors of the crown so that the king might be answered first, to spiritual corporations, and to others.

Replevin
To release of a distress effected by a sheriff either in response to a writ out of king's bench or common please, or upon a reasonable complaint made directly by the party. 'When the king is party, or the taking is in right of the crown, in these cases the Sheriff is to surcease'.

Rescue
The forcible, and illegal, re-possession of a distress.

Scire facias
'a writ judicial most commonly to call a man to shew cause to the court when it issues, why execution of a judgment passed should not be made out.' Also used to summon to show cause why certain duties should not be performed, or issues forfeited.

Wager of law (Vadiare legem)
This is where an action of debt is brought against a man upon a simple contract between the parties, without deed or record; and the defendant swears in court in the presence of his purgators, that he oweth the plaintiff nothing in the manner and form as he hath declared; and the reason of waging of law is, because the defendant may pay the plaintiff his debt in private, or before witnesses who may be all dead, and therefore the law allows him to wage his law in discharge; and his oath shall rather be accepted to discharge himself, than the law will suffer him to be charged upon the bare allegation of the plaintiff.'

Bibliography

Manuscripts

TNA The National Archives, Kew, Richmond, Surrey

C1	Chancery, Judicial Proceedings (Equity side), Proceedings, Early
C33	Chancery, Judicial Proceedings (Equity side), Decrees and Orders, Entry Books of
C60	Chancery, Rolls (Enrolments), Fine Rolls
C66	Chancery, Rolls (Enrolments), Patent Rolls
C78	Chancery, Rolls (Enrolments), Decree Rolls
C193	Chancery, Crown Office Records, Miscellaneous Books
DL5	Duchy of Lancaster, Decrees and Orders, Entry Books of
E13	Exchequer, Exchequer of Pleas, Plea Rolls
E36	Exchequer, Treasury of the Receipt, Miscellaneous Books
E101	Exchequer, King's Remembrancer, Accounts, Various
E111	Exchequer, King's Remembrancer, Bills, Answers and Depositions (Early)
E114	Exchequer, King's Remembrancer, Bonds
E159	Exchequer, King's Remembrancer, Memoranda Rolls
E164	Exchequer, King's Remembrancer, Miscellaneous Books, Series I
E175	Exchequer, King's Remembrancer, Parliamentary and Council Proceedings
E179	Exchequer, King's Remembrancer, Subsidy Rolls Etc.
E202	Exchequer, King's Remembrancer, Writs
E321	Exchequer, Augmentation Office, Proceedings of the Court of Augmentations
E359	Exchequer, Lord Treasurer's Remembrancer, Enrolled Accounts, Subsidies
E363	Exchequer, Lord Treasurer's Remembrancer, Exannual Rolls
E364	Exchequer, Lord Treasurer's Remembrancer, Foreign Accounts, Rolls of
E368	Exchequer, Lord Treasurer's Remembrancer, Memoranda Rolls
E371	Exchequer, Lord Treasurer's Remembrancer, Originalia Rolls
E372	Exchequer, Lord Treasurer's Remembrancer, Pipe Rolls
E379	Exchequer, Lord Treasurer's Remembrancer, Sheriffs' Accounts of Seizures
E401	Exchequer, Exchequer of Receipt, Receipts, Enrolments and Registers
E402	Exchequer, Exchequer of Receipt, Receipts, Original
E404	Exchequer, Exchequer of Receipt, Issues, Writs and Warrants
E405	Exchequer, Exchequer of Receipt, Receipts and Issues, Rolls of
E407	Exchequer, Exchequer of Receipt, Miscellanea

IND   Indexes: 1-9, Court of Common Pleas, Plea Rolls, Docket Rolls; 1325-37,
       Court of King's Bench, Crown Side, Plea Rolls, Coram Rege Rolls, Docket
       Rolls (Civil Pleas).
REQ1   Court of Requests, Miscellaneous Books
REQ2   Court of Requests, Proceedings
SC1   Special Collections, Ancient Correspondence
SP1   State Paper Office, Domestic and Foreign, State Papers, Henry VIII, General
       Series
SP2   State Paper Office, Domestic and Foreign, State Papers, Henry VIII, Folios
SP6   State Paper Office, Domestic and Foreign, State Papers, Henry VIII,
       Theological Tracts
St. Ch. 1 Court of Star Chamber, Proceedings (Henry VII)
St. Ch. 2 Court of Star Chamber, Proceedings (Henry VIII)
Wards 9 Engrossed accounts

BLO Bodleian Library, Oxford

Dodsworth MSS

BM British Museum, London

Additional MSS
Cottonian MSS
Lansdowne MSS
Stowe MSS

Microfilms of Salisbury MSS, Hatfield House

CLRO Corporation of London Record Office

Journals of the Common Council
Repertories of the Court of Aldermen

GMR Guildford Muniment Room, Castle Arch, Guildford

Loseby MSS

HLRO House of Lords Record Office

Acts of Parliament, Original, Subsidy Acts

LAC Lincolnshire Archives Committee, The Castle, Lincoln

L1/1/1 Corporation of Lincoln, Minute Books

UL University of London, Senate House Library

1921 Catalogue No. 9. Treatise on the exchequer

WA Westminster Abbey, London

The Westminster Abbey Collection

Unpublished works

Kelly, M.J. 'Canterbury jurisdiction and influence during the episcopate of William Warham, 1503–32', Ph.D. dissertation, Cambridge University, 1963.

Published Works, Original Material

(Listed in alphabetical order as cited in the footnotes. Place of publication is London, unless otherwise indicated.)

Acts of the Privy Council of England, ed. J. R. Dasent, 32 vols, 1890–1907.

Brinkelow, Henry, *Complaynt of Roderyck Mors*, ed. J. M. Coopers, Early Engl. Text Soc., extra series, XXII (1874).

Calendar of Patent Rolls, Henry VII, I: 1485–94: II: 1494–1509, 2 vols, 1914–16.

Calendar of State Papers, Milan (1385–1618), A.B. Hinds, 1912.

Calendar of State Papers, Spanish, 13 vols and 2 supplements, 1862–1954.

Calendar of State Papers, Venetian, 9 vols, 1202–1603, Rawdon Brown, Cavendish Bentinck, Horatio Brown, 1862–1954.

Calendar of the Fine Rolls, 22 vols, 1911–. Vol. 22.

Campbell, William, *Materials for a History of the Reign of Henry VII*, 2 vols, Rolls series, 1873.

Chibnall, A. C. and Woodman, A. V., *Subsidy Roll for the County of Buckingham, Anno 1524*, Buckinghamshire Record Society, VIII (1950).

Christ Church Letters, ed. J. S. Sheppard, Camden Society, N. S. XIX (1877).

Chronicles of London, ed. C. L. Kingsford, Oxford, 1905.

CJ: *Journals of the House of Commons*, s. l., s. a., 1803 ff.

Colchester, The Red Paper Book of, ed. W. G. Benham, Colchester, 1902.

Cornwall, Julian, *Lay Subsidy Rolls for . . . Sussex*, Sussex Record Society Publications LVI (1956).

D'Ewes, Simonds, *The Journals of all the Parliaments during the reign of Queen Elizabeth*, 1682.

_____ *Dialogus Scaccarii, (De necessariis observantiis Scaccarii dialogus)*

_____ *The Course of the Exchequer by Richard [of Ely], son of Nigel, Treasurer of England and Bishop of London*, trans. with introduction and notes by C. Johnson, 1950.

Ellis, Sir Henry, *Original Letters Illustrative of English History*, 1824.

[Fitzherbert, Anthony], *In this book is conteyned the offices of sheryffes, bailiffes, escheatours, constables, and coroners*. [1538].

Fortescue, Sir John, 'De Dominio Regali et politico', *The Works of Sir John Fortescue, knight*, ed. Thomas Lord Claremont, 1869.

Gairdner, James, *Letters and Papers Illustrative of the reigns of Richard III and Henry VII*, 2 vols, Rolls series, 1861–3.

Great Chronicle of London, ed. A. H. Thomas and I. D. Thornley, 1938.

Grey Friars of London Chronicle, ed. J. G. Nicholas, Camden Society LIII (1852).

[Hales, John], *A discourse of the common weal of this realm of England*, ed. Elizabeth Lamond, Cambridge, 1929.

Hall, Edward, *Chronicle*, 1809.

Hamilton Papers, ed. Joseph Bain, 2 vols, Edinburgh, 1890.

Harvey, S. H. A., *Suffolk in 1524*, Suffolk Green Books, X (1909).

HMC Historical Manuscripts Commission, *Reports 1–*, 1870–.

Holinshed, Raphael, *Chronicles*, ed. Henry Ellis, 6 vols, 1807–8.

Jessop, Augustus, ed., *The Oeconomy of the Fleete*, Camden Society, N. S., XXV (1879).

Johnson, H. C., *Surrey Taxation Returns, Part (B)*, Surrey Record Society, XI (1932).

Kaulek, J., *De Castillon et de Marillac, Correspondence politique*. Paris, 1885.

Lists and Indexes, [to manuscripts in the PRO], 55 vols, 1892–1936.

LJ *Journals of the House of Lords*, 1509–, s. l., s. a.

LJ (RP) Rotuli Parliamentorum, as printed in *Journals of the House of Lords*, vol. 1.

Lord Herbert of Cherbury, *The Life and Reign of King Henry the Eighth*, 1572.

LP *Letters and Papers, Foreign and Domestic, of the Reign of Henry VIII, 1509–47*; J. S. Brewer, James Gairdner, R. H. Brodie. 21 vols, in 33 parts, 1862–1910; also vol. I in 3 parts, 1920; addenda vol. I, pts i, ii, 1929–32.

Nicholas, N. H., *Proceedings and Ordinances of the Privy Council of England, 1386–1542*, 7 vols, 1834–37.

Nottingham Records, *Records of the Borough of Nottingham*, W. H. Stevenson *et al.*, 6 vols., Nottingham, 1882–1914.

Paston Letters, 1442–1509, ed. James Gairdner, 6 vols, 1904.

Plumpton Correspondence, ed. Thomas Stapleton, Camden Society, IV (1839).

Pollard, A. F., *The Reign of Henry VII from contemporary sources*, 3 vols, University of London Historical Series, No. 1, 1913–14.

Polydore Vergil, *Anglica Historia*, ed. and transl. by Denys Hay, Camden Society, 3rd Series, LXXIV (1950).

Ramsay, G. D. *Two Sixteenth Century Taxation Lists, 1545 and 1576*. Wiltshire Archaeological and Natural History Society, Records Branch, X (1954).

Red Book of the Exchequer, ed. Hubert Hall, 3 vols, 1896–97.

Roper, William, *The Lyfe of Sir Thomas Moore, knighte*, Early Engl. Text Soc., Original series, CXCVII (1935).

Rot. Parl., *Rotuli Parliamentorum: ut et petitiones et placita in parliamento*, (1278–1504), 6 vols, s. a., s. l.

Stat. Realm, *Statutes of the Realm*, ed. A. Luders, T. E. Tomlins, J. Raithby *et al.*, 11 vols, 1810–28.

Steele, Robert, *Tudor and Stuart Proclamations 1485–1714*, 2 vols, Oxford, 1910.

Stow, John, *Annales*, 1631.

Tait, James, *Taxation in Salford Hundred, 1524–1802*, Chetham Society, N. S. 83 (1924).

Trevelyan Papers, ed. J. P. Collier, 3 vols, Camden Society, CV (1872).

Two London Chronicles, ed. C. L. Kingsford, Camden Society Miscellany, XII (1910).

Wake, Joan, *A Copy of Papers relating to Musters, Beacons, Subsidies & c., in the County of Northampton, A. D. 1586–1623*, Northampton Record Society, III (1926).

Wilkins, David, *Concilia Magnae Britanniae et Hiberniae ... 446–1718*, 4 vols, 1737.

Wriothesley, Charles, *A Chronicle of England*, ed. W. D. Hamilton, 2 vols, Camden Society, N. S. XI (1875–77).

Year Books, *Les Reportes des Cases En les Ans des Roys Edward v. Richard iij, Henri vij, & Henrie viij.*, printed by George Sawbridge, William Rawlins, and Samuel Roycroft, 1679. For fifteenth century cases see below, Chrimes, *Constitutional Ideas*, Appendix.

Published Works, Secondary Authorities

Alsop, D., 'The theory and practice of Tudor taxation', *Eng. Hist. Rev.*, xcvii (1982), 19–30.

_____ 'Innovation in Tudor Taxation', *Eng. Hist. Rev.*, xcix (1984), 83–93.

Bell, H.E., *An Introduction to the History and Records of the Courts of Wards and Liveries*, Cambridge, 1953.

Bibliography of Early English Law Books, compiled for the Ames Foundation by Joseph Henry Beale, Cambridge (Mass.), 1926.

Brooke, George C., *English Coins from the Seventh Century to the Present Day*, 1950.

Bush, M. L., ' "Up for the Commonweal" : The Significance of Tax Grievances in the English Rebellions of 1536', *Eng. Hist. Rev.*, cvi (1991), 314–15.

Chapman, D., 'Wealth and Trade in Leicester in the Early Sixteenth Century', *Transactions of the Leicestershire Archaeological Society*, XXV (1949), 69–97.

Chrimes, S. B., *English Constitutional Ideas in the Fifteenth Century*. Cambridge, 1936.

Coke, Sir Edward, *Institutes of the Laws of England*; 1st and 2nd parts, 1797; 4th part, 1629.

Cooper, J. P., 'Henry VII's last years reconsidered', *Historical Journal*, II (1959), 103–29.

Cornwall, Julian, 'English County Towns in the 1520s', *Econ. Hist. Rev.*, 2nd series, XV (1962).

Cowell, John, *A Law Dictionary*, 1727.

Craig, Sir John, *The Mint*, Cambridge, 1953.

Dictionary of National Biography [compact edn.], Oxford Univ. Press, 1975.

Dietz, Frederick C., *English Government Finance, 1485–1588*. University of Illinois Studies in the Social Sciences, IX (1920), No. 3.

DNB *Dictionary of National Biography*, Leslie Stephen and Sidney Lee, 63 vols, 1885–1900; 1st supplement, 3 vols, 1901: Index and epitome, 1903.

Dodds, M. H. and Ruth, *The pilgrimage of grace 1536–7, and the Exeter conspiracy, 1538*, 2 vols, Cambridge, 1915.

Dowell, Stephen, *A History of Taxation and Taxes in England*, 4 vols, 1888.

Elton, G. R., 'The Evolution of a Reformation Statute', *Eng. Hist. Rev.*, lxiv (1949), 174–97.

_____ 'The Exchequer: War in the Receipt', *Elizabethan Government and Society*, being essays presented to Sir John Neale, ed. S. T. Bindoff, J. Hurstfield, C. H. Williams, 1961, 213–48.

_____ 'Henry VII; Rapacity and Remorse', *Hist. Journal*, I (1958), 21–39.

_____ 'Henry VII: A Restatement', *Hist. Journal*, IV (1961), 1–29.

_____ 'Parliamentary Drafts, 1529–1540', *BIHR*, XXV (1952), 117–32 and further note *ibid.*, XXVII (1954), 198–200.

_____ Taxation for War and Peace in Early-Tudor England', in *War and Economic Development: Essays in Memory of David Joslin*, ed. J. M. Winter, (1975) Cambridge, rep. in his *Studies in Tudor and Stuart Politics and Government*, (Cambridge, 1974–92), iii, 216–33.

_____ *The Tudor Constitution: Documents and commentary*, Cambridge, 1960.

_____ *The Tudor Revolution in Government*, Cambridge, 1953.

Fanshawe, Thomas, *The Practice of the Exchequer Court with its severall officers*, 1658.

Foss, Edward, *Judges of England, with sketches of their lives and notices connected with the courts at Westminster, 1066–1864*, 9 vols, 1848–64.

Gilbert, Geoffrey, *A Treatise on the Court of the Exchequer*, 1758.

Giuseppi, M. S., *Guide to the Manuscripts preserved in the Public Office*, 1923.

Goldscheid, R., 'A sociological approach to problems in public finance', in R. A. Musgrave and A. T. Peacock, eds, *Classics in the Theory of Public Finance*, pp. 203–13.

Gray, H. L., 'Incomes from Land in England in 1435', *Eng. Hist. Rev.*, xlix (1934), 607–39.

Guy, John, 'Wolsey and the Parliament of 1523', in Claire Cross, David Loades, and J. Scarisbrick, eds, *Law and Government under the Tudors*, Cambridge, (1988), 1–18.

Handbook of British Chronology, ed. Sir F. Maurice Powicke and E. B. Fryde, 1961.

Handbook of Dates, ed. C. R. Cheney, Royal Historical Society guides and handbooks, No. IV, 1955.

Harris, G. L., '*Aids, loans and benevolences*', *Historical Journal*, 6 (1963), 1–19.

———— 'Theory and Practice in Royal Taxation: Some Observations', *Eng. Hist. Rev.* xcii (1978), 1–30.

———— 'Thomas Cromwell's "New principle of Taxation"', *Eng. Hist. Rev.* xciii (1978), 721–38.

Holdsworth, W. S., *History of English Law* (3rd ed.), 1923.

Hoskins, W. G., 'Early Tudor Towns', *Trans. Roy. Hist. Soc.*, 5th series, vol. 6, 1–19.

Hoyle, Richard W. 'The Crown, parliament and Taxation in sixteenth century England', *Eng. Hist. Rev.*, cix, (1994), 992–1196.

———— 'Taxation and the mid-Tudor crisis', *Econ. Hist. Rev.* li (1998), 649–75.

———— *Tudor Taxation Records: a guide for users*, Public Record Office Readers' No 5., 1994.

Jacob, Giles, *A New Law Dictionary* (9th ed.), 1772.

Jenkinson, H., 'Exchequer Tallies', *Archaeologia*, LXII (1911), 367–80.

Jordan, W. K., *The Charities of London, 1480–1660*, 1960.

———— *The Charities of Rural England, 1480–1660*, 1961.

———— *Philanthropy in England, 1480–1660*, 1959.

Kennedy, W., *English Taxation 1640–1799: an Essay on Policy and Opinion* (London, 1913; reprinted 1964).

Knowles, David and Hadcock, R. N., *Medieval Religious Houses: England and Wales*, 1953.

Lang, R. G., *Two Tudor assessment tolls for the City of London: 1541 and 1582*, ed. for the London Record Soc., 1993.

Maxwell-Lyte, H. C., *Historical notes on the use of the great seal of England*, 1926.

Medieval Latin Word List, from British and Irish sources, prepared by J. H. Baxter and C. Johnson, with the assistance of P. Abrahams, under the direction of a committee appointed by the British Academy, 1934.

Miller, Helen, 'Subsidy Assessments of the Peerage in the Sixteenth Century', *BIHR*, xxviii (1955), 15–34.

Neale, J. E., *The Elizabethan House of Commons*, 1949.

———— *Elizabeth and her Parliaments, 1559–1581*, 1953.

———— *Elizabeth and her Parliaments, 1584–1601*, 1957.

Overton, M., 'Estimating crop yields from probate inventories: an example from East Anglia, 1575–1735', *Journal of Economic History*, 39 (1979).

Phelps Brown, E. H. and Hopkins, Sheila V., 'Seven Centuries of the Prices of Consumables, compared with Builders' Wage-rates', *Economica*, N. S. XXIII (1956), 296–314.

Pickthorne, K. W. M., *Early Tudor Government: 1: Henry VII, 2: Henry VIII*, 2 vols, Cambridge, 1934.

Plucknett, Theodore F. T., 'The Lancastrian Constitution', in *Tudor Studies presented to A. F. Pollard*, ed. R. W. Seton-Watson, 1924.

Pollard, A. F., *The Evolution of Parliament*, 1926.

Pugh, T. B. and Ross, C. D., 'The English Baronage and the Income Tax of 1436', *BIHR*, XXVI (1953), 1–28.

Ramsey, J. H., *Lancaster and York*, Oxford, 1892.

Schofield, R.S., 'Parliamentary lay taxation, 1485–1547', unpublished Ph.D. dissertation, University of Cambridge, 1963.

_____ 'Taxation and the political limits of the Tudor state', in Claire Cross, David Loades, and J. Scarisbrick, eds, *Law and Government under the Tudors*, Cambridge, (1988), 227–55.

Shorter Oxford English Dictionary, ed. C. T. Onions, Oxford, 1956.

Siegel, Sidney, *Nonparametric Statistics for the Behavioural Sciences*, Tokyo, 1956.

Smith, R. B., *Land and Politics in the England of Henry VIII: the West Riding of Yorkshire, 1530–1546*, Oxford, 1970.

Steel, Anthony, *The Receipt of the Exchequer, 1377–1485*, Cambridge, 1954.

Swinburne, H., *Brief Treatise of Testaments and Last Willes*, 1590.

Thomas, F. S., *The Ancient Exchequer of England*, 1848.

Vernon, Christopher, *Considerations for Regulating the Exchequer*, 1642.

Vickers, Kenneth H., *England in the Later Middle Ages*, 1913.

Willard, James Field, *Parliamentary Taxes on Personal Property, 1290–1334*, Cambridge (Mass.), 1934.

_____ 'The Taxes upon Moveables of the Reign of Edward III', *Eng. Hist. Rev.*, xxx (1915), 69–74.

Index

Printed and bound by CPI Group (UK) Ltd, Croydon, CR0 4YY

23/04/2025

14660944-0003